Le

University of
fordshire

International Review of
Industrial
and Organizational
Psychology
2010   Volume 25

International Review of Industrial and Organizational Psychology
2010 Volume 25

Edited by

Gerard P. Hodgkinson
The University of Leeds, UK

and

J. Kevin Ford
Michigan State University, USA

WILEY-BLACKWELL

A John Wiley & Sons, Ltd., Publication

This edition first published 2010
© 2010 John Wiley & Sons Ltd.

Wiley-Blackwell is an imprint of John Wiley & Sons, formed by the merger of Wiley's global Scientific, Technical, and Medical business with Blackwell Publishing.

Registered Office
John Wiley & Sons Ltd, The Atrium, Southern Gate, Chichester, West Sussex, PO19 8SQ, UK

Editorial Offices
The Atrium, Southern Gate, Chichester, West Sussex, PO19 8SQ, UK
9600 Garsington Road, Oxford, OX4 2DQ, UK
350 Main Street, Malden, MA 02148-5020, USA

For details of our global editorial offices, for customer services, and for information about how to apply for permission to reuse the copyright material in this book please see our website at www.wiley.com/wiley-blackwell.

Library of Congress Cataloging-in-Publication Data

International review of industrial and organizational psychology.
   —1986—Chichester; New York; Wiley, c1986–
   v.: ill.; 24cm.
   Annual.
   ISSN 0886-1528 $1/4$ International review of industrial and organizational psychology
   1. Psychology, Industrial—Periodicals.   2. Personnel management—Periodicals.
   [DNLM: 1. Organization and Administration—periodicals.   2. Psychology, Industrial—periodicals. W1IN832UJ]
   HF5548.7.157   158.7005—dc 19 86-643874   AACR 2 MARC-S
   Library of Congress [8709]

ISBN: 9780470682593

A catalogue record for this book is available from the British Library.

Set in 10/12 pt Plantin by Aptara® Inc., New Delhi, India
Printed in the United Kingdom

1   2010

CONTENTS

ABOUT THE EDITORS

Gerard P. Hodgkinson   *Leeds University Business School, The University of Leeds, Leeds, LS2 9JT, UK*

J. Kevin Ford   *Department of Psychology, 135 Psychology Research Building, Michigan State University, E. Lansing, MI 48824, USA*

Gerard P. Hodgkinson is Professor of Organizational Behaviour and Strategic Management and Director of the Centre for Organizational Strategy, Learning and Change (COSLAC) at the University of Leeds, UK. He earned his BA, MSc, and PhD degrees at Wolverhampton Polytechnic and the Universities of Hull and Sheffield, respectively. He has (co-)authored three books and over 60 scholarly journal articles and chapters on topics of relevance to the field of industrial and organizational psychology. A Fellow of both the British Psychological Society and the British Academy of Management, and an Academician of the Academy of Social Sciences, his work centres on the analysis of cognitive processes in organizations and the psychology of strategic management. In recent years, his work on these topics has been taken forward through the award of a Fellowship of the Advanced Institute of Management Research (AIM), the UK's research initiative on management funded by the Economic and Social Research Council (ESRC) and Engineering and Physical Sciences Research Council (EPSRC). From 1999 to 2006 he was the editor-in-chief of the *British Journal of Management* and currently serves on the Editorial Boards of the *Academy of Management Review, Journal of Management, Journal of Organizational Behavior* and *Organization Science*. A chartered occupational psychologist, registered with the UK Health Professions Council as a practitioner psychologist, he has conducted numerous consultancy assignments for leading private and public sector organizations. Further information about Gerard and his work can be found at the following addresses: (1) http://www.leeds.ac.uk/lubs/coslac/ (2) http://www.aimresearch.org.

J. Kevin Ford is a Professor of Psychology at Michigan State University. His major research interests involve improving training effectiveness through efforts to advance our understanding of training needs assessment, design, evaluation and transfer. Dr. Ford also concentrates on understanding change dynamics in organizational development efforts and building continuous learning and improvement orientations within organizations. He has published over 50 articles and chapters and four books relevant to industrial and organizational psychology. Currently, he serves on the editorial boards of the *Journal of Applied Psychology* and *Human Performance*. He is an active consultant with private industry and the public sector on training, leadership, and organizational change issues. Kevin is a Fellow of the American Psychological Association and the Society of Industrial and Organizational Psychology. He received his BS in psychology from the University of Maryland and his MA and PhD. in psychology from The Ohio State University. Further information about Kevin and his research and consulting activities can be found at http://www.io.psy.msu.edu/jkf.

CONTRIBUTORS

Derek R. Avery

Department of Psychology, University of Houston, 126 Heyne Building, Houston, TX 77024, USA

James Campbell Quick

College of Business, The University of Texas at Arlington, PO Box 19377, 701 South West Street, Suite 334, Arlington, TX 76019-0377, USA

Michael J. Cavanagh

School of Psychology, University of Sydney, Sydney, NSW 2006, Australia

Cary L. Cooper

Lancaster University Management School, Lancaster University, Lancaster, LA1 4YXX, UK

Olga Epitropaki

Work and Organisational Psychology Group, Aston Business School, Aston University, Birmingham, B4 7ET, UK

Philip C. Gibbs

Centre for Organisational Health & Well-Being, School of Health & Medicine, Lancaster University, Lancaster, LA1 4YD, UK

Anthony M. Grant

School of Psychology, University of Sydney, Sydney, NSW 2006, Australia

Paul R. Jackson

Manchester Business School, University of Manchester, Booth Street West, Manchester, M15 6PB, UK

Laura M. Little

Terry College of Business, University of Georgia, 425 Brooks Hall, Athens, GA 30602, USA

Robert G. Lord

Department of Psychology, University of Akron, Arts & Sciences Building, 3rd Floor, Akron, OH 44325-4301, USA

Robin Martin

Work and Organisational Psychology Group, Aston Business School, Aston University, Birmingham, B4 7ET, UK

Patrick F. McKay

School of Management and Labor Relations, Rutgers, The State University of New Jersey, Janice H. Levin Building, 94 Rockafeller Road, Piscataway, NJ 08854, USA

Debra L. Nelson   *Department of Management, Spears School of Business,
Oklahoma State University, Stillwater, OK 74078, USA*

Deniz S. Ones   *Department of Psychology, University of Minnesota, N218
Elliott Hall, 75 East River Road, Minneapolis, MN
55455-0344, USA*

Helen M. Parker   *School of Psychology, University of Sydney, Sydney, NSW
2006, Australia*

Jonathan Passmore   *School of Psychology, University of East London, Stratford
Campus, Water Lane, London, E15 4LZ, UK*

Sara J. Shondrick   *Department of Psychology, University of Akron, Arts &
Sciences Building, 3rd Floor, Akron, OH 44325-4301, USA*

Geoff Thomas   *Work and Organisational Psychology Group, Aston Business
School, Aston University, Birmingham, B4 7ET, UK*

Anna Topakas   *Work and Organisational Psychology Group, Aston Business
School, Aston University, Birmingham, B4 7ET, UK*

Sjir Uitdewilligen   *Department of Organization and Strategy, Maastricht
University, Tongersestraat 53, 6211 LM Maastricht,
The Netherlands*

Chockalingam   *Department of Psychology, Florida International University,*
Viswesvaran   *University Park Campus, 11200 S. W. 8th Street, Miami,
FL 33199, USA*

Mary J. Waller   *Schulich School of Business, York University, 4700 Keele
Street, Toronto, Ontario M3J 1P3, Canada*

Fred R.H. Zijlstra   *Department of Work & Social Psychology, Maastricht
University, P.O. Box 616, 6200 MD Maastricht, The
Netherlands*

EDITORIAL FOREWORD

The present volume marks the twenty-fifth anniversary of the *International Review of Industrial and Organizational Psychology*. For a quarter of a century, this series has provided authoritative, state-of-the-art overviews of the major developments at the forefront of the field, covering the full range of established and emerging topics.

Several chapters in the present volume revisit topics surveyed on previous occasions in the series, exemplified by the opening chapters on leadership by Sara Shondrick and Robert Lord ('Implicit Leadership and Followership Theories: Dynamic Structures for Leadership Perceptions, Memory, and Leader–Follower Processes') and Robin Martin, Olga Epitropaki, Geoff Thomas, and Anna Topakas ('A Review of Leader–Member Exchange Research: Future Prospects and Directions'). Other topics revisited in the present volume include diversity management ('Doing Diversity Right: An Empirically Based Approach to Effective Diversity Management' by Derek Avery and Patrick McKay), team cognition ('Team Cognition and Adaptability in Dynamic Settings: A Review of Pertinent Work' by Sjir Uitdewilligen, Mary Waller, and Fred Zijlstra) and personnel selection ('Employee Selection in Times of Change' by Chockalingam Viswesvaran and Deniz Ones).

New topics are surveyed in the present volume by Paul Jackson ('Corporate Communications') and James Campbell Quick, Cary Cooper, Phillip Gibbs, Laura Little, and Debra Nelson ('Positive Organizational Behavior at Work'). Also new to the series is the topic of coaching ('The State of Play in Coaching Today: A Comprehensive Review of the Field' by Anthony Grant, Jonathan Passmore, Michael Cavanagh, and Helen Parker).

Having established itself as the primary source of scholarly reviews in the related fields of organizational behavior and industrial and organizational psychology, we look forward to the series' fiftieth anniversary celebration.

GPH
JKF
October 2009

Chapter 1

IMPLICIT LEADERSHIP AND FOLLOWERSHIP THEORIES: DYNAMIC STRUCTURES FOR LEADERSHIP PERCEPTIONS, MEMORY, AND LEADER-FOLLOWER PROCESSES

Sara J. Shondrick and Robert G. Lord

Department of Psychology, University of Akron, Akron, OH, USA

In this review, we address implicit leadership theories (ILTs) and implicit followership theories (IFTs). Both types of implicit theories are important because leadership and followership are dynamic, socially constructed processes (Meindl, 1995) in which a leader's perceptions of followers are as critical as followers' perceptions of leadership. Both types of perceptions elicit confirming responses from the person being perceived, helping to create a dynamic leadership process in which relatively stable social structures emerge over time as leader and follower roles become differentiated. ILTs (and IFTs), which are a fundamental part of this process, are also dynamic in that they can be tuned automatically to particular contexts (Lord, Brown, and Harvey, 2001). In this dynamic process, both parties use their implicit theories to make sense of and react to the other party's behavior, creating an evolving basis for further interaction. In this sense, leadership is an ongoing, dynamic, two-way exchange between leaders and followers that is structured by both parties' implicit theories. Shamir (2007) provided an example of how important this process can be. He noted that Adolf Hitler perceived himself to be merely a drummer gathering the masses for the arrival of the "great leader" (the *Führer*) until his 30s, when he began to view himself as Germany's rightful leader. This shift in his self-perception may have been largely influenced by the way his followers responded to him.

Within this chapter, we discuss three broad areas of research that emphasize perceptual processes that are central to this dynamic leadership process. First,

International Review of Industrial and Organizational Psychology, 2010, Volume 25.
Edited by G. P. Hodgkinson and J. K. Ford. Copyright © 2010 John Wiley & Sons, Ltd

we consider research on the social construction of leadership and followership, specifically focusing on how dynamic leadership-oriented schemas influence both cognition and action. Next, we review research on behavioral measurement and sensemaking, highlighting how followers' cognitive and emotional processes color their interpretation and ratings of leadership behavior. Finally, we conclude by taking a closer look at perceptual and memory processes and the nature of knowledge while developing a more integrative perspective.

Thus, one major contribution of our review is to provide an integrated theoretical perspective in which both leadership and followership can be understood by incorporating the cognitive and affective structures that guide the perceptions and reactions of both leaders and followers. This approach facilitates our understanding of the follower's role in leadership processes because we can generalize many of the findings derived from the extensive research on follower's perceptions of leaders to our emerging understanding of how followers are perceived. Another major contribution is to extend our understanding of social cognitions to include recent arguments that cognitions are embodied and embedded in specific contexts (Neidenthal et al., 2005). Also, we use this recent perspective to help understand how leadership measurement can be improved. Finally, we show how many well-replicated findings concerning ILTs are consistent with the integrated perspective we develop.

Before proceeding further, it is important to note that the processes of leadership and followership are dynamic in three very different but related ways. One is that, as mentioned earlier, these processes take place within an emerging social structure. The second is that the ILTs and IFTs that guide perceptions and reactions are by themselves dynamic in that they can be adjusted to fit changing contexts and changing input patterns. However, once ILTs have been used for sensemaking, one's understanding of that situation is relatively stable. Thus, there is both plasticity and stability in the application of implicit theories to social perceptions. The third dynamic aspect is the knowledge we access (or recreate) is sensitive to the embodied emotions experienced in a particular situation. For example, a leader's facial expressions may be mimicked by followers, creating an emotion in followers that is similar to that felt by the leader. These emotions, in turn, can affect followers' perceptions of the leader and their willingness to accept the goals or motivational orientations of a leader. These three processes combine to create a dynamic, embodied, evolving understanding for both leaders and followers that guides the actions and reactions of both parties.

THE SOCIAL CONSTRUCTION OF LEADERSHIP AND FOLLOWERSHIP

Leadership and followership are now accepted as being perceptual and behavioral social constructs, existing only when others perceive one's behaviors to be role congruent. There is extensive research on the emergence of leadership and the processes used by followers to perceive (or infer) leadership, yet little attention has been given to the companion process by which followership emerges when a leader views others to be followers (Uhl-Bien and Pillai, 2007). However, these perceptual processes are both likely to be based on the cognitive categorization process described by Rosch (1977, 1978) more than 30 years ago. In the following sections, we begin by reviewing the development of categorization theory before discussing the dynamic nature of person schemas, such as those of a leader or follower.

Categorization Theory: From Rosch to the Present

The Structure of Cognitive Categories

In order to be economical perceivers of our world, we develop cognitive shortcuts that allow us to simplify information processing to focus on the broader picture. *Schemas*, which are knowledge structures that develop through experience (e.g., categories, scripts, plans, implicit theories, and heuristics), provide one such cognitive shortcut. Without schemas, we would be overwhelmed by the plethora of information we encounter every day. After encoding initial person-based information, Rosch (1977, 1978; Rosch and Mervis, 1975) maintained that we engage in a limited search through long-term memory for an adequately matching schema. Successful matches result in the person being labeled as a categorical member and subsequently treated and recalled as such. With unsuccessful matches, the search continues until a match is made. As a result, cognitive categories play a predominant role in information processing.

Rosch's (1978) research describes the nature of cognitive categories. Categories tend to develop around a prototype, which is the most abstract yet representative example of a category. Prototypical features are widely shared among category members, but they are much less common in contrasting categories. For this reason, they are very useful cues regarding category membership. Categories are organized horizontally with respect to contrasting interpretations of a stimuli (e.g., a leader vs a non-leader) and hierarchically around levels of abstraction within a particular category (e.g., leader). The *basic level* (e.g., business leader or political leader) is the most commonly used and the most useful for understanding one's world. *Superordinate level* categories are more abstract and inclusive (e.g., leaders), whereas *subordinate level* categories are more concrete and exclusive (e.g., top-level business leaders, lower-level business leaders) than basic level categories. Categories contain information about the physical form of the concept and the *affordances* offered by the concept (e.g., what purposes it serves for the perceiver; *cf.* Lance *et al.*, 2008).

Interestingly, Rosch (1977) recognized that schemas are constructed around information that is environmentally useful for the perceiver, maintaining that biological, social, and cultural needs heavily influence human's schema construction. Thus, as we describe more fully near the end of this review, rather than being created in a vacuum, schematic knowledge is constrained by the perceiver's perceptual, motor, and introspective systems, and it is situated in a specific context (Barsalou, 1999; Neidenthal et al., 2005; Wheeler, 2005).

Leader Categorization Theory

On the basis of Rosch's work (Rosch & Mervis, 1975, 1977, 1978), Lord and his colleagues (Lord, 1985; Lord, Foti, and de Vader, 1984; Lord, Foti, and Phillips, 1982; Lord and Maher, 1991) developed a recognition-based theory of leadership that describes how categorization influences one's perceptions, memory, and interactions with a potential leader. They proposed that when we encounter a person who exhibits characteristics or behaviors that are particularly salient or vivid, we engage in search for a matching category. If the search produces a match to a leader category, then the person is perceived as being a leader. The nature and automaticity of these searches can be influenced by factors such as the introduction of evaluative information about the target person (Cronshaw and Lord, 1987), the perceptual salience of information (Phillips and Lord, 1981), the ambiguity of information (Lord and Smith, 1983), and the perceiver's goals (Foti and Lord, 1987; Murphy and Jones, 1993), culture (Ensari and Murphy, 2003; Hanges, Lord and Dickson, 2000), and affect (Medvedeff and Lord, 2007).

Exemplar Models of Leadership Perception

Rosch's (1977; 1978) theory and related leadership research emphasizes category prototypes as the central construct defining a category, but there is also a long history of research using exemplar models to define categories in terms of specific individuals (Hintzman and Ludlam, 1980; Medin and Schaffer, 1978). When we think about leaders, we activate not only our abstract representations of typical leaders but also our firsthand experiences with specific leaders. Moreover, these experiences may transfer from one leader to another (Ritter and Lord, 2007).

The work of Smith and Zárate maintained that exemplars influence social judgments even beyond the effect of prototypes that are acquired through social learning. For instance, Smith and Zárate (1990) found that our social judgments rely on exemplar and prototype comparisons differently depending on whether exemplars or prototypes are learned first. When perceivers were not familiar with the prototypical attributes of a social group before making judgments, their social categorizations of target individuals were more likely to be based on experience with exemplars. Consistent with this argument, Matthews, Lord, and Walker (unpublished manuscript) examined leadership categorization in students of different ages, finding that young children defined leadership in terms of specific exemplars (e.g., their teacher, mother, or father), but by high school, most students defined leadership in terms of a more abstract prototype. In their later model, Smith and Zárate (1992) argued that exemplars are retrieved from memory and used for judgments when salient characteristics of a target individual match those of the exemplar. For instance, when perceivers are preoccupied with the gender of a target individual (e.g., a female superior), stored exemplars matching the target's gender are retrieved and compared, while other attributes of the target individual (e.g., the female superior's agentic personality) may be ignored.

Smith and Zárate (1992) contended that exemplar-based models of categorization are complementary to, rather than a replacement for, prototype models. Earlier research often favored prototype models for explaining categorization processes (e.g., Hampton, 1993; Lakoff, 1987; Rosch and Mervis, 1975), but in some circumstances exemplar models can outperform prototype models in explaining perception and judgment (Voorspoels, Vanpaemel, and Storms, 2008). It may be more reasonable to conceptualize person schema like leadership as existing on a continuum of exemplar to prototype models (Vanpaemel, Storms, and Ons, 2005; Verbeemen et al., 2007).

Taken together, the inconsistencies in research comparing the categorization prototype and exemplar models suggest that there may be important moderators determining the nature of the schema that is used for categorization. Likely moderators include the availability of exemplars, the perceiver's affect and motivation, perceiver's experience in the domain of a social category, or one's knowledge about the target category. Despite potential moderator effects, this research suggests that judgments about leadership may be colored by readily accessible information about prior supervisors that is coupled with our long-standing beliefs about leadership. Indeed, Verbeemen et al. (2007) suggest that our judgments may be especially influenced by a representation of leaders that involves a set of highly salient exemplar characteristics that are embedded within more abstract beliefs that are acquired through social learning.

Consequences of Cognitive Categorization

Leader categorization has important cognitive consequences. Once an adequate match to a leader category is made, the person is labeled as a leader, and the label is stored in long-term memory. Subsequently, judgments about the individual are made by assessing the leader category and inferring the individual's traits on the basis of what is typical of a leader, not just on what was actually observed. This process significantly reduces encoding and memory demands. When the leader category becomes activated by contextual cues, perceivers begin to selectively attend to, encode, and retrieve information that is consistent with their impressions, and they fill in gaps in their knowledge with schema-consistent information (Phillips and Lord, 1982; Phillips, 1984). Interestingly, social impressions tend to automatically develop very quickly and then stabilize (Ambady and Rosenthal, 1992), suggesting that once a person has been labeled as a leader or non-leader, this perception will persevere even if conflicting information is encountered. Research examining the dynamics of changing leadership perceptions in groups shows precisely this pattern, with changes in perceptions occurring substantially later than changes in behavioral patterns (Brown et al., 1998).

Additionally, leadership judgments influence social interactions through behavioral *script* activations, which connect cognition with action (Gioia and Manz, 1985). Scripts, like schemas, simplify and guide information processing and are structurally organized around common features. Script activation (through goals or contextual cues) prompts script-concordant behavior (Lord and Kernan, 1987), and it influences memory, causing raters to remember more script-relevant behavior (Foti and Lord 1987). Additionally, scripts and ILTs are used to interpret the behavior of others (Wofford and Goodwin, 1994; Wofford, Joplin, and Cornforth, 1996) and to generate one's own behaviors (Lord and Maher, 1991; Wofford, Goodwin, Whittington, 1998). For instance, Engle and Lord (1997) showed that when supervisors and subordinates share schemas, they have better quality exchanges and typically like each other more. Additionally, Neuberg (1996) maintains that our expectations about people cause us to treat them in a way that leads them to engage in expectancy-confirming behaviors. Thus, the combination of person categorization and script activation influences both cognition and action.

Moving From a Static to a Dynamic View of ILTs

Context-based Changes in Leadership Prototypes

The classical perspective of categorization maintained that ILTs were relatively fixed, context-specific categories that shared a family resemblance type of structure across contexts (e.g., lower, middle, and higher level leaders or military vs business vs religious leaders), but more recent research suggests that ILTs are dynamic. The classic perspective, which held that each new context evoked a different but stable prototype that had been learned over time (Lord et al., 1984), has been replaced by a view of emergent ILTs that are created dynamically on the basis of contextual input.

Cross-cultural research within the classical perspective indicated substantial consistency in ILT content across cultures (at least at the superordinate level), but notable differences as well (Gerstner and Day, 1994). The GLOBE (Global Leadership and Organizational Behavior Effectiveness) project led by Bob House, which investigated the content of ILTs across numerous cultures, found that in general the contents and structure of ILTs appear to hold across cultures (Den Hartog et al., 1999; House et al., 1999). However, the GLOBE project gathered ratings of ideal leaders without specifying context, suggesting that ILTs were being measured at the superordinate rather than at the basic level. Thus, they did not investigate whether culture moderated the sensitivity of leadership prototypes to situational cues (e.g., level in an organization or type of leadership context). Similarly, Epitropaki and Martin (2004) did not find differences in the factor structure of ILTs for different groups of workers, but again they did not investigate context-specific changes in ILTs.

Other research has investigated the sensitivity of ILTs to situational cues. Although the superordinate level of an ILT (i.e., a typical leader) appears to be relatively resistant to cultural differences, basic-level categorical instances of a leader (e.g., religious leaders or female leaders) tend to differ depending on the situation. For instance, Solano (2006) found that in civilian contexts, the ideal leader is someone who is participative, democratic, and has a high regard for followers' welfare, yet in a military context, the ideal leader is someone who makes self-focused autocratic decisions. Ritter and Yoder (2004) showed that a woman's, but not a man's, ability to emerge as a leader depends on the nature of the task being performed (see also Hall, Workman and Marchioro, 1999). These effects of task context are often described in terms of Eagly and Karau's (2002) role congruity theory, in which the stereotypic role of a leader (being agentic) clashes with the stereotypic role of a female (being communal) but is congruent with the stereotypic role of a male (being assertive, controlling, and confident). This male-consistent aspect of leadership prototypes puts females at a noticeable disadvantage for competitive leadership roles. Additionally, Dickson, Resick, and Hanges (2006) found that prototypes of effective leadership that are shared within an organization vary to some extent on the degree to which the organization reflects mechanistic or organic forms. Thus, interpretations of the stability of ILTs need to be qualified by the level of analysis used (i.e., basic, superordinate, or subordinate).

Dynamics of Flexible Prototype Activation

Because prototypes exhibit sensitivity to context, Lord and colleagues revised leader categorization theory (Hanges *et al.*, 2000; Lord *et al.*, 2001; Lord, Brown, Harvey, & Hall, 2001) to explain how leadership prototypes could change in response to many contextual differences. Using a connectionist rather than a symbolic model of knowledge representation (see "Conclusions" of this chapter for a fuller discussion of this distinction), they maintained that prototypes were attractor regions (i.e., regions of stability) in neural networks. Further, they proposed that these stable regions were sensitive to (1) contextual constraints, (2) input patterns of traits or behaviors exhibited by social targets, and (3) individual differences in perceivers' network structures. These three factors dynamically interact to create the attractor region used to interpret social stimuli. Thus, they theorized that the meaning of leadership as well as the perceptions of particular leaders could change over time or across contexts.

The gender and race of potential leaders and one's cultural background, momentary affect, and identification with one's current group were critical factors thought to affect these dynamic aspects of ILTs. Thus, this dynamic perspective on ILTs was able to integrate research showing that the gender (Heilman et al., 1989) and race (Rosette, Leonardelli, and Phillips, 2008) of potential leaders affect the ILTs used to assess their leadership. For example, Scott and Brown (2006) showed that varying the gender of a potential leader affected the ease with which perceivers could encode agentic leadership behaviors, supporting the notion that agentic behaviors would be less prototypical for female than for male leaders.

An additional constraint on the prototypes which define ILTs is the active identity of perceivers. Considerable research shows that as one's group membership becomes increasingly salient, group members typically adopt a collective identity and begin to base leader categorization on group prototypicality rather than on leader typicality (e.g., Fielding and Hogg, 1997; Hains, Hogg, and Duck, 1997; Hogg et al., 2006; Hogg, Hains, and Mason, 1998). Interestingly, fitting a group prototype can allot a perceived leader a lot of forgiveness, essentially giving them a "license to fail" as long as the failure can be interpreted in multiple ways (van Knippenberg, van Knippenberg, and Giessner, 2007).

Another consequence of a collective identity is that followers typically prefer a depersonalized leadership style that treats all group members similarly over a personalized leader–member exchange in which leader behavior varies depending on the specific group member (Hogg et al., 2005). This contrasts with prescriptions from the leader–member exchange theory that maintains that differentiated roles develop among followers (Graen and Scandura, 1987), but this may be more appropriate when individual identities predominate.

Stability Versus Plasticity in ILTs and Social Perceptions

An important issue associated with the connectionist-based theory of ILTs concerns what exactly changes. In connectionist systems, the weights connecting units within a pattern change very slowly, creating stability in what has been learned. However, the pattern that is *activated* using those weights can change as different inputs and constraints are encountered. It is this active pattern that reflects the dynamic aspects of ILTs and the contextualized meaning attached to a particular leader. Yet, once an interpretation is constructed in a particular situation, it also functions as an attractor, creating a degree of stability in perceptions and social processes as long as the situation remains constant. For this reason, social perceptions like leadership exhibit stability, and they change less rapidly than one might expect. In other words, there is considerable "cognitive inertia" associated with categorizing an individual. Consequently, change in social perceptions over time, but within context, is likely to be discontinuous. Moreover, the degree of discontinuity over time may vary with the strength of the attractors created by neural networks (Hanges *et al.*, 2002).

In support of this reasoning, several studies have found that shifts in leadership perceptions typically occur in a sudden, discontinuous manner. For instance, Brown *et al.* (1998) had participants observe a series of nine videotapes of a business meeting in which either a man or a woman was clearly engaging in leaderlike behaviors initially. However, through the course of the video series, the demonstration of leadership shifted slowly in a way that, by the end of the videotape, another person was clearly the new leader (in this case, leadership shifted either from a man to a woman or from a woman to a man). Interestingly, when both a man and a woman were equally exhibiting moderate displays of leadership during the fifth vignette, participants' perceptions of leadership still favored the initial leader.

Using a similar research paradigm that focused on followers' perceptions of emerging male and female leaders, Foti, Knee, and Backert (2008) found that emerging male leaders are more likely to be perceived in terms of gradual shifts in leadership perceptions, whereas emerging female leaders are more likely to be perceived in terms of discontinuous shifts in perceptions. Foti and her colleagues reasoned that this occurred because the activation of a male stereotype increases the accessibility of a leader schema, whereas the activation of a female stereotype inhibits the accessibility of ILTs. Other research has found that individual differences predict catastrophic shifts in perceptions of leadership, including one's beliefs in sexism and one's need for closure (Brown *et al.*, 1998; Hanges *et al.*, 1997).

In sum, much has been learned regarding the nature of leadership categories and their role in leadership perception. As described in "The Social Construction of Follwership", contemporary research is beginning to focus on the explicit and implicit processes that define followership.

The Social Construction of Followership

The social construction of followership involves the emergence of a leadership relationship that occurs when (1) a potential leader perceives or infers a group of individuals to be his or her followers or (2) when individuals in a group begin to view themselves as members of a larger group led by a leader. Rather than being confined to the role of a passive participant under the control of a leader, followers are able to actively construct and shape the leader's perceptions and their self-perceptions through interactions with the leader and each other. Indeed, "followers" may view themselves as leaders momentarily joining forces with others who share their goals (Mccaw, 1999). This perspective in line with Rost's (2008) argument in which followers are reconceived as being active, intelligent, responsible, and involved in interests shared with the leader (see also Chaleff, 1998; Hollander, 1992), although some followers choose to assume a more passive or negative role within a group (Kelley, 2008). To provide an elementary framework for investigating the social construction of followership, we extend the research discussed earlier to the topic of followership.

Follower Categorization Theory

As we have argued, follower categorization is equally as important as leader categorization (Uhl-Bien and Pillai, 2007). In this section, we apply categorization theory to show how follower categorization influences perceptions, memory, and interactions, and we discuss the nature of IFTs, which involve the implied beliefs that perceivers have about the prototypical characteristics of followers. Although we confine our discussion to a recognition-based process of followership, it is expected that followership can also be inferred based on performance information. For instance, followership may be inferred if group performance improves following the implementation of someone's suggestions.

Salient group behaviors or characteristics cue perceivers (whether a bystander or a group member) to search through memory for a matching social category to make sense of the situation. Behavior could be understood in terms of situationally guided scripts (Gioia and Sims, 1985; Foti and Lord, 1987), conformity to group prototypes (Hogg, 2001; van Knippenberg and Hogg, 2003), or personal attributions like perceptions of followership. For group members, this process can activate a follower identity, although it can also be activated through the perception that someone else is the leader (Uhl-Bien and Pillai, 2007) or through a leader's activities (Lord and Brown, 2001; 2004; Shamir, House, and Arthur, 1993). In short, there is a dynamic interplay between perceptions of leadership and perceptions of followership.

Rosch's theory of cognitive categorization implies that IFTs are hierarchically organized around a basic level category, which may include a general context-specific concept of someone who shows deference to a leader (Uhl-Bien and Pillai, 2007). As with other categories, IFTs can be expected to develop around prototypes or exemplars. Exemplar matching may occur if a perceiver has limited previous experiences with followers or if relevant episodic memories are particularly salient. Exemplar follower categories may be based on observations of other followers, or one's own experience with similar leaders (Ritter and Lord, 2007). With additional exposure to followers, IFTs become refined and tied to more well-defined contexts. Also, IFTs may become defined in terms of prototypes linking a category across contexts.

Rosch's theory also implies that the follower category includes information about a follower's physical form and the affordances that accompany followership, such as social capital or goal attainment. IFTs may include information regarding followers' location in space compared with leaders' (Giessner and

Shubert, 2007) appearance, voice (e.g., Bolinger, 1964, found that one's vocal pitch is associated with perceived submissiveness), race, gender, emotional expressions (Tiedens, 2001), or behavior such as when cooperating, listening, participating in decision-making, providing constructive feedback, or showing interest in the leader's goals.

The process of follower categorization is expected to have several important cognitive consequences. Because people are reluctant to change categories, a follower label may outlive its usefulness, preventing followers from exhibiting leadership qualities when needed. IFTs may also guide the sensemaking of both leaders and followers, producing inferences and role definitions that are unwarranted (e.g., Kipnis, 1976). Follower construction also interacts with the construction of leadership. Perceiving a leader within one's group may activate follower-centered scripts within that individual, which may then cause the "leader" to apply a follower category to the group after observing follower-like behaviors. Conversely, perceiving followership can activate leadership scripts in a potential leader, which may then increase the likelihood that others apply a leadership category to that individual. However, empirical support of this process is still needed. In addition, it remains unknown whether IFTs exhibit cross-cultural stability or whether stability exists at various levels of a schema's hierarchy. Future research needs to address these issues and identify the behavioral and perceptual components of IFTs.

Ironically, necessary research on followership and leadership is complicated by the effects of ILTs on the measurement of social processes. In the following section, we discuss research on the measurement of leadership as a joint construction of leaders and followers, highlighting how followers' cognitive and emotional processes influence ratings. We expect the same processes to operate when leaders are asked to describe followers' behaviors, as some research on performance appraisal has suggested (Feldman, 1981).

ILTS, SENSEMAKING, AND BEHAVIORAL MEASUREMENT

As in many leadership processes, leadership measurement involves a joint construction of leaders and followers. Although researchers may be primarily concerned with qualities or behaviors of leaders when they ask for follower ratings, ratings are colored and in some cases created by the follower's cognitive and emotional processes that are used to make sense of leadership processes. This has been known for many years (Eden and Leviatan, 1975; Staw, 1975), yet its consequences are still not widely appreciated. This issue is important because, as Hunter, Bedell-Avers, and Mumford (2007) noted, most leadership studies begin with a predeveloped, behaviorally based questionnaire given to subordinates to measure their leader's qualities. Correlations between such questionnaire ratings and other dependent variables are then thought to reflect the effects of leader behaviors rather than followers' potential contributions. For example, the correlation between transformational leadership behavioral ratings and reports of satisfaction by subordinates has been interpreted as reflecting the effects of transformational leadership behavior. However, these correlations are much higher when subordinates provide both the satisfaction and leadership measures than when independent sources provide behavioral ratings (Lowe, Kroeck, and Sivasubramaniam, 1996). Such results suggest that subordinates' affect and cognition could have influenced descriptions of leader behaviors.

The potential of follower affect to influence such ratings is clearly illustrated by a recent study of the Multifactor Leadership Questionnaire (MLQ) by Brown and Keeping (2005). These authors used structural equation modeling techniques to examine the effects of rater mood on the item loadings in the MLQ. Although general affect had very little effect on loadings for specific dimensions, affect directed towards the leader in the form of liking ratings had a substantial effect, which was roughly equal to the size of the dimension loadings on their indicators. This result shows that affective and cognitive processes are often integrated in ways that are hard to separate as Damasio (1994) has stressed, and that affective reactions to leaders must be taken into account when we attempt to assess leadership processes. In the following section, we take a closer look at such follower or rater effects, which often reflect processes that occur implicitly as followers make sense of, react to, remember, and rate leadership processes. We begin by summarizing some of the earlier literature documenting the effects of raters on "behavioral ratings," then we turn to more recent research that extends our understanding of such processes.

Early Research on ILTs

Reconstructed Rather Than Remembered Ratings

Research conducted in the 1970s and 1980s on ILTs had three important implications for leadership behavior measurement. First, the research clearly showed that perceivers do not operate like objective data-recording devices, storing independent slices of a leader's behavior so that it can be accurately recalled later for leader evaluation. Rather, perceivers subjectively organize behavioral information when it is encountered, assimilating it with existing knowledge structures as part of an ongoing sensemaking process. This process often assimilates rated behaviors with affective reactions such as liking the leader. Once this sensemaking occurs, it generally is not possible to *directly* retrieve the original behavioral information. Instead, raters rely on their implicit theories to retrieve behaviors that were likely to have occurred given their currently held leader evaluations. In other words, behavioral ratings reflected the nature of raters' currently held interpretive schema and only indirectly the effects of prior behavior.

This general process of immediately encoding information into global evaluations has been termed *on-line encoding* by Hastie and Park (1986), who distinguished this process from memory-based encoding in which behaviors are stored independent of an overall evaluation of another person. They emphasized that normally, perceivers recall prior on-line judgments when making a subsequent judgment rather than retrieve specific behaviors. Thus, on-line encoding in terms of leadership or followership and the subsequent use of ILTs or IFTs is likely to have important influences on behavioral ratings. Because person-based encoding is the normal default in social perceptions, at least in Western cultures, we tend to use person schema such as leadership to make sense of social behavior. And, as we have discussed in the previous section, this means that we typically categorize leaders in terms of their match to available prototypes and exemplars, which then influence the behavioral information we can later access. This process helps to explain the other two important implications for behavioral measurement.

Common Sense Science and Questionnaire Measures of Behavior

The second implication pertains to methodological processes that are normally used to construct behavioral questionnaires and evaluate their accuracy. Typically, behavioral scientists develop measuring instruments by having domain experts (e.g., managers) generate items and then giving these items to a large group of raters (e.g., subordinates) before using psychometric techniques such as factor analysis to refine these measures by dropping out items that do not load on appropriate scales. If ratings reflect the actual behaviors of leaders, these techniques might help produce purer measures of behavioral tendencies on the part of leaders. However, if ratings also reflect the sensemaking processes of perceivers, then these techniques might instead primarily reflect the structure in constructs held by perceivers on how leaders should behave.

Early research supported this latter interpretation (Eden and Leviatan, 1975; Rush, Thomas, and Lord, 1977; Weiss and Adler, 1981). These studies showed that the factor structures of popular leadership measures could be obtained from raters who were only rating hypothetical leaders, or from individuals who had limited exposure to a leader's behavior. Such results undercut the interpretation that leadership questionnaires were primarily measures of actual leadership behaviors and instead suggested that the structure of leadership questionnaires could reflect the relation of behavioral items to raters' ILTs. However, as Weiss and Adler (1981) noted, this does not mean that ILTs are inaccurate descriptions of general patterns of leader behavior, but it does mean that questionnaire descriptions may not accurately describe the behavior of a specific leader.

Along with undermining measurement processes, such research echoed a general criticism of applied social science research raised by Calder (1977). He argued that there was an over-reliance on common sense (e.g., implicit theories) as the basis for generating research theories and an under-reliance on more scientifically based constructs. The danger Calder saw was that if common sense ideas were used to generate theory, then tests of theory could also be supported by the common sense ideas of raters. One common sense theory fitting this scenario is that leaders who exhibit normative leadership styles (i.e., they behave in prototypical ways) will produce good performance in their organizations or work groups. As Meindl (1995) noted, the actual determinants of performance are too complex for most observers in real organizations to objectively evaluate. Instead, people rely on common sense–romanticized beliefs about causality in which leaders are the cause of very good (or very bad) organizational performance.

Performance as a Cue for Behavioral Ratings

Using this common sense theory, Staw (1975) recognized that it could create a reverse causality artifact in ratings in which knowledge of performance affects descriptions of prior behaviors. Focusing on group rather than on leadership processes, he showed that knowledge of group performance had significant effects on ratings of many types of group processes. Staw's research manipulated performance knowledge to determine its causal effect on ratings of group processes. However, in cross-sectional, correlational research, causality is unclear; thus, correlations between performance and group processes could reflect performance-influencing group process ratings, with rated processes actually having caused group performance, or a combination of both of these effects.

Extensive researchers showed that Staw's concern applied to the leadership field as well. For example, Rush et al. (1977) instructed participants to rate hypothetical leaders after being told that the leader's group performed well or poorly. As predicted, performance information had broad and substantial effects on all 10 behavioral scales of the Leader Behavior Description Questionnaire, which they labeled a performance cue effect (PCE). Mitchell, Larsen, and Green (1977) also reported consistent PCEs in studies using audio, video, and group interactions as stimulus materials to be rated. They also gave performance cues before groups interacted (which could affect both encoding and retrieval processes) or only after groups interacted (which could affect only retrieval processes). Because this timing manipulation did not alter PCEs substantially, they theorized that PCEs were produced mainly by retrieval processes. Subsequent research (Rush, Phillips, and Lord, 1981), which showed participants videotapes of group behavior and then gave them bogus performance feedback before behavioral ratings, also found a PCE. Specifically, their feedback manipulation was significantly correlated with global leadership ratings made immediately after viewing the videotape ($r = 0.31$) or after a 48-hour delay ($r = 0.40$), even though subjects shown good and bad performance information saw exactly the same behavior. Research by Binning and Lord (1980) also showed that PCEs occurred when leadership ratings were provided by members of groups who actually interacted on multiple occasions. Many other researchers also replicated the PCE under various conditions (Butterfield and Powell, 1981; Gioia and Sims, 1985; Larson, 1982; Larson, Lingle, and Scerbo, 1984; Lord et al., 1978; Mitchell et al., 1977; Rush and Beauvais, 1981), demonstrating a very robust effect. Thus, as Staw (1975) had suggested, the rater's implicit theories provided an alternative interpretation for the relation of behavioral ratings to performance. In other words, the rater's sensemaking processes could create correlations between performance and rated behavior that were interpreted by typical leadership researchers as the effects of leaders on performance, not rater-induced artifacts.

Recent Research on ILTs

The distinction between early and recent ILT research is somewhat arbitrary, but we use this classification to separate research demonstrating that PCEs occurred under various conditions from research aimed at explaining why PCEs occurred or how they could be eliminated. The two major theories explaining why PCEs occurred were provided by attribution theory and categorization theory. More recent research on how memory functions indicates several ways to eliminate PCEs.

Attribution Theory

Sensemaking processes are closely related to one's understanding of causal events in a situation, and leaders are often assumed to have a causal impact on outcomes (Meindl, 1995). Recognizing the importance of causal attributions, several studies have manipulated factors that increase attributions to leaders for performance outcomes. In general, PCEs are enhanced when leaders are seen as being more causal. For example, when situational factors augment causal ascriptions to leaders or when the perceptual salience of leaders is enhanced, both causal attributions to the leader and PCEs are increased (Phillips and Lord, 1981). Although one might think of attributional processes as involving explicit reasoning processes, conscious processes do not have to be involved for such effects to occur as was shown by Phillips and Lord's (1981) manipulation of visual salience.

Other research examining leadership perceptions has contrasted attributional explanations with those based on categorization theory, with results generally favoring categorization theory (Cronshaw and Lord, 1987). What does seem to be critical for the use of ILTs, whether in recognition-based or inferential processing, is that events and behaviors are interpreted using a person schema and that a trait-based interpretation is developed. This idea was clearly demonstrated in a study by Murphy and Jones (1993), which induced raters to use either event-focused (e.g., script-based) or person-focused encoding. Significant PCEs were found under person-focused conditions; however, under event-focused conditions, PCEs were reduced to nonsignificant levels for most dependent measures. In a later study, Ensari and Murphy (2003) extended these findings showing that PCEs (and prototypicality manipulations) affected charismatic leadership perceptions only when raters made dispositional attributions. Their study was also unique in employing a cross-cultural perspective. In short, these studies show that use of a person-based schema and interpretation of outcomes in terms of personal qualities are needed for PCEs, to affect leadership ratings. These findings are consistent with the general importance of person-based trait ascriptions in explaining leadership emergence in groups (Lord, De Vader, and Aliger, 1986).

Categorization Theory

As discussed earlier, leader categorization theory (Lord et al., 1982, 1984) posits that after one is classified as a leader, generic category information is used to guide subsequent ratings of behavior. Theory and research show that when a person is classified as a leader, prototypical leader behaviors are more likely to be recognized as having been seen, and antiprototypical leader behaviors are less likely to be recognized, with exactly the opposite pattern occurring when individuals are seen as being ineffective leaders. When accuracy is defined as the ability to differentiate seen from unseen behavior, then it is generally low for both prototypical and antiprototypical leadership behaviors (Binning, Zaba, and Whattam, 1986; Foti and Lord, 1987; Phillips and Lord, 1982; Phillips, 1984). Further, performance information, which affects leadership categorization, also indirectly affects memory through its influence on categorization processes (Binning et al., 1986; Phillips and Lord, 1982; Downey, Chacko, and McElroy, 1979). Using a correlational methodology in a sample of real work supervisors, Rush and Russell (1988) found that affective evaluations of leaders seemed to cue appropriate prototypes and that agreement in supervisor ratings can be produced by similar implicit theories.

Interestingly, several of these studies show that items that are neutral with respect to leadership categories are responded to most accurately (Phillips and Lord, 1982; Phillips, 1984; Foti and Lord, 1987). However, there is also evidence that when behavioral items are very specific and clear behavior is observed, the effects of performance information on ratings are reduced (Downey et al., 1979; Binning et al., 1986; Gioia and Sims, 1985), but this does not also imply that responses are more accurate, a point addressed more thoroughly in section "An Integrative Perspective on Social Perceptions and Measurement."

A common theme among all of these studies is the importance of the rater's leadership categories in guiding leader behavior descriptions. Research shows that ILTs are multidimensional, trait-based knowledge structures that guide sensemaking and behavioral encoding (Epitropaki and Martin, 2004; Offerman, Kennedy, and Wirtz, 1994). Interestingly, Foti and Lord (1987) found results paralleling those for ILTs when examining behavioral items related to scripts – the more prototypical an item, the more likely it was to be falsely recognized as having been previously observed – which replicates previous findings for script-related items (Graesser *et al.*, 1980). Such findings indicate that integration with a schema, whether event- or person-based, *diminishes* the rater's ability to distinguish observed from unobserved behaviors. Similar results occur in the performance appraisal area where frame-of-reference training has been shown to *decrease* behavioral-level accuracy (Sulsky and Day, 1992), while at the same time increasing the ability to correctly classify ratees as good or bad performers. In sum, cognitive categories aid in sensemaking, helping assimilate observed behavior with accumulated knowledge in a given domain. However, categories can also distort memory, inducing raters to falsely recognize category-consistent behaviors that did not occur as having occurred previously.

Semantic Versus Episodic Memory

The effect of ILTs on ratings can also be better understood by applying constructs and techniques developed by research in human memory. Memory researchers typically distinguish between *semantic memory,* which stores general information that accumulates with experience (e.g., dark clouds and thunder usually mean that rain is likely), and *episodic memory,* which stores context-specific memories of a particular events, such as an event with high emotional impact or vivid perceptual qualities (e.g., the black clouds and hard rain during my camping trip to Yellowstone Park last summer). ILTs reflect the effects of semantic memory, which uses categorical structures such as leadership to make sense of events. Episodic memory, which may involve a specific exemplar in a specific context, may provide more accurate but less general descriptions of leadership. Because semantic leadership knowledge seems so plausible and is so easily accessible, given the performance information or information about prototypical qualities of a leader, it is confused by raters with episodic information, and it is thought to have occurred.

One way to assess whether memory reflects a direct recollection of prior experience (episodic memory) or more general sensemaking processes associated with semantic memory is to use signal detection theory (Lord, 1985). This approach uses two parameters to separate accurate signals from background noise created by the rater's implicit theories. The first parameter, *memory sensitivity*, reflects the raters' ability to distinguish behavioral items that correspond to previously observed behaviors from similar items that correspond to unobserved behaviors. Because this distinction reflects the grounding of ratings in a specific context, it is a good indicator of episodic memory. The second parameter, *bias*, reflects a change in the threshold used in making judgments, such as an increased tendency to respond that a behavior previously occurred. Bias can be caused by a type of behavior being consistent with one's implicit understanding of a situation, such as prototypically effective leadership behavior being consistent with good performance. In a series of innovative studies Martell (Martell and Guzzo, 1991; Martell and Willis, 1993) used signal detection theory to show that PCEs were associated with the bias but not the memory sensitivity parameter. Martell and Willis (1993) also showed that bias completely mediated the relationship between PCEs and ratings. Martell and DeSmet (2001) have also shown that gender-related effects on leadership ratings operate through the bias rather than the memory sensitivity component.

We have already seen that PCEs do not occur when leaders are not seen as being the cause of performance, but Martell's research suggests that techniques that would eliminate memory bias could eliminate PCE-related distortions in leadership ratings. Martell and Evans (2005) reasoned that this bias could be eliminated by training raters to use episodic memory as a basis for ratings. In their study, participants observed a videotaped group exercise and then received bogus good or bad performance cues. Before eliciting ratings, Martell and Evans (2005) trained raters in a reality-monitoring technique aimed at eliminating memory bias. Specifically, they trained raters to distinguish between judgments that reflect a vivid memory of a specific action (*remember judgments*) from those that reflect a general feeling of knowing or familiarity (*know judgments*). Subjects may be highly confident in both remember and know judgments, but remember judgments are thought to better reflect episodic memory (Gardiner and Richardson-Klavehn, 2000). In Martell and Evans' (2005) study, participants were instructed to only respond with a "yes" to remember judgments. This source-monitoring technique completely eliminated the memory bias component associated with PCEs, but it had no effect on memory sensitivity, suggesting that appropriate rater training can eliminate bias, but it still does not enhance accuracy as indexed by memory sensitivity.

Baltes and Parker (2000) also examined rater-training approaches to eliminate PCEs. They investigated two training techniques. One trained raters to eliminate halo error (i.e., seeing universally good or bad qualities in ratees). The other involved structured-recall memory training that defines rating dimensions before viewing stimulus videotapes and also asks raters to recall behaviors relevant to each dimension before making ratings. Compared with a no-training control group in which 45% of the variance in behavioral ratings was associated with performance cues, much less variance was explained by the PCE in both the halo-effect training (3%) and the structured-recall training (4%) groups. Consistent with Martell's research, both these training techniques also reduced memory bias to nonsignificant levels, but they had no effect on memory sensitivity.

As is evident, rater training can help reduce the reliance on semantic memory in making leadership ratings, but it does not increase the reliance on episodic memory. Are there factors that can increase the use of episodic memory? Surprisingly, memory research indicates that more emotionally arousing events (Allen, Kaut, and Lord, 2009) and individuals who react more emotionally (Lord, Hall, Schlauch, Chang, & Allen, unpublished manuscript) tend to produce more accurate episodic memories. This is because emotional reactions increase attention to events and their context, producing an encoding that is more episodic. However, emotions can also bias retrieval processes in semantic memory and can be associated with halo error. Thus, more emotional memories will not be more accurate unless these emotions are used to access episodic rather than semantic memory.

One technique, visualization of prior experiences, shows some promise in facilitating the use of episodic memory. In two separate studies, Naidoo, Kohari, Lord, and Dubois (in press) compared ratings when raters visualized their leader with when they did not. This visualization procedure was designed to provide more vivid cues for retrieving behaviors that are based on perceptual aspects of the leader and context and *the rater's own feelings* more vivid cues for retrieving behaviors. The first study involved perceptions of employee's actual work supervisor, and the second had participants watch an engaging and dramatic videotape before making leadership ratings immediately and also one to three weeks later. Results from both studies showed that, as predicted, visualization made affect a more central component in ratings. Interestingly, the second study also showed that under visualization conditions, delayed ratings of leaders were more consistent with ratings made immediately after viewing the videotape and, perhaps more importantly, episodic memory recall was better in the leader visualization condition.

To summarize briefly, research shows that typical behavioral measurement is dependent on the ILTs that people use to construct on-line interpretations of social processes such as leadership. ILTs reflect general knowledge stored in semantic memory, and categorization processes seem to tap into this general knowledge when ratings are made. More episodic memory can be relied on for ratings under special circumstances, such as when raters are trained in reality monitoring (Martell and Evans, 2005), and this process can reduce memory biases associated with semantic knowledge, but it does not necessarily make ratings more accurate. To increase behavioral accuracy, both encoding and memory retrieval processes need to use episodic memory. This may occur when behavior is especially vivid or when intense emotions are aroused.

AN INTEGRATIVE PERSPECTIVE ON SOCIAL PERCEPTIONS AND MEASUREMENT

As evident, leadership perceptions and leader behavior measurement are complex, dynamic processes that involve both aspects of leaders and processes specific to followers. Perceivers (leaders or followers) use schema derived from experience but tuned to a particular context to make sense of behavior in an ongoing manner and to form social perceptions. Many of the effects illustrated in the earlier review can be understood by taking a closer look at theory, addressing what knowledge actually is and how perceptual/memory processes operate. In this final section, we address these two issues, simultaneously showing how a more precise specification of these cognitive processes helps us understand many of the effects research has shown to be associated with ILTs. These effects and associated explanations are shown in Table 1.1.

Sensemaking and the Nature of Knowledge

Classical, Symbolic View of Knowledge

In what has been labeled the classical view, knowledge is thought to be represented in the form of symbols (e.g., letters and words) that are distinct from the perceptual structures on which they are based. Thus, perceivers were thought to translate observed behavior into more abstract symbolic representations that had a generalized meaning, such as cognitive categories and ILTs. Using this translation process, perceivers seem to shift from a more episodic to a semantic memory representation to undergird their understanding of leadership. This symbolic representation was thought to be guided by leadership prototypes that were relatively stable (Epitropaki and Martin, 2004).

Connectionist View of Knowledge

Two important changes in this view of ILTs have occurred that question the classical view of knowledge. Following cognitive research (i.e., connectionism) that emphasizes more microlevel processes produced by associative networks, Lord *et al.* (2001) maintained that neural networks integrate many features in an ongoing manner in forming leadership perceptions. Thus, Lord *et al.* (2001) saw leadership categories as being defined by neural networks rather than prototypes which are symbolic and permanently stored in long-term memory. Research by Foti *et al.* (2008) supports this perspective showing that personal relevance moderated the extent to which the connectionist networks guiding person perception changed during a task.

This more dynamic view of leadership perceptions helps us to understand how performance cues could retrospectively bias what is retrieved from memory (Finding 1 in Table 1.1). It is likely that performance information

Table 1.1 Explanation of implicit leadership theory (ILT) effects based on different views of knowledge and adaptive resonance theory (ART)

Finding from Prior Leadership Research	Explanation Based on Knowledge View or ART
1. PCE affects descriptions of schema-consistent behaviors	Performance inferences or behavioral recognition both activate categories; descriptions are then based on category content
2. Affect and vividness of stimuli can affect memory sensitivity	Both affect and vividness can capture attention, and they are part of an embodied, context-specific episodic representation
3. Followers' perceptual schemas and affective states affect leadership perceptions	Perceptions reflect embodied as well as symbolic knowledge in perceivers
4. ILTs (IFTs) and associated leadership processes have an embodied component that is not symbolically represented	Sensemaking, reactions to leaders (followers), and contextual stimuli are embodied; we understand through perceiving, reacting, and acting
5. Perceptions of leadership are more strongly tied to patterns than individual features	Patterns of inputs provide multiple routes to access leadership schema and they resonate more strongly with these schema
6. Memory sensitivity (ability to distinguish seen from unseen behaviors) is low for schema-consistent behaviors	On-line encoding is based on resonating interpretations between a pattern of inputs and previously learned schema; individual inputs are not noticed or encoded; an interpretation's pattern is stored in semantic memory
7. Once formed, leadership perceptions are slow to change and change in a discontinuous manner	Resonating interpretations of stimuli receive both top–down and bottom–up activation; new inputs must overcome top–down schematic activation
8. Discontinuities in changing perceptions can vary in strength	Vigilance parameters alter the degree of fit needed for resonance to occur; liberal parameters allow many partially competing patterns to resonate, making misfits harder to detect
9. Context determines basic level categories	Context and prototypical patterns are assimilated in convergence zones and are learned together
10. Categorization can be based on a continuum from exemplar to prototype models	Stringent vigilance parameters may require precise fit on many or very specific features, requiring exemplar-based categorization; liberal vigilance parameters may allow fewer or more abstract features to fit, allowing for a prototype-based process

not only makes leadership categories more accessible, increasing the ease with which prototypical behaviors can be retrieved, but also activates an entire prototype, making unseen but plausible behaviors as active as behaviors that were actually observed on a previous occasion. In other words, the connection of leadership behaviors and performance expectations is a two-way street. Activation can flow in either direction: We can recognize leadership when a pattern of traits and behaviors activates a network of prototypical qualities (Smith and Foti, 1998; Foti and Hauenstein, 2007), with the resulting leadership perceptions fostering high performance expectations; or alternatively, we can infer leadership and activate the network of underlying prototypical qualities given the high performance information. In either case, perceptions, performance, and behavior are activated together, and raters have limited ability to separate seen from unseen, but prototype-consistent, behaviors.

Embodied, Embedded View of Knowledge

A more contemporary view of knowledge emphasizes that not only are the perceiver's abstract mental structures involved in the perceptual processes but knowledge is also literally embodied in that it is dependent on the perceptual structures, the anticipated motor responses to these structures, and affective reactions in the perceiver (Neidenthal et al., 2005); that is, the mind and body are both involved in sensemaking processes. This embodied view of knowledge implies that perceptions arise in a fundamental sense from the physical experience of a perceiver in a particular context. Consistent with this view, qualities like gender (Scott and Brown, 2006) or race (Rosette et al., 2008) can have subtle effects on how perceivers see and interpret leadership behaviors because they create salient perceptual structures that underlie information stored in episodic memory, and they also have important implications for how to act and what reactions to expect.

This embodied perspective also emphasizes that abstract (i.e., amodal) knowledge, such as that tapped by most questionnaires purporting to measure behavior, is fundamentally different from the embodied knowledge that drives sensemaking procedures. In a literal sense, sensemaking is embodied because a physical, living, and feeling person is embedded in the sensemaking context. As such, meaning construction takes into account potential harm or benefit to that person. Potential harm or benefit produces affective reactions and activates motor programs related to appropriate responses. Consequently, accurate, context-specific knowledge is grounded in perceptual, affective, and motor structures; when these components are vivid, they can be bound together to create a specific episodic memory (Allen et al., 2009). Rating procedures, such as visualization, can help raters tap into previous episodic memory; however, asking for the frequency of leadership behaviors is much more likely to access more general semantic knowledge (Finding 2 in Table 1.1) and ratings may merely reflect the accessibility of that semantic knowledge (Lord et al., 1984; Lore and Foti, 1987).

This embodied perspective helps us understand why visualization procedures can be helpful in retrieving prior experience (Naidoo et al., in press) and also helps explain why affective reactions to a leader are an important part of rating processes (Brown and Keeping, 2005). But, it also has additional complications; for example, it suggests that factors such as perceptual salience will be an important component of our understanding of leadership as in Phillips and Lord's (1981) study, which showed that visual salience can affect both causal attributions and leadership ratings. Factors that merely prime perceptual structures, like orientation along a vertical dimension, can also affect leadership perceptions (Giessner and Schubert, 2007). Similarly, processes that elicit affective reactions in perceivers (Bono and Ilies, 2006; Naidoo and Lord, 2008) can influence perceptions of leadership. In short, followers' embodied responses are part of the process of leadership perception (Finding 3 in Table 1.1). Embodied responses also go beyond perceptual processes, providing an important basis for decision making based on somatic markers (Bechara and Damasio, 2005).

An additional advantage of an embodied, embedded perspective on knowledge is that it focuses on sensemaking processes that involve real people with powerful emotions in real contexts (O'Malley et al., 2008). Perceptions, affective reactions, motor behaviors, and understanding all emerge in a dynamic, ongoing process (Weick, 1995). This suggests that the embodied knowledge of these individuals is a fundamental part of the leadership process. Leadership theories that emphasize such components rather than just abstract, behavioral knowledge have the potential to be more valid (See Naidoo et al., in press, for an illustration of such an effect) (Finding 4, in Table 1.1).

The Importance of Schemas during Perceptual Processes

It is widely recognized that schemas are necessary to help simplify information processing, but their precise role in guiding perceptions is usually glossed over. Schemas not only provide ready-made constructs for encoding observed behavior, but also provide a filtering system that helps individuals notice and interpret some aspects of their context while ignoring others. They do this by accentuating the activation of information relevant to schema, making them more likely to be consciously noticed. Grossberg's (1999) adaptive resonance theory (ART) provides a detailed explanation of this selection process.

ART and Top–Down Influence on Perception

ART contends that mental representations, such as ILTs, are an important top–down influence that interacts with bottom–up processes, such as patterns of traits or behaviors, during perception and information processing. If this interaction creates a resonance state with sufficiently high activation, the created pattern (i.e., an interpretation of the stimulus) gains access to working memory. This is an important point, because what is noticed is a pattern or interpretation, not the isolated inputs that help create this pattern. Thus, only this interpretive pattern can be encoded consciously and stored in memory.

In more concrete terms, information from external stimuli, such as observed leader behaviors, is automatically compared with cognitive categories held in long-term memory, such as a leader prototype, via bidirectional feedback loops. Only successful top–down and bottom–up matches are brought into working memory, creating an emergent interpretive structure that identifies a person as a leader or a follower. Unsuccessful matches result in either the comparison of observed behavior with a different representation in long-term memory or, if sufficiently interesting, the learning of a new cognitive category. Consistent with this reasoning, research has found that patterns have greater effects than their independent constituent elements (Smith and Foti, 1999; Foti and Hauenstein, 2007) in predicting leadership perceptions, which makes sense because the pattern of characteristics creates resonance, not individual elements (Finding 5 in Table 1.1).

Further, because the pattern of inputs resonates with a perceiver's ILT (or IFT), it is hard to distinguish characteristics consistent with the perceiver's implicit theories that were not part of the input pattern from actual inputs (Finding 6 in Table 1.1). This is because as schemas resonate (i.e., using con-nectionist terms, settle in to an interpretation), gap-filling occurs and aspects of schemas not present in input patterns become activated. This gap-filling should be less extreme for aspects that are closely tied to perceptual features of a stimulus, but it may be substantial for more abstract features. Thus, we would not encode a female leader as being a male because leadership prototypes con-tain many masculine features, but we may perceive her as being intelligent or decisive regardless of whether we actually observe behavior related to these characteristics.

Search for Appropriate Categories

According to Grossberg, a *vigilance parameter* monitors the process by which stimulus input is matched to a prototype. When the vigilance parameter is more stringent, a stricter match between stimulus input and a relevant schema is required for resonance to occur. With a more liberal vigilance parameter, a looser match may be sufficient to create resonance. For instance, Barack Obama's ability to gain the popular presidential vote may have depended in part on how well he fitted Americans' expectations of an ideal presidential leader – yet the strictness of the match that is required can vary across and within individuals. With very strict vigilance parameters, Obama may have a hard time overcoming racial biases that are incorporated into ILTs, as a near-exact match may be required. If he is unable to match our expectations of a leader, we may attempt to match him to a non-leader category, perhaps revolving around his race or youthfulness. As noted by Medvedeff and Lord (2007), affect may influence the strictness of the vigilance parameter, with positive affect inducing less stringent vigilance than negative affect.

However, once a match is found and resonance occurs – that is, an inter-pretation of a person as being a leader is created – input patterns can change without the resonant pattern being altered very much. Thus, as we have al-ready noted, cognitive categories create inertia in social perceptions, causing changes in leadership perceptions to be discontinuous (Finding 7 in Table 1.1). As well as modulating the nature of perceptions, vigilance parameters could modulate the nature of change by altering the degree of fit required to create a new interpretation of a stimulus. With a liberal vigilance parameter, which allows many competing patterns to be interpreted similarly, interpre-tations would have more inertia because many aspects of the stimulus would have to change before the interpretive category would change (Finding 8 in Table 1.1).

According to ART, if all of the accessible categories are exhausted without leading to a successful match with a stimulus, a new prototype may be cre-ated. Importantly, prototype learning occurs as a whole. After stimuli reach our senses and are interpreted by feature detectors, conjunction neurons store contextual information from multiple modalities in parallel (Neidenthal et al., 2005). With repeated exposure to a stimulus over time, populations of conjunc-tion neurons converge within association areas of the brain called *convergence zones* to represent the stimulus (Damasio, 1989). These convergence zones can later be reactivated without any of the original stimulus input and are contextually dependent. In this sense, we recreate perceptual images when we remember something (Payne et al., 1999) and retrieval of information occurs as a whole. With repeated activation over time, the pattern gets strengthened, creating a prototype that can guide perceptions.

Learned prototypes can later be refined through experience to slowly change to accommodate repeatedly encountered new information. However, the stim-ulus' context, which is bound to the prototype in convergence zones that are reactivated to create memories, guides our expectations and interpretations when bottom–up information is ambiguous or when a similar context occurs in the future. Thus, the theory suggests, as Rosch's categorization theory has found, that it is the combination of context and stimulus features that creates a basic or fundamental level of categorization (Finding 9 in Table 1.1).

With a strict vigilance parameter, a near-exact match between the stimulus' context and a matching category's context may be required for categorization to occur. That match may include enough perceptual and contextual features to require an exemplar-based match. However, more liberal vigilance param-eters may overlook contextual inconsistencies during category searches, thus allowing for a wider range of potential target categories to be considered. In other words, the continuum from exemplar to prototype models proposed by some researchers (Vanpaemel et al., 2005; Verbeemen et al., 2007) may also reflect the effects of stringent versus liberal vigilance parameters (Finding 10 in Table 1.1). In this way, prototype matching or accessibility is strongly tied to contextual information, but what is critical about context will be defined by an embodied perceiver, who has a particular history and physical perspective, relevant affect, and ongoing somatic or motor reactions during sensemaking. Extending the reasoning of Medvedeff and Lord (2007) to this issue, the effect of perceivers' affective states on vigilance parameters may help determine whether exemplar or prototype models are used.

Because ART is capable of accommodating new information without eradicating existing knowledge structures, this theory is capable of reconciling the stability and plasticity of ILTs. Stability involves matching existing structure, but plasticity occurs when we create new schema because matches to extant schemas cannot be found. Through its introduction of vigilance parameters that control the stringency of schema matches and its emphasis on prototype learning as a whole, ART should prove noteworthy within the study of leadership and followership. Indeed, it has received recent attention though its application to gender biases (Hogue and Lord, 2007), leadership categorization and affect (Medvedeff and Lord, 2007), and goal striving (Johnson, Chang, and Lord, 2006).

CONCLUSIONS

As shown in Table 1.1, we can deepen our understanding of the effects associated with ILTs or IFTs by considering the nature of knowledge and the dynamics of ART processes. In conjunction, these two theories imply that knowledge, perceptions, and memory are actually by-products of an embodied agent who is situated in a particular context and is attempting to adapt to that context while meaning is being created. Perception, action, and understanding are dynamically interrelated over time. Leadership processes reflect this dynamic, embodied, evolving understanding of both leaders and followers.

REFERENCES

Abelson, R. P. (1981). Psychological status of the script concept. *American Psychologist,* 7, 715–29.

Allen, P., Kaut, K., & Lord, R. (2009). Emotion and episodic memory. In E. Dere, A. Easton, & J. Huston (Eds), *Handbook of Behavioral Neuroscience: Episodic Memory Research* (pp. 115–32). Amsterdam: Elsevier Science.

Ambady, N., & Rosenthal, R. (1992). Thin slices of behavior as predictors of interpersonal consequences: A meta-analysis. *Psychological Bulletin,* **111**, 256–74.

Baltes, B. B., & Parker, C. P. (2000). Reducing the effects of performance expectations on behavioral ratings. *Organizational Behavior and Human Decision Processes,* **82**, 237–67.

Barsalou, L. W. (1999). Perceptual symbol systems. *Behavioral and Brain Sciences,* **22** (4), 577–660.

Bechara, A., & Damasio, A. (2005). The somatic marker hypothesis: A neural theory of economic decisions. *Games and Economic Behavior*, **52**, 336–72.

Binning, J. F., & Lord, R. G. (1980). Boundary conditions for performance cue effects on group process ratings: Familiarity versus type of feedback. *Organizational Behavior & Human Performance*, **26**, 115–30.

Binning, J. F., Zaba, A. J., & Whattam, J. C. (1986). Explaining the biasing effects of performance cues in terms of cognitive categorization. *Academy of Management Journal*, **29**, 521–35.

Bolinger, D. L. (1964). Intonation across languages. In: J. H. Greenberg, C. A. Ferguson & E. A. Moravcsik (Eds), *Universals of human language, Vol. 2: Phonology*. Stanford, CA: Stanford University Press, pp. 471–524.

Brown, D. J., & Keeping, L. M. (2005). Elaborating the construct of transformational leadership: The role of affect. *Leadership Quarterly*, **16**, 245–273.

Brown, D., Marchioro, C., Tan, J. A., & Lord, R. G. (April 1998). *Individual difference variables and leadership perceptions: Linear or catastrophic relationship?* Poster paper presented at the annual meeting of the Society for Industrial and Organizational Psychology, Dallas, TX.

Butterfield, D. A., & Powell, N. (1981). Effect of group performance, leader sex, and rater sex on ratings of leader behavior. *Organizational Behavior & Human Performance*, **28** (1), 129–41.

Calder, B. J. (1977). Attribution theory: Phenomenology or science? *Personality and Social Psychology Bulletin*, **3** (4), 612–15.

Cantor, N., & Mischel, W. (1979). Prototypicality and personality: Effects on free recall and personality impressions. *Journal of Research in Personality*, **13**, 187–205.

Chaleff, I. (1998). *The courageous follower: Standing Up to and for Our Leaders*. San Francisco, CA: Berrett-Koehler Publishers.

Cronshaw, S. F., & Lord, R. G. (1987). Effects of categorization, attribution, and encoding processes on leadership perceptions. *Journal of Applied Psychology*, **72** (1), 97–106.

Damasio, A. R. (1994). *Descartes' Error: Emotion, Reason, and the Human Brain*. New York: Grosset/Putnam.

Damasio, A. R. (1989). The brain binds entities and events by multiregional activation from convergence zones. *Neural Computation*, **1** (1), 123–32.

Den Hartog, D. N., House, R. J., Hanges, P. J., et al. (1999). Culture specific and cross-culturally generalizable implicit leadership theories: Are the attributes of charismatic/transformational leadership universally endorsed? *Leadership Quarterly*, **10**, 219–58.

Dickson, M. W., Resick, C., & Hanges, P. J. (2006). Systematic variation in organizationally-shared cognitive prototypes of effective leadership based on organizational form. *Leadership Quarterly*, **17**, 487–505.

Downey, H. K., Chacko, T. I., & McElroy, J. C. (1979). Attribution of the "causes" of performance: A constructive, quasi-longitudinal replication of the Staw (1975) study. *Organizational Behavior & Human Performance*, **24** (3), 287–99.

Eagly, A. H., & Carli, L. L. (2003). The female leadership advantage: An evaluation of the evidence. *The Leadership Quarterly*, **14**, 807–37.

Eagly, A. H., & Karau, J. (2002). Role congruity theory of prejudice toward female leaders. *Psychological Review*, **109** (3), 573–98.

Eden, D., & Leviatan, U. (1975). Implicit leadership theory as a determinant of the factor structure underlying supervisory behavior scales. *Journal of Applied Psychology*, **60** (6), 736–41.

Engle, E. M., & Lord, G. (1997). Implicit theories, self-schemas, and leader-member exchange. *Academy of Management Journal*, **40** (4), 988–1010.

Ensari, N., & Murphy, S. E. (2003). Cross-cultural variations in leadership perceptions and attribution of charisma to the leader. *Organizational Behavior and Human Decision Processes*, **92**, 52–66.

Epitropaki, O., & Martin, R. (2004). Implicit leadership theories in applied settings: Factor structure, generalizability, and stability over time. *Journal of Applied Psychology*, **89**, 293–310.

Feldman, J. (1981). Beyond attribution theory: Cognitive processes in performance appraisal. *Journal of Applied Psychology*, **66**, 127–48.

Fielding, K. S., & Hogg, A. (1997). Social identity, self-categorization, and leadership: A field study of small interactive groups. *Group Dynamics: Theory, Research, and Practice*, **1** (1), 39–51.

Foti, R. J., & Lord, R. G. (1987). Prototypes and scripts: The effects of alternative methods of processing information on rating accuracy. *Organizational Behavior and Human Decision Processes*, **39**, 318–40.

Foti, R. J., Knee Jr., R. E., & Backert, R. S. G. (2008). Multi-level implications of framing leadership perceptions as a dynamic process. *The Leadership Quarterly*, **19**, 178–94.

Foti, R. J., & Hauenstein, A. (2007). Pattern and Variable Approaches in Leadership Emergence and Effectiveness. *Journal of Applied Psychology*, **92** (2), 347–55.

Gardiner, J. M., & Richardson-Klavehn, A. (2000). Remembering and knowing. In E. Tulving & F. I. M. Craik, (Eds), (*The Oxford Handbook of Memory* (pp. 229–44). London: Oxford University Press.

Gerstner, C. R., & Day, V. (1994). Cross-cultural comparison of leadership prototypes. *Leadership Quarterly*, **5** (2), 121–34.

Giessner, S. R., & Schubert, T. W. (2007). High in the hierarchy: How vertical location and judgments of leaders' power are interrelated. *Organizational Behavior and Human Decision Processes*, **104**, 30–44.

Gioia, D. A., & Manz, C. C. (1985). Linking cognition and behavior: A script processing interpretation of vicarious learning. *Academy of Management Review*, **10**, 527–39.

Gioia, D. A., & Poole, P. P. (1984). Scripts in organizational behavior. *Academy of Management Review*, **9** (3), 449–59.

Gioia, D. A., & Sims, P. (1985). On avoiding the influence of implicit leadership theories in leader behavior descriptions. *Educational and Psychological Measurement*, **45** (2), 217–232.

Graen, G. B., & Scandura, A. (1987). Toward a psychology of dyadic organizing. *Research in Organizational Behavior*, **9**, 175–208.

Graesser, A. C., Woll, S. B., Kowalski, D. J., & Smith, D. A. (1980). Memory for typical and atypical actions in scripted activities. *Journal of Experimental Psychology: Human Learning and Memory*, **6**, 503–15.

Grossberg, S. (1999). The link between brain learning, attention, and consciousness. *Consciousness and Cognition*, **8**, 1–44.

Hains, S. C., Hogg, M. A., & Duck, J. M. (1997). Self-categorization and leadership: Effects of group prototypicality and leader stereotypicality. *Personality and Social Psychology Bulletin*, **23** (10), 1087–99.

Hall, R. J., Workman, J. W., & Marchioro, C. A. (1998). Sex, task, and behavioral flexibility effects on leadership perceptions. *Organizational Behavior and Human Decision Processes*, **74** (1), 1–32.

Hampton, J. (1993). Prototype models of concept representation. In I. Van Mechelen, J. Hampton, R. S. Michalski, & P. Theuns (Eds), *Categories and Concepts: Theoretical Views and Inductive Data Analysis* (pp. 67–95). San Diego, CA: Academic Press.

Hanges, P. J., Lord, R. G., & Dickson, M. W. (2000). An information processing perspective on leadership and culture. A case for connectionist architecture. *Applied Psychology: An International Review*, **49**, 133–61.

Hanges, P. J., Lord, R. G., Day, D. V., Sipe, W. P., Smith, W. G., & Brown, D. J. (1997, April). Leadership and gender bias: Dynamic measures and nonlinear modeling. *Paper presented at 12th Annual Conference of the Society for Industrial and Organizational Psychology, St. Louis, MO.*

Hanges, P. J., Lord, R. G., Godfrey, E. G., & Raver, J. L. (2002). Modeling nonlinear relationships: Neural networks and catastrophe analysis. In S. Rogelberg (Ed.), *Handbook of Research Methods in Industrial/Organizational Psychology.* (pp. 431–55) Oxford, UK: Blackwell.

Hastie, R., & Park, B. (1986). The relationship between memory and judgment depends on whether the judgment task is memory-based or on-line. *Psychological Review*, **93**, 258–68.

Heilman, M. E., Block, C. J., Martell, R. F., & Simon, M. C. (1989). Has anything changed? Current characterizations of men, women, and managers. *Journal of Applied Psychology*, **74** (6), 935–42.

Hintzman, D. L., & Ludlam, G. (1980). Differential forgetting of prototypes and old instances: Simulation by an exemplar-based classification model. *Memory & Cognition*, **8** (4), 378–82.

Hogg, M. A. (2001). A social identity theory of leadership. *Personality and Social Psychology Review*, **5** (3), 184–200.

Hogg, M. A., Fielding, K. S., Johnson, D., Masser, B., Russell, E., & Svensson, A. (2006). Demographic category membership and leadership in small groups: A social identity analysis. *The Leadership Quarterly*, **17**, 335–50.

Hogg, M. A., Hains, S. C., & Mason, I. (1998). Identification and leadership in small groups: Salience, frame of reference, and leader stereotypicality effects on leader evaluations. *Journal of Personality and Social Psychology*, **75** (5), 1248–63.

Hogg, M. A., Martin, R., Epitropaki, O., Mankad, A., Svensson, A., & Weeden, K. (2005). Effective leadership in salient groups: Revisiting leader-member exchange theory from the perspective of the social identity theory of leadership. *Personality and Social Psychology Bulletin*, **31** (7), 991–1004.

Hogue, M., & Lord, R. G. (2007). A multilevel, complexity theory approach to understanding gender bias in leadership. *The Leadership Quarterly*, **18**, 370–90.

Hollander, E. P. (1992). Leadership, followership, self, and others. *Leadership Quarterly*, **3** (1), 43–54.

House, R. J., Hanges, P. J., Ruiz-Quintanilla, *et al.* (1999). Cultural influences on leadership and organizations: Project GLOBE. *Advances in Global Leadership*, **1**, 171–233.

Hunter, S. T., Bedell-Avers, K. E., & Mumford, M. D. (2007). The typical leadership study: Assumptions, implications, and potential remedies. *Leadership Quarterly*, **18** (5), 435–46.

Johnson, R. E., Chang, C. H., & Lord, R. G. (2006). Moving from cognition to behavior: What the research says. *Psychological Bulletin*, **90**, 381–415.

Kelley, R. E. (2008). Rethinking followership. In B. Shamir, R. Pillai, M. C. Bligh, & M. Uhl-Bien (Eds), *Follower-Centered Perspectives on Leadership: A Tribute to the Memory of James R. Meindl* (pp. 5–15). Greenwich, CT: Information Age Publishing.

Kipnis, D. (1976). *The Powerholders*. Oxford, England: University of Chicago Press.

Lakoff, G. (1987). Cognitive models and prototype theory. In U. Neisser (Ed.), *Concepts and Conceptual Development: Ecological and Intellectual Factors in Categorization* (pp. 63–100). New York: Cambridge University Press.

Lance, C. E., Hoffman, B. J., Gentry, W. A., & Baranik, L. E. (2008). Rater source factors represent important subcomponents of the criterion space, not rater bias. *Human Management Review*, 18, 223–32.

Larson, J. R. (1982). Cognitive mechanisms mediating the impact of implicit theories of leader behavior on leader behavior ratings. *Organizational Behavior & Human Performance*, 29 (1), 129–40.

Larson, J. R., Lingle, J. H., & Scerbo, M. M. (1984). The impact of performance cues on leader-behavior ratings: The role of selective information availability and probabilistic response bias. *Organizational Behavior & Human Performance*, 33 (3), 323–49.

Lord, R. G. (1985). An information processing approach to social perceptions, leadership and behavioral measurement in organizations. In B. M. Staw & L. L. Cummings (Eds), *Research in Organizational Behavior* (Vol. 7, pp. 87–128). Greenwich, CT: JAI Press.

Lord, R. G., Binning, J. F., Rush, M. C., & Thomas, J. C. (1978). The effect of performance cues and leader behavior on questionnaire ratings of leadership behavior. *Organizational Behavior & Human Performance*, 21 (1), 27–39.

Lord, R. G., & Brown, J. (2001). Leadership, values, and subordinate self-concepts. *Leadership Quarterly*, 12 (2), 133–52.

Lord, R. G., & Brown, D. J. (2004). *Leadership Processes and Follower Self-Identity*. Mahwah, NJ: Erlbaum.

Lord, R. G., Brown, D. J., & Harvey, J. L. (2001). System constraints on leadership perceptions, behavior and influence: An example of connectionist level processes. In M. A. Hogg & R. S. Tindale (Eds), *Blackwell Handbook of Social Psychology: Group Processes* (pp. 283–310). Oxford, UK: Blackwell Publishers.

Lord, R. G., Brown, D. J., Harvey, J. L., & Hall, R. J. (2001). Contextual constraints on prototype generation and their multilevel consequences for leadership perceptions. *The Leadership Quarterly*, 12, 311–38.

Lord, R. G., de Vader, C. L., & Alliger, G. M. (1986). A meta-analysis of the relation between personality traits and leadership perceptions: An application of validity generalization procedures. *Journal of Applied Psychology*, 71 (3), 402–10.

Lord, R. G., Foti, R. J., & de Vader, C. L. (1984). A test of leadership categorization theory: Internal structure, information processing, and leadership perceptions. *Organizational Behavior & Human Performance*, 34, 343–78.

Lord, R. G., Foti, R. J., & Phillips, J. S. (1982). A theory of leadership categorization. In J. G. Hunt, U. Sekeran, C. Schriesheim (Eds), *Leadership: Beyond Establishment Views* (pp.104–21). Carbondale, IL: Southern Illinois University.

Lord, R. G., & Hall, R. J. (2003). Identity, leadership categorization, and leadership schema. In D. van Knippenberg & M. A. Hogg (Eds.), *Leadership and Power: Identity Processes in Groups and Organizations* (pp. 48–64). Newbury Park, CA: Sage.

Lord, R. G., & Kernan, M. C. (1987). Scripts as determinants of purposeful behavior in organizations. *Academy of Management Review*, 12, 265–77.

Lord, R. G., & Maher, K. J. (1991). *Leadership and Information Processing: Linking Perceptions and Performance*. Boston: Routledge.

Lord, R. G., & Smith, E. (1983). Theoretical, information processing, and situational factors affecting attribution theory models of organizational behavior. *Academy of Management Review*, 8 (1), 50–60.

Lowe, K. G., Kroeck, K. G., & Sivasubramaniam, N. (1996). Effectiveness correlates of transformational and transactional leadership: A meta-analytic review of the MLQ literature. *Leadership Quarterly*, 7, 385–425.

Martell, R. F., & Evans, D. P. (2005). Source-monitoring training: Toward reducing rater expectancy effects in behavioral measurement. *Journal of Applied Psychology*, **90**, 956–63.

Martell, R. F., & Guzzo, R. A. (1991). The dynamics of implicit theories of group performance: When and how do they operate? *Organizational Behavior and Human Decision Processes*, **50**, 51–74.

Martell, R. F., & DeSmet, L. (2001). A diagnostic-ration approach to measuring beliefs about the leadership abilities of male and female managers. *Journal of Applied Psychology*, **86** (6), 1223–31.

Martell, R. G., & Willis, C. E. (1993). Effects of observers' performance expectations on behavior ratings of work groups: Memory or response bias? *Organizational Behavior and Human Decision Processes*, **56**, 91–109.

Mccaw, W. (1999). The perception of followers. *Dissertation Abstracts International*, **60**, 6B. 2998.

Medin, D. L., & Schaffer, M. (1978). Context theory of classification learning. *Psychological Review*, **85** (3), 207–38.

Medvedeff, M. E., & Lord, R. G. (2007). Extending the follower-centered perspective on leadership: A social identity analysis of followers' role in leadership effectiveness. In B. Shamir, R. Pillai, M. C. Bligh, & M. Uhl-Bien (Eds), *Follower-centered Perspectives on Leadership: A Tribute to the Memory of James R. Meindl* (pp. 19–50). Charlotte, NC: Information Age Publishing.

Meindl, J. R. (1995). The romance of leadership as a follower-centric theory: A social constructionist approach. Leadership Quarterly, **6**, 329–41.

Mitchell, T. R., Larson, J. R., & Green, S. (1977). Leader behavior, situational moderators, and group performance: An attributional analysis. *Organizational Behavior & Human Performance*, **18**, 254–68.

Murphy, M. R., & Jones, A. P. (1993). The influence of performance cues and observational focus on performance rating accuracy. *Journal of Applied Social Psychology*, **23**, 1523–45.

Naidoo, L. J., Kohari, N. E., Lord, R. G., & DuBois, D. (in press). 'Seeing' is retrieving: Recovering emotional content in leadership processes through visualization. *The Leadership Quarterly*.

Neidenthal, P. M., Barsalou, L. W., Winkielman, P., Krauth-Gruber, S., & Ric, F. (2005). Embodiment in attitudes, social perception, and emotions. *Personality and Social Psychology Review*, **9** (3), 184–211.

Neuberg, S. L. (1996). Social motives and expectancy-tinged social interactions. In R. M. Sorrentino & T. E. Higgins, (Eds), (*Handbook of Motivation and Cognition, Vol. 3: The interpersonal context*. New York, NY: Guilford Press.

O'Malley, A., Ritchie, S. A., Lord, R. G., Gregory, J. B., & Young, C. (2008, August). *Incorporating embodied cognition into sensemaking theory: A theoretical examination of embodied processes in a leadership context*. Paper presented at the Academy of Management Convention, Anaheim, CA.

Offerman, L. R., Kennedy, J. K., & Wirtz, P. W. (1994). Implicit leadership theories: Content, structure, and generalizability. *Leadership Quarterly*, **5**, 43–58.

Payne, D. G., Klin, C. M., Lampinen, J. M., Neuschatz, J. S., & Lindsay, D. S. (1999). Memory applied. In F. T. Durso (Ed.), *Handbook of Applied Cognition* (pp. 83–113). Binghamton, NY: John Wiley & Sons.

Phillips, J. S. (1984). The accuracy of leadership ratings: A cognitive categorization perspective. *Organizational Behavior & Human Performance*, **33**, 125–38.

Phillips, J. S., & Lord, G. (1981). Causal attributions and perceptions of leadership. *Organizational Behavior & Human Performance*, **28** (2), 143–63.

Phillips, J. S., & Lord, R. G. (1982). Schematic information processing and perceptions of leadership in problem-solving groups. *Journal of Applied Psychology*, 67, 486–92.

Ritter, B. A., & Lord, R. G. (2007). The impact of previous leaders on the evaluation of new leaders: An alternative to prototype matching. *Journal of Applied Psychology*, 92 (6), 1683–95.

Ritter, B. A., & Yoder, D. (2004). Gender differences in leader emergence persist even for dominant women: An updated confirmation of role congruity theory. *Psychology of Women Quarterly*, 28 (3), 187–93.

Rosch, E., & Mervis, C. B. (1975). Family resemblances: Studies in the internal structure of categories. *Cognitive Psychology*, 7, 573–605.

Rosch, E. (1977). Human categorization. In N. Warren (Ed.), *Advances in Cross-Cultural Psychology (Vol. 1)*. London: Academic Press.

Rosch, E. (1978). Principles of categorization. In E. Rosch & B. B. Lloyd (Eds), *Cognition and Categorization*. Hillsdale, NJ: Erlbaum.

Rosette, A. S., Leonardelli, G. J., & Phillips, K. W. (2008). The white standard: Racial bias in leader categorization. *Journal of Applied Psychology*, 93 (4), 758–77.

Rost, J. (2008) Followership: An outmoded concept. In B. Shamir, R. Pillai, M. C. Bligh, & M. Uhl-Bien (Eds), *Follower-Centered Perspectives on Leadership: A Tribute to the Memory of James R. Meindl* (pp. 53–64). Greenwich, CT: Information Age Publishing.

Rush, M. C., & Beauvais, L. (1981). A critical analysis of format-induced versus subject-imposed bias in leadership ratings. *Journal of Applied Psychology*, 66 (6), 722–27.

Rush, M. C., Phillips, J. S., & Lord, R. G. (1981). Effects of a temporal delay in rating on leader behavior descriptions: A laboratory investigation. *Journal of Applied Psychology*, 66 (4), 442–50.

Rush, M. C., Thomas, J. C., & Lord, R. G. (1977). Implicit leadership theory: A potential threat to the internal validity of leader behavior questionnaires. *Organizational Behavior & Human Performance*, 20 (1), 93–110.

Rush, M. E., & Russell, J. E. A. (1988). Leader prototypes and prototype-contingent consensus in leader behavior descriptions. *Journal of Experimental Social Psychology*, 24, 88–104.

Scott, K. A., & Brown, D. J. (2006). Female first, leader second? Gender bias in the encoding of leadership behavior. *Organizational Behavior and Human Decision Processes*, 101, 230–42.

Shamir, B. (2007). From passive recipients to active co-producers: Followers' roles in the leadership process. In B. Shamir, R. Pillai, M. C. Bligh, & M. Uhl-Bien (Eds), *Follower-Centered Perspectives on Leadership: A Tribute to the Memory of James R. Meindl* (pp. ix–xxxix). Greenwich, CT: Information Age Publishing.

Shamir, B., House, R. J., & Arthur, M. B. (1993). The motivational effects of charismatic leadership: A self-concept based theory. *Organization Science*, 4 (4), 577–594.

Smith, J. A., & Foti, J. (1998). A pattern approach to the study of leader emergence. *Leadership Quarterly*, 9 (2), 147–60.

Smith, E. R., & Zárate, M. A. (1992). Exemplar-based model of social judgment. *Psychological Review*, 99 (1), 3–21.

Smith, E. R., & Zárate, A. (1990). Exemplar and prototype use in social categorization. *Social Cognition*, 8 (3), 243–62.

Solano, A. C. (2006). Motivacion para liderar y efectividad del lider. *Revista de Psicologia General y Aplicada*, 59 (4), 563–77.

Staw, B. M. (1975). Attribution of the "causes" of performance: A general alternative interpretation of cross-sectional research on organizations. *Organizational Behavior & Human Performance*, 13 (3), 414–32.

Sulsky, L. M., & Day, D. V. (1992). Frame-of-reference training and cognitive categorization: An empirical investigation of rater memory issues. *Journal of Applied Psychology*, 77, 501–10.

Tiedens, L. Z. (2001). Anger and advancement versus sadness and subjugation: The effect of negative emotion expressions on social status conferral. *Journal of Personality and Social Psychology*, **80** (1), 86–94.

Uhl-Bien, M., & Pillai, R. (2007). The romance of leadership and the social construction of followership. In B. Shamir, R. Pillai, M. Bligh, & M. Uhl-Bien (Eds), *Follower-centered Perspectives on Leadership: A Tribute to the Memory of James R. Meindl* (pp. 187–209). Greenwich, CT: Information Age Publishing.

van Knippenberg, D., & Hogg, M. A. (2003). A social identity model of leadership effectiveness in organizations. In R. M. Kramer & B. M. Staw (Eds), *Research in Organizational Behavior: An Annual Series of Analytical Essays and Critical Reviews*, **25** (pp. 243–95). Oxford, England: Elsevier Science.

van Knippenberg, D., van Knippenberg, B., & Giessner, S. R. (2007). Extending the follower-centered perspective: Leadership as an outcome of shared social identity. In B. Shamir, R. Pillai, M. C. Bligh, & M. Uhl-Bien (Eds), *Follower-centered Perspectives on Leadership: A Tribute to the Memory of James R. Meindl* (pp. 51–70). Greenwich, CT: Information Age Publishing.

Vanpaemel, W., Storms, G., & Ons, B. (2005). A varying abstraction model for categorization. In B. G. Bara, L. Barsalou & M. Bucciarelli (Eds), *Proceedings of the 27th Annual Conference of the Cognitive Science Society* (pp. 2277–82). Mahwah, NJ: Erlbaum.

Verbeemen, T., Vanpaemel, W., Pattyn, S., Storms, G., & Verguts, T. (2007). Beyond exemplars and prototypes as memory representations of natural concepts: A clustering approach. *Journal of Memory and Language*, **56**, 537–54.

Voorspoels, W., Vanpaemel, W., & Storms, G. (2008). Exemplars and prototypes in natural language concepts: A typicality-based evaluation. *Psychonomic Bulletin & Review*, **15** (3), 630–37.

Weick, K. E. (1995). *Sensemaking in Organizations*. Thousand Oaks, CA: Sage.

Weiss, H. M., & Adler, S. (1981). Cognitive complexity and the structure of implicit leadership theories. *Journal of Applied Psychology*, **66**, 69–78.

Wheeler, M. (2005). *Reconstructing the Cognitive World: The Next Step*. Cambridge, MA: The MIT Press.

Wofford, J. C., & Goodwin, V. L. (1994). A cognitive interpretation of transactional and transformational leadership theories. *Leadership Quarterly*, **5**, 161–86.

Wofford, J. C., Goodwin, V. L., & Whittington, J. L. (1998). A field study of a cognitive approach to understanding transformational and transactional leadership. *Leadership Quarterly*, **9**, 55–84.

Wofford, J. C., Joplin, J. R., W. & Cornforth, B. (1996). Use of simultaneous verbal protocols in analysis of group leaders' cognitions. *Psychological Reports*, **79**, 847–58.

Chapter 2

A REVIEW OF LEADER–MEMBER EXCHANGE RESEARCH: FUTURE PROSPECTS AND DIRECTIONS

Robin Martin, Olga Epitropaki, Geoff Thomas and Anna Topakas

Work and Organisational Psychology Group, Aston Business School, Aston University, Birmingham, UK

PREAMBLE

On the basis of our review of the literature, we view the relationship with one's supervisor as a lens through which the entire work experience is viewed (Gerstner and Day, 1997, p. 840).

The topic of leadership remains one of the most researched areas in industrial and organizational psychology (I/O psychology). The popularity of the topic is, no doubt, linked to the belief that leadership effectiveness is one of the most important determinants of organizational performance (Bass, 1990). Of the numerous definitions of organizational leadership, the one provided by the GLOBE (Global Leadership and Organizational Behavior Effectiveness) project, which resulted out of a meeting of 54 researchers from 38 countries, is very comprehensive: "*The ability of an individual to influence, motivate, and enable others to contribute toward the effectiveness and success of the organizations of which they are members*" (House and Javidan, 2004. p. 15). Definitions of leadership tend to emphasize that it is a process of influence with the aim of helping people achieve some individual, team, and organizational work goals.

International Review of Industrial and Organizational Psychology, 2010, Volume 25.
Edited by G. P. Hodgkinson and J. K. Ford. Copyright © 2010 John Wiley & Sons, Ltd

According to Yukl (2010), there are about five major paradigms in the development of leadership theories, namely trait, behavior, power–influence, situational, and integrative approaches (for recent reviews see Avolio, Walumbwa, and Weber, 2009; Bass and Bass, 2008; Chemers, 2001; Hogg, in press;). This chapter reviews a specific approach to leadership that originated in the mid 1970s, which examines the *quality of the relationship* between a leader and a subordinate. As the quote by Gerstner and Day (1997) aforementioned highlights, the relationship people have with their supervisor (or leader) is crucial in shaping their understanding of, and therefore reactions to, their work experience. By emphasizing the relationship between leaders and subordinates, we are acknowledging that leadership is not simply a top–down process, as characterized by much of the early research in leadership, nor is it bottom–up, but it is a reciprocal relationship where each person plays an active role.

Before we begin the review, it is necessary to clarify the terminology that we will employ. By "leader" we refer to the person who has direct responsibility over another person in the organization. In most cases this will be the direct manager or supervisor and is the person who has legitimate authority over other people in the organization as defined by the organizational structure. Traditionally, the term given for the person who is "led" by the manager in the leadership literature is "subordinate" or "follower." The potential problem with the connotations of these terms is that they inevitably place the person who is "led" in a passive role where they have little impact on the leader. Sometimes, the terminology employed is "leader" and "employee," but this suggests that the former is not an employee of the organization but is the employer. These terms emphasize the top–down perspective noted earlier, which is at odds with the leader–member exchange (LMX) approach that suggests that leadership is a relationship between two people and is not a unidirectional but a reciprocal process. LMX theory uses the term "member" to distinguish from the leader presumably to reflect the person is a member of the group the leader manages. However, the term "member" is not used in other areas of I/O psychology. Recognizing the many problems associated with these terms, in this review we will employ the term "subordinate" because it is well used in the leadership literature. This does not avoid the problem of suggesting leadership is a top–down process, but these terms are commonly used in the I/O psychology literature. The "subordinate" is the person who, according to the organizational structure, reports directly to a specific supervisor or manager (the "leader"). We therefore define "leader" and "subordinate" with reference to their position in terms of legitimate (but not necessary other forms of) power that is inherent within the formal organizational structure.

The chapter is organized into three main sections. The first section outlines the concept of LMX, and how it has developed historically and also deals with measurement and levels of analysis issues. The second reviews LMX research according to the four stages of research evolution outlined by Graen and

Uhl-Bien (1995). The third provides some summary conclusions, reflections and directions for future research.

LMX THEORY: BASIC CONCEPTS, MEASUREMENT AND LEVELS OF ANALYSIS

LMX: Basic Concepts

LMX theory was introduced by Graen and colleagues during the 1970s (Dansereau, Graen, and Haga, 1975; Graen and Cashman, 1975). At this time, LMX theory was referred to as the vertical dyad linkage (VDL) approach to leadership (the VDL name was "discarded early because of its unexpected connotations of venereal disease," Graen, 2005, p. 207). The theory has made a major contribution to the existing leadership literature by proposing that leaders adopt different leadership styles when dealing with different subordinates. Or, in other words, leaders treat subordinates differently from each other. LMX theory therefore viewed leadership as a dyadic process between a leader and each subordinate.

Schriesheim, Castro, and Cogliser (1999) view early VDL as evolving into two separate theoretical approaches (LMX and individualized leadership). They differentiate VDL from LMX as follows: "The VDL approach has employed negotiating latitude as its key variable and has focused on differentiated dyads in groups as its level of analysis." The LMX approach has used measures of leader–member exchange as its central variable and has left the level of analysis open or unspecified "despite using the terms 'dyad' and 'dyadic', LMX theory and research has typically been unclear as to whether dyads in groups, dyads independent of groups or some other level of analysis is involved" (p. 79). Schriesheim et al. (1999) also contend that one of the clearest statements of the LMX concept comes from Scandura, Graen, and Novak (1986) "leader member exchange is (a) a system of components and their relationships (b) in both members of a dyad (c) involving interdependent patterns of behavior and (d) sharing mutual outcome instrumentalities and (e) producing conceptions of environments, cause maps, and value" (p. 580).

According to LMX theory, effective leadership is achieved via the dyadic leadership relationship. These relationships develop through a series of social exchanges and are defined as the quality of the exchange relationship between a leader and a subordinate (Schriesheim et al., 1999). LMX relationships develop via a process of exchanging a variety of tangible and intangible commodities within a leader–member dyad. For example, a leader may exchange resources such as, information, influence, desired tasks, latitude, support and attention, for the services of the employee, which may include task performance, commitment, loyalty, and citizenship.

The resulting LMX relationships range on a continuum from those with exchanges based mainly on the employment contract (low-quality LMX, originally called "out-group" relationships) to those with exchanges extending beyond the formal job contract where the aim is to develop the person's ability to perform on the job (high-quality LMX, originally called "in-group" relationships). Both Graen and Uhl-Bien (1995) and Liden and Maslyn (1998) proposed that high-quality LMX relationships consists of many underlying dimensions but differ in the nature of these dimensions: the former stating mutual respect, trust and obligation, and the latter refering to affect, loyalty, contribution, and professional respect.

Since the development of LMX research, there has been a lot of ambiguity about the nature of the LMX construct. Schriesheim *et al.* (1999) noted that during the 1980s alone, 11 different theoretical definitions and 35 different subdimensions of LMX were employed in the literature. Definitions included, "negotiating latitude," "trust in supervisor," "opportunities for influence," and "leadership attention"; however, the authors noted that "quality of the exchange relationship" was the most frequently cited definition of LMX. In regards to the 35 different subdimensions noted by Schriesheim *et al.* (1999) to describe LMX, the most common dimensions were mutual support, trust, liking, latitude, attention, and loyalty; however dimensions also included reciprocal influence, respect, satisfaction, shared values, authority, information, innovation, and affect. In an attempt to clarify the nature of the LMX construct, Graen and Scandura (1987) theorized that LMX consisted of two higher-order factors, which they labeled "quality" and "coupling." The quality factor refers to the attitudinal components of the relationships (e.g. mutual respect, trust, and obligation), whereas the coupling factor refers to the behavioral aspects of the relationship (e.g., latitude, delegation of responsibility, decision influence, and innovativeness). More recently, researchers have acknowledged the important role of trust between the leader and subordinate as an important dimension in LMX quality (Gómez and Rosen, 2001; Scandura and Pellegrini, 2008).

In summary, the central tenet of LMX theory is that leaders develop *different* quality relationships with each of their subordinates. That is, a leader may develop a poor LMX relationship with some subordinates, but a high LMX relationship with other subordinates. This assumption of relationship heterogeneity distinguishes LMX from more traditional leadership theories (e.g., trait, behavioral theories), which assume that leaders developed fairly homogeneous relationships with all of their members; otherwise known as an Average Leadership Style approach (Dansereau *et al.*, 1975).

LMX: Measurement Issues

The measurement of LMX remains an area of ongoing concern in the literature (Avolio *et al.*, 2009). It is interesting to note that LMX research tends to focus on the "quality" factor to measure LMX, whilst treating aspects of the "coupling" factor as antecedents to and outcomes of the "quality" factor. Further work to clarify the LMX construct was undertaken by Liden and Maslyn (1998). Through literature reviews and qualitative interviews, they extended work initially conducted by Dienesch and Liden (1986) to suggest four dimensions of LMX relationships: contribution (or task-related behaviors), loyalty (including aspects of trust), affect, and professional respect. Although Liden and Maslyn (1998) employed a rigorous scale development process to arrive at their four-factor model, LMX researchers have not readily embraced their model or the corresponding measurement instrument (i.e., the LMX Multi-Dimensional Measure; LMX-MDM).

After reviewing the LMX literature over 25 years, Graen and Uhl-Bien (1995) concluded that "the LMX construct has multiple dimensions, but these dimensions are so highly correlated they can be tapped into with the single measure of LMX" (p. 237). They went on to suggest that LMX consists of three underlying dimensions: mutual respect, trust, and obligation. Accordingly, Graen and Uhl-Bien (1995) recommended the use of a unidimensional measure of LMX (i.e., the seven-item LMX-7 scale). Research by Keller and Dansereau (2001) also supports the utility of a unidimensional measure of LMX. Their research shows that the centroid item of the LMX-7 scale (i.e., single-item measuring overall relationship effectiveness) produced a full set of significant correlations with known LMX correlates. They concluded that this centroid item was an acceptable short measure of LMX; thus supporting the notion that LMX could be adequately measured by a unidimensional scale.

More recently, a number of measurement issues have been identified. Bernerth et al. (2007), for example, note that most measures of LMX focus on the quality of the relationship and specifically on the social exchanges (that might lead to them). They specifically examined two of the most employed measures (LMX-7 and LMX-MDM), and, through content analysis procedures using 25 LMX experts, judged whether each scale item could be classified as referring to social exchange, affect, loyalty or was unidentifiable. They found that very few of the items were classified as referring to social exchanges (e.g., for the LMX-7 less that 8% of classifications indicated the items referred to social exchanges). From this set of findings, they developed a new 8-item scale they term "leader–member social exchange" (LMSX) to directly examine the nature of the social exchanges between leaders and subordinates.

Another measurement issue is that LMX measures have been developed from the subordinate perspective (even though the supervisor might employ the same items to judge the relationship). Greguras and Ford (2006) noted this problem and developed a measure of LMX, based on Liden and Maslyn's (1998) LMX-MDM scale, which accommodates the supervisor's perspective. Factor analysis of the scale reveals four dimensions: affect, loyalty, contribution, and professional respect. Importantly, the authors show that these subdimensions differentially predict work reactions.

A major criticism of LMX measurement is that although LMX is theorized at the dyadic level, most studies have tended to collect LMX data from only the subordinate's perspective. One problem with this approach is that there is typically a lack of consensus between leaders and members in their appraisal of the relationship. For example, in their meta-analysis Gerstner and Day (1997) reported that leaders and members demonstrated low to moderate agreement ($r = .29$, corrected for unreliability). Sin, Nahrgang, and Morgeson (2009) report a meta-analysis of 64 independent samples ($N = 10,884$ dyads) examining agreement between leader and subordinate relationships. The overall agreement was moderate, and the highest levels of agreement were observed when relationship tenure was long in time, relationship dimensions were affectively oriented, and ad hoc sampling techniques were used.

Virtually all measures of LMX have been developed using psychometric procedures that rely on total scale scores and means and the assumption that the observed score is an amalgam of the true score for that construct and measurement error. However, advances in measurement theory have not generally been adopted in developing leadership measures (Scherbaum et al., 2006). One such measurement development that has been applied to LMX measurement is item response theory (IRT; Scherbaum, Naidoo, and Ferreter, 2007). IRT allows the generation of latent parameters for the persons and items using the responses from the sample of data. Scherbaum et al. (2007) discuss a number of advantages of using IRT in measuring LMX. For example, in traditional psychometric approaches, measurement error is considered standard across all levels of a characteristic. However, it is possible that measurement error is less for those with low LMX quality than those with high LMX quality. IRT overcomes this problem and allows a consideration of measurement error at different levels of LMX quality. This might be particularly important in studies that divide a sample into low versus high LMX groups. However, Scherbaum et al. (2007) claim that both psychometric and IRT approaches can be appropriate but in different situations depending on the type of study and research questions examined.

All measures described so far have focused on LMX as the unique relationship between the leader and the subordinate as that was the main theoretical focus of the research. However, as demonstrated elsewhere in this review, LMX research has expanded to examine how LMX relationships are perceived within the wider group context. This change in research focus has lead to the development of new ways to measure relationship quality amongst group members. These measure focus on *relationship variation*, the amount of variability in relationship quality between subordinates and/or with the manager.

Two types of LMX variation measures have been developed. One set of measures employs self-reports of the subordinate's judgment of the *quality of the relationship between all subordinates* within their work group. For instance the LMX-7 measure has been rephrased to cover all group members (Graen and Uhl-Bien, 1995). Additional measures focus on other members of the work group (e.g., CWX, coworker exchanges; Sherony and Green, 2002), and specific scales have been devised that focus on the perceived quality of the exchanges between subordinates (e.g., "team–member exchange," TMX; Seers, 1989). Finally, another type of measure employs a social network matrix approach and involves questions focusing on how frequently the subordinates engage in a number of activities (e.g., Gerstner and Tesluk, 2005).

A second set of measures of LMX variation relies on the perceived *range of LMX relationships* the manager has with his or her work team (which is referred to as "LMX differentiation"). This has been achieved by using techniques such as computing individual LMX minus group average LMX scores (e.g., Henderson *et al.*, 2008), variability or aggregate scores for LMX of individual subordinates in a work group (e.g., Boies and Howell, 2006; Liden *et al.*, 2006) and evaluating subordinates' perceptions of LMX variation within their work team, for example, by comparing LMX scores across coworkers within a given team (e.g., Sherony and Green, 2002). Other approaches to the assessment of within-team LMX variations that capture group variability include the use of the coefficient of variation based on estimate of LMX quality for each member of the workteam (e.g., Hooper and Martin, 2006, 2008). Interestingly, we are not aware of a measure that captures the leaders' perception of their different LMX relationships.

In summary, issues concerning LMX measurement continue to be discussed in the literature. These issues are determined in part by a lack of consensus as to what the LMX construct is and what its key dimensions are. Most measures of LMX tend to focus on a narrow construal of the LMX concept and collapse across measurement dimensions to provide an overall evaluation of LMX on a global scale, ranging from low to high quality. Recent research is advancing the measurement of LMX in three important ways, namely, (1) better alignment between LMX theory and measurement to include theoretically related dimensions, (2) improvements in statistical and measurement techniques in scale construction, and (3) expanding the assessment of LMX to the group level to examine within-groups relationship variation.

LMX: Levels of Analysis

The issue concerning levels of analysis has become increasingly important in leadership research (see Dansereau and Yammarino, 1998a, b). Levels of analysis are entities (in this case human beings) that are examined, and these entities are typically located in hierarchical order such that higher levels (e.g., work teams) include lower levels (e.g., subordinates). With respect to leadership research, the key levels of analysis are the individuals or persons (independent subordinates, or leader), dyads (leader–subordinate, subordinate–subordinate relationships), groups (work groups and teams), and organizations (collectives larger than groups and groups of groups). Although it is possible to examine a single level of analysis, increasingly researchers are examining multiple levels of analysis in combination or simultaneously, using multilevel modeling techniques. A simple example can highlight some of the problems of an inappropriate consideration of levels of analysis. A common practice among researchers is to measure a given variable (e.g., the leader's delegation style) by sampling the judgments of subordinates and then correlating the resulting data with the leader's report of the subordinates' job performance. Correlations obtained in this way might be used to draw inferences concerning the linkages between leader delegation styles and subordinate performance more generally. However, the results of such a study may be misleading because of potential correlated error in either or both measures (and because of some unmeasured variables not included in the analyses), leading to biases in the parameter estimates. To further demonstrate this problem, imagine that two subordinates work for the same leader. Although the leader might treat each subordinate differently (as expected by LMX theory), he or she is also likely to exhibit some common leadership behaviors to both subordinates, not least behaviors arising from their basic task duties. This source of common variance across subordinates constitutes an unmeasured variable, the work team, which conceivably could be correlated significantly with the dependent and independent variables under investigation. This problem is potentially acute in LMX research, where the focus is on dyadic relationships, but where the samples of participants typically comprise multiples of subordinates reporting to a smaller subset of leaders.

One analytical technique that has been employed to examine such dyadic relationships is Within- And Between-entities Analysis (WABA: Dansereau, Alutto, and Yammarino, 1984). In WABA a distinction is made between an "entity" (e.g., work group) and a "part" (e.g., subordinate members of the work group). Each subordinate response can then be represented at two levels: as part of the entity (average of all subordinates in the work group) and as a part within the entity (subordinate's score minus the average for their work group). By partitioning the subordinate's score into within- and between-group parts allows for testing effects at these different levels. In addition to using WABA, some researchers have employed within-group agreement scores (r_{wg}) with the same data (e.g., Cogliser and Schriesheim, 2000) to compare the efficacy of different techniques. However, the use of WABA analysis in LMX and leadership research more widely has been criticized by Graen and Lau (2005) on the grounds that within- and between-relationships typically coexist. Hence, it does not make sense to examine if one of these relationships is stronger than the other. As an alternative, they suggest the use of hierarchical linear modeling (HLM) techniques for examining cross-level effects.

The issue of levels of analysis in leadership research has been examined by Yammarino et al. (2005) who reviewed 348 leadership articles across 17 areas of leadership research, published from 1995 (as a follow-on from their re-view books Dansereau and Yammarino, 1998a, b). Each article was coded in terms of the level of analysis it employed with respect to theory formation, construct/variable measurement, the data analytic techniques employed and the kinds of inferences drawn. A total of 35 empirical studies pertaining to LMX research were identified. In terms of incorporating appropriate levels of analysis the following results were found (number of articles and percent-age of total for LMX in parentheses): theoretical and hypothesis development (7, 20%), measurement (6, 17%), and data analytic techniques (5, 14%). Finally, in terms of alignment between theory and data at the appropriate level for analysis, only five papers met all the criteria (14%) and are included amongst 19 from the whole leadership area as a "template or 'best practices' approach for researchers to follow in their own work" (p. 905). (These papers are Cogliser and Schriesheim, 2000; Hofmann, Morgeson, and Gerras, 2003; Schriesheim *et al.* 2000; Schriesheim *et al.*, 2001; Schriesheim, Neider, and Scandura, 1998.) The findings from the LMX area showed one of the lowest uses of appropriate levels of analysis across the 17 areas of leadership research surveyed by Yammarino *et al.* (2005).

It is clear that researchers need to be very careful while interpreting the results from LMX studies, especially when they test cross-level effects. We are sure the debate over which are the most appropriate analytical techniques will continue. At this stage we wish to add just one observation. The levels of analysis approach assume that the different levels are consensually agreed by members of the organization. This might not be necessarily true. Consider a simple example where a researcher is examining the relationship between sub-ordinates' perceived work group conflict and supervisors' ratings of work group performance. Aggregating the subordinates into the organizationally defined work group might be very different from each subordinate's psychologically defined work group. In other words, each subordinate might include different subordinates in their work group, and this judgment itself could covary by an additional factor (e.g., their identification with the group).

LMX THEORY DEVELOPMENT AND RESEARCH

The literature examining LMX is extensive and is increasing over time. There have been a number of narrative (e.g., Breukelen, Schyns, and LeBlanc, 2006; Erdogan and Liden, 2002; Graen and Uhl-Bien, 1995; Liden, Sparrowe, and Wayne, 1997; Schriesheim *et al.*, 1999) and meta-analytic (e.g., Gerstner and Day, 1997; Ilies, Nahrgang and Morgeson, 2007; Sin *et al.*, 2009) reviews of the LMX literature. Some narrative reviews report lists of individual studies and enumerate the specific features of each study. For example, Schriesheim *et al.* (1999) list 147 individual studies, which they document in terms of the theoretical definition of LMX employed, the subdimensions they examine, the measures used, and the analytic methodology employed. In another narrative review, which builds on a previous one by Liden et al. (1997), Erdogan and Liden (2002) document 57 individual studies in terms of the LMX antecedents and outcomes investigated and the sample characteristics of each study. Meta-analytic reviews have addressed specific relationships involving LMX by statistically combining the results of many studies addressing common issues. For example, Gerstner and Day (1997) report the results of 79 studies (85 independent samples) examining the relationship between LMX and a range of outcomes, while Ilies et al. (2007) report 50 studies examining the relationship between LMX and organizational citizenship behavior (OCB).

Given the aforementioned reviews of the LMX literature, it is important to avoid duplication. Accordingly, in the present case we adopted a different approach, based on the categorization system proposed by Graen and Uhl-Bien (1995). Graen and Uhl-Bien (1995) described four stages through which LMX research has progressed since its inception: (1) the discovery of differential dyads, (2) a focus on the LMX relationship and its outcomes, (3) description of dyadic partnership building, and (4) examining LMX at the group and network levels. Although these are called "stages" they do not refer to developmental stages in the sense that later stages are more important than the initial stages. Instead they refer to different levels (or areas) of research enquiry and that all stages are important for understanding LMX processes. Each of these four stages is described later, along with a review of the most significant findings that have emerged over the 14 years that have elapsed since the publication of this framework.

Stage 1: Discovery of Differentiated Dyads

Stage 1 of LMX theory development involved the discovery that leaders differentially treated their subordinates in terms of relationship quality (e.g., Graen, Orris, and Johnson, 1973; Johnson and Graen, 1973). Some of this research examined the development of LMX relationships over time and showed that leaders develop different quality relationships with each of their subordinates. During this stage, research indicated that approximately 85–90% of leaders developed relationships of differing quality with their subordinates (e.g., Dansereau et al., 1975; Liden and Graen, 1980). In a longitudinal study that examined LMX development Nahrgang, Morgeson, and Ilies (2009) examined LMX quality in leader and subordinate relationships, commencing with the initial interaction and then weekly, over eight consecutive weeks. The leaders were MBA students at a university who led a group of undergraduate students, and the leader was responsible for all aspects of team formation, development, and performance (this, the authors argue, is similar to the processes involved in managing entry-level people in an organization). In line with expectations from theory, the leaders developed variable-quality LMX relationships with the members of their groups. Furthermore, leader–subordinate agreement on LMX quality converged over time.

Differences in self-ratings of LMX across employees within the same team are typically taken to indicate LMX differentiation by the leader. Another line of research examined this issue from a different perspective. Hooper and Martin (2006, 2008) asked subordinates to estimate the different LMX relationships they thought each team member had with their leader. They found strong evidence that subordinates believed that their leader had different quality relationships with those people they managed.

One of the reasons why leaders might develop different quality relationships is that resource constraints cause leaders to be more selective in whom they invest their limited time and resources. This would lead to different quality relationships ranging from low to high LMX quality (as described earlier). The leaders might develop low-quality relationships with some subordinates who are seen as "hired hands" (Graen and Uhl-Bien, 1995, p. 227) who only work to fulfill the requirements of their job description. However, the leader might also develop higher-quality LMX relationships with a subgroup of people seen as "trusted assistants" (Graen and Uhl-Bien, 1995, p. 227) with such relationships marked by high degrees of mutual respect, trust, and obligation.

If leaders develop different quality relationships with each of their subordinates, then it follows that leaders use different styles of leadership for different members of their work group. This is a very important observation because it contradicts the view proposed in the leadership styles approach that leaders use the same style of leadership for all their subordinates (the "average leadership style" approach). An alternative perspective is that leaders do use the same style with all their subordinates, but each subordinate reacts differently to the leader's behavior resulting in different quality relationships. The contribution to LMX quality from (1) the leader using different styles or (2) differential reactions by the subordinates to the same leadership style remains unknown.

Utilizing differences in self-ratings of LMX to denote leader differentiation is commonly practiced throughout the LMX literature (e.g., Dansereau *et al.*, 1975; Kinicki and Vecchio, 1994; McClane, 1991; Sherony and Green, 2002). A pertinent limitation of this methodology, however, is that differences in self-ratings may reflect differences in each employee's response style, rather than *real* or *perceived* differences in treatment by the leader (see Cronbach and Meehl, 1955). One possible solution to this problem would be for researchers to supplement subordinate ratings with leader ratings of the relationship quality with each of his or her direct reports (see the section "LMX: Measurement Issues" discussed earlier in this review).

Stage 2: Focus on the Relationship and Its Outcomes

Stage 2 of theory development, the one that has attracted the most research, has involved examining the correlates of LMX quality. Although only a few studies have directly investigated the causal direction between LMX and associated variables (see Epitropaki and Martin, 2005, for an exception), this stage of LMX theory development is mainly based on cross-sectional research designs with a priori causal logic to demarcate antecedents from outcomes of LMX. Specifically, LMX has been consistently linked to a wide variety of important individual and organizational variables, including employee benefits, and positive attitudinal and behavioral outcomes for employees. We now consider research that examines the antecedents and outcomes of LMX.

Antecedents of LMX

Research examining the antecedents of LMX, views LMX quality as a dependent variable with some antecedent factor as the independent (or predictor) variable that causes LMX (for reviews see Erdogan and Liden, 2002; Liden *et al.*, 1997). Liden *et al.* (1997) groups the antecedent variables into four main categories: subordinate characteristics, leader characteristics, interactional variables, and contextual variables. Research relevant to each of these four antecedent categories is discussed subsequently.

Subordinate characteristics

A range of subordinate characteristics have been investigated as potential antecedents to LMX. For example, Kinicki and Vecchio (1994) and Martin *et al.* (2005) reported a positive relationship between subordinate locus of control and LMX while Phillips and Bedeian (1994) reported a positive relationship between subordinate extraversion and LMX. Other individual difference factors that have been examined including subordinates' cognitive style (Allinson, Armstrong, and Hayes, 2001), self-efficacy (Murphy and Ensher, 1999), personality traits (Bernerth *et al.*, 2007; Lapierre and Hackett, 2007) and implicit leadership theories (Engle and Lord, 1997; Epitropaki and Martin, 2005). In each case, the studies have found evidence of individual difference factors predicting LMX ratings.

Finally, some studies have examined specific issues to do with the characteristics of the subordinate that might not be considered to be directly relevant to the work place. For example, Colella and Varma (2001) examined the role of subordinate disability on LMX development. They reasoned that subordinate disability might influence a supervisor's attributions of the level of work contribution. They hypothesized that a subordinate's disability might hinder LMX development as supervisors might perceive them as "different" from themselves and other members of the work team (as we highlight later, perceived similarity between leader and subordinate is an important predictor of the quality of LMX relationship). The results of a simulation experiment and cross-sectional survey with employees supported this hypothesis showing that supervisors reported worse LMX relationships with subordinates who had indicated they had a disability than those subordinates that had indicated they did not have a disability. The aforementioned relationship was moderated by subordinates' perceived use of ingratiation tactics (i.e., seeking opportunities to admire the supervisor) such that supervisors reported the worse LMX relationships for subordinates reporting they were disabled and who did *not* engage in ingratiation. To some extent ingratiation tactics by the subordinate overcame some of the negative consequences of being disabled. It would be premature to generalize too much from one study; nevertheless, this research raises a very important issue for leaders dealing with disabled subordinates and suggests such people may engage in ingratiation tactics to overcome the potential disadvantage their disability gives them in developing good-quality LMX relationships.

Leader characteristics

There has been relatively less research examining leader factors as antecedents of subordinate LMX than there has been examining subordinate factors. Research has examined the ability of the leader to use a number of power strategies (e.g., Borchgrevink and Boster, 1997), leader agreeableness (Nahrgang *et al.*, 2009), downward influence tactics (e.g., Sparrowe, Soetjipto, and Kraimer, 2006), appearing to be intuitive (Allinson *et al.*, 2001) and their affectivity (Day and Crain, 1992). Not surprisingly, the more the leader can control important factors that directly affect the workplace, the greater is the quality of the LMX relationship they develop with others. For example, Aryee and Chen (2006), in a Chinese sample of employees from a manufacturing organization, found that the more the subordinates believed that the supervisor could control valuable rewards (such as promotion or pay levels), the greater the quality of the LMX relationship was. While the mechanism for this is not known, the most likely explanation is that if one's leader can directly control important work outcomes, the more the subordinate will try and develop good LMX relations to try and secure these valued outcomes. Conversely, if the leader has low positional power, then there is little motivation on the subordinate's part to develop good-quality relationships.

Interactional variables

It has been suggested that interactional variables, such as leader–subordinate similarity and liking, play a more crucial role in LMX development than many subordinate or leader characteristics do alone. However, some of these proposed antecedents have also yielded unreliable relationships with LMX quality. For example, several studies have revealed a positive relationship between leader–subordinate demographic similarity, in that the leader and subordinate are similar on a range of dimensions, including gender, age, race, education (e.g., Duchon *et al.*, 1986; Epitropaki and Martin, 1999; Green *et al.*, 1996; Pelled and Xin, 2000; Turban and Jones, 1988; Varma and Stroth, 2001), leader–subordinate tenure (e.g., Somech, 2003), and LMX quality; however, other studies have found no relationship between demographic similarity and LMX quality (e.g., Bauer and Green, 1996; Liden, Wayne, and Stilwell, 1993; McClane, 1991; Murphy and Ensher, 1999).

Some studies have investigated the relationship between personality similarity and LMX quality. This line of research has yielded mixed findings. For example, Bauer and Green (1996) reported a positive relationship between leader–subordinate similarity in terms of positive affectivity and LMX quality. McClane (1991), on the other hand, reported a positive relationship between need for power similarity and LMX quality, but no effect of locus of control similarity, need for achievement similarity or least preferred coworker similarity. Ashkanasy and O'Connor (1997), however, found a positive association between value similarity (i.e., compatibility on valuing obedience, achievement, and mateship or friendship) and high LMX quality. One explanation for this variable pattern of results is that different researchers have focused on different personality characteristics; perhaps some of these characteristics are more salient than others in the determining of the quality of LMX.

Some researchers have suggested that it may not be *actual* similarity but rather *perceived* similarity that is related to LMX quality. This is consistent with the general trend in the social cognition literature that feeling similar to others is often more important than actually being similar. This is either partly because of perceptual bias or because perceptions may be more proximal to relationship outcomes in that actual similarity creates the perception of similarity (see Kenny and Acitelli, 2001; Reis, 2007). Indeed, several researchers have reported a positive relationship between perceived similarity (e.g., Liden *et al.*, 1993; Murphy and Ensher, 1999; Phillips and Bedeian, 1994) and LMX quality. In addition, other researchers have found a positive relationship between perceived value similarity, that is, the extent the subordinate believes he or she has similar values to their leader) and LMX quality (e.g., Dose, 1999). Furthermore, Liden *et al.* (1993), in a longitudinal study, found that perceived similarity between the subordinate and the leader predicted future reports of LMX quality. More recent research has highlighted the need to examine potential moderators, determining when similarity between leader and subordinate affects LMX quality (e.g., Brouer *et al.*, 2009).

With regard to leader–subordinate liking as a potential antecedent to LMX quality, several studies have shown a positive relationship between leader and/or subordinate liking and LMX quality (e.g., Engle and Lord, 1997; Liden *et al.*, 1993; Varma and Stroth, 2001; Wayne and Ferris, 1990; Wayne, Shore, and Liden, 1997). For example, Wayne and Ferris (1990) drew on the theoretical work by Dienesch and Liden (1986) to test the prediction that leaders' liking of subordinates and their perceptions of the subordinates' performance both contribute to the development of high-quality LMX relationships. In an experimental study that more clearly delineated the direction of effects, leaders' ratings of the extent to which they liked their subordinates and their ratings of their subordinate's performance were both positively linked to LMX quality. Furthermore, the findings suggested that leaders' ratings of their subordinates' performance were influenced by their liking of them. A follow-up field study similarly indicated that liking was positively related to LMX quality and leader-rated performance; however, in this study, leader-rated performance was not significantly linked to LMX quality. In summary, Wayne and Ferris' (1990) research shows a positive relationship between leader's liking of the subordinate and LMX quality and suggests that liking (more than leader's perceptions of employee competence) may be the initial driving force behind the development of LMX.

Overall, there is mixed evidence concerning a range of interactional variables predicting LMX quality. On balance, there is some evidence showing that the more similar the leader and subordinate are on a range of demographic and personal factors, the better is the quality of LMX that develops. It is plausible that actual (and especially perceived) similarity leads to enhanced liking, which in turn leads to better-quality LMX (i.e., the similarity-attraction effect, Byrne, 1971). The inconsistencies in this body of work as a whole might be explained by the fact that research assumes that each of the various similarity dimensions investigated is equally important to the leader and subordinate. A better approach would be to examine the potential moderating role of similarity dimension importance to the leader and subordinate vis-à-vis LMX quality. This would lead to the prediction that leader/subordinate similarity leads to better LMX quality on dimensions that are perceived as important to the leader and/or subordinate than on dimensions that are perceived as less important. Related to this issue is the finding that the degree the subordinate believes their manager fits their implicit theory of what constitutes an effective leader, the more positive is LMX quality (Engle and Lord, 1997; Epitropaki and Martin, 2005). Similarity on conceptions of desired member competencies and key performance indicators are likely to be important to both leaders and subordinates because it should help predict future subordinate performance, and hence may influence leaders' initial decisions concerning who to focus their limited resources on.

Contextual variables

With regard to contextual variables predicting LMX quality, some studies have examined the impact of the leader's workload. Graen *et al.* (1986) found a negative relationship between leader workload and LMX, such that as the leader's workload increased, LMX quality decreased (but see also Kinicki and

Vecchio, 1994). Another contextual variable that has been examined as a potential antecedent of LMX is the number of subordinates a leader manages. Research has shown that as the number of subordinates a leader manages increases, the more negative is the LMX quality (Green, Anderson, and Shivers, 1996; Schriesheim et al., 2000; Schyns et al., 2005). This might be expected. Leaders have limited time to spend with subordinates, and with the increase in the number of subordinates, the leader has less time to develop good-quality relationships with all group members. Therefore, when the leader has a large group of people to manage, it is likely that different quality relationships will develop leading to subgroups of subordinates with low- and high-quality LMX relationships. The relationship between leadership span and LMX might be better conceptualized, and analyzed, as a nonlinear relationship; as leadership span increases, the greater the likelihood of a bimodal distribution of LMX quality. Finally, some recent research has examined the role of organizational (e.g., Tordera, González-Romá, and Peiró, 2008) and team (e.g., Tse, Dasborough, and Ashkanasy, 2008) climate on LMX. Given the paucity of studies in this area, it is difficult to draw firm conclusions.

Summary

In summary, a range of factors have been shown to be potential antecedents of LMX quality. For ease of presentation these were grouped according to their main focus on subordinate characteristics, leader characteristics, interaction variables, and finally, contextual factors. In fact, most of the studies reviewed earlier have examined multiple antecedents within one research design, sometimes making it difficult to determine the unique impact of any given predictor. While these studies reliably show associations between a variety of factors and LMX, because they mainly rely on cross-sectional research designs, they do establish that the factors in question *determine* LMX quality. The status of these factors as antecedents is assumed through logically reasoning that stable factors that are beyond the control of the leader–subordinate relationship (such as personality, relational demography, team size) are causally implicated in quality of the LMX relationship. However, in relation to some of these factors, competing hypotheses can be derived. For instance, it is possible that leaders choose team members that they intuitively believe they will have a good relationship with (e.g., certain personality profile, same gender) and this leads to a good-quality relationship. The number of studies examining antecedents is increasing, and we believe that this area will benefit from a clearer understanding of the theoretical status of the key variables.

Outcomes of LMX

A considerable amount of research has been conducted into the consequences of having a low- or high-quality LMX relationship. A meta-analysis of 85 samples from publications published between 1984 and 1996 by Gerstner and Day (1997), showed that LMX quality as perceived by the subordinate was related to the leader's rating of performance, objective performance (although the effect size was less than for supervisor-rated performance), satisfaction with the leader, overall satisfaction, organizational commitment, role conflict, role clarity, and turnover intentions (but not actual turnover). The pattern of results led the authors to conclude that "having a high-quality relationship with one's supervisor can affect the entire work experience in a positive manner, including performance and affective outcomes" (Gerstner and Day, 1997, p. 835). In order to avoid duplication, we focus on research mainly conducted subsequent to the Gerstner and Day's (1997) review. We organize this research into the main type of outcome examined: attitudes and perceptions, behaviors, and task performance.

Attitudes and perceptions
More recent research confirms the positive benefits of having high-quality LMX relationships with a range of attitudinal benefits that were initially reported in the Gerstner and Day (1997) meta-analysis. A number of studies show that a high-quality LMX relationship is related to the following:

- *At the individual level*: employee job satisfaction (Aryee and Chen, 2006; Epitropaki and Martin, 2005; Lapierre and Hackett, 2007; Liden, Wayne, and Sparrowe, 2000; Major *et al.*, 1995; Mardanov, Heischmidt, and Henson, 2008; Martin *et al.*, 2005; Masterson, Lewis, Goldman, and Taylor, 2000; Murphy and Ensher, 1999), job-related well-being (Bernas and Major, 2000; Epitropaki and Martin, 1999, 2005; Martin *et al.*, 2005; Sparr and Sonnentag, 2008), lower job stress (Bernas and Major, 2000), increased organizational commitment (Epitropaki and Martin, 2005; Kacmar, Carlson and Brymer, 1999; Liden *et al.*, 2000; Major *et al.*, 1995; Martin *et al.*, 2005; Wayne *et al.*, 1997), positive self-efficacy (Murphy and Ensher, 1999), employee empowerment (Gómez and Rosen, 2001; Keller and Dansereau, 1995; Liden *et al.*, 2000), and lowered turnover intentions (Bauer *et al.*, 2006; Major *et al.*, 1995; Vecchio and Gobdel, 1984; Wayne *et al.*, 1997, but see also Harris, Kacmar and Witt, 2005).
- *At the dyad level*: workplace friendships (Tse *et al.*, 2008), perceived leader support (Bauer and Green, 1996), and perceived leader delegation and consultation (Yukl and Fu, 1999).
- *At the organizational level*: perceived justice (Andrews and Kacmar, 2001; Erdogan, 2002) and perceived transformational leadership (Howell and Hall-Merenda, 1999; Pillai, Schriesheim, and Williams, 1999).

Without doubt, research consistently shows the positive benefits of having a good LMX relationship in relation to a wide range of work-related attitudes and reactions. However, on occasions it should be noted that high LMX has also been associated with negative nonwork outcomes, not the least an increase in work–family conflict (Bernas and Major, 2000).

Behaviors

There are many favorable *employee behavioral outcomes* associated with high LMX quality. These include increased time and effort devoted to the job (Liden and Graen, 1980), greater likelihood of engaging in a wider job breadth (Hsiung and Tsai, 2009), increased innovative behaviors (Janssen and Van Yperen, 2004; Scott and Bruce, 1998; Tierney, Farmer, and Graen, 1999) and reduced actual turnover (Graen, Liden, and Hoel, 1982).

One of the most examined behaviors is organizational citizenship behaviors (OCBs), that is, discretionary behaviors that are beneficial to the organization, but which are not directly or explicitly recognized by the formal reward system. In a recent meta-analysis, Ilies *et al.* (2007) examined 50 published studies and concluded that LMX is reliably related to OCBs. Interestingly, the LMX–OCB relationship was moderated by the nature of the target of the citizenship behavior. The impact of LMX was stronger when the citizenship behaviors were targeted at individuals (i.e., individual-targeted OCBs that benefit specific individuals, such as altruism, helping, or courtesy) than when they were targeted at the organization (i.e., organizational-targeted OCBs that benefit the entire organization, such as conscientiousness, job dedication, or civic virtue).

A number of *leader behavioral outcomes* have been associated with high LMX quality, including a greater supply of resources and leader support for innovations (Scott and Bruce, 1998), more contingent rewards (Wayne *et al.*, 2002), influence (Dansereau *et al.*, 1975; Scandura, Graen, and Novak, 1986), and leader support, attention, more information, confidence, and concern from the leader (Dansereau *et al.*, 1975). High LMX quality is also associated with more positive communication experiences with the leader, including more participative communications (Yrle, Hartman, and Galle, 2002), less autocracy (Schriesheim *et al.*, 1992), and less antagonistic and adversarial communications (Fairhurst, 1993).

Task performance

Task performance refers to output that is directly related to the job itself. Gerstner and Day (1997), in the meta-analysis described earlier, found a reliable relationship between LMX and task performance, with the relationship being stronger for supervisor rated than for objective performance. More recently, researchers have examined the role of a number of moderator variables on the LMX–task performance relationship. A number of reliable moderators have been found and the pattern of these effects is as one would expect. The moderator variables can be grouped into three categories, namely, subordinate characteristics, work-related characteristics, and aspects of supervision.

The relationship between LMX and performance was greater in terms of the following:

- *Subordinate characteristics:* when the subordinate was characterized by high conscientiousness (Kamdar and Van Dyne, 2007), low extraversion (Bauer, *et al.*, 2006), high employee growth need strength (Graen, Novak and Sommerkamp, 1982), high goal commitment (Klein and Kim, 1998), and internal locus of control (Ozer, 2008).
- *Work-related* characteristics: when the work was characterized by low role conflict (Dunegan, Uhl-Bien, and Duchon, 2002), high task autonomy (Ozer, 2008), and a high degree of working virtually (Golden and Veiga, 2008).
- *Aspects of supervision:* when the leader had a low span of supervision (Schriesheim *et al.*, 2000), engaged in communication with high frequency (Kacmar *et al.*, 2003), enjoyed high perceived organizational support (Erdogan and Enders, 2007), and held middle-high levels of management responsibility (Fernandez and Vecchio, 1997).

Some studies have examined the role of mediators in the LMX–task performance relationship. For example, Chen, Lam, and Zhong (2007) examined the role of negative feedback-seeking behavior (the extent to which subordinates asked for feedback on inadequate performance) in mediating the LMX–task performance relationship. They found that supervisors' ratings of subordinates' negative feedback-seeking behavior mediated the relationship between LMX and both supervisor-rated and objective (monthly piece-rate wages paid in proportion to the quantity and quality of work) measures of performance. This suggests that subordinates who have a good relationship with their supervisor are more likely to seek feedback on poor performance (and presumably make appropriate corrections to their work) leading to enhanced task performance (see also Janssen and Van Yperen, 2004).

It has also been popular to examine the role of LMX as mediating between the use of a transformational leadership style and performance (e.g., Howell and Hall-Merenda, 1999; Wang, 2005). Since one of the subdimensions of transformational leadership directly relates to the leader being concerned about each of their subordinates (individualized consideration), it is not surprising that there is a strong link between transformational behaviors and LMX quality.

The amount of research examining the relationship between LMX and performance is increasing. We wish to make two observations on this research. First, a noticeable feature in most of the aforementioned studies is that performance has been measured by supervisors' ratings of subordinates' performance, typically using a global rating scale not linked to specific job dimensions. Some studies have examined objective measures of performance (such as, Chen *et al.*, 2007; Duarte, Goodson, and Klich, 1993; Graen *et al.*, 1982; Klein and Kim, 1998) but as noted by Gerstner and Day (1997) the strength of the relationship between LMX quality and objective performance, whilst reliable, is not as strong as it is for supervisor-rated performance. The potential problem of using subjective, supervisor-rated performance measures in these sorts of studies was well documented by Duarte *et al.* (1993). In a study of employees in a telephone company, Duarte *et al.* (1993) obtained for each subordinate both a subjective supervisor-rated judgment (on a single 7-point scale concerning "quantity of performance") and an objective measure of performance averaged over six months (e.g., time taken to complete a call, time taken to complete assignments). When the LMX quality was high, supervisors' ratings of subjective performance were not affected by the objective performance level. In other words, high LMX subordinates were given high performance ratings by their supervisor regardless of their actual performance. However, low LMX subordinates' supervisor ratings were consistent with the actual, objective performance. There are many potential explanations for these results, including the possibility that the supervisors' ratings included a wider range of job-related performance criteria than did the objective measure. However, it is also likely that a number of attribution biases might affect supervisors' ratings. For instance, it is likely that supervisors will attribute the causes of poor performance of people they like (high LMX subordinates) to external factors beyond their control in order to maintain a positive view of the person (see Maio and Thomas, 2007, for a review of this and other self-persuasion tactics). In other words, supervisors might be more forgiving of poor performance from high than low LMX subordinates and deem that such performance is not their fault (see also Wilhelm, Herd, and Steiner, 1993).

The second point we wish to raise concerns the measurement timing of LMX and performance. Virtually all the studies reviewed earlier in this chapter were cross-sectional in nature and therefore the direction of the effects is unclear. However, since one would expect LMX quality to vary over time and that LMX quality takes time to manifest itself onto performance, one would expect current LMX quality to predict future performance. A few of the studies' authors do specify that they examined future performance (e.g., over a one-year period, Howell and Hall-Merenda, 1999). A few studies have examined changes in both LMX and performance over time (e.g., Bauer and Green, 1996; Bauer *et al.*, 2006; Graen *et al.*, 1982; Nahrgang, *et al.*, 2009). The Bauer *et al.* (2006) longitudinal study is particularly interesting as it examined new recruits in a pharmaceutical organization and data were obtained pre-entry to the job and three months after being in the job, while managers' ratings of their performance were taken six months into the job and data from company records (e.g., turnover data) three-and-a-half years later. They found that subordinates' extraversion moderated the relationship between LMX and performance. In particular, subordinates low (but not high) in extraversion showed a relationship between LMX, performance and turnover intentions. Longitudinal studies can give a causal understanding of the relationship between LMX and performance that is not possible with cross-sectional designs, especially if multiple measurements of key theoretical variables are taken to allow for causal modeling techniques to be employed (e.g., Nahrgang *et al.*, 2009).

Summary

In summary, recent research continues to demonstrate a strong association between LMX and a range of important individual and organizational outcomes. A noticeable difference in recent research is a more sophisticated examination of the relationship between LMX and attitudinal reactions. This new research represents a second generation of research efforts that can advance our understanding of when and why LMX leads to beneficial outcomes in three specific ways. First, the testing of *mediation/process models* of LMX: for example, Lapierre and Hackett (2007) compared two processes models connecting trait conscientiousness, LMX, job satisfaction and OCBs (one linking trait conscientiousness to job satisfaction and the other LMX to OCB). In fact, the final model had LMX directly predicting job satisfaction. Second, examining LMX as *moderating different aspects of outcome factors*: for example, van Dyne, Kamdar, and Joireman (2008) examined the effect of LMX on two aspects of OCBs (in-role vs extra-role) and the moderating role of role perceptions on these relationships. Third, testing *nonlinear* relationships between LMX and outcomes: for example, Harris *et al.* (2005) examined the relationship between LMX and turnover intentions as a curvilinear as opposed to the traditional negative linear relationship. They found that turnover intentions increased at high levels of LMX. The authors propose that this might be because individuals with a high LMX perceive they are more "attractive" as employees in other organisations and that their career aspirations could be achieved through such a move.

Stage 3: Description of Dyadic Partnership Building

Stage 3 of LMX theory development and research concerns describing the development of LMX relationships and how managers work with each subordinate to develop effective relationships. The key difference in this stage is that research moves away from examining leaders having different quality relationships with their subordinates to how leaders develop these relationships and can provide all subordinates with the opportunity to develop effective LMX quality.

Development of LMX Relationships

Several longitudinal studies have investigated how LMX relationships develop over time (e.g., Bauer and Green, 1996; Bluedorn and Jaussi, 2008; Boyd and Taylor, 1998; Graen *et al.*, 1982; Hochwarter and Castro, 2005; Liden *et al.*, 1993; Major *et al.*, 1995; Maslyn and Uhl-Bien, 2001; Maurer, Pierce, and Shore, 2002; Nahrgang *et al.*, 2009; Scandura and Graen, 1984).

From the empirical evidence, it appears that the relationship between new leader–subordinate dyads takes shape remarkably quickly, over the first few weeks and even days of working together (Bauer and Green, 1996; Liden et al., 1993), and may even have its roots in the recruitment and selection process (Parsons, Liden, and Bauer, 2001). Once established, the trajectory of LMX appears to remain fairly stable over time. For example, Liden et al. (1993) found that LMX measured after the first five days of leader and subordinate dyads working together was a moderately high predictor of LMX quality six months later ($r = .45$). Further research is needed, however, to track the process by which LMX quality develops and is maintained across the life cycle of the relationship to examine relationship development and partnership building. In this section we consider the role of social exchanges and attributional processes in shaping LMX development.

Role of social exchanges
It is clear that the development of LMX relationships occurs through various social exchanges between the leader and subordinate over time. However, what is less clear is the actual content of these exchanges and there is a dearth of research on this issue. One exception is the study by Maurer et al. (2002), which examined the role of a range of "development activities" undertaken by the subordinates (e.g., taking job-related courses to enhance performance, being on a task force to examine difficult work issues). The benefits of these activities can be construed on three dimensions according to the potential beneficiary of the activity (subordinate, supervisor or organization), and the likelihood of engaging in these activities will be determined by the overall quality of the LMX relationship. For example, if LMX quality is high, then subordinates are more likely to engage in activities that are beneficial to the supervisor and/or organization than if it is low.

The most popular theoretical model to explain LMX development is the "Leadership-Making Model" (Graen and Uhl-Bien, 1991; Uhl-Bien and Graen, 1995). This model was based on the earlier Role-Making Model of Leadership proposed by Graen (1976), which in turn was based on Kahn and colleagues' role theory (see Kahn et al., 1964; Katz and Kahn, 1978). The role theory describes the process through which individuals develop roles via dyadic exchanges (see Graen, 2005, for comparison of different approaches).

Three stages make up the Leadership-Making Model: the "stranger stage" (role taking), the "acquaintance stage" (role making), and the "maturity stage" (role routinization) (see also the three-phase model of LMX development by Scandura and Lankau, 1996). The first stage is the stranger stage (role taking), where the leader and subordinate have little knowledge of each other and occupy interdependent roles. The nature of the exchanges between the leader and subordinate are based on the job description and requirements of the work. Leaders provide sufficient resources required for the subordinate to do their work and, in turn, the subordinate only does what his or her job requires. Exchanges are based strictly on the employment contract, and exchange reciprocation is essentially immediate. From this situation the leader or subordinate might make, "an 'offer' for an improved working relationship through career-orientated social exchange" (Graen and Uhl-Bien, 1995, p. 230). The leader or subordinate might initiate social exchanges that can lead to a relationship that goes beyond the stranger stage, e.g., the leader might give a challenging task to the subordinate. Whether or not the subordinate accepts this "offer," the relationship can move to the second stage of development.

The acquaintance stage (role making) is when the nature of the leader–subordinate relationship becomes defined. Role making is strengthened through the mutual and equitable exchange of resources within the dyad. In this stage, interactions become more frequent, with social exchanges extending beyond the formal employment contract to include the sharing of information and resources at both the personal and work levels. However, these social exchanges are based on the principle of equity between both members of the dyad who are still testing to determine an acceptable role relationship.

Stage 3 of the Leadership-Making Model is the maturity stage (role routinization). The exchanges between the leader and subordinate are highly developed and each person can count on the other for loyalty and support. In this stage, the leader–subordinate relationship is characterized by mutual respect, trust, and obligation. The leader and subordinate become more interdependent, and their expectations stabilize over time. The maturity stage is characterized by a high frequency of exchanges that extend beyond the formal employment contract and prolonged time spans of reciprocation. When people reach this level of LMX development they correspond to a high LMX relationship.

Inherent in Role theory is the assumption that exchanges are based on the principle of equity; that is, exchanges are perceived as fair if the ratio of inputs to outputs for both individuals in a dyad is equal (cf. Adams, 1965). In line with equity theory and more recent justice theoretic conceptions (e.g., Greenberg), if exchanges are not perceived as fair, the aggrieved dyad member may seek additional compensation from the other member of the dyad, or alternatively reduce his or her contributions to the relationship to achieve equity. These exchanges may involve different commodities being contributed by each member of the dyad. For example, leaders may offer information (e.g., Krammer, 1995), latitude and desired tasks in exchange for an employee's performance, loyalty, and citizenship. Although the exchange commodities may differ, they should be of equal value to the members of the dyad in order for equity to be achieved. Despite the assumption that LMX relationships are governed by equity principles, as observed by van Breukelen, Konst, and Van Der Vlist (2002) little empirical work has been conducted on this issue (but see Maslyn and Uhl-Bien, 2001, for a notable exception).

Role of attributions

Attributions may come into play in several ways with regard to exchanges between leaders and subordinates and, thus, attribution theory is useful in understanding LMX dynamics (Dasborough and Ashkanasy, 2002; Davis and Gardner, 2004; Lam, 2007; Martinko *et al.*, 2007). Green and Mitchell (1979) proposed a model depicting how subordinate's behavior led to informational cues that influenced leader attributions, which in turn influenced leaders' behaviors toward members. They generated more than 20 different hypotheses, which in general state how different patterns of attributions lead to different types of leader behavior. The leader's attributions of subordinates' performance concern whether the subordinate has adequate ability or motivation (internal attribution) or whether something in the situation caused the observed behavior (external attribution). Generally, internal attributions lead to behaviors directed to the subordinate, such as coaching or changing the work assignment, whereas external attributions result in behaviors directed toward the situation, such as providing more resources or changing the task (Martinko *et al.*, 2007; Mitchell *et al.*, 1981; Steiner, 1997).

Dienesch and Liden's (1986) model also incorporates attributional processes in the LMX context. They have suggested that there are two paths to LMX development. In the first, salient behaviors occurring in the initial interaction between a leader and a subordinate may have immediate implications for the nature of the exchange. The leader's initial liking for subordinates and perceptions of their ability appear to be very influential factors in early LMX development (Dockery and Steiner, 1990; Steiner, 1997). In the alternative path, the initial interaction may not lead to immediate categorization but rather to the superior's assigning some initial responsibilities to the subordinate. Attributions then enter the process for both members of the dyad. On the one hand, subordinates try to understand their initial assignments and make attributions about leader behavior. These attributions influence how they perform for the leader and whether or not they respond with loyalty and attempt to achieve high performance, characteristic of a high LMX exchange. On the other hand, their performance on the initial assignments allows the leader to make attributions regarding this performance. These leader attributions influence the assignment of subsequent responsibilities to subordinates. If leaders make internal attributions about good performance and external attributions about poor performance, the development of high LMX is likely. Once the exchange is established, attributional processes continue to operate. In other words, supervisors make attributions about subordinate performance, and these attributions influence their behavior toward subordinates. Supervisors give challenging assignments to high LMX subordinates, prepare them for difficult responsibilities and talk about their strengths to upper management (Graen, 1990; Steiner, 1997) all actions consistent with attributing good performance to internal factors.

Another approach to LMX development explicitly examines the process from the subordinate's perspective. For example, Hochwarter and Castro (2005) examined the role of a number of subordinate needs (e.g., need for belongingness and love), emotions, influence tactics, and presentation styles in shaping LMX development. Of particular interest is the role emotional regulation (a construct that has similarity to social competence in emotional intelligence) plays in the effectiveness of influence tactics engaged in by the subordinate in determining the LMX development. They found that emotional regulation can have two main impacts; first, in terms of the choice of tactic to engage in and second, how well the tactic is delivered.

Integration of LMX and Interpersonal Relationship Research

The evolution of stage 3 LMX theory and research has coincided with the rapid growth of a multidisciplinary science of *close interpersonal relationships* (for reviews see Berscheid, 1994, 1999; Berscheid and Reis, 1998; Reis, 2007). Given that both of these research traditions are quintessentially relationship based, it is perhaps surprising that they have developed more in parallel than in tandem. While some distinctions can be made between personal and workplace relationships in terms of their nature and functions (see Duck, 2007; Graen and Uhl-Bien, 1995; Van Lear, Korner, and Allen, 2006), there are more similarities than differences between LMX and close personal relationships. For example, both high-quality LMX and nonwork friendships are characterized by mutual influence, reciprocal liking, high trust, mutual disclosure of privileged information, and the provision of various kinds of support (Boyd and Taylor, 1998; Fehr, 2008). More importantly, certain generic processes and knowledge may transcend almost all kinds of relationships (Berscheid and Reis, 1998; Clark and Reis, 1988). We maintain, therefore, that there is potential for the LMX literature to be informed by (and to inform) the interpersonal relationships literature. Later in the chapter, we discuss some possible benefits of cross-fertilization between the LMX and close relationships approaches.

Complementary theoretical and methodological approaches
While both the LMX and interpersonal relationships research traditions have been heavily influenced by social exchange theory (Homans, 1961; Thibaut and Kelley, 1959), the interpersonal relationships literature conceptualizes relationships as more than just patterns of behavioral exchanges within dyads; they involve pre-existing schemas and beliefs, memories, emotions, and judgments about each other (Hinde, 1996; Fletcher and Thomas, 1996). For example, interdependence theory (Kelly *et al.*, 1983; Rusbult and Arriaga, 1997) and the communal relationship approach (Clark and Mills, 1979; Mills and Clark, 1994), both of which are germane to the analysis of LMX relationships, extend the notion of social exchange in important ways. Interdependence

theory defines relationships in terms of their closeness, which is the degree of interdependence of people's behavior, including their cognitions and emotions. Close relationships typically involve frequent, strong and diverse influence, synchronized goals and plans, shared feelings and emotional responses, enhanced liking, trust and commitment, and an appreciation of the uniqueness of the relationship (Berscheid and Reis, 1998; Burgess and Huston, 1979); each of these features are characteristic of high-quality LMX relationships, especially those that reach the (previously described) dyadic partnership building stage. The importance of the dimension of relationship closeness and interdependence is that it underlies most relationship phenomena of interest, regardless of relationship form or type (Berscheid and Reis, 1998; Clark and Reis, 1988).

According to the communal relationship approach, social exchanges can be governed by norms other than equity or the quid pro quo that has been presumed to characterize LMX relationships (see Clark and Reis, 1988, for a review). For example, in communal relationships members feel a mutual responsibility for the welfare of each other, and benefits are given noncontingently on a needs basis. The norm of reciprocity is more implicit than explicit in communal relationships (Harvey and Weber, 2002). Communal strength, the motivation to adopt a needs-based rule in the context of a particular relationship, is likely to be determined by (1) higher levels of perceived relationship closeness (Mills et al., 2004), (2) the salience of cooperative or socioemotional (over economic productivity) goals (Deutsch, 1975), and (3) higher levels of communal orientation, that is, the general tendency of each dyad member to follow communal rules in relationships (Clark et al., 1987). These moderating conditions of communal strength seem relevant to LMX relationships. High-quality LMX relationships, particularly those at the mature stage, are characterized by a significant degree of closeness (i.e., liking) and a concern for mutual support and development, and therefore are likely to be influenced by communal norms. Hence, we expect that high-quality LMX relationships, such as friendships, constitute a form of hybrid or blended relationship in which both exchange and communal elements coexist (Boyd and Taylor, 1998; Bridge and Baxter, 1982).

Relationship initiation

More recent conceptualizations of relationships have emphasized the complexity of relationship processes as they extend over time. In particular, a good deal of theory and research has focused on the genesis of relationships, which seems relevant to understanding the process of LMX initiation and differentiation. Broadly speaking, close relationship selection appears to involve a two-stage process (Fehr, 2008). The first is an *exclusion process*, whereby people make intuitive, and often affectively driven, judgments based on initial impressions and quickly eliminate those that they dislike or disregard (Denrell, 2005; Gouldner and Strong, 1987). The notion that not everyone is afforded a genuine chance to impress runs counter to early LMX theorizing about role taking (e.g., Graen and Uhl-Bien 1995), but is consistent with the social cognition literature on impression formation (see Fiske and Taylor, 1991). The final selection stage is an *inclusion process* and often involves more deliberative, in-depth cognitive processing. For example, relationship discrepancy models view the motivation to forge a close relationship as strategically driven by the perceived consistency between a priori standards or expectations and perceptions of the prospective partner relative to those standards (Fletcher, Simpson, and Thomas, 2000; Fletcher *et al.*, 1999). Such standards may comprise one's partner and relationship ideals (Fletcher and Thomas, 1996; Simpson, Fletcher, and Campbell, 2001) or what one could realistically expect, that is, compared to potentially available alternative partners (Kelly *et al.*, 1983).

Friendship researchers have identified a wide range of characteristics that predict friendship desirability and formation, including physical attractiveness, social skills, perceived responsiveness, reciprocity of liking, mutual self disclosure, warmth and agreeableness, shared fun and humor, frequency of exposure, familiarity, and similarity (for a review see Fehr, 2008). Many of these factors are likely to combine to form the building blocks of a rapport and knowledge generation phase (Bredow, Cate and Huston, 2008). For example, research examining the acquaintanceship process has shown that friends develop a greater understanding of each other's traits, attitudes, motives, thoughts, and feelings compared to that of strangers (e.g., Blackman and Funder, 1998; Colvin, Vogt, and Ickes, 1998; Kenny, 1994; Thomas and Fletcher, 1997, 2003). In terms of more distal characteristics, there is widespread recognition of the importance of personal relationship history in determining relationship formation processes (Berscheid, 1994). For instance, people's earlier experience of trusting and supportive relationships instills a sense of felt security and a positive working model of themselves and others in relationships in general, which in turn affects the propensity to initiate and build rapport in prospective relationships (see Berscheid and Reis, 1998; Popper, Mayseless, and Castelnovo, 2000; Simpson, 2008). Apart from the effect of similarity, many of these characteristics are yet to be systematically examined as antecedents of LMX formation.

In summary, while clearly not all relationships are created equal, and a good deal of relationship knowledge is not easily generalized across relationship type, there is generic relationship knowledge and processes featured in the interpersonal relationships literature that are sufficiently promising to warrant more attention by LMX researchers. In this review, we have briefly discussed just a few such examples. We believe that there is much to be gained by LMX research from drawing on the insights of relationship research, especially in terms of understanding more fully the social exchange process and the development and maintenance of LMX over the relationship life cycle.

Stage 4: LMX at the Group and Network Levels

Stage 4 of LMX theory development recognizes that LMX relationships are not just isolated dyads (leader–subordinate) but occur within a network of other relationships within the context of a wider organizational setting. This leads to the expansion of research from the dyadic level of analysis to the group and network levels of analyses, a move that is advocated by many LMX theorists (e.g., Gerstner and Day, 1997; Graen and Scandura, 1987; Graen and Uhl-Bien, 1995; Kinicki and Vecchio, 1994; Liden *et al.*, 1997; Mayer and Piccolo, 2006; Sparrowe and Liden, 1997; Van Breukelen *et al.*, 2002). Graen and Uhl-Bien (1995) identified three levels of potential inquiry for research at stage 4 of LMX development, and for each propose example research questions: *work group* (e.g., how do subordinates with low- and high-quality LMX relationships interact and work together?), *beyond immediate work group* (e.g., how does LMX quality affect relationships in other areas of the organization?), and *crossing organizational boundaries* (e.g., how does LMX quality affect relationships with people outside the organization, such as customers?). At the time of their review, Graen and Uhl-Bien (1995) noted that they were not aware of much, or indeed any, empirical research in this stage of LMX development. Since their review, there has been considerable attention, both empirical research and theory development, extending LMX beyond the dyadic level with respect to the application of social network analysis, relational leadership, and relationship variation. We describe some of the developments in each of these areas.

Social Network Analysis

The approach adopted by social network analysis (Burt and Minor, 1983; Granovetter, 1985), with its emphasis on the effects of the structure of relationships on important outcomes, offers a means for extending the domain of LMX research beyond the vertical dyad linkage. The central argument of social networks research is that actors are embedded in networks of interconnected social relationships that offer opportunities for and constraints on behavior. From this perspective, individuals' positions within social networks can offer advantages, such as organizational assimilation (Sparrowe and Liden, 1997) and promotions (Burt, 1992), or lead to disadvantages, such as organizational exit (Krackhardt and Porter, 1986). Centrality, the extent to which a given individual is connected to others in a network is the structural property most often associated with instrumental outcomes such as power (Brass, 1984), influence in decision making (Friedkin, 1993), and innovation (Ibarra, 1993).

In the context of LMX, research has generally supported the salience of the formal leader in providing subordinates with desired resources; however, informal social networks and horizontal exchanges are also likely to be critical in the provision of resources as well as in determining outcomes. Research on the effects of individuals' social networks in organizations indicates that the structural configuration of relationships (ties) with others beyond their immediate superiors has positive effects on promotions (Burt, 1992) influence (Brass, 1984; Brass and Burkhardt, 1992; Friedkin, 1993; Mardsen and Friedkin, 1993), reputation (Kilduff and Krackhardt, 1994), turnover (Krackhardt and Porter, 1986), and career progression (Sparrowe and Popielarz, 1995). (See also Mayer and Piccolo, 2006, for an examination of LMX using both social network and multilevel perspectives.)

Early formulations of LMX theory (e.g., Cashman et al., 1976; Graen et al., 1977) focused only on the leader–subordinate dyad and highlighted the role of the formal leader because she or he was seen to be the "linking pin" connecting members to the resources that flow through the reporting relationships of the organizational hierarchy, but later discussions of LMX theory have extended its basic ideas to "dyadic subassemblies" (Graen and Scandura, 1987) and social networks (Sparrowe and Liden, 1997; Uhl-Bien, Graen, and Scandura, 2000).

Sparrowe and Liden (1997) were the first to stress the importance of studying LMX relationships within the context of the organization as a whole (see also Gibbons and Grover, 2006). They noted that LMXs are embedded in larger networks of informal relationships whose structure is important for understanding the differentiation process. They portrayed differentiation in leader–subordinate exchange as a dynamic process, the outcomes of which are shaped by the quality of leader–subordinate exchange and the structure of the emergent informal networks in which both parties are embedded. They developed a series of propositions concerning the quality of leader–member relations and their connection to the organization and its informal networks. They proposed that a subordinate's "assimilation" into the organization depends on the sponsorship of his or her leader, that is, the leader's incorporation of subordinates into his or her own network of close relations. They also suggested that sponsorship depends on the quality of members' relationships with their leaders. In Sparrowe and Liden's (1997) model, sponsorship connoted intentionality on the part of the leader. Although leaders do in fact intentionally incorporate subordinates into their trust networks, sponsorship need not rely solely on the leader's intentional initiatives. Balance theory (Heider, 1958; Newcomb, 1961) suggests that members who have high-quality exchange relationships with their leaders will be accepted as trustworthy by the leaders' own trusted contacts, thereby increasing the extent of shared trust relationships. This "transfer" of trustworthiness can occur even if the leader's contact and the member have not physically met (Ferrin, Dirks, and Shah, 2006). Within the context of a high-quality exchange each individual's social capital becomes important as it enables the opportunity for mutual benefits in the relationship. Social capital is often operationalized as network centrality, or the number of connections between an individual and others in a network, which grants the central actor access to those individuals and their resources (Brass, 1984).

Individuals who are central within a network have connection benefits that may provide the basis for power because of the dependence others have on their access to people or information. The social capital of the leader or the subordinate may therefore be a valuable resource to the other, and this benefit may influence the maintenance of a close LMX relationship.

Despite the theoretical work suggesting that organizational networks are important to the LMX relationship, only a few studies have addressed this issue directly. Mehra *et al.* (2006) found differences in leader's social networks were related to differences in the economic performance of their units as well as to their personal reputations as leaders. They specifically found that embeddedness of leaders in the friendship networks of their subordinates, peers, and supervisors had implications for objective group performance and the leaders' reputations. The group leaders' centrality scores vis-à-vis internal and external friendship networks were directly related to group performance and their personal reputations as leaders.

Sparrowe and Liden's (2005) study of influence furthered the understanding of LMX by examining it relative to informal networks within the organization. They found that follower LMX and advice centrality related to influence within the organization, but this relationship depended on sponsorship (the extent to which a given follower shared ties within the leader's trust network) and the leader's centrality in the advice network. If the leader was central, his or her sponsorship was positive for the subordinate's advice centrality and influence. If the leader was not central, sponsorship was not beneficial to the subordinate's advice centrality and influence. Sparrowe and Liden concluded that it is not just the formal hierarchical relationship between leaders and their subordinates that determines the extent to which the latter have influence within the organization, the leader's informal network ties to others throughout the organization also plays a crucial role.

Finally, Goodwin, Bowler, and Whittington (2009) tested components of LMX theory within the context of informal organizational networks, finding support for the importance of instrumental components within quality LMX relationships. They found that when a subordinate was sought for work-related advice by many employees, that is, the subordinate's advice centrality in informal networks was high, the subordinate's leader reported a high LMX quality. They also found that leaders and subordinates use a different basis for the evaluation of LMX quality when both the social and instrumental aspects of the relationship are considered. For followers, perceptions of similarity to the leaders were what mattered and consideration of instrumental advantages through association with the leader did not affect their evaluation of LMX quality. Leaders, on the other hand, seemed to be more concerned with the instrumental value of the relationship with the subordinate. When leaders perceived that they were dissimilar to their subordinates, their evaluations of the quality of the LMX relationship were invariant – regardless of whether subordinate advice centrality was low or high. When, however, they perceived themselves to be similar to their subordinates along this (these) dimension(s), they rated the quality of the relationship higher when the subordinate was central in the advice network, but lower when the subordinate was not central.

It becomes apparent from the aforementioned discussion that integrating LMX theory and research with work on the analysis of social networks is a fruitful line for future inquiry (see also Gibbons and Grover, 2006; Mayer and Piccolo, 2006). As observed by Gibbons and Grover (2006), ongoing research on LMX theory should continue to incorporate network variables as a means of identifying formal and informal structural influences on the LMX relationship, along the lines of the recent study by Gibbons and Grover (2006). In our view, this line of inquiry could usefully be extended further, for example by investigating the impact of structural holes (Burt, 1992) and broadening the range of informal networks considered (for example by incorporating networks based on friendship). Work-related networks characterized by high versus low trust and negative networks should also be considered.

Relational Leadership

In recent years, there has been an increase in interest in what is referred to as the "relational perspective on leadership," as distinct from the more traditional "entity approach" (see, e.g., Brower, Shoorman, and Tan, 2000; Hosking, Dachler, and Gergen, 1995; Murrell, 1997; Uhl-Bien, 2006). LMX theory and research falls within the traditional, entity approach because it focuses on individual entities (leaders, subordinates, colleagues, and environment), predicted on the assumption that individuals in a relationship are separate, that is, bounded, entities. In this context there is a separation between the "internal self" of the individual and their "external environment." People's knowledge of "reality" comes from their ability to engage in internal thought processes. As reality resides within the mind of the individual and is a result of internal cognitive processes (that are distinct from external influences), the level of analysis is focused on the individual and their characteristics. According to Dachler and Hosking (1995) the "relationship" part of LMX theory can be viewed in terms of a "subject–object" understanding. The individual is seen as the "subject," which is a different entity from other aspects in the environment and which is passive and controllable by the subject. The object in this sense is the relationship that resides in the mind of the subject (individual).

While the entity approach focuses on the attributes and behaviors of people in the LMX dyad, the relational approach focuses on the social construction processes that determine the understanding of leadership within a particular context. Social realities concerning the self, other people, and the wider social environment are interdependent, social constructions. Since social constructions of leadership are created and recreated through communication processes, the latter forms the main unit of analysis within the relational approach. In other words, the key emphasis within this perspective is on relationships and communication processes to understand better how people interact to construct knowledge systems and create social order, thereby transcending the individual level of analysis that has been the hallmark of the entity perspective.

While both the entity and relational perspectives focus on leadership relationships, they differ in some very important ways. One major distinction is how each approach conceptualizes "relationships." In entity perspectives such as LMX theory, the emphasis in on interpersonal processes between the leader and subordinate, whereas within the relational approach the emphasis is on "relating," which involves a consideration of the subordinate in relation to others and the role of the social system in developing the meaning of leadership. This is studied through examining processes of interaction, communication and narration.

Uhl-Bien (2006) provides a framework for a relational approach termed "relational leadership theory". She defines relational leadership as "*a social influence process through which emergent coordination (i.e., evolving social order) and change (i.e., new values, attitudes, approaches, behaviors, ideologies, etc) are constructed and produced*" (p. 668). She then focuses on two aspects of the framework: first, "relationships as outcomes," centered on the question of how leadership relationships emerge from social interactions; second, "relational dynamics as a process of structuring," with a view to understanding how relational interactions contribute to the emergence of social order.

Uhl-Bien (2006) does not reject prior research on LMX based on the entity approach, but suggests that this needs to "evolve into more sociological or social–psychological orientations and go beyond the limited focus on dyadic or leader–follower singular relationships" (p. 672). Accordingly, she offers some potentially insightful ways to examine new leadership research questions using methodologies commensurate with entity, relational, and hybrid approaches, the latter seeking to combine the strengths of the former. In our view, the relational perspective offers many interesting opportunities to explore the development of relationships between leaders and subordinates and, in so doing, address recent calls in the literature to examine LMX relationships in ways that go beyond the dyadic level, to consider the role of the larger social system. By way of illustration, Huang *et al.* (2008) used the repertory grid technique to examine how leaders and subordinates develop different "relational schemas" (cognitive representations of exchange experiences) of the relationship.

Relationship Variation

According to Graen and Uhl-Bien (1995) a very important issue for research in stage 4 of LMX development is to examine "how high-quality and lower-quality exchanges are aggregated within a single work unit and what their combined effect is on group-level work processes and outcomes" (p. 234). This question has arisen following recognition that relationship quality varies considerably within the work group (between subordinates and with their leader). This can be examined in two ways: relationship variation between subordinates and relationship variation with the same leader. Both these conceptualizations of relationship variation are attracting research attention and are described later.

Researchers have examined *relationship variation between subordinates,* using the "team–member exchange" (TMX: Seers, 1989). As described earlier, in the measurement section, the TMX measure focuses on the perceived quality of relationships among subordinates within the work team, as opposed to the quality of relations between subordinates and their leader, the latter being the focus of conventional LMX research. The utility of the TMX construct has been demonstrated by studies showing that TMX explains additional variance in subordinates' work reactions (e.g., lower job satisfaction and organizational commitment) beyond that explained by LMX alone (Liden, Wayne and Sparrowe, 2000; Seers, 1989). Gerstner and Tesluk (2005) further developed the TMX construct by adopting a social network analysis in developing their measure of member–member exchanges (MMX). The social network matrix approach involves subordinates answering questions about how frequently they engaged in various activities with other subordinates (e.g., the frequency they rely on others to solve work-related problems and talk to others about nonwork issues). These questions assessed dimensions concerning relationships, friendship patterns, and trust.

The theoretical relationship between LMX and TMX remains unclear. Researchers have examined the links between these constructs in a variety of different ways. In some studies TMX has been incorporated as an additional predictor variable, in an attempt to explain variance beyond LMX per se in the prediction of work-related outcomes (e.g., Liden *et al.,* 2000; Seers, 1989). In other studies LMX has been investigated as a predictor of TMX (e.g., Tse *et al.,* 2008). Still other studies have examined the differential validity of LMX and TMX as joint predictors of various outcomes (e.g., Ford and Seers, 2006), as separate moderators (e.g., Major *et al.,* 1995), and the interaction between them (e.g., Dunegan, Tierney and Duchon, 1992) in predicting outcomes.

With respect to examining the *relationship variation with the leader,* researchers have focused on "LMX differentiation," that is, the extent to which subordinates believe that their leader has different quality relationships with the subordinates they manage (Henderson *et al.,* 2009). Most managers do seem to have different LMX quality relations with subordinates. However, this is seen as potentially leading to negative consequences because of feelings of unfair or inequitable treatment (Erdogan and Liden, 2002). Furthermore, if subordinates see their manager treat others in their group unfairly then this violates the expectation of leader neutrality, a vital prerequisite for procedural justice (Scandura, 1999; Tyler, 1989) and perceptions of trust (Gómez and Rosen, 2001; Scandura and Pellegrini, 2008). Given these observations, one might also expect to find evidence of a link between LMX differentiation and a variety of negative work reactions among subordinates.

To examine LMX differentiation, many researchers have employed various within-group agreement or coefficient of variability scores, based either on LMX scores for the whole group or on an individual subordinate's perceptions of other subordinates' LMX quality. Consistent with the aforementioned TMX findings, this research shows that LMX differentiation explains additional variance to that explained by the quality of LMX per se in the prediction of job satisfaction and well-being, with greater differentiation associated with negative outcomes in both cases (Boies and Howell, 2006; Hooper and Martin, 2008; Sherony and Green, 2002). Other research has shown a link between LMX differentiation and negative work reactions (Boies and Howell, 2006; Henderson et al., 2008; Ford and Seers, 2006; Liden et al., 2006; van Breukelen et al., 2002). As LMX differentiation runs counter to principles of equality and consistency, which are important for maintaining social harmony in groups, it is not surprising that this leads to negative effects on a number of group processes, such as team potency (Boies and Howell, 2006) and team conflict (Hooper and Martin, 2008). Hooper and Martin (2008) found that LMX differentiation negatively predicted job satisfaction and that this relationship was mediated by team conflict. Finally, some studies have examined the interaction between LMX and LMX differentiation, but the results, at this stage, have not been consistent (Boies and Howell, 2006; Henderson et al., 2008; Liden et al., 2006).

In summary, while stage 4 of LMX development has received the least amount of research attention (as one would expect because it builds on the earlier stages), it is currently receiving a lot of attention, a trend that we expect will continue in the future. Within this stream of work as a whole, we have highlighted three areas of development—social network analysis, relational leadership, and relationship variation–which we believe will add greatly in contextualizing LMX relationships both within the work-group and the wider organization. This is very important as organizational leadership is not restricted to dyadic relationships, rather, it embraces wider relationships that span a complex array of social structures, which in turn shape and give the leadership process meaning.

FINAL REFLECTIONS

In this section, we make some final reflections concerning the aforementioned review of the LMX literature with respect to observations on current research, future research directions, and leadership as a "lens".

Observations on Current Research

Our first observation is that research into LMX is flourishing and that the number of published scientific papers is increasing. Indeed, Yammarino *et al.* (2005) observed that LMX is currently the second most researched theory of leadership, and our expectation is that this trend is likely to continue. Research papers addressing LMX theory and research tend to be published in some of the world's most prestigious journal outlets, reflecting its overall importance and impact within the wider leadership literature and, indeed, the position of leadership as a topic within the field of I/O psychology as a whole. Our review shows that the nature of LMX research is also diverse in terms of occupational samples, cultural context, measurement instruments, research designs, and statistical approaches. This diversity gives increased confidence of the generalizability of research findings.

We note a welcome increase in the number of longitudinal studies. Unlike cross-sectional research, longitudinal studies offer the opportunity to examine the dynamic nature of LMX over time and the testing of causal hypotheses. However, virtually all the research we reviewed is quantitative in nature, i.e. too little qualitative research has been conducted. Given that LMX is a relational construct, we would welcome more diverse research methods, ones that can potentially reveal fresh insights into what is in essence a complex notion. For example, interviews, diaries, and observation of subordinate–subordinate, subordinate–leader, and leader–leader interactions could each provide a rich data source to complement the questionnaire-based empirical studies that have thus far dominated the field, opening up key areas of LMX (e.g., LMX development) to much-needed fine-grained analyses.

There has also been a very significant increase in statistical sophistication in analyzing LMX. As illustrated in the earlier sections of our review, advanced statistical techniques such as WABA and HLM can help partition variance between the individual, dyad, and group levels—essential when examining a complex, multifaceted notion like LMX, which is multilevel in nature.

For simplicity, we organized our review of the literature around the four stages of LMX development outlined by Graen and Uhl-Bien (1995). We did this to emphasize the most important developmental trends in the research and to highlight areas for future research activity. In reality, many of the papers surveyed cover more than one of the stages. For example, some studies examine both the correlates of LMX and LMX differentiation within the same paradigm and, therefore, there is already some integration across the stages. As observed earlier, some stages of research (such as in stage 2: identifying LMX antecedents and outcomes) are well advanced, while others (such as in stage 4: examining LMX at the group level) are still in their infancy. This is only to be expected, as is typical of the evolutionary development of research in all topic areas of all fields. Accordingly, as research on LMX continues apace, we anticipate that there will be an increased shift in emphasis toward work falling within the third and fourth stages of the Graen and Uhl-Bien (1995) taxonomy, especially studies examining LMX at the group level.

In reviewing this area, we were impressed by the consistency of many of the findings, especially in terms of the magnitude (or in statistical terms, the "effect size") of the relationship between LMX and many important work-related outcomes. It is likely that this has contributed to the popularity of the area. On the basis of the large literature that has now been amassed, we have a good idea of at least some of the main antecedents of LMX (subordinate characteristics, leader characteristics, interactional variables, and contextual variables), and an even better knowledge of the outcomes of LMX quality (especially of its impact on attitudes and perceptions, behaviors, and task performance). The evidence base concerning LMX antecedents is not as strong as it is for LMX outcomes because very few studies actually measure antecedents before LMX formation, partly because LMX forms so quickly. Therefore, many antecedents are deduced on the basis of theoretical reasoning, rather than inferred from statistical evidence gathered empirically in longitudinal studies based on designs that can enable the testing of causal relationships between hypothesized antecedents and outcomes with precision.

If one were to be critical, one might observe that there is a bewildering array of factors that have been identified as antecedents and outcomes of LMX. Indeed, one might be hard pressed to identify any variables within the I/O psychology literature that have not, in some way, been linked to LMX. This state of affairs can be interpreted in one of two ways: positive or negative, respectively. The more positive interpretation is that LMX is such an important variable that its influence pervades all areas of I/O psychology. The more negative interpretation is that LMX has become an easy "add on" for many research programs, one that provides a "safe bet" when seeking potentially significant (and hence potentially publishable) results. In reading some elements of the voluminous LMX literature in preparation for the drafting of this chapter we have identified many studies that appear to support the latter viewpoint. One obvious way to deal with a research concept that is linked to many variables is to identify key moderators that determine when these variables will have an effect. To this end, recent researchers have begun to identify some of the main moderators of established relationships between LMX antecedents and outcomes, especially with respect to task performance outcomes. We are also witnessing a growth in the use of the aforementioned advanced statistical techniques to develop and test multilevel models incorporating complex moderators and mediators of LMX antecedents and outcomes. Given the shared variance between many of the putative antecedents identified in the literature, we do not yet have a sufficient body of evidence to determine robustly their relative effect sizes or incremental predictive power in the prediction of an equally diverse array of outcomes. Knowledge of which antecedents and outcomes are more important than others would help further LMX theory development.

For example, we do not know whether interactional/relationship variables are more important than individual-level leader and subordinate variables. There is a potential danger that a reader of this chapter will be left with the impression that the authors believe that LMX research is without criticism. It is true that we have sought to celebrate the many valuable contributions of the area. However, we are aware that there have been many justifiable criticisms of LMX research in terms of concept definition, measurement, statistical procedures, and interpretation of findings. We do not wish to convey the impression of wanting to brush these criticisms aside. Indeed, we have addressed several of these concerns in various sections of this review. At this point, however, we wish to focus on two criticisms in particular.

Our first criticism concerns the *dearth of theoretical understanding*. The vast majority of the research is descriptive in nature and atheoretical in approach. Put simply, the area lacks an integrative theory that explains the causes and effects of LMX. As noted earlier, there is a smorgasbord of variables that have been shown to be linked to LMX, but we do not yet have a clear theory as to how these variables link together. Apart from the use of social exchange theory, LMX theory has become something of a theoretical island. We would encourage researchers to be bold on this front and to develop integrative theories that link together many of the well-established findings in the area. In our review, we have suggested that LMX research could benefit considerably by utilizing theoretical approaches that have been developed in related areas. In this respect we have identified research on close interpersonal relationships as a potentially important area to draw on in developing LMX theory. Work and non-workplace relationships share many similar characteristics. Accordingly, we maintain that there is tremendous potential to apply concepts and theories from the close relationships literature to enrich understanding of LMX in the workplace, and in earlier sections of this chapter we have highlighted what we consider some of the most immediately promising areas of application.

Our second criticism is that there have been *very little practical developments* from the LMX literature (for some notable exceptions, however, see the review of leadership development techniques by Avolio and Chan, 2008). This major omission is surprising, given the consistency of findings in the literature and the clear prediction that improving LMX quality should lead to a number of important work-related benefits (such as improved job satisfaction and task performance). Indeed, some studies show the benefits of increasing LMX on a variety of outcomes (e.g., Graen *et al.*, 1982; Graen, Scandura, and Graen, 1986). However, very little applied research has been conducted that explicitly aims to improve LMX quality and relate these to work outcomes. In terms of practical implications, some authors have argued that managers should try to avoid having different quality relationships with their subordinates (especially negative ones); instead, they should try to develop high-quality LMX relationships with all subordinates (Graen and Uhl-Bien, 1995). The likelihood that a manager could successfully implement this prescriptive advice has been questioned in the light of several practical constraints, not least variations in span of control, time constraints on the part of the leader and the potential scarcity of required material resources (van Breukelen *et al.*, 2006). It is disappointing that an area that has shown the importance of LMX quality for subordinate well-being and performance has not led to proven training programmes to enhance LMX quality, and we hope that future research will address this gap.

Future Research Directions

The aims of this chapter were twofold: to conduct an up-to-date survey of the area and, in so doing, to provide some pointers for future research. We have described many potential avenues for future research in various sections of this review. In this penultimate subsection we wish to touch on two further areas for future research that is particularly pertinent to the authors.

Development and Maintenance of Relationship Quality

We have already proposed that the LMX area could benefit from closer integration with research into close interpersonal relationships. One particular issue concerns how LMX relationships are maintained and enhanced over time, an issue that has not been systematically examined by LMX researchers (Erdogan and Liden, 2002). A useful way to view relationship maintenance is Harvey and Omarzu's (1997) concept of *minding*, which refers to an array of cognitive and behavioral activities that people can employ to regulate and sustain their close relationships. For example, minding can involve proactively managing and promoting relationship quality and the experience of positive affect, using tactics such as eliciting greater mutual self-disclosure, conveying respect and acceptance for one's partner, generating benevolent and benign relationship attributions, acknowledging the significance of partner's and joint contributions to the relationship, and adopting and communicating optimistic views of the relationship's future (see Harvey and Omarzu, 1997; Simpson, Ickes and Orina, 2001). The first component of the minding process is reducing the ambiguity of meaning during relationship interactions by exhibiting the motivation and ability to accurately read the significant other's thoughts and feelings, commonly referred to as empathic accuracy or mind-reading accuracy (e.g., Ickes, 2003; Simpson *et al.*, 2001; Thomas and Fletcher, 1997; Thomas and Maio, 2008).

Using the aforementioned mind-reading skills, minding also involves preemptively dealing with and regulating negative affect and relationship conflict so as to prevent the deterioration of relationship quality. Partners in high-quality relationships are more willing to accommodate and constructively deal with minor relationship-based problems before they escalate into more serious problems (e.g., Fletcher and Thomas, 2000; Fletcher, Thomas, and Durant, 1999). In particular, mind-reading skills can effectively be used to avert and diffuse problems that inevitably arise in relationships (e.g., Thomas, Fletcher, and Lange, 1997); a maintenance process that is especially evident in high-quality relationships (Thomas and Fletcher, 2003; cf. Simpson, Ickes, and Blackstone, 1995). We suspect that greater mind-reading accuracy would also be demonstrated in high-quality LMX relationships, but because of the power differential, subordinates may be more motivated to accurately read the leader's thoughts and feelings than vice versa (see Thomas and Maio, 2008, for a discussion on motivated accuracy).

Finally, if relationship problems cannot be nipped in the bud, and partners hurt and offend each other, thereby threatening the quality of the relationship, then more reactive relationship repair strategies such as forgiveness are likely to become important for restoring relationship stability (Fincham, 2000; Maio et al., 2008). It should be noted, however, that the effectiveness of such maintenance and repair strategies is likely to be moderated by individual's implicit relationship theories and beliefs about relationship development. For example, Knee and his colleagues have found that those who harbor destiny beliefs view relationships as generally fixed and stable, and believe that relationship quality is determined at the initiation stage by finding a compatible partner. In contrast, those who hold growth beliefs are more focused on relationship maintenance and enhancement, and believe that relationships can be cultivated not despite relationship problems, but partly because of the opportunities that such problems provide for further relationship development (Knee, 1998; Knee and Bush, 2008).

Group-Level Perspective

It is now widely recognized that one of the limitations of LMX theory is its sole focus on dyadic leader–subordinate relations (Avolio et al., 2009). Although important in their own right, dyadic relationships occur within a wider context of shared group membership, that is, subordinates interact with one another as group members and the quality of those relationships is influenced by their perceptions of the leader's relations with the wider group (Hogg, Martin, and Weeden, 2004). Accordingly, as described earlier, LMX research is increasingly considering dyadic and group-level perspectives not as contradictions but as complementary approaches to examine leadership phenomena. In this section we outline some recent developments of conceptualizing LMX as occurring within a group context that merit more systematic research.

The first development concerns the issue of *LMX differentiation* (i.e., the extent to which leaders have different quality relationships with the subordinates they manage) that was described earlier in the review. As noted earlier, LMX differentiation is associated with negative work reactions amongst subordinates

(Boies and Howell, 2006; Henderson *et al.*, 2008, 2009; Ford and Seers, 2006; Liden *et al.*, 2006; van Breukelen *et al.*, 2002) because LMX differentiation breaks norms of leader nonneutrality and equity (Colquitt, 2004; Leventhal, 1980; Scandura, 1999). The original perspective of LMX theory proposed that leaders develop individual, and unique, relationships with each subordinate, which ignores the fact that leaders lead groups of subordinates who communicate with each other. One of the reasons why it is important to acknowledge that leadership occurs within a group context is because group members engage in various social comparison processes (Festinger, 1954) where they compare themselves with significant others on important dimensions.

In the context of work organizations, subordinates will most likely compare their LMX relationship with that of other subordinates within their work group and these comparisons will affect the self-concept and perceptions of fairness (e.g., Buunk *et al.*, 1990; Leventhal, 1980; Masterson *et al.*, 2000; Tyler, 1989; Tyler, Degoey, and Smith, 2001). These comparisons give meaning to people's social world and are open to a number of attributional biases. This is nicely shown in a qualitative study by Sias and Jablin (1995) who found that subordinates engaged in various attributional biases to interpret the reasons for people having low- and high-quality LMX relationships in their work team. For example, subordinates who had a high LMX relationship viewed the differential treatment by the leader as fair, while those subordinates that had a low LMX relationship viewed the leader's differential treatment as unfair. On the basis of this pattern of findings, we believe more research should be directed at understanding the role of social comparison processes, the person chosen for comparison, the types of comparisons engaged in (upward, downwards, lateral), the types of biases that can occur and the outcomes of these processes in terms of subordinates' work reactions.

The second development concerns the *social identity theory of leadership* (Hogg, 2001; in press; van Knippenberg *et al.*, 2004). Leaders are significant in shaping the social identity of group members. In situations where group membership is important, and members identify with the group, leaders who are perceived as being more group prototypical (i.e., embody the key characteristics that represent group members) are more effective than leaders who are perceived to be less prototypical of the group. This is because prototypical leaders are more able to influence group members (because they are perceived as being similar to the group members) compared to nonprototypical leaders. Hogg *et al.* (2005) used social identity theory to examine some of the boundary conditions for LMX theory. Across two cross-sectional surveys, they found that when group membership was not salient, a personalized style that emphasized leader–member relations was most effective. However, when group membership was salient (and presumably identification with the group was high), a depersonalized leadership style that empathized being a group member was most effective. This suggests that the LMX approach might not be effective in situations that emphasize high group identification and the feeling that one is part of a group rather than a collection of individuals. In this situation, a more group-orientated leadership style might be appropriate. The social identity approach to leadership is gaining a lot of research attention, and we believe that this approach has much to offer in understanding LMX processes.

Concluding Thoughts (Leadership as a "Lens" Revisited)

We end this chapter by revisiting the quote by Gerstner and Day (1997) we cited at the outset. The quote suggested that the relationship a person has with their supervisor is a "lens" through which they perceive their work experience. The research reviewed in this chapter shows that the quality of one's LMX is indeed a powerful lens that significantly shapes the experience of work. We wish to take the lens analogy further than originally introduced by Gerstner and Day. First, we suggest that the lens is, metaphorically speaking, bidirectional in nature; LMX relations shape not only the subordinate's experience of work, but also that of the leader. Building on the spirit that LMX emphasizes that leadership is a relationship between leader and subordinate, it also follows that the impact of these relationships should affect both parties (albeit not to the same extent, because of the power differential that exists). Second, people often work for many managers in an organization (other than their direct manager) and they can be both subordinate and leader to different people. Therefore, there are multiple lenses (like a kaleidoscope), with each lens casting a different image on the experience of work. Finally, we suggest that the leadership lens is not static but dynamic; it changes over time, reflecting the varied experiences people have of their work. We hope this review has provided a glimpse into one important leadership lens and, in so doing, provided insights for future research and theoretical development.

REFERENCES

Adams, J.S. (1965). Inequity in social exchange. In L. Berkowitz (Ed), *Advances in Experimental Social Psychology* (vol. 2) (pp. 267–99). New York, NY: Academic Press.

Allinson, C.W., Armstrong, S.J., & Hayes, J. (2001). The effects of cognitive style on leader-member exchange: A study of manager-subordinate dyads. *Journal of Occupational and Organizational Psychology*, **74**, 201–20.

Andrews, M.C., & Kacmar, M. (2001). Discriminating among organizational politics, justice and support. *Journal of Organizational Behavior*, **22**, 347–66.

Aryee, S., & Chen, Z.X. (2006). Leader-member exchange in a Chinese context: Antecedents, the mediating role of psychological empowerment and outcomes. *Journal of Business Research*, **59**, 793–801.

Ashkanasy, N.M., & O'Connor, C. (1997). Value congruence in leader-member exchange. *Journal of Social Psychology*, **137**, 647–62.

Avolio, B.J., & Chan, A. (2008). The dawning of a new era for genuine leadership development. In G.P. Hodgkinson & J.K. Ford (Eds), *International Review of Industrial and Organizational Psychology* (Vol. 23, pp. 197–238). Chichester, UK: Wiley.

Avolio, B.J., Walumbwa, F.O., & Weber, T.J. (2009). Leadership: Current theories, research, and future directions. *Annual Review of Psychology*, 60, 421–49.

Bass, B.M. (1990). *Bass & Stodgill's Handbook of Leadership. Theory, Research & Managerial Applications*. New York: Free Press.

Bass, B.M., & Bass, R. (2008). *Handbook of Leadership: Theory, Research, and Application*. New York: Free Press.

Bauer, T.N., Erdogan, B., Liden, R.C., & Wayne, S. (2006). A longitudinal study of the moderating role of extraversion: Leader-member exchange, performance, and turnover during new executive development. *Journal of Applied Psychology*, 91, 298–310.

Bauer, T.N., & Green, S.G. (1996). Development of leader-member exchange: A longitudinal test. *Academy of Management Journal*, 39, 1538–67.

Bernas, K.H., & Major, D.A. (2000). Contributions to stress resistance: Testing a model of women's work-family conflict. *Psychology of Women Quarterly*, 24, 170–8.

Bernerth, J.B., Armenakis, A.A., Feild, H.S., Giles, W.F., & Walker, H.J. (2007). Is personality associated with perceptions of LMX? An empirical study. *Leadership and Organization Development Journal*, 28, 613–31.

Berscheid, E. (1994). Interpersonal relationships. *Annual Review of Psychology*, 45, 79–129.

Berscheid, E. (1999). The greening of relationship science. *American Psychologist*, 54, 260–6.

Berscheid, E., & Reis, H.T. (1998). Attraction and close relationships. In D.T. Gilbert, S.T. Fiske & G. Lindzey (Eds), *Handbook of Social Psychology* (Vol. 2, 4th Ed., pp. 193–281). Boston, MA: McGraw-Hill.

Blackman, M.C., & Funder, D.C. (1998). The effect of information on consensus and accuracy in personality judgment. *Journal of Experimental Social Psychology*, 34, 164–81.

Bluedorn, A.C., & Janussi, K.S. (2008). Leaders, followers, and time. *Leadership Quarterly*, 19, 654–68.

Boies, K., & Howell, J.M. (2006). Leader-member exchange in teams: An examination of the interaction between relationship differentiation and the mean LMX in explaining team-level outcomes. *Leadership Quarterly*, 17, 246–57.

Borchgrevink, C.P., & Boster, F.J. (1997). Leader-member exchange development: A hospitality antecedent investigation. *International Journal of Hospitality Management*, 16, 241–59.

Boyd, N.G., & Taylor, R.R. (1998). The developmental approach to the examination of friendship in leader-follower relationships. *Leadership Quarterly*, 9, 1–25.

Brass, D.J. (1984). Being in the right place: A structural analysis of individual influence in an organization. *Administrative Science Quarterly*, 29, 518–39.

Brass, D.J., & Burkhardt, M.E. (1992). Centrality and power in organizations. In N. Nohria & R. Eccles (Eds), *Networks and organizations: Structure, form, and action* (pp. 191–215). Boston: Harvard Business School Press.

Bredow, C.A., Cate, R.M., & Huston, T.L. (2008). Have we met before? A conceptual model of first romantic encounters. In S. Sprecher, A. Wenzel & J. Harvey (Eds), *Handbook of Relationship Initiation* (pp. 3–29). New York: Psychology Press.

Bridge, K., & Baxter, L.A. (1982). Blended relationships: Friends as work associates. *Western Journal of Communication*, 56, 220–5.

Brouer, R.L., Duke, A., Treadway, D.C., & Ferris, G. (2009). The moderating effect of political skill on the demographic dissimilarity – Leader-member exchange quality relationship. *Leadership Quarterly*, 20, 61–9.

Brower, H.H., Schoorman, F.D., & Tan, H.H. (2000). A model of relational leadership: The integration of trust and leader-member exchange. *Leadership Quarterly*, **11**, 227–50.

Burgess, R.L., & Huston, T.L. (1979). *Social Exchanges in Developing Relationships*. New York: Academic Press.

Burt, R.S. (1992). *Structural Holes: The Social Structure of Competition*. Cambridge, MA: Harvard University Press.

Burt, R.S., & Minor, M.J. (1983). (Eds.) *Applied network analysis. A methodological introduction*. London, Thousand Oaks, CA: Sage publications.

Buunk, B.P., Collins, R.L., Taylor, S.E., VanYperen, N.W., & Dakof, G.A. (1990). The affective consequences of social comparison: Either direction has its ups and downs. *Journal of Personality and Social Psychology*, **59**, 1238–49.

Byrne, D. (1971). *The Attraction Paradigm*. New York: Academic Press.

Cashman, J., Dansereau, F., Graen, G., & Haga, W.J. (1976). Organizational structure and leadership: A longitudinal investigation of the managerial role-making process. *Organizational Behavior and Human Performance*, **15**, 278–96.

Chemers, M.M. (2001). Leadership effectiveness: An integrative review. In M.A. Hogg & R.S. Tindale (Eds), *Blackwell Handbook of Social Psychology: Group Processes* (pp. 376–99). Oxford, UK: Blackwell.

Chen, Z., Lam, W., & Zhong, J.A. (2007). Leader-member exchange and member performance: A new look at individual-level negative feedback-seeking behavior and team-level empowerment climate. *Journal of Applied Psychology*, **92**, 202–12.

Clark, M.S., & Mills, J. (1979). Interpersonal attraction in exchange and communal relationships. *Journal of Personality & Social Psychology*, **37**, 12–24.

Clark, M.S., Oullette, R., Powell, M., & Milberg, S. (1987). Relationship type, recipient mood, and helping. *Journal of Personality and Social Psychology*, **53**, 94–103.

Clark, M.S., & Reis, H.T. (1988). Interpersonal processes in close relationships. *Annual Review of Psychology*, **39**, 609–72.

Cogliser, C.C., & Schriesheim, C.A. (2000). Exploring work unit context and leader-member exchange: A multi-level perspective. *Journal of Organizational Behavior*, **21**, 487–511.

Colella, A., & Varma, A. (2001). The impact of subordinate disability on leader-member exchange relationships. *Academy of Management Journal*, **44**, 304–15.

Colquitt, J.A. (2004). Does the justice of the one interact with the justice of the many? Reactions to procedural justice in teams. *Journal of Applied Psychology*, **89**, 633–46.

Colvin, C.R., Vogt, D., & Ickes, W.J. (1997). Why do friends understand each other better than strangers? In W.J. Ickes (Ed.), *Empathic Accuracy* (pp. 169–93). New York: Guilford.

Cronbach, L.J., & Meehl, P.E. (1955). Construct validity in psychological tests. *Psychological Bulletin*, **52**, 281–302.

Dachler, H.P., & Hosking, D.M. (1995). The primacy of relations in socially constructing organizational realities. In D.M. Hosking, H.P. Drachler & K.J. Gergen (Eds), *Management and Organization: Relational Alternatives to Individualism* (pp. 1–29). Aldershot, UK: Avebury.

Dansereau, F., Alutto, J.A., & Yammarino, F.J. (1984). *Theory Testing in Organizational Behavior: The Variant Approach*. Englewood Cliffs, NJ: Prentice Hall.

Dansereau, F., Graen, G.B., & Haga, W. (1975). A vertical dyad linkage approach to leadership in formal organizations. *Organizational Behavior and Human Performance*, **13**, 46–78.

Dansereau, F., & Yammarino, F.J. (Eds) (1998a). Leadership: The multiple-level approaches (Part A: Classic and new wave). *Monographs in Organizational Behavior and Industrial Relations*, Vol. **24**. Stamford, CT: JAI Press.

Dansereau, F., & Yammarino, F.J. (Eds) (1998b). Leadership: The multiple-level approaches (Part B: Contemporary and alternative). *Monographs in Organizational Behavior and Industrial Relations*, Vol. 24. Stamford, CT: JAI Press.

Dasborough, M.T., & Ashkanasy, N.M. (2002). Emotion and attribution of intentionality in leader-member relationships. *Leadership Quarterly*, 13, 615–34.

Davis, W.D., & Gardner, W.L. (2004). Perceptions of politics and organizational cynicism: An attributional and leader-member exchange perspective. *The Leadership Quarterly*, 15, 439–65.

Day, D.V., & Crain, E.C. (1992). The role of affect and ability in initial exchange quality perceptions. *Group and Organization Management*, 17, 380–97.

Denrell, J. (2005). Why most people disapprove of me: Experience sampling in impression formation. *Psychological Review*, 112, 951–78.

Deutsch, M. (1975). Equality, equality, and need: What determines which value will be used as the basis of distributive justice? *Journal of Social Issues*, 31, 37–149.

Dienesch, R.M., & Liden, R.C. (1986). Leader-member exchange model of leadership: A critique and further development. *Academy of Management Review*, 11, 618–34.

Dockery, T.M., & Steiner, D.D. (1990). The role of the initial interaction in leader member exchange. *Group and Organization Studies*, 15, 395–413.

Dose, J.J. (1999). The relationship between work values similarity and team-member and leader-member exchange relationships. *Group Dynamics: Theory, Research, and Practice*, 3, 20–32.

Duarte, N.T., Goodson, J.R., & Klich, N.R. (1993). How do I like thee? Let me appraise the ways. *Journal of Organizational Behavior*, 14, 239–49.

Duchon, D., Green, S.G., & Taber, T.D. (1986). Vertical dyad linkage: A longitudinal assessment of antecedents, measures and consequences. *Journal of Applied Psychology*, 71, 56–60.

Duck, S. (2007). Commentary: Finding connections at the individual/dyadic level. In J.E. Dutton & B.R. Ragins (Eds), *Exploring Positive Relationships at Work* (179–86). Mahwah, NJ: Erlbaum.

Dunegan, K.J., Tierney, P., & Duchon, D. (1992). Perceptions of an innovative climate: Examining the role of divisional affiliation, work group interaction, and leader/subordinate exchange. *IEEE Transactions on Engineering Management*, 39, 227–36.

Dunegan, K.J., Uhl-Bien, M., & Duchon, D. (2002). LMX and subordinate performance: The moderating effects of task characteristics. *Journal of Business and Psychology*, 17, 275–85.

Engle, E.M., & Lord, R.G. (1997). Implicit theories, self-schemas, and leader-member exchange. *Academy of Management Journal*, 40, 988–1010.

Epitropaki, O., & Martin, R. (1999). The impact of relational demography on the quality of leader-member exchanges (LMX) and employees' work attitudes and well being. *Journal of Occupational and Organizational Psychology*, 72, 237–40.

Epitropaki, O., & Martin, R. (2005). From ideal to real: A longitudinal study of the role of implicit leadership theories on leader-member exchanges and employee outcomes. *Journal of Applied Psychology*, 90, 659–76.

Erdogan, B. (2002). Antecedents and consequences of justice perceptions in performance appraisals. *Human Resource Management Review*, 12, 555–78.

Erdogan, B., & Enders, J. (2007). Support from the top: Supervisors' perceived organizational support as a moderator of leader-member exchange to satisfaction and performance ratings. *Journal of Applied Psychology*, 92, 321–30.

Erdogan, B., & Liden, R.C. (2002). Social exchanges in the workplace: A review of recent developments and future research directions in Leader-Member Exchange theory. In L.L. Neider & C.A. Schriescheim (Eds), *Leadership* (pp. 65–114). Greenwich, CT: Information Age Publishing.

Fairhurst, G.T. (1993). The leader-member exchange patterns of women leaders in industry: A discourse analysis. *Communication Monograph*, **60**, 321–51.

Fehr, B. (2008). Friendship formation. In S. Sprecher, A. Wenzel & J. Harvey (Eds), *Handbook of Relationship Initiation* (pp. 29–55). New York: Psychology Press.

Fernandez, C.F., & Vecchio, R.P. (1997). Situational leadership theory revisited: A test of an across-jobs perspective. *Leadership Quarterly*, **8**, 67–84.

Ferrin, D.L., Dirks, K.T., & Shah, P.P. (2006). Third party relationships and interpersonal trust. *Journal of Applied Psychology*, **91**, 870–83.

Festinger, L. (1954). A theory of social comparison processes. *Human Relations*, 7, 117–40.

Fincham, F.D. (2000). The kiss of the porcupines: From attributing responsibility to forgiving. *Personal Relationships*, 7, 1–23.

Fiske, S.T., & Taylor, S.E. (1991). *Social Cognition* (2nd Ed.). New York: McGraw-Hill.

Fletcher, G.J.O., Simpson, J.A., & Thomas, G. (2000). Ideals, perceptions, and evaluations in early relationship development. *Journal of Personality and Social Psychology*, **79**, 933–40.

Fletcher, G.J.O., Simpson, J.A., Thomas, G., & Giles, L. (1999). Ideals in intimate relationships. *Journal of Personality and Social Psychology*, **79**, 72–89.

Fletcher, G.J.O., & Thomas, G. (1996). Close relationship lay theories: Their structure and function. In G.J.O. Fletcher & J. Fitness (Eds), *Knowledge Structures in Close Relationships: A Social Psychological Approach* (pp. 3–24). Mahwah, NJ: Erlbaum.

Fletcher, G.J.O., & Thomas, G. (2000). Behavior and on-line cognition in marital interaction. *Personal Relationships*, 7, 111–30.

Fletcher, G.J.O., Thomas, G., & Durant, R. (1999). Cognitive and behavioral accommodation in close relationships. *Journal of Social and Personal Relationships*, **16**, 705–30.

Ford, L.R., & Seers, A. (2006). Relational leadership and team climate: Pitting differentiation versus agreement. *Leadership Quarterly*, **17**, 258–70.

Friedkin, N.E. (1993). Structural bases of interpersonal influences in groups: A longitudinal case study. *American Sociological Review*, **58**, 861–72.

Gerstner, C.R., & Day, D.V. (1997). Meta-analytic review of Leader-Member Exchange Theory: Correlates and construct issues. *Journal of Applied Psychology*, **82**, 827–44.

Gerstner, C.R., & Tesluk, P.E. (2005). Peer leadership in self-managing teams: Examining team leadership through a social network analytic approach. In G.B. Graen (Ed.), *Global Organizing Designs* (pp. 131–51). Greenwich, CT: Information Age Publishing.

Gibbons, D.E., & Grover, S.L. (2006). Network factors in Leader-Member relationships. In G.B. Graen (Ed.), *Sharing Network Leadership* (pp. 63–93). Greenwich, CT: Information Age Publishing.

Golden, T.D., & Veiga, J.F. (2008). The impact of superior-subordinate relationships on the commitment, job satisfaction, and performance of virtual workers. *Leadership Quarterly*, **19**, 77–88.

Gómez, C.A., & Rosen, B. (2001). The leader-member exchange as a link between managerial trust and employee empowerment. *Group & Organizational Management*, **26**, 53–69.

Goodwin, V.L., Bowler, W.M., & Whittington, J.L. (2009). A social network perspective on LMX relationships: Accounting for the instrumental value of leader and follower networks. *Journal of Management*, **35**, 954–80.

Gouldner, H., & Strong, M.S. (1987). *Speaking of Friendship: Middle-Class Women and Their Friends*. New York: Greenwood Press.

Graen, G.B. (1976). Role-making processes within complex organizations. In M.D. Dunnette (Ed.), *Handbook of Industrial and Organizational Psychology* (pp. 1201–45). Chicago: Rand McNally.

Graen, G.B. (1990). Designing productive leadership systems to improve both work motivation and organizational effectiveness. In U. Kleinbeck, H.H. Quast, H. Thierry & H. Hacker (Eds), *Work Motivation* (pp. 133–56). Hillsdale, NJ: Erlbaum.

Graen, G.B. (2005). Three dyadic leadership theories: Comparative multiple hypotheses testing. In G.B. Graen (Ed.), *Global Organizing Designs* (pp. 205–15). Greenwich, CT: Information Age Publishing.

Graen, G.B., & Cashman, J.F. (1975). A role-making model of leadership in formal organisations: A developmental approach. In J.G. Hunt & L.L. Larson (Eds), *Leadership Frontiers* (pp. 143–65). Kent, OH: Kent State University Press.

Graen, G.B., Cashman, J.F., Ginsburgh, S., & Schiemann, W. (1977). Effects of linking-pin quality on the quality of working life of lower participants. *Administrative Science Quarterly*, 22, 491–504.

Graen, G.B., & Lau, D. (2005). Proper levels of analysis, hierarchical linear models, and leadership theories. In G.B. Graen (Ed.), *Global Organizing Designs* (pp. 235–69), Greenwich, CT: Information Age Publishing.

Graen, G.B., Liden, R.C., & Hoel, W. (1982). Role of leadership in the employee withdrawal process. *Journal of Applied Psychology*, 67, 868–72.

Graen, G.B., Novak, M.A., & Sommerkamp, P. (1982). The effects of leader-member exchange and job design on productivity and satisfaction: Testing a dual attachment model. *Organizational Behavior and Human Performance*, 30, 109–31.

Graen, G.B., Orris, D., & Johnson, T. (1973). Role assimilation processes in a complex organization. *Journal of Vocational Behavior*, 3, 395–420.

Graen, G.B., & Scandura, T. (1987). Toward a psychology of dyadic organizing. In B. Staw & L.L. Cummings (Eds), *Research in Organizational Behavior* (pp. 175–208). Greenwich, CT: JAI Press.

Graen, G.B., Scandura, T.A., & Graen, M. R. (1986). A field experimental test of the moderating effects of GNS on productivity. *Journal of Applied Psychology*, 71, 484–91.

Graen, G.B., & Uhl-Bien, M. (1991). Partnership-making applies equally well to team mate-sponsor team mate-competence network, and team mate-team mate relationships. *Journal of Management Systems*, 3, 33–48.

Graen, G.B., & Uhl-Bien, M. (1995). Relationship-based approach to leadership: Development of leader-member exchange (LMX) theory of leadership over 25 years: Applying a multi-level multi-domain perspective. *Leadership Quarterly*, 6, 219–47.

Granovetter, M. (1985). Economic action and social structure: The problem of embeddedness. *American Journal of Sociology*, 91, 481–510.

Green, S.G., Anderson, S.E., & Shivers, S.L. (1996). Demographic and organizational influences on leader-member exchange and related work attitudes. *Organizational Behavior and Human Decision Processes*, 66, 203–14.

Green, S.G., & Mitchell, T.R. (1979). Attributional processes of leaders in leader-member interactions. *Organizational Behavior and Human Performance*, 23, 429–58.

Greguras, G.J., & Ford, J.M. (2006). An examination of the multidimensionality of supervisor and subordinate perceptions of leader-member exchange. *Journal of Occupational and Organizational Psychology*, 79, 433–65.

Harris, K.J., Kacmar, K.M., & Witt, L.A. (2005). An examination of the curvilinear relationship between leader-member exchange and intent to turnover. *Journal of Organizational Behavior*, 26, 363–78.

Harvey, J.H., & Omarzu, J. (1997). Minding the close relationship. *Personality and Social Psychology Review*, 1, 224–40.

Harvey, J.H., & Weber, A.L. (2002). *Odyssey of the Heart: Close Relationships in the 21ˢᵗ Century* (2nd Ed.). Mahwah, NJ: Erlbaum.

Heider, F. (1958). *The Psychology of Interpersonal Relations*. New York: Wiley.

Henderson, D.J., Liden, R.C., Glibkowski, B.C., & Chaudhry, A. (2009). LMX differentiation: A multilevel review and examination of its antecedents and outcomes. *Leadership Quarterly*, 20, 517–34.

Henderson, D.J., Wayne, S.J., Shore, L.M., Bommer, W.H., & Tetrick, L.E. (2008). Leader-Member Exchange, differentiation, and psychological contract fulfillment: A multilevel examination. *Journal of Applied Psychology*, 93, 1208–19.

Hinde, R.A. (1996). Describing relationships. In A.E. Aughagen & M. Von Salisch (Eds), *The Diversity of Human Relationships* (pp. 7–35). Cambridge, UK: Cambridge University Press.

Hochwarter, W.A., & Castro, S.L. (2005). Social influence from the bottom up: A process model of LMX development. In G.B. Graen (Ed.), *Global Organizing Designs* (pp. 43–71). Greenwich, CT: Information Age Publishing.

Hofmann, D.A., Morgeson, F.P., & Gerras, S.J. (2003). Climate as a moderator of the relationship between leader-member exchange and content specific citizenship: Safety climate as an exemplar. *Journal of Applied Psychology*, 88, 170–8.

Hogg, M.A. (2001). A social identity theory of leadership. *Personality and Social Psychology Review*, 5, 184–200.

Hogg, M.A. (in press). Influence and leadership. In S.T. Fiske, D.T. Gilbert & G. Lindzey (Eds), *Handbook of Social Psychology* (5th Ed.). Hoboken, NJ: Wiley.

Hogg, M.A., Martin, R., Epitropaki, O., Mankad, A., Svensson, A., & Weeden, K. (2005). Effective leadership in salient groups: Revisiting leader-member exchange theory from the perspective of the social identity theory of leadership. *Personality and Social Psychology Bulletin*, 31, 991–1004.

Hogg, M.A., Martin, R., & Weeden, K. (2004). Leader-member relations and social identity. In D. van Knippenberg & M.A. Hogg (Eds), *Leadership and Power: Identity Processes in Groups and Organizations* (pp. 18–33). London: SAGE.

Homans, G.C. (1961). *Social Behavior: Its Elementary Forms*. New York: Harcourt, Brace & World.

Hooper, D., & Martin, R. (2006). Beyond personal LMX quality: The effects of perceived LMX variability on employee reactions. In A.I. Glendon, B. Myors & B.M. Thompson (Eds), *Advances in Organizational Psychology: An Asia-Pacific Perspective*. Brisbane: Australian Academic Press.

Hooper, D., & Martin, R. (2008). Beyond personal Leader-Member Exchange (LMX) quality: The effects of perceived LMX variability on employee reactions. *Leadership Quarterly*, 19, 20–30.

Hosking, D.M., Dachler, H.P., & Gergen, K.J. (1995). *Management and Organization: Relational Alternatives to Individualism*. Aldershot: Avebury.

House, R.J., & Javidan, M. (2004). Overview of GLOBE. In R.J. House, P.J. Hanges, M. Javidan, P. Dorfman & V. Gupta (Eds), & GLOBE associates, *Leadership, Culture, and Organizations: The GLOBE Study of 62 Societies* (pp. 9–28). Thousand Oaks, CA: Corsage.

Howell, J.M., & Hall-Merenda, K.E. (1999). The ties that bind: The impact of Leader-Member Exchange, transformational and transactional leadership, and distance on predicting follower performance. *Journal of Applied Psychology*, 84, 680–94.

Hsiung, H-H., & Tsai, W-C. (2009). Job definition discrepancy between supervisors and subordinates: The antecedent role of LMX and outcomes. *Journal of Occupational and Organizational Psychology*, 82, 89–112.

Huang, X., Wright, R.P., Chiu, W.C.K., & Wang, C. (2008). Relational schemas as sources of evaluation and misevaluation of leader-member exchanges: Some initial evidence. *Leadership Quarterly*, **19**, 266–82.

Ibarra, H. (1993). Network centrality, power and innovation involvement: Determinants of technical and administrative roles. *Academy of Management Journal*, **36**, 471–501.

Ickes, W.J. (2003). *Everyday Mind Reading: Understanding what Other People Think and Feel*. Amherst, NY: Prometheus Books.

Ilies, R., Nahrgang, J.D., & Morgeson, F.P. (2007). Leader-Member Exchange and citizenship behaviors: A meta-analysis. *Journal of Applied Psychology*, **92**, 269–77.

Janssen, O., & Van Yperen, N.W. (2004). Employees' goal orientations, the quality of leader-member exchange, and the outcomes of job performance and job satisfaction. *Academy of Management Journal*, **47**, 368–84.

Johnson, T., & Graen, G.B. (1973). Organizational assimilation and role rejection. *Organizational Behavior and Human Performance*, **10**, 72–8.

Kacmar, K.M., Carlson, D.S., & Brymer, R.A. (1999). Antecedents and consequences of organizational commitment: A comparison of two scales. *Educational and Psychological Measurement*, **59**, 976–94.

Kacmar, K.M., Witt, L.A., Zivnuska, S., & Gully, S.M. (2003). The interactive effect of leader-member exchange and communication frequency on performance ratings. *Journal of Applied Psychology*, **88**, 764–72.

Kahn, R.L., Wolfe, D.M., Quinn, R.P., Snoek, J.D., & Robert, A. (1964). *Organizational Stress: Studies in Role Conflict and Ambiguity*. New York: Wiley.

Kamdar, D., & Van Dyne, L. (2007). The joint effects of personality and workplace social exchange relationships in predicting task performance and citizenship performance. *Journal of Applied Psychology*, **92**, 1286–98.

Katz, D., & Kahn, R.L. (1978). *The Social Psychology of Organizations* (2nd Ed.). New York: Wiley.

Keller, T., & Dansereau, F. (1995). Leadership and empowerment: A social exchange perspective. Human Relations, **48**, 127–46.

Keller, T., & Dansereau, F. (2001). The effect of adding items to scales: An illustrative case of LMX. *Organizational Research Methods*, **4**, 131–43.

Kelly, H.H., Berscheid, E. Christensen, A. *et al.* (1983). *Close Relationships*. San Francisco: Freeman.

Kenny, D.A. (1994). *Interpersonal Perception*. New York: Guilford.

Kenny, D.A., & Acitelli, L.K. (2001). Accuracy and bias in perceptions of the partner in close relationships. *Journal of Personality and Social Psychology*, **80**, 439–48.

Kilduff, M., & Krackhardt, D. (1994). Bringing the individual back in: A structural analysis of the internal market for reputation in organizations. *Academy of Management Journal*, **37**, 87–108.

Kinicki, A.J., & Vecchio, R.P. (1994). Influences on the quality of supervisor-subordinate relations: The role of time-pressure, organizational commitment, and locus of control. *Journal of Organizational Behavior*, **15**, 75–82.

Klein, K.J., & Kim, J.S. (1998). A field study of the influence of situational constraints, leader-member exchange, and goal commitment on performance. *Academy of Management Journal*, **41**, 88–9.

Knee, C.R. (1998). Implicit theories of relationships: Assessment and prediction of romantic relationship initiation, coping and longevity. *Journal of Personality and Social Psychology*, **74**, 360–70.

Knee, C.R., & Bush, A.L. (2008). Relationship beliefs and their role in romantic relationship initiation. In S. Sprecher, A. Wenzel & J. Harvey (Eds), *Handbook of Relationship Initiation* (pp. 471–86). New York: Psychology Press.

Krackhardt, D., & Porter, L.W. (1986). The snowball effect: Turnover embedded in communication networks. *Journal of Applied Psychology*, **71**, 50–5.

Krammer, M.W. (1995). A longitudinal study of superior-subordinate communication during job transfers. *Human Communication Research*, **22**, 39–64.

Lam, W. (2007). Attribution and LMX theory. In G.B. Graen & J.A. Graen (Eds), *New Multinational Network Sharing* (pp. 79–91). Greenwich, CT: Information Age Publishing.

Lapierre, L.M., & Hackett, R.D. (2007). Trait conscientiousness, leader-member exchange, job satisfaction and organizational citizenship behaviour: A test of an integrative model. *Journal of Occupational and Organizational Psychology*, **80**, 539–54.

Leventhal, G.S. (1980). What should be done with equity theory? New approaches to the study of fairness in social relationships. In K.J. Gergen, M.S. Greenberg & R.H. Willis (Eds), *Social Exchange: Advances in Theory and Research* (pp. 27–55). New York: Plenum.

Liden, R.C., Erdogan, B., Wayne, S.J., & Sparrowe, R.T. (2006). Leader-member exchange, differentiation and task interdependence: Implications for individual and group performance. *Journal of Organizational Behavior*, **27**, 723–46.

Liden, R.C., & Graen, G. (1980). Generalizability of the vertical dyad linkage model of leadership. *Academy of Management Journal*, **23**, 451–65.

Liden, R.C., & Maslyn, J.M. (1998). Multidimensionality of Leader-member exchange: An empirical assessment through scale development. *Journal of Management*, **24**, 43–72.

Liden, R.C., Sparrowe, R.T., & Wayne, S.J. (1997). Leader-member exchange theory: The past and potential for the future. *Research in Personnel and Human Resources Management*, **15**, 47–119.

Liden, R.C., Wayne, S.J., & Sparrowe, R.T. (2000). An examination of the mediating role of psychological empowerment on the relations between the job, interpersonal relations, and work outcomes. *Journal of Applied Psychology*, **85**, 407–16.

Liden, R.C., Wayne, S.J., & Stilwell, D. (1993). A longitudinal study on the early development of leader-member exchanges. *Journal of Applied Psychology*, **78**, 662–74.

Maio, G.M., & Thomas, G. (2007). The epistemic-teleologic model of deliberate self persuasion. *Personality and Social Psychology Review*, **11**, 1–22.

Maio, G.M., Thomas, G., Fincham, F.D., & Carnelley, K.B. (2008). Unravelling the role of forgiveness in family relationships. *Journal of Personality and Social Psychology*, **94**, 307–19.

Major, D.A., Kozlowski, S.W.J., Chao, G.T., & Gardner, P.D. (1995). A longitudinal investigation of newcomer expectations, early socialization outcomes, and the moderating effects of role development factors. *Journal of Applied Psychology*, **80**, 418–31.

Mardanov, I.T., Heischmidt, K., & Henson, A. (2008). Leader-member exchange and job satisfaction bond and predicted employee turnover. *Journal of Leadership & Organizational Studies*, **15**, 159–75.

Martin, R., Thomas, G., Charles, K., Epitropaki, O., & McNamara, R. (2005). The role of leader-member exchanges in mediating the relationship between locus of control and work reactions. *Journal of Occupational and Organizational Psychology*, **78**, 141–7.

Martinko, M.J., Moss, S.E., Douglas, S.C., & Borkowski, N. (2007). Anticipating the inevitable: When leader and member attributions clash. *Organizational Behavior and Human Decision Processes*, **104**, 158–74.

Maslyn, J.M., & Uhl-Bien, M. (2001). Leader-member exchange and its dimensions: Effects of self-effort and other's effort on relationship quality. *Journal of Applied Psychology*, **86**, 697–708.

Masterson, S.S., Lewis, K., Goldman, B.M., & Taylor, M.S. (2000). Integrating justice and social exchange: The differing effects of fair procedures and treatment on work relationships. *Academy of Management Journal*, 43, 738–48.

Maurer, T., Pierce, H., & Shore, L. (2002). Perceived beneficiary of employee development activity: A three-dimensional social exchange model. *Academy of Management Review*, 27, 432–44.

Mayer, D.M., & Piccolo, R.F. (2006). Expanding the scope: Social network and multilevel perspectives on Leader-Member Exchange. In G.B. Graen (Ed.), *Sharing Network Leadership* (pp. 37–62). Greenwich, CT: Information Age Publishing.

McClane, W.E. (1991). The interaction of leader and member characteristics in the leader-member exchange (LMX) model of leadership. *Small Group Research*, 22, 283–300.

Mehra, A., Dixon, A.L., Brass, D.J., & Robertson, B. (2006). The social network ties of group leaders: Implications for group performance and leader reputation. *Organization Science*, 17, 64–79.

Mills, J., & Clark, M.S. (1994). Communal and exchange relationships: Controversies and research. In R. Erber & R. Gilmour (Eds), *Theoretical Frameworks for Personal relationships* (pp. 29–42). Hillsdale, NJ: Erlbaum.

Mills, J., Clark, M.S., Ford, T.E., & Johnson, M. (2004). Measurement of communal strength. *Personal Relationships*, 11, 213–30.

Mitchell, T.R., Green, S.G., & Wood, R.E. (1981). An attributional model of leadership and the poor performing subordinate: Development and validation. *Research in Organizational Behavior*, 3, 197–234.

Murphy, S.E., & Ensher, E.A. (1999). The effects of leader and subordinate characteristics in the development of leader-member exchange quality. *Journal of Applied Social Psychology*, 29, 1371–94.

Murrell, K.L. (1997). Emergent theories of leadership for the next century: Towards relational concepts. *Organizational Development Journal*, 15, 35–42.

Nahrgang, J.D., Morgeson, F.P., & Ilies, R. (2009). The development of leader – member exchanges: Exploring how personality and performance influence leader and member relationships over time. *Organizational Behavior and Human Decision Processes*, 108, 256–66.

Newcomb, T.M. (1961). *The Acquaintance Process*. New York: Holt, Reinhart & Winston.

Ozer, M. (2008). Personal and task-related moderators of leader-member exchange among software developers. *Journal of Applied Psychology*, 93, 1174–82.

Parsons, C.K., Liden, R.C., & Bauer, T.N. (2001). Person perception in employment interviews. In M. London (Ed.), *How People Evaluate Others in Organizations* (pp. 67–90). Mahwah, NJ: Lawrence Erlbaum Associates, Inc.

Pelled, L.H., & Xin, K.R. (2000). Relational demography and relationship quality in two cultures. *Organizational Studies*, 21, 1077–94.

Phillips, A.S., & Bedeian, A.G. (1994). Leader-follower exchange quality: The role of personal and interpersonal attributes. *Academy of Management Journal*, 37, 990–1001.

Pillai, R., Schriesheim, C., & Williams, E.S. (1999). Fairness perceptions and trust as mediators for transformational and transactional leadership: A two-sample study. *Journal of Management*, 25, 897–933.

Popper, M., Mayseless, O., & Castelnovo, O. (2000). Transformational leadership and attachment. *Leadership Quarterly*, 11, 267–89.

Reis, H.T. (2007). Steps toward the ripening of relationship science. *Personal Relationships*, 14, 1–23.

Rusbult, C.E., & Arriaga, X.B. (1997). Interdependence theory. In S. Duck (Ed.), *Handbook of Personal Relationships: Theory, Research, and Interventions* (2nd Ed., pp. 221–50). Chichester, UK: Wiley.

Scandura, T.A. (1999). Rethinking leader-member exchange: An organizational justice perspective. *Leadership Quarterly*, 10, 25–40.

Scandura, T.A., & Graen, G.B. (1984). Moderating effects of initial leader-member exchange status on the effects of a leadership intervention. *Journal of Applied Psychology*, 69, 428–36.

Scandura, T.A., Graen, G.B., & Novak, M.A. (1986). When managers decide not to decide autocratically: An investigation of leader-member exchange and decision influence. *Journal of Applied Psychology*, 71, 579–84.

Scandura, T.A., & Lankau, M.J. (1996). Developing diverse leaders: A leader-member exchange approach. *Leadership Quarterly*, 7, 243–263.

Scandura, T.A., & Pellegrini, E.K. (2008). Trust and leader-member exchange: Acloser look at relational vulnerability. *Journal of Leadership & Organizational Studies*, 15, 101–10.

Scherbaum, C.A., Finlinson, S., Barden, K., & Tamanini, K. (2006). Applications of item response theory to measurement issues in leadership research. *Leadership Quarterly*, 17, 366–86.

Scherbaum, C.A., Naidoo, L.J., & Ferreter, J.M. (2007). Examining component measures of team leader-member exchange: Using item response theory. In G.B. Graen & J.A. Graen (Eds), *New Multinational Network Sharing* (pp. 129–56). Greenwich, CT: Information Age Publishing.

Schriesheim, C.A., Castro, S.L., & Cogliser, C.C. (1999). Leader-member exchange (LMX) research: A comprehensive review of theory, measurement, and data-analytic practices. *Leadership Quarterly*, 10, 63–113.

Schriesheim, C.A., Castro, S.L., & Yammarino, F.J. (2000). Investigating contingencies: An examination of the impact of span of supervision and upward controllingness on leader-member exchange using traditional and multivariate within- and between-entities analysis. *Journal of Applied Psychology*, 85, 659–77.

Schriesheim, C.A., Castro, S.L., Zhou, X.T., & Yammarino, F.J. (2001). The folly of theorizing "A" but testing "B". A selective level-of-analysis review of the field and a detailed leader-member exchange illustration. *Leadership Quarterly*, 12, 515–51.

Schriesheim, C.A., Neider, L.L., & Scandura, T.A. (1998). Delegation and leader-member exchange: Main effects, moderators, and measurement issues. *Academy of Management Journal*, 41, 298–318.

Schriesheim, C.A., Neider, L.L., Scandura, T.A., & Tepper, B.J. (1992). Development and preliminary validation of a new scale (LMX-6) to measure leader-member exchange in organizations. *Educational and Psychological Measurement*, 52, 135–47.

Schyns, B., Paul, T., Mohr, G., & Blank, H. (2005). Comparing antecedents and consequences of leader-member exchange in a German working context to findings in the US. *European Journal of Work and Organizational Psychology*, 14, 1–22.

Scott, S.G., & Bruce, R.A. (1998). Following the leader in R&D: The joint effect of subordinate problem-solving style and leader-member relations on innovative behaviors. *IEEE Transactions on Engineering Management*, 45, 3–10.

Seers, A. (1989). Team-member exchange quality: A new construct for role-making research. *Organizational Behavior and Human Decision Processes*, 43, 118–35.

Sherony, K.M., & Green, S.G. (2002). Coworker exchange: Relationships between coworkers, leader-member exchange, and work attitudes. *Journal of Applied Psychology*, 87, 542–8.

Sias, P.M., & Jablin, F.M. (1995). Differential superior-subordinate relations, perceptions of fairness, and coworker communication. *Human Communication Research*, 22, 5–37.

Simpson, J.A. (2008). Foundations of interpersonal trust. In A.W. Kruglanski & E.T. Higgins (Eds), *Social Psychology: A Handbook of Basic Principles* (2nd Ed.) (587–607). New York: Guilford.

Simpson, J.A., Fletcher, G.J.O., & Campbell, L. (2001). The structure and function of ideal standards in close relationships. In G.J.O. Fletcher & M.S. Clark (Eds), *Blackwell Handbook of Social Psychology* (pp. 86–106). Oxford: Blackwell.

Simpson, J.A., Ickes, W., & Blackstone, T. (1995). When the head protects the heart: Empathic accuracy in dating relationships. *Journal of Personality and Social Psychology*, 69, 629–41.

Simpson, J.A., Ickes, W.J., & Orina, M. (2001). Empathic accuracy and preemptive relationship maintenance. In J.H. Harvey & A. Wenzel (Eds), *Close Romantic Relationships: Maintenance and Enhancement* (27–46). Mahwah, NJ: Erlbaum.

Sin, H-P., Nahrgang, J.D., & Morgeson, F.O. (2009). Understanding why they don't see eye-to-eye: An examination of leader-member exchange (LMX) agreement. *Journal of Applied Psychology*, 94, 1048–57.

Somech, A. (2003). Relationships of participative leadership with relational demography variables: A multi-level perspective. *Journal of Organizational Behavior*, 24, 1003–18.

Sparr, J.L., & Sonnentag, S. (2008). Fairness perceptions of supervisor feedback, LMX, and employee well-being at work. *European Journal of Work and Organizational Psychology*, 17, 198–225.

Sparrowe, R.T., & Liden, R.C. (1997). Process and structure in leader-member exchange. *Academy of Management Review*, 22, 522–52.

Sparrowe, R.T., & Liden, R.C. (2005). Two routes to influence: Integrating leader-member exchange and social network perspectives. *Administrative Science Quarterly*, 50, 505–35.

Sparrowe, R.T., & Popielarz, P.A. (1995). Weak ties and structural holes: The effects of network structure on careers. Paper presented at the annual meetings of the Academy of Management.

Sparrowe, R.T., Soetjipto, B.W., & Kraimer, M.L. (2006). Do leaders' influence tactics relate to members' helping behavior? It depends on the quality of the relationship. *Academy of Management Journal*, 49, 1194–208.

Steiner, D.D. (1997). Attributions on leader-member exchanges: Implications for practice. *European Journal of Work and Organizational Psychology*, 6, 59–71.

Thibaut, J.W., & Kelley, H.H. (1959). *The Social Psychology of Groups*. New York: Wiley.

Thomas, G., & Fletcher, G.J.O. (1997). Empathic accuracy in close relationships. In W.J. Ickes (Ed.) *Empathic Accuracy* (pp. 194–217). New York: Guilford.

Thomas, G., & Fletcher, G.J.O. (2003). Mind-reading accuracy in intimate relationships: Assessing the roles of the relationship, the target, and the judge. *Journal of Personality and Social Psychology*, 85, 1079–94.

Thomas, G., Fletcher, G.J.O., & Lange, C. (1997). On-line empathic accuracy in marital interaction. *Journal of Personality and Social Psychology*, 72, 839–50.

Thomas, G., & Maio, G.M. (2008). Man I feel like a woman: When & how gender-role motivation helps mind-reading. *Journal of Personality and Social Psychology*, 95, 1165–79.

Tierney, P., Farmer, S.M., & Graen, G.B. (1999). An examination of leadership and employee creativity: The relevance of traits and relationships. *Personnel Psychology*, 52, 591–620.

Tordera, N., González-Romá, V., & Peiró, J.M. (2008). The moderator effect of psychological climate on the relationship between leader-member exchange (LMX) quality and role overload. *European Journal of Work and Organizational Psychology*, **17**, 55–72.

Tse, H.H.M., Dasborough, M.T., & Ashkanasy, N.M. (2008). A multi-level analysis of team climate and interpersonal exchange relationships at work. *Leadership Quarterly*, **19**, 195–211.

Turban, D.B., & Jones, A.P. (1988). Supervisor-subordinate similarity: Types, effects and mechanisms. *Journal of Applied Psychology*, **73**, 228–34.

Tyler, T.R. (1989). The psychology of procedural justice: A test of the group-value model. *Journal of Personality and Social Psychology*, **57**, 830–8.

Tyler, T.R., Degoey, P., & Smith, H. (2001). Understanding why the justice of group procedures matters: A test of the psychological dynamics of the group-value model. In M.A. Hogg & D. Abrams (Eds), *Intergroup Relations: Essential Readings* (pp. 205–27). Philadelphia: Psychology Press.

Uhl-Bien, M. (2006). Relational leadership theory: Exploring the social processes of leadership and organizing. *Leadership Quarterly*, **17**, 654–76.

Uhl-Bien, M., Graen, G., & Scandura, T.A. (2000). Implications of leader-member exchange (LMX) for strategic human resource management systems: Relationships as social capital for competitive advantage. In G.R. Ferris (Ed.), *Research in Personnel and Human Resource Management* (Vol. **18**, pp. 137–85). New York: Elsevier.

van Breukelen, W., Konst, D., & Van Der Vlist, R. (2002). Effects of LMX and differential treatment on work unit commitment. *Psychological Reports*, **91**, 220–30.

van Breukelen, W., Schyns, B., & LeBlanc, P. (2006). Leader-member exchange theory and research: Accomplishments and future challenges. *Leadership*, **2**, 295–316.

van Dyne, L., Kamdar, D., & Joireman, J. (2008). In-role perceptions buffer the negative impact of low LMX on helping and enhance the positive impact of high LMX on voice. *Journal of Applied Psychology*, **93**, 1195–207.

van Knippenberg, D., van Knippenberg, B., De Cremer, D., & Hogg, M.A. (2004). Leadership, self, and identity: A review and research agenda. *Leadership Quarterly*, **15**, 825–56.

Van Lear, C.A., Koerner, A., & Allen, D.M. (2006). *Relationship typologies*. In A.L. Vangelista & D. Perlman (Eds), *The Cambridge Handbook of Personal Relationships* (pp. 91–111). New York: Cambridge University Press.

Varma, A., & Stroth, L.K. (2001). The impact of same-sex LMX dyads on performance evaluations. *Human Resource Management*, **40**, 309–20.

Vecchio, R.P., & Gobdel, B.C. (1984). The vertical dyad linkage model of leadership: Problems and prospects. *Organizational Behavior and Human Performance*, **34**, 5–20.

Wang, H., Law, K.S., Hackett, R.D., Wang, D., & Chen, Z.X. (2005). Leader-member exchange as a mediator of the relationship between transformational leadership and followers' performance and organizational citizenship behavior. *Academy of Management Journal*, **48**, 420–32.

Wayne, S.J., & Ferris, G.R. (1990). Influence tactics, affect, and exchange quality in supervisor-subordinate interactions: A laboratory experiment and field study. *Journal of Applied Psychology*, **75**, 487–99.

Wayne, S.J., Shore, L.M., Bommer, W.H., & Tetrick, L.E. (2002). The role of fair treatment and rewards in perceptions of organizational support and leader-member exchange. *Journal of Applied Psychology*, **87**, 590–8.

Wayne, S.J., Shore, L.M., & Liden, R.C. (1997). Perceived organizational support and leader-member exchange: A social exchange perspective. *Academy of Management Journal*, **40**, 82–111.

Wilhelm, C.C., Herd, A.M., & Steiner, D.D. (1993). Attributional conflict between managers and subordinates: An investigation of leader-member effects. *Journal of Organizational Behavior*, **14**, 531–44.

Yammarino, F.J., Dionne, S.D., Chun, J.U., & Dansereau, F. (2005). Leadership and levels of analysis: A state-of-the-science review. *Leadership Quarterly*, **16**, 879–919.

Yrle, A.C., Hartman, S., & Galle, W.P. (2002). An investigation of relationships between communication style and leader-member exchange. *Journal of Communication Management*, **6**, 257–68.

Yukl, G. (2010). *Leadership in Organizations* (7th Ed.). New Jersey: Pearson.

Yukl, G.A., & Fu, P.P. (1999). Determinants of delegation and consultation by managers. *Journal of Organizational Behavior*, **20**, 219–232.

Chapter 3

CORPORATE COMMUNICATIONS

Paul R. Jackson

Manchester Business School, University of Manchester, Manchester, UK

INTRODUCTION

Communication is ubiquitous: it is the lifeblood of all our actions whether corporate or personal, and without it there are no relationships. Globalization and accompanying changes in technologies have fundamentally altered our perceptions of space and time: distance is no longer a barrier, and the Internet has allowed more or less instantaneous communication regardless of distance. The effects of these developments on communication both within and between organizations are profound; there are many more actors in an organization's communication network together with denser and more varied kinds of linkages between them. Communication professionals have recognized these effects, but theoretical development has lagged behind the developments in technology.

The argument that will be developed in this chapter is as follows. First, corporate communications is a specialism that focuses on the management of the relationship between organizations and their stakeholders. Second, its core proposition is that effective corporate communications contribute to the competitive advantage of organizations. The responsibility of corporate communications professionals is to maintain and develop communication as a capability which enables organizations to compete effectively in their markets and reconfigure their internal resources in the face of changes in the competitive landscape. The third element is that it does this in a variety of ways, both directly and indirectly. It enables the organization to formulate and implement its strategic goals; it contributes towards building a positive reputation among important stakeholders (and thereby influence the financial bottom line); it protects the organization against external threats which could damage its reputation or financial viability; and it enables the organization to identify

International Review of Industrial and Organizational Psychology, 2010, Volume 25.
Edited by G. P. Hodgkinson and J. K. Ford. Copyright © 2010 John Wiley & Sons, Ltd

opportunities in its external competitive environment and respond effectively to them. Each element of this argument will be examined in turn.

The next section proposes a definition of corporate communications in terms of its role in managing the relationship between an organization and its stakeholders, leading to a conceptual analysis of the contribution of stakeholder relationships to organizational competitive advantage. I view organizations and their stakeholders as communities consisting of actors linked in networks, and the major part of the chapter presents an analysis of these network communities. I begin at the lowest level, with a consideration of the network actors themselves and address the question of who are an organization's stakeholders. Next, I consider the characteristics of the linkages between network members, paying particular attention to the symmetrical model of public relations (Grunig, Grunig, and Dozier, 2002). The next section moves on to an analysis of communication flows through network linkages. The penultimate section brings it all together showing the role of corporate communications in the orchestration of organizational resources and external messages. The final section presents some conclusions and implications for future research.

Defining Corporate Communications

First, it is necessary to delimit the scope of the chapter since the concept of communication itself is so broad. Communication occurs at different levels – between organizations, between groups and between individuals – and involves different modalities (one-to-one, one-to-few, one-to-many) as well as a wide diversity of media (both direct and intermediated; and including written, visual and aural). The primary domain of corporate communications is the corporate level between an organization and its stakeholders; intergroup and interpersonal communication have not generally been considered as part of corporate communications. Thus, for example Welch and Jackson (2007) did not include topics such as appraisal and interpersonal skills training under the heading of corporate communications, because these are concerned with communication among internal stakeholders rather than between the organization and its internal stakeholders. Rather, they included within corporate communications those interactions which involved managers who could be taken to be acting on behalf of the corporate entity itself rather than simply speaking on their own behalf. Other communications scholars have taken a similar view.

However, this distinction becomes less clear-cut when different kinds of external communication are examined. Consider the conversation between an employee working in a call centre and a customer of the organization. At first glance, this does not seem to be an example of corporate communications. Nevertheless, for organizations such as First Direct Bank, this is almost exclusively the way that customers can deal personally with the bank and so such conversations are powerful ways whereby First Direct shapes its image and reputation with a vital stakeholder. Even though call centre employees are not

Table 3.1   Definitions of the field of corporate communications

'as the sum of communication activities brought under one banner' (Christensen, Morsing, and and Cheney, 2008) (p. 2). The aim of corporate communications is to 'speak to many audiences *at once* with a consistent set of messages' (p. vi, italics in original)
'a management function that offers a framework for the effective coordination of all internal and external communication with the overall purpose of establishing and maintaining favourable reputations with stakeholder groups upon which the organization is dependent' (Cornelissen, 2008, p. 5)
'image and identity, corporate advertising, media relations, financial communications, employee relations, community relations and corporate philanthropy, government relations and crisis communications' (Argenti, 1996, p. 77)
'a framework in which all communication specialists integrate the totality of the organizational message, thereby helping to define the corporate image as a means to improving corporate performance' (van Riel, 1995, p. xi); 'an instrument of management by means of which all consciously used forms of internal and external communication are harmonised as effectively and efficiently as possible, so as to create a favourable basis for relationships with groups upon which the company is dependent' (p. 26)

in a senior position within the organization, they can reasonably be said to be acting on behalf of the organization and therefore their actions could be interpreted as corporate communications. There is thus a key difference between peer-to-peer communications among employees and employee–customer communications. In the former case, the image which is created is that of the employee, while in the latter case the image created is of both the employee and the organization. A call handler who loses his temper with a customer creates an impression not only of a person who is rude but also of a company that does not care about its customers. Two employees talking to each other do not necessarily represent the organization (their 'voice' is their own), while an employee talking to a customer speaks with the 'voice' of the employing organization. Whether recognized or not, employees in such situations create an impression both of themselves and of their employing organization.

The literature offers a variety of definitions of corporate communications (see Table 3.1), and common elements among these definitions are:

- corporate communications encompasses the *totality* of all forms of communication (both intended and unintended);
- its focus is on the communication of organizational *messages*;
- it is the management function responsible for the *integration* of communication efforts;
- its aim is to *create favourable images* with key stakeholders in order to enhance corporate performance.

A synthesis of the definitions in Table 3.1 gives the following: corporate communications is concerned with the management of relationships between organizations and their stakeholders within which inferences about communications may legitimately be made about the organization as a whole, rather than just about the individuals concerned.

I now use a brief case study based on van Exel and Fisher (2005) to illustrate the elements of this definition and the themes to be examined in the rest of the chapter. In 2004, United Airlines launched Ted as a low-fare airline-within-an-airline. (It was subsequently shut down in 2009 and the aircraft were returned to service within United Airlines.) The task of the communications team was to work with two key stakeholder groups, employees and customers, to support the introduction of the new low-cost service while at the same time protecting the parent brand. For the company's main products, the launch was potentially highly damaging: why would passengers pay United's higher prices when the same company was offering flights at lower prices? On the other hand, the risk of launching a new service would be much lower if they could take advantage of the positive aspects of the United brand. The senior management team recognized the importance of employees in ensuring that the low-fare airline was effective, since it required changes in their working practices in order to reduce costs, and they could also play a major advocacy role in selling the product to paying customers.

The priority of the communication team was to concentrate on domestic employee stakeholders and create a strong commitment to the new strategy. They first defined what they needed to know, and they set out to change their opinions through a programme of education. They used a variety of communication channels (face-to-face meetings, newsletters, or emails) to help employees 'interact with the product and senior management in a positive way'. They used staff surveys in the prelaunch stage to identify the most effective way to communicate messages to employees and to monitor how effectively they had managed to convey those messages. It is quite clear that the communications team were following a transmission model of communication (Shannon and Weaver, 1949), as they sought to find effective ways of ensuring that the desired messages from senior management were communicated to employees. Having built a strong relationship with United's domestic employees around commitment to the new product, the team then worked hard to build effective relationships with potential customers. While the main focus of the team's activities was United's employees, they also recognized that the new airline needed customers to succeed. They set up employees as what they called "brand ambassadors" in order to tell them about the new product, and the communications team set out to teach employees about the product's core values and how they could communicate those values to customers. In all of their efforts, the team were strongly committed to the orchestration of communication. They continually met with the Ted senior leadership team to ensure that it was always 'on message'; and they prepared standard presentations for use by managers at each airport so that there was consistency of messages across employee groups.

The communications team targeted salient stakeholder groups (in this case, employees and customers) and sought to build good relationships with them. They followed an explicit communication model and demonstrated the importance of actively orchestrating messages about the strategy to achieve consistency. The case thus shows how communication can enable a firm to achieve a strategic objective, and each of the steps that the team followed will be considered below.

Stakeholder Relationships and Organizational Competitive Advantage

Donaldson and Preston (1995) presented an instrumental justification for stakeholder relationship management, arguing that organizations should develop and maintain effective relationships with their stakeholders because they will achieve performance benefits by doing so. Berman *et al.* (1999) refined the instrumental model into two versions of the way in which stakeholder relationships might relate to strategy and financial performance. The *direct effects* model conceptualizes the management of stakeholder relationships as one of many strategic objectives for an organization, but one which is not integrated into its other objectives. Examples of such initiatives might be corporate sponsorship of local community projects or subsidy of employees' educational development programmes. An organization which follows this model will pursue stakeholder relationships as long as they benefit the bottom line, while those that do not will be discontinued. The second model is a *moderation* model which proposes a stronger integration between strategic objectives and stakeholder relationship management role. Here, stakeholder relationships play an important role in strategy execution by moderating its impact on financial performance. Thus, the model proposes that good relationships with stakeholders enable the organization to achieve its strategic objectives more effectively, while poor relationships impede its ability to do so.

A strong basis for organizations to achieve an enduring competitive advantage is through the internal capabilities that they can draw upon (Barney, 1991; Wernerfelt, 1984), but communication is either absent or marginal to debates within the strategic management literature on capabilities as a source of competitive advantage. Existing literature on corporate strategy implementation tends to focus on organizational structure and processes, reward systems and resource allocation; and there is little literature which emphasizes communication capability as a source of competitive advantage. Helfat *et al.* (2007) argue that seeing organizations as bundles of capabilities which can be deployed in adaptive ways can bridge the artificial divide that exists in the strategic management literature between content and process. Understanding how organizations can survive and thrive in highly changeable environments clearly requires knowledge of what their capabilities are (content) and also how they are deployed (process). Effective corporate communications has a crucial role in both aspects. Writers on organizational change management (e.g. Burnes, 2004; Deetz, Tracy, and Simpson, 2000) place a strong emphasis on the role of communication in both the formulation and the implementation of strategic change. The instrumental models of Berman *et al.* (1999) are appealing because they position corporate communications as part of the bundle of capabilities of organizations which may contribute to enduring competitive advantage (Barney, 1991; Barney and Clark, 2007).

Tucker, Meyer, and Westerman (1996) develop this theme further in an article that places communication systems at the core of the organization's internal strategic capability which leads in turn to the delivery of competitive advantage. Following Barney (1991), they propose that organizations which possess hard-to-imitate configurations of internal capabilities will perform better and that effective organizational communication systems play a key role in building those configurations. They emphasize the mediational role of communication systems in turning both tacit and explicit knowledge into internal strategic capabilities. They conceptualize *communicated knowledge* as 'the single most important source of competitive advantage into the 21st Century' (p. 55). They consider a twofold taxonomy of knowledge as individual versus collective and as tacit versus explicit. At the macro-level of the organization, effective communication systems can promote the development of organizational routines (Nelson and Winter, 1982) by providing vehicles for the institutionalization of tacit knowledge through such mechanisms as cultural messages and rituals. Effective communication processes also enable top-level leaders to coordinate explicit knowledge in support of organizational goals. At the micro-level of the *individual*, effective communication processes can enhance the frequency, intensity and quality of interactions between people and thus support effective and efficient integration of tacit knowledge within an organizational culture. Communication systems also make individuals' explicit knowledge available to others through such mechanisms as management information systems, intranets, emailing and instant messaging technologies.

Argenti and Forman (2000) offer a different approach to the relationship between strategy and communication, building on rhetoric as the theoretical basis for linking the two based on co-creation processes within the dialogue between an organization and its stakeholders. The fundamental principle of rhetoric was first developed by Aristotle in ancient Greece is persuasion, which they define as 'a process of discovery and interaction with the audience by which the speaker both creates a message collaboratively with the audience and communicates that message to the audience' (p. 234). The starting point for rhetorical practices is the organization's strategic goals which help to define relevant stakeholder groups (Argenti and Forman call them 'constituencies') and also the messages which are appropriate for each group. Strategy formulation and implementation then depends crucially on how effectively the organization works with its stakeholder groups in the collaborative co-creation of a future strategic position which meets the objectives of the organization's senior management. 'The leaders in expressive organizations, like the individual speaker in the public assemblies of Athens, advance their strategic agendas by attending to their significant constituencies as collaborators in the creation of meaning and as parties to be influenced and moved to carry out those agendas' (p. 244).

An important question for research is whether organizations whose managers adopt principles and practices which are sensitive to the interests of their stakeholders perform better financially than those that do not. This question is difficult to answer, and Donaldson and Preston (1995) say it has never been addressed effectively. Doing so requires sensitive performance indicators at an appropriate aggregation level – the business unit, the corporation and so on) and a clear specification of appropriate stakeholder management indicators (again at an appropriate aggregation level).

Organizations as Members of Multilevel Network Communities

Organizations operate in networks of stakeholders where network actors seek to pursue their own interests and influence the actions of other network members. In formal terms, networks are made up of actors (nodes or agents) and linkages (or ties) between them. Networks vary in various ways, notably in size (the number of actors) and density (the number and patterning of linkages between actors). Moreover, organizations and stakeholders are intrinsically multilevel in structure, and research needs to reflect this fundamental property. Much of the existing research is limited in scope because it is confined to a single level of analysis. Building on the microfoundations concept in the strategic management literature (Abell, Felin, and Foss, 2008; Teece, 2007), I maintain that the linkage between macro-level strategic initiatives and corporate performance is only partly achieved through direct relationships at the macro-level.

There are also input–output linkages at meso- and micro-levels which can have macro-level impacts on organizational performance. There are also cross-level influences (both upwards and downwards) on performance at different levels. Finally, there is an aggregate influence on performance of the consistency of communications within and between levels. Building on Klein and Kozlowski (2000), it is possible to conceptualize three formal kinds of model for the role of communication in achieving an impact of strategy on performance. *Single-level* models contain only constructs measured at a single hierarchical level: person, group or organization level. Applying models developed at one level to phenomena at another level is inappropriate and can lead to different kinds of fallacy. The ecological fallacy refers to assuming that relationships identified at the group level apply in the same way at the individual level. The atomistic fallacy refers to the opposite assumption: that relationships identified at the individual level apply in the same way at the group level. *Cross-level models* conceptualize constructs measured at different levels, with hypothesized causal influences of variables at (usually) a higher level on variables measured at a lower level. *Homologous multilevel* models are models of relationships among variables measured at the same level, where the same relationships are assumed to apply at all levels within a multilevel hierarchy. An example of a homologous model could be the conceptualization of communication routines as following the same causal processes whether measured at the macro-, meso- or micro-levels. As observed by Monge and Contractor (2003) processes within levels may be influenced by factors within levels, microdeterminants (factors from lower levels), macrodeterminants (factors from higher levels), as well as by factors outside the network (externalities).

Adopting a multilevel lens for viewing members of network communities leads to a recognition that organizations communicate with their stakeholders at different levels. At the *macro-level* are communications through press releases from a central corporate communications function, the annual company report or by direct communication between senior executives such as the CEO and external stakeholders. The *meso-level* encompasses communication between internal functional specialisms and their counterparts outside the company. These include a marketing group dealing with customers, as well as specialist groups that deal with suppliers, regulators, shareholders and so on. At the *micro-level* lie a myriad of interactions between individual company employees and representatives of outside stakeholder groups. While the macro-level is the traditional domain of corporate communications, I will show that the meso- and the micro-levels are also relevant to an organization's relationships with its stakeholders. Although they have generally been left to other specialisms (both at an academic and a professional level), there is an increasing realization that this fragmentation is inadequate. I consider later the three aspects of networks: network actors, network linkages and communication flows through network linkages.

NETWORK COMMUNITIES: WHO ARE AN ORGANIZATION'S STAKEHOLDERS?

The globalization of organizations (Dicken, 2003) exposes them to a hugely wider array of groups with whom they have to engage in order to pursue their strategic objectives. Moreover, the diversity of those groups is much greater in a global economy in terms of culture, language and institutional frameworks (Whitley, 2007). Organizations which operate globally face formidable challenges in how they can communicate effectively across national boundaries and within a wide diversity of local communities. There is also a communication challenge brought about by the rapid convergence of communication technologies through the Internet which has greatly accelerated the globalization process. Advances in Internet technologies have created hugely greater convergence among communities of relevance to organizations, enabling rapid and rich communication among them. Thus organizations can communicate speedily regardless of distance, and stakeholder groups can also communicate with each other in ways that were unthinkable 20 years ago. No organization can expect to keep secrets about how it acts in any part of the world. Moreover, it can no longer deal separately with different stakeholder groups with the expectation that those groups will be unaware of how it acts elsewhere. The consequence is that corporate communications is becoming widely recognized as fundamental to helping an organization achieve its strategic objectives.

The idea that organizations have stakeholders has become commonplace since Freeman's (1984) book, and indeed the term 'stakeholder' has acquired a taken-for-granted status that runs the risk of making it meaningless. In part, this arises from the very broad definition that Freeman offered: 'a stakeholder is any group or individual who can affect or is affected by the achievement of the organization's purpose and objectives' (p. 6). This definition does not give priority to any group or individual: all those with an interest in the firm should participate to obtain benefits, and none has a higher priority over others. There has been a spirited debate among management scholars (Donaldson and Preston, 1995; Freeman, 1999; Jones and Wicks, 1999; Mitchell, Agle, and Wood, 1997), initially centred on the view offered by Friedman (1970) that organizations do not have a responsibility to any group other than their owners. More recently, the attention of scholars has broadened to consider how the multiple responsibilities that organizations have towards their interest groups can be discharged, while still serving the primary purpose of making a profit and remaining in business. From both a practical and a conceptual point of view, Freeman's definition of stakeholders is too broad to be useful, and others have been proposed. The most helpful is that by Mitchell *et al.* (1997) which defines three attributes of stakeholders, power, legitimacy and urgency, as a basis for organizations to prioritize among the interests of groups with which they deal.

The first attribute of *power* is defined by Salancik and Pfeffer (1974) as 'the ability of those who possess it to bring about the outcomes they desire' (p. 3), and following Etzioni (1964), we can see that there are different kinds of resources which may be used to exercise power. Power may be coercive, based on the actual or threatened use of physical resources through violence or force, it may be utilitarian, based on awarding material or financial resources, and it may be normative, based on symbolic rather than material resources such as prestige, esteem or acceptance.

The second attribute of *legitimacy* is central to most narrow definitions of the concept of stakeholder, and refers to 'a generalized perception or assumption that the actions of an entity are desirable, proper, or appropriate within some socially constructed system of norms, values, beliefs, and definitions' (Suchman, 1995). Thus, the rights of a group to have its interests taken into account by an organization arise not from intrinsic characteristics but rather out of socially defined views of those interests. While the idea of legitimacy has a superficial attractiveness about it, its application to specific interest groups is much more difficult.

First, the concept relies to a degree at least on the existence of a shared view of the interests at stake, and the acceptance of a group as having legitimate claims may be strongly contested. For example, the concept of 'the deserving poor' has a long history in English society, and is embodied in the 1601 Act for the Relief of the Poor. It distinguished between those people who were unable to support themselves for reasons beyond their control (through infirmity or misfortune) and those people whose poverty was regarded as being within their control (perhaps through idleness or drink). The 1601 law placed responsibilities on civil authorities to support the first group, but not the second; and the distinction still resonates through political debate in the UK and beyond. The labelling of a group as 'deserving' or 'undeserving' is itself an example of framing (see later), and the example shows how the stakeholder concept itself is socially defined.

Second, legitimacy is both temporally and culturally bound, and so is subject to change as a result of alterations either in the standing of the interest group itself or in society's views of the group. When organizations consider which interest groups are their legitimate stakeholders, they have to take into account what may be changing social norms. Consider the difficulty that organizations have in working out how they need to operate when faced with issues such as HIV/AIDS or genetically modified (GM) foods, where social consensus is difficult to achieve. The same volatility in consensus is evident with regard to the legitimate responsibilities of organizations for the actions of their suppliers as employers. For many years, Marks & Spencer (M&S) imposed strict production and HR standards on those companies which supplied products for sale within M&S stores. It is only much more recently, that companies such as Nike have come under fire because of working conditions within the factories of their supplier companies. Nike has no legal responsibility there, but supplier employees have acquired at least a degree of legitimacy in the eyes of Nike customers in many Western countries.

The third attribute is *urgency*, defined as 'the degree to which stakeholder claims call for immediate action' (Mitchell *et al.*, 1997, p. 867). Some claims of interest groups may be high in criticality through their potential for harm to the group, and examples include shareholdings that cannot be disposed of without loss of value, employees' expectations of benefits from a company pension scheme and the importance attached by an interest group to risks to which they have been exposed. The collapse of the global financial system has brought about dramatic loss of value of the savings of millions of people, and the actions of governments around the world have given high priority to protecting as far as possible those whose interests suddenly became urgent. The urgency of claims may also arise from time sensitivity, where a delay in organizational action would be unacceptable to an interest group. Although this

Table 3.2 Taxonomy of stakeholder classes

Latent stakeholders
  Dormant – power alone
  Discretionary – legitimacy alone
  Demanding – urgency alone

Expectant stakeholders
  Dominant – power plus legitimacy
  Dependent stakeholders – legitimacy plus urgency
  Dangerous stakeholders – urgency plus power
Definitive stakeholders – urgency plus legitimacy plus power

attribute is not often considered in the general stakeholder literature, it is an important focus for issues management and crisis management. For example, it is increasingly common to read about product recalls as a precautionary measure. Johnson & Johnson famously ultimately enhanced their reputation by immediately withdrawing all Tylenol products from the shelves in 1982 when cyanide found in the product led to the death of seven people. The risk to customers was statistically very low, but no one knew the extent of the risk at the start of the crisis, and the potential harm if exposed was very high. This case illustrates how both aspects of urgent claims can coincide to make company action a priority. In contrast, Cadbury's came under fire when salmonella was found in its chocolate products in January 2006, but the company did not make any public announcement or withdraw infected products from shops until June (long after children had eaten Easter eggs which were made with the contaminated chocolate). They argued that the level of contamination was well below levels which were a danger to health and had already found the source of the problem and corrected it; even so they were strongly criticized because they did not respond to a problem in a time-sensitive way. While the claims of consumers were not as critical as in the Tylenol case – sickness rather than death, the timing of the company response was widely seen as inappropriate.

Combining the three attributes outlined earlier gives seven classes of stakeholder, plus an additional category of non-stakeholder defined by the absence of all three attributes (see Table 3.2). Mitchell *et al.* argue that the salience of a stakeholder group depends on the number of attributes it possesses at a specific time. Latent stakeholders are those groups who possess only one of the three attributes; expectant stakeholders are those groups who possess two attributes; while the highest priority would be given to what they call definitive stakeholders; that is stakeholders who possess all three attributes.

Latent stakeholders are those who possess only one attribute. *Dormant* stakeholders are those who possess power alone, but it is not being used. They may be people who could mount costly and embarrassing lawsuits or could command the attention of the media. They might be former employees with a grievance, who may file for wrongful dismissal or perhaps return to shoot people indiscriminately (as has happened from time to time in a number of different countries). *Discretionary* stakeholders are those whose sole claim is legitimacy, but they have neither power nor urgency to claims. *Demanding* stakeholders are those whose sole relevant attribute is urgency, and they possess neither power nor legitimacy: they are irritating but not more. Broadly, organizations will only consider the interests of latent stakeholders when their standing changes: 'legitimacy gains rights through power and voice through urgency' (Mitchell *et al.*, 1997, p. 870).

Expectant stakeholders possess two of the three attributes. *Dominant* stakeholders are labeled thus because they tend to form the dominant coalition of the organization by virtue of possessing both power and legitimacy. They will 'matter' to managers, and managing their interests will usually be formally recognized. Owners, important creditors and community leaders are often explicitly represented on corporate boards, while the interests of other dominant stakeholder groups are managed by internal specialist functions – for example, investor relations office (investors), HR department (employees) or public affairs office (local, national or regional government). *Dependent* stakeholder groups are those with legitimate and urgent claims but who lack power. For example, residents of Prince William Sound suddenly became dependent stakeholders of Exxon in 1989 following the oil spillage from the Exxon Valdez. Dependent stakeholders are reliant on powerful others to pursue their claims, either through advocacy (by government, special interest groups) or through the voluntary exercise of management's values. *Dangerous* stakeholders are those groups which lack legitimacy but possess urgency and power; examples include groups that use unlawful coercion through wildcat strikes or kidnapping of company employees for financial or political gain. Global employers such as Shell have long experience of planning for the protection of their employees when working in countries such as Nigeria and Colombia.

Finally, *definitive* stakeholders are those groups which possess all three attributes. Dominant stakeholders, such as major stockholders, can acquire definitive status when major declines in share values lead them to challenge company management through an extraordinary general meeting. The dependent stakeholder groups resident in Prince William Sound acquired definitive status when US government acted on their behalf. The African National Congress became a definitive stakeholder in multinational enterprises (MNEs) operating in South Africa following its election victory in 1994; and a similar change has occurred in the standing of Sinn Fein in Northern Ireland in the last 10 years.

Implications for Research

A major contribution of the stakeholder taxonomy is in defining the actors in the competitive environment within which organizations seek to achieve their strategic objectives. Stakeholders who occupy different regions of the taxonomy will contribute in quite different ways to an organization's competitive advantage, and we need to know much more about how to map and monitor them. Stakeholder mapping tools (e.g. Eden and Ackerman, 1998) can be effective for helping organizations to define which stakeholders are important in achieving competitive advantage. While corporate communications scholars have discussed its strategic role, theory development and empirical study of corporate communications in strategy formulation and implementation is sparse. Further work is also needed on the environmental scanning role of corporate communicators (Monge and Poole, 2008), since they are in a unique position on the boundary of the organization, with responsibilities for dealing with both internal and external stakeholders. Moreover, it is quite clear that stakeholder network communities are fluid rather than static, and stakeholder groups can occupy different regions of the typology depending on social, economic and political forces operating upon them. Recognizing the dynamic nature of stakeholder networks sets major challenges to a scholarly community that is most familiar with thinking of networks as static entities.

NETWORK LINKAGES: THE RELATIONSHIP BETWEEN AN ORGANIZATION AND ITS STAKEHOLDERS

In common with other areas of management, corporate communications scholars (e.g. Grunig, 1992; Ledingham and Bruning, 2000) see organizations and their stakeholders not just as senders and receivers of messages but also as linked to each other through relationships. Just as there is a vigorous debate in marketing over the validity and meaningfulness of the concept of customer relationship management (how many of us feel that we have a relationship with our preferred supermarket, rather than simply see it as a place where we buy what we need to live?), so there is plenty of room for questioning what it means to say that an organization can have a relationship with either a person or a group. Nevertheless, the use of the concept does lead to a focus on the character of the linkage between the organization and salient stakeholder groups rather than simply on exchanges of messages between them. A number of authors (Goodman, 2000; Grunig, 2000; Grunig and Huang, 2000) have argued that corporate communications is about relationship building, and adopting this view means that an important indicator of the success of an organization's corporate communications function is the quality of the relationships that the organization can maintain with its stakeholders.

The influence of a stakeholder through its relationship with an organization can be seen as the total of two influences: *direct* effects and the *indirect* effect (which is the sum total of all indirect ties involving other network members).

The direct impact of a non-governmental organization (NGO) stakeholder might be very low, but its indirect effect could be much higher through its influence in shaping public policy on an issue of social importance. This explains why many organizations place great importance on monitoring issues as well as stakeholders, since recognizing issues of increasing social and political importance will allow for more effective preparation than simply monitoring the activities of stakeholder groups which might at some time become salient. This is reflected in a shift in focus within the corporate communications literature away from crisis management (with its emphasis on how to respond to an unforeseen event) to issues management. Scholars such as Coombs (1999) have shown the importance of the need for an organization to continually scan its external environment to identify issues that might impact on the organization. Building on the issues management perspective, Deephouse and Heugens (2009) looked at issue adoption by an organization and argued that it is necessary to go beyond a focus on the issue and the organization. They argue that issue adoption is a socially constructed process mediated by third parties, called infomediaries, and present a model of the role of infomediaries in establishing credible linkages between organizations and social issues.

A major theme of corporate communications research has been the analysis of the linkages between organizations and the stakeholders who are members of their network community. While a simplistic approach would just focus on whether or not there is a linkage between two network members, a more realistic approach recognizes that network ties vary along a number of dimensions, namely stability, frequency, multiplexity, strength and symmetry (Brass, 1995; Monge and Contractor, 2003). Ties vary in their *stability*, such that some relationships are enduring over time, whereas others are short-lived and transient. Exchanges between two network members may be either *frequent* or irregular. A relationship between two network members may be narrowly focused on a single project (uniplex) or be broader based (*multiplex*). Neville and Menguc (2006) report an interesting study of a related construct which they call stakeholder multiplicity: "the degree of multiple, conflicting, complementary, or cooperative stakeholder claims made to an organization"(p. 377). Ties between network members will be *stronger* where they spend more time working together, where there is higher emotional intensity in the relationship and where there is greater intimacy in the relationship. Finally, network ties can differ in their *symmetry*, the extent to which the relationship is bidirectional, and it is this characteristic of organization–stakeholder relationships that has been the primary focus of corporate communications research.

The Symmetrical Model of Organization–Stakeholder Relationships

The traditional practice model for both corporate communications and its external face, public relations is one of one-way communication, with an emphasis on how an organization can most effectively persuade or influence others. The modern view among the professional bodies is rather different as we will see later in the chapter, but most communications professionals see themselves as functioning primarily to support the interests of their employing organization, through either advocacy or persuasion. Early typologies of communication capture this through the distinction between *synchronic* and *diachronic* communication. The purpose of *synchronic* communication is to align the behaviour of a stakeholder group with the interests of the organization, whereas the purpose of *diachronic* communication is to negotiate a state of affairs that benefits both parties (Grunig and Grunig, 1992). Neither model allows for the possibility that organizations might exist to serve the interests of external stakeholder groups. In a further development of this distinction, Grunig and Hunt (1984) proposed two dimensions reflecting whether communication is one or two way, and the extent of symmetry or asymmetry in the relationship. They used these two dimensions to derive a fourfold taxonomy of communications practice within public relations, which is also relevant to corporate communications.

The first element of the taxonomy and the earliest form of communications practice is one-way asymmetrical communication, represented by the *press agentry* model. The most famous press agent was P.T. Barnum, the nineteenth century American showman who is reputed to have said 'there is a sucker born every minute'. Barnum's goal was publicity in aid of persuading a gullible public to buy products as long as there was profit in it for him. The press agent function still survives in sport or theatrical promotion, and the world of celebrities is supported by agents who are paid to create favourable publicity for their clients and to hide anything that does not favour the client. This is one-way asymmetrical communication: a monologue which seeks to change the public.

The second element of the taxonomy is the *public information* model, which is also one-way communication targeted at a specific audience, but is more symmetrical in that it recognizes the interests of both parties to the relationship and values truth and accuracy in communications. Campaigns by government agencies on such issues as child vaccination, drink driving, healthy eating and online completion of tax returns are all examples of the public information model of communications practice. This is one-way communication because there is no true dialogue between the parties to the communication: the aim is to change public understanding of an issue while leaving the source organization essentially unchanged. However, it is more symmetrical than the press agent model in so far as the interests of the target audience are what motivates and directs the communication effort.

The third element of the taxonomy is the *two-way asymmetrical* model where communication is used to influence a stakeholder group on the basis of first-seeking information from the group about their opinions and values on a specific issue. Public debate on issues such as GM ingredients in foods, renewable energy, recycling, and organ donation reflect the operational form of this communications model. The debate includes large corporations as well as citizens and communities, and such agencies will often have great power to promote their own interests. However, these agencies can only achieve their interests by listening to and influencing public opinion. Two case examples show this communications model in action.

The first case is Shell's plan to decommission the Brent Spar oil storage platform through deep-sea disposal on the basis of a three-year scientific investigation of the risks and costs of several alternative options and extensive consultation with governments in northwestern Europe (Fombrun and Rindova, 2000; Wei-Skillern, 2004). Unfortunately, Shell completely misjudged public opinion with respect to using the ocean as a 'dumping ground' for waste; and the environmental campaigning group Green Peace quickly became the voice for public awareness of environment issues through peaceful occupancy of the platform and extensive political lobbying of governments in several western European countries. One of the indicators of Green Peace's success was the occurrence of noisy demonstrations in Germany and the Netherlands around Shell petrol stations. (A less attractive consequence was the throwing of a petrol bomb at a Shell petrol station in Germany.) Shell was forced to reverse its policy decision, and the platform was eventually towed to a Norwegian fjord where it now forms part of a harbour quay at Mekjavik near Stavanger. Shell's communication policy was one of widespread (but it turns out biased and partial) consultation, followed by efforts to persuade affected parties of the validity of its proposed action. Although Shell thought that it had taken public opinion very seriously, through a process of consultation and dialogue, the organization was forced to recognize it had made fundamental mistakes.

The second case is similar in that it illustrates the failure of an organizational communications effort to support a practice in the face of changing public sensitivities, in this case with regard to organ retention. Alder Hey Hospital is a world-class research hospital in Liverpool, Merseyside, where Professor Van Velzen was located while employed by the University of Liverpool as a pathologist. In the course of a public inquiry into excessive death rates during operative procedures at another hospital, it came to light that Van Velzen had been accumulating a large collection of body parts acquired during his pathology practice from children who had died at Alder Hey Hospital. People in the UK were shocked that almost all of this material had been retained without the informed consent of the parents of the dead children. Van Velzen justified his actions on the basis that the tissue bank was necessary for medical research that would bring long-term benefit to others and that he was following accepted medical practice regarding informed consent. It quickly became impossible for either the hospital or the university employer to defend his actions, and a public inquiry was set up alongside the doctor's suspension. He subsequently left the UK, and has been struck off by the British Medical Association so that he can no longer practice medicine in the UK. The Alder Hey scandal and the Redfern Report that arose out of it had widespread consequences (Dewar Boddington, 2004). Autopsy practices changed to reflect a greater public insistence on the need for consent. Consequently, however, there was a greater reluctance on the part of doctors to make requests of the relatives of those who had just died. Organ donations became much less frequent (with consequential effects on those in need of organ transplants). Practices enshrined in the Human Tissue Act 1961 were modified by the Human Tissue Act 2004 to bring medical practice more closely into line with changes in public attitudes. This case illustrates the ineffectiveness of the operation of a two-way asymmetrical model in the face of major change in attitudes towards an issue of societal concern.

The final element of the taxonomy of communications practice is the *two-way symmetrical* model of dialogue and balanced communication between the organization and its stakeholder groups. In contrast to the one-way communication models reviewed earlier, the aim is to facilitate mutual understanding, rather than for one party to persuade the other. Grunig regards the symmetrical model as the ideal of communications practice, especially for organizations operating in Western societies. The prevalence of the four models have been subject to empirical testing through what has become known as The Excellence Project, a large research programme sponsored by the International Association of Business Communications (IABC), which involved over 300 organizations in the UK, Canada and the US (Dozier, Grunig, and Grunig, 1995; Grunig *et al.*, 1992; Grunig *et al.*, 2002). As part of the study, scales were developed to measure the extent to which each of the four models is practiced in a particular organization, and the authors claim adequate technical quality for the scales. The symmetrical model has been further elaborated and tested in a number of studies (Toth, 2007). The conclusion of the project was that two-way symmetrical relationships are the ideal, but this has been subject to criticism on a variety of grounds. Organizations in their communications practices rarely operate in the unitary way implied by neat taxonomies, and it is quite usual to find hybrid practices which utilize elements of more than one model, although Grunig and Grunig respond that the four models in their taxonomy can be seen as ideal types rather than descriptive realities in their pure form. Furthermore, the relationship of an organization with its stakeholders is likely to be dynamic in nature, depending on circumstances and the pressures of external events. Finally, while the Excellence Project was conducted only in three Anglo-Saxon countries (US, UK and Canada), its conclusions were proposed as universal, and the cultural universality of the symmetrical model has also been challenged.

Cancel *et al.* (1997) have been vigorous proponents of a contingency theory of organizations' dealings with their stakeholders. They argue that the symmetrical model of dialogue to build healthy relationships with stakeholders cannot be taken as an ideal but rather that the communication professional's role lies on a continuum from pure *advocacy* on behalf of the employing organization at one extreme to pure *accommodation* through a mutual relationship of trust at the other extreme (Murphy, 1991). They argue that the position to adopt in order to achieve organizational objectives depends upon a wide variety of contingency factors, both internal and external to the company. Interviews with public relations practitioners followed by content analysis produced a list of 86 factors which respondents reported as influences on their practice (see also Cameron, Cropp, and Reber, 2001; Cancel, Mitrook, and Cameron, 1999; Jin and Cameron, 2006; Murphy, 2000; Reber and Cameron, 2003; Shin, Cameron, and Cropp, 2006). Table 3.3 organizes these contingency factors according to levels (macro, meso and micro) and whether each factor relates to the focal organization, the stakeholder group or the relationship between them.

Stakeholder Network Characteristics

The members of network communities seek to optimize and protect their political and economic interests through direct interactions with each other (Ferrary, 2009; Frooman, 1999), and these interactions can be fundamental in shaping the parameters of the relationship between the focal organization and its stakeholders. Stakeholder groups will be bound together where they share common interests, and an exclusive focus on the dyadic linkages of an organization with individual stakeholders will miss much of the richness of the network (see Fassin, 2008 for a graphical representation of the structure of stakeholder networks). Furthermore, stakeholder group may have overlapping memberships: employees may be owners through an employee equity scheme as well as customers and members of a local community which is affected by the organization's operations.

The first characteristic of stakeholder networks is that they are *complex*, in that they consist of many different stakeholder groups, which in turn are linked to each other through patterns of interdependencies. In the language of the NK model from complexity theory (Jackson, 2006; Kauffman, 1993), the stakeholder network of most organizations is a highly *complex* one with both high N (a count of the number of salient stakeholder groups) and high K (the number of linkages or interdependencies among groups). Rowley (1997) argues that complex networks with many linkages among network members should have more efficient communication flows than sparsely connected networks; this in turn fosters the development of shared norms leading to higher consistency in how different stakeholders relate to the focal organization. This argument presupposes that the members of the stakeholder network have a common incentive to cooperate with each other. A particularly interest perspective is that offered by Roloff (2008) who analysed what she called multi-stakeholder

Table 3.3 Contingency factors affecting the character of the relationship between an organization and a specific stakeholder group

Level	Organization	Stakeholder Group	Relational Factors
Environmental context			
Network community level	Embeddedness within social and political structures: societal support, lobbying connexions to government	Embeddedness within social and political structures: societal support, lobbying connexions to government	Degree of environmental dynamism and competition
Macro-level – organization	Structure of decision-making; geographical dispersion; use of technology	Legitimacy of the activist's cause	
Meso-level – group	Size and structure of PR department; location within organizational hierarchy; experience; resource availability	Size and structure of PR department; advocacy practices	Negotiating tactics
Micro-level – individual	Capabilities – personal, relational, cognitive Amount of professional experience	Capabilities – personal, relational, cognitive Amount of professional experience	Personal liking between representatives

Adapted from Shin, J.-H., Cameron, G. T., & Cropp, F. (2006). Occam's razor in the contingency theory: A national survey on 86 contingent variables. *Public Relations Review*, 32, 282–6 (Elsevier).

networks, defined as 'networks in which actors from civil society, business and governmental institutions comes together to find a common approach to an issue that affects them all' (p. 238). Where such conditions exist, there is an important role for corporate communications scholars in understanding how organizations can work cooperatively with their stakeholder networks to solve tough problems (Kahane, 2004). However, it is more likely that organizations have to manage relationships with multiple stakeholders, each of which is seeking to protect interests which are inconsistent with each other and perhaps also with those of the organization. Following the NK model, the most likely effect of high network complexity is that it is difficult for organizations to predict the consequences of actions involving any specific stakeholder (technically, this is referred to as a rugged fitness landscape).

The second characteristic of stakeholder networks is that they are *dynamic* and volatile, reflecting the unpredictability of the global world within which organizations operate. While some things are predictable ('death and taxes'), others are not, and the salience of stakeholders can vary dramatically over time. A major role for corporate communications professionals is to act as watchkeepers, keeping an eye out for potential hazards that may impact on the organization. Following Weick (1995), their role is to make sense of the external environment within their privileged position dealing with the variety of external stakeholders. A promising area for future research is the evolution of network relationships.

The third characteristic of relationships within stakeholder networks is that they are highly *variable* in character: stakeholder groups have varying and contradictory interests which need to be managed in different ways. Moreover, organizations themselves are not monolithic and unitary (Clarkson, 1995), but rather are networks of interests which may be contradictory. As a result, the organization's relationship with an external stakeholder group is actually a nexus of multiple (perhaps contradictory) strands. This implies that the corporate communications function is a complex and demanding one, which draws upon a wide variety of capabilities required to manage relationships effectively.

Implications for Research

Building on the multilevel perspective of Monge and Contractor (2003), linkages between network members need to be examined at multiple levels: at the micro-level between individuals in networks of personal contacts, at the meso-level between groups working on joint projects, and at the macro-level between organizations engaged in alliances. Important issues to address include defining the linkages and dependencies between levels, assessing whether the same relationships apply at different hierarchical levels, and examining the performance implications of consistency or inconsistency between communication flows at different levels. One active area of research where a multilevel perspective would be especially valuable is in corporate social responsibility where inconsistencies in organization–stakeholder relationships between different levels are likely to be particularly damaging. For example, a press release (organization-level communication) may emphasize the ethical commitment of the company in corporate social responsibility programmes, while organizational subunits may contract with suppliers on the basis of cheapest price and disregard ethical considerations (work-group level), and employees may ignore corporate ethical codes in their dealings with customers (individual level).

COMMUNICATION FLOWS IN NETWORKS

Having considered the membership of stakeholder networks and the relationships among network members, I now turn to an examination of the communication flows which occur through the linkages between network members. Within both the academic literature and the professional practice community, we can see a strong emphasis on the message. For example, van Riel (1995) defines the responsibilities of the corporate communications function as integrating 'the totality of the organizational *message*' (p. xi, emphasis added). In contrast, a smaller but growing stream of research emphasizes *meaning* – its construction, management and contested nature (Putnam and Fairhurst, 2001; Putnam, Phillips, and Chapman, 1996). I consider both perspectives later in the chapter, taking first the transmission models which underpin much of corporate communications practice and then moving on to explore corporate communication as a co-creation process based on dialogue within a relationship.

Communication Flows as Transmission of Messages

All of the transmission models build on the pioneering work of Shannon and Weaver (1949) who reported on Bell Labs' research on ways of maximizing the engineering efficiency of communication channels such as telephone cables and radio waves. The key elements of their model are sender and receiver, message and communication channel. The process they set out to understand was how to ensure that information was accurately transmitted from the sender to the receiver, having been encoded by the sender for transmission through a communication channel and then decoded by the receiver. Later developments of this model include the work of Gerbner (1956), Schramm (1955) and Berlo (1960).

Encoding/Decoding Processes

In the classical Shannon and Weaver model both the encoding and the decoding are technical matters. Thus telephone conversations involve encoding of sound into electrical signals, which are then transmitted through the telephone system from the sender's handset to that of the receiver where the electrical signals are decoded into sound which can be heard by the receiver. Gerbner (1956) recognized the narrowness of this exclusively technical focus and expanded on the encoding/decoding element of the original model in his universal communication model. On the encoding side, he distinguished between an event (E) and the perception of the event (E_1), and he recognized the idea familiar to psychologists that perception is an active process. The relationship between E and its percept E_1 is not a simple one-to-one mapping but involves active *selection* of features of the event. Furthermore, selection is based on *pattern recognition* through hypothesis testing processes of matching against internal templates or patterns. The final element of Gerbner's model links the receiver to what is perceived (the signal about an event), and selection and pattern recognition are once again an integral part of this decoding process. Within the model, the active process of perception of an event by the message sender and the perception by the message receiver of signals about the event are influenced by experience, history and culture.

The concept of message framing is an application of the active encoding element of this framework which has been important in crisis and issues management research. Framing is defined as 'ways leaders can use their language to shape or modify particular interpretations of organizational events' (Deetz *et al.*, 2000). Properties of psychological frames are described by Rees, Gandy, and Grant (2001). The metaphor of a frame is one that draws a boundary around a body of material; as such it is both inclusive (by restricting which messages or actions are incorporated within a given frame) and exclusive (by virtue of what is left out). A frame draws attention to what is inside it and defines the premises on which recipients are expected to interpret what is inside. The power of framing was shown by El Sawy and Pauchant (1988) in a laboratory study of the power of initial information to frame later decision-making. They first gave participants information about strategic opportunities in the cell phone market, indicating the huge potential of the market. Participants were then informed that cell phones could be dangerous while driving, and they asked whether people would change their framing given by the initial information or reinterpret the information. The clear finding was that study participants did not reject the initial information, rather, they found ways of defending the frame, by such interpretations as cell phone owners are safer drivers (and therefore would be less likely to have accidents anyway), hands-free capabilities were being developed that would obviate any problems of using phones within vehicles and cell phone could be used in cases of accident. Entman (1991) further illustrates the properties of the framing process in a comparison between two stories: the shooting down of Iran Air Flight 655 by a US Navy ship in 1988 and the shooting down of Korean Airlines Flight 007 by a Soviet fighter in 1983. Entman describes how the US media portrayed the first as 'a technical problem', whereas the second was portrayed as a 'moral outrage'. No doubt, the media in the then USSR displayed a similar asymmetry in their reporting of these same stories.

Communication Channel

Shannon and Weaver considered features of a communication channel such as its capacity to transmit signals and the influence of noise, defined as anything added to the signal which was not intended by the sender. The signal-to-noise (S/N) ratio measures the quality of what passes through the communication channel. A high ratio would be shown by a clear signal with little degradation by noise, while a low ratio would be shown by a poor signal. The S/N ratio can be used to identify ways in which poor quality transmission could be rectified: it can be made higher either by increasing the strength of the signal (subject to the capacity of the channel itself) or by decreasing the strength of the noise (perhaps by improving the medium used by the communication channel). Where the S/N ratio cannot easily be changed, effective transmission is still possible by increasing the redundancy of the message through repeating elements of the text or through including words which could be deleted without removing the essential meaning. Thus a degree of degradation of signal still allows the message to be transmitted successfully. Prose text in any language is highly redundant, while users of instant messaging, short message service (SMS) texts and other text-based media have developed a great variety of shorthand forms which have much lower levels of redundancy.

Critiques of Transmission Models

Given the dominance of the focus on the message in corporate communi-cations, it is not surprising that transmission models (and in particular the Shannon and Weaver model) heavily inform both research and professional practice. However, transmission models are limited in a number of important ways, and their key assumptions have been subject to strong criticism (Heath and Bryant, 2000; Putnam, Phillips, and Chapman, 1996). The most obvious assumption is that communication is defined within the models as a linear process of messages from sender to receiver. The only role of feedback in these models is through reversing the roles of sender and receiver, in the same way that speakers take turns in a conversation. Thus the models cannot account for the turn-taking process itself or the ways in which the parties to a conversation actively respond to previous turns.

A second fundamental assumption of transmission models is that there is such a thing as the message which is knowingly present in the mind of a sender and is then encoded ('wrapped' like a parcel) for transmission and finally decoded ('unwrapped') by the receiver to reveal the intended message

(Reddy, 1979). This neglects the fact that the encoding transmission and decoding processes all contribute meaning and become intrinsically part of the message. For example, it is widely accepted that messages of high personal significance should be transmitted face to face. So, we are generally critical of using text messages to ask one's partner for a divorce or inform staff that they have been made redundant or that their salaries will not be paid for the month. The message is indeed in the medium as well as in the words themselves.

A third major assumption of transmission models is that only the sender of messages is active, and the role of the receiver is simply to receive and unwrap the message. This fundamental failing of such models has led to the development of a second approach which gives an active role to all participants.

Communication Flows as Co-creation of Meaning

So, communication is more than simply the transmission of messages between network members such that knowledge exists in network nodes and is passed as messages more or less well through linkages between them, but rather exists in the network itself and is co-constructed by network actors. Motion and Leitch (2002) argue that corporate communications needs to focus on 'the production of meanings' (p. 58) rather than the transmission of messages. Deetz (1992) proposes a participative approach to communication theorizing and suggests that 'this will require a consideration of the *production* of understanding through communication as distinct from the strategic *reproduction* of meaning' (p. 160). The role of communication is 'not so much to transmit one person's knowledge to others as to permit both together to construct interactively a basis of knowledge' (Taylor and van Every, 2000, p. 3). Major developments have also been made by organizational communication scholars such as those in the Montreal School (Cooren, Taylor, and Van Every, 2006; Taylor and van Every, 2000), but this research has yet to make a major impact within corporate communications.

One way in which these ideas have been applied is through rhetorical processes. Public relations scholar Robert Heath has long been an advocate of rhetoric, the theory and practice of persuasion, as a strong basis for understanding the dialogue between organizations and their stakeholders (Heath, 1994, 2001). Rhetorical processes consist of contested dialogue between organizations and those who have a stake in an issue through which shared meaning is co-created. The relative power of parties to a process of dialogue (and therefore the symmetry of their relationship) lies not so much in their size or their communications budgets but rather in the relative strength of their ideas which are contested publicly. From this perspective it is entirely appropriate that stakeholders speak out from their self-interested positions, and such advocacy is 'a necessary part of the process of co-creating meaning' (Heath, 2001, p. 32; see also L'Etang, 1996; Putnam and Fairhurst, 2001). Argenti and Forman (2000, p. 234) pose the question: '[H]ow can senior management use communication effectively to formulate strategy and to ensure that the strategy is implemented?' (see also Argenti, 1996), and they base their answer on two elements. The first is deliberative rhetoric, within which debate over alternative strategic positions for the organization leads to a process of emergence of a specific position through interaction between the organization and its stakeholders. The speaker creates a message collaboratively with the audience and communicates that message to the audience. The second element is a strong constituency focus, by which they mean the centrality of the audience to persuasive discourse. Stakeholder audiences have an important role for organizations as judges of their strategic plans, vision statements and key corporate actions. There is thus a key responsibility for organizational leaders to know how to motivate key internal and external stakeholders to engage in dialogue in order to help formulate, accept and implement the strategic change or vision that the leader advocates. Strategic positions should thus arise out of the contested dialogue of ideas, through a process of advocacy and critical listening, such that the strongest idea prevails.

Implications for Research

Fruitful avenues for future research will build on the Grunig symmetrical model of organization–stakeholder relationships and bring to it a focus on dialogue with stakeholders within which meanings emerge through co-construction processes. What is needed is a process approach similar to that which is already used widely within the strategy literature, but one which recognizes the dynamic and contested nature of meaning construction. It will need to recognize that communication flows are multilevel and meanings are co-created within and between levels.

BRINGING IT ALL TOGETHER: THE ORCHESTRATION OF COMMUNICATION

The Communication Challenge

The communication challenge that organizations face is now immensely greater, since the corporate function is not the sole means by which the organization communicates with its stakeholders. As Freeman (1984) put it, 'internal stakeholders must be seen as the conduit through which managers reach other external stakeholders.' (p. 18). Arguably this has always been the case, but organizational structures have undergone considerable change driven by a number of forces. The need for agility in responsiveness to technological change and environmental uncertainty leads to radical changes in internal organizational forms (Volberda, 1998) and boundaries are becoming unclear as organizations change from vertical, function-based structures to horizontal, process-based structures (Daft, 2001). Process-based forms of work organization have greatly weakened traditional definitions of jobs in terms of functional specialisms, and job descriptions are now much more fluid; workers are expected to do whatever it takes to get the job done (Parker, Wall, and Jackson, 1997). Employees are much more likely to deal directly with external stakeholders such as customers or suppliers, rather than have their communication mediated through a specialist function. There is less and less buffering of internal organizational actors (Pratt and Foreman, 2000), with insiders increasingly visible to outsiders to the extent that Kiriakidou and Millward (2000) conclude that 'the management of external relations is now an integral part of the daily life of nearly all organizational members' (p. 49).

More and more companies are seeking strategic alliances (Child and Faulkner, 1998), and so organizational employees may find themselves working more closely with members of another organization (which may even be a competitor) than with people inside their own organization. Such arrangements are enhanced by lean production systems (Womack and Jones, 2003) which depend heavily on long-term trusting relationships between members of supply chains. Companies are seeking to reduce the number of their suppliers, preferring close working relationships with fewer suppliers to competitive relationships among many. These patterns of working relationships are such that a company may have employees who work all of their time on the premises of a supplier, and a customer may have a much greater impact on working practices within a company (and therefore on employees) than the formal employer.

Similarly, outsourcing of support functions leads either to core elements of a company's business being provided externally (perhaps on sites alongside similar functions for other companies) or to employees of another organization working within a company's premises. An example of this can be seen in call centres. Call centres are an increasingly important way of using communication technology to provide flexibility of service to customers. In some organizations, such services are supplied by outsourcing the function to specialist suppliers, and advances in telephone and networking technology allow call centres to be located almost anywhere in the world. The role of employees in a call centre is particularly important, since they are often the only human contact between the customer and the organization. From this point of view, they are the custodians of the corporate brand. It is all the more surprising, therefore, that working conditions in call centres are so poor (Sprigg and Jackson, 2006), leading to them being described as 'electronic sweatshops' (D'Cruz and Noronha, 2007).

In a variety of ways, then, it is becoming less and less clear where organizational boundaries are, and thus harder and harder to exert control over the ways in which the organization communicates its messages to others. Organizational boundaries have become increasingly open to external scrutiny (Cross, Yan, and Louis, 2000). Furthermore, Hatch and Schultz (2002) note that organization boundaries are becoming more and more transparent as external stakeholders take a greater interest in their internal workings. The effects of these changes are many. First, the organization through its senior management is seen as having greater responsibility than before to account for how they work. Second, there is a greater responsibility on employees for how they represent the employing organization. Finally, it is no longer possible for the corporate communications function to act as an intermediary between the organization and its external stakeholders. It is no longer the gatekeeper which controls the organization's external messages. Instead, corporate communicators coordinate and integrate the actions of others in their management of relationships between the organization and its stakeholders. We next consider two aspects of the integration which is now required: first, the orchestration of internal organizational resources and second, the orchestration of messages with external stakeholders.

Orchestration of Organizational Resources

One of the major roles of strategic communication managers is to achieve an appropriate alignment among processes, systems, organizational elements in order to equip the organization to respond effectively to external challenges (Helfat et al., 2007, Chapter 3; Siggelkow, 2001). Communication is not just one of the key capabilities of an organization; it also plays a vital role in the deployment of other organizational capabilities. Communication between an organization and its stakeholders has been spread out among a wide variety of specialist functions, such as marketing, human resources, finance and media relations, each of which deals with specific stakeholder groups (Will, 2000). While this has some benefits through allowing the development of specialist knowledge of the characteristics of particular stakeholders, the great danger which has become increasingly clear is the fragmentation that it leads to and the potential for inconsistency and contradiction in messages sent and received. Such a differentiation is now untenable, and indeed Cheney and Christensen (2001) propose that internal and external communications no longer constitute separate fields of practice. Similarly, Will (2000) argues for a new professional discipline of communications management, which he sees as a part of strategic management: 'a holistic approach to managing a company's communication requirements with all external and internal targets and intermediaries' (p. 46).

Orchestration of Messages

Integration is about consistency of messages to different stakeholder groups and a primary role for communication managers is the coordination of those messages to achieve the desired corporate goals. However, the *integration* concept presupposes that organizations can control their messages and speak through only limited voices: those of the CEO or of specialist communicators representing the organization. Similarly, organizations need to ensure consistency in the messages they send to their external stakeholders. Between-level consistency refers to whether CEO-level messages about corporate performance are matched by the communications of specialist functions and individual employees within the company. The Gerald Ratner's infamous 'joke' in a speech at the UK Institute of Directors in 1991 that his products were 'crap' clearly undermined what his sales employees were saying to customers in their efforts to sell those same products. The consequence was a severe loss of confidence in the company, which soon after went out of business, and it took Ratner many years to relaunch himself successfully. An example of within-level inconsistency was reported by van Riel (1995) from *Het Financieele Dagblad* (the Dutch *Financial Times*) on 25 November 1989. The tobacco company BAT placed an advertisement aimed at shareholders extolling a 22% increase in profits. On the front page of the same issue was the announcement of the closure of a cigarette factory in Amsterdam with the loss of 123 jobs. The co-occurrence of these two articles in the same issue of the newspaper presented a clear but unintended message of a company making profits on the backs of employees losing their jobs.

The scope of activities which fall under the heading of corporate communications has expanded considerably that it now includes much more than corporate messages in the form of press releases or annual reports. Organizations express themselves in many ways and use diverse media: accounting practices express the organization as 'ethical', human resource practices express the organization as a 'good' employer, waste management practices express the organization as 'green' and business relationships with suppliers express the organization as 'responsible'. In each of these respects, an organization communicates through what it does and how it does it, and thereby says something about what kind of organization it is. For these reasons, efforts to channel all communication through a single function are doomed to failure. Instead, Gronstedt (1996) and van Riel (2000) argue that the role of communications is to coordinate the messages that organizations send across all levels to their stakeholder groups. However, technological change makes it impossible to control how different parts of an organization communicate with their diverse stakeholders. Indeed, Christensen, Morsing, and Cheney (2008) and Hazen (1993) suggest that organizations consist of multiple dialogues or polyphonic voices which cannot be controlled or integrated into a single 'voice'. An organization then can be thought of as an orchestra with many instruments, each of which is playing its own part of the total melody. The artistic merit of a piece of music lies in large part on both diversity in the different parts and the ways in which harmony among them is achieved (Christensen, Firat, and Torp, 2008).

Communications technologies now offered many more media, and the Internet has made unmediated communication much easier – consumers and citizens can now get information directly from sources without it being channeled through broadcast or print media. Organizations have taken advantage of these new technologies by changing their internal architecture such that boundaries (internally and externally) are now both different in kind and more porous. The consequence of these changes is that organizations no longer communicate with their stakeholders primarily through professional communicators; rather, all employees are now communicators with a responsibility for how the identity of the organization is expressed through their actions. The concept of the expressive organization is a powerful means of emphasizing that organizations compete on the basis of their ability to express who they are and what they stand for (Schultz, Hatch, and Larsen, 2000). Building on this concept, Jackson (2006) proposed a model of the holographic organization, which offers that a deeper approach to orchestration is to think in terms of coherence of values within the organization.

The Holographic Metaphor

The increased fluidity of organizational boundaries creates much greater internal complexity, which brings with it higher management costs and greater risk of disjointedness or incoherence (Pratt and Foreman, 2000), where the experience of a specific stakeholder of the organization is quite different in different places and at different times. Jackson (2006) uses the metaphor of the hologram to express the importance of a holistic approach to relationships with external stakeholders. The hologram is a special form of photographic image which uses laser light to record an image as an interference pattern on a light-sensitive plate. Parts of a normal photographic negative have a one-to-one correspondence to the original object, while each part of the interference pattern for the holographic image contains information about the whole object. In a hologram, therefore, the whole is enfolded in every component part just as every human cell contains all of the genetic code for the whole human body. The individual parts of the holographic image are not redundant: the picture recreated from one small part of a holographic image of, for example, a vase of flowers contains less detail than that from the whole image and from a different point of view. Nevertheless, what we get is a vase containing a bunch of flowers, not just one daisy.

Applying the holographic metaphor to organizations implies an integrated approach to corporate communications within which the same fundamental values are expressed throughout the organization's culture (Hatch and Schultz, 2002). One basis for the holographic organization is the concept of Common Starting Points (CSPs: van Riel, 1995): 'central values which function as the basis for undertaking any kinds of communication envisaged by an organization. Establishing CSPs is particularly useful in creating clear priorities, e.g. to facilitate an eventual control and evaluation of the total communication policy' (p. 185). The CSP notion is extended by Motion and Leitch (2002) by their idea of multiple identity enactments. Shared employee identification with a set of core values does not imply that employees are clones or that every employee needs to behave in a uniform way. Rather, it means that the same common values are embodied perhaps in very different but appropriate ways throughout the organization. For example, an organization may have putting customers first as a core value. A design engineer could express that value by focusing primarily on what customers look for in a new product. Sales staff might express the same value by ensuring that customer needs are explored thoroughly before advice is given on choice of product. Dispatchers may seek to identify the delivery mode which best suits the lifestyle of the customer. The same fundamental values can thus be expressed throughout the organization, but in very different ways using the diverse skill sets that employees possess. Although these employees share the same values, they are not substitutable one for another and cannot be considered as clones.

CONCLUDING REMARKS

We have seen that organizations are multilevel entities and that communications between organizations and their external stakeholders take place at multiple levels and not just at the corporate level. Organizations seek to achieve their strategic objectives by acting within networks of stakeholders and their success in so doing depends fundamentally on the quality of the relationships that they maintain with salient stakeholder groups. However, the linkages between strategy, communication and performance have not been explicated precisely and this is a key priority for future research. Efforts to fill this gap will need to draw upon the recent developments in the strategic management literature emphasizing the microfoundations of organizational capabilities and are likely to require a synthesis of hitherto disparate literatures on strategy content and strategy process. Future programs will also need to use more complex multilevel research designs (Drnevich and Shanley, 2005) to capture both organization-level features of network communities and the nuances of intraorganization communication processes. Such research will also require the use of analytical methods which are currently unfamiliar to most management scholars (Walls and Schafer, 2005).

Researcher will also need to venture outside the comfort of their disciplinary boundaries in order to make progress in this multilevel adventure. For the most part, economists tend to work at the firm level, while psychologists are most familiar with individual- or group-level constructs. The dangers of this narrowness are threefold. First, those who work exclusively within a level of analysis end up (either by deliberate choice or out of ignorance) making sweeping assumptions about phenomena at other levels which are likely to be at least partly erroneous. Second, scholarly communities develop their own technical terms which acquire constellations of meaning that are helpful to insiders but can be dangerously misleading when outsiders use them. The dangers lay both in scholars using the same terms but defining them differently and in using different terms for the same phenomena. The third danger of continuing to operate within disciplinary silos is that causal influences do not exclusively run within the levels each of us is familiar with, so we are in grave danger of missing the most important aspects of what we seek to understand. As I have argued elsewhere (Jackson, 2005), there is strong potential for rewarding progress for those who are able to build diverse research communities. Just as organizations can protect and promote their competitive advantage through fruitful dialogues with their immense array of stakeholders, so scholars who seek to link together strategy, corporate communications and financial performance will need to work together in the pursuit of novel theoretical perspectives.

REFERENCES

Abell, P., Felin, T., & Foss, N. (2008). Building micro-foundations for the routines, capabilities, and performance links. *Managerial and Decision Economics*, **29**, 489–502.

Argenti, P.A. (1996). Corporate communication as a discipline. *Management Communication Quarterly*, **10**(1), 73–97.

Argenti, P.A., & Forman, J. (2000). The communication advantage: A constituency-focused approach to formulating and implementing strategy. In M. Schultz, M.J. Hatch & M. Holten Larsen (Eds), *The Expressive Organization: Linking Identity, Reputation and the Corporate Brand* (pp. 233–245). Oxford: Oxford University Press.

Barney, J.B. (1991). Firm resources and sustained competitive advantage. *Journal of Management*, **17**, 99–120.

Barney, J.B., & Clark, D.N. (2007). *Resource-Based Theory: Creating and Sustaining Competitive Advantage*. Oxford: Oxford University Press.

Berlo, D. (1960). *The Process of Communication*. New York: Holt, Rinehart and Winston, Inc.

Berman, S.L., Wicks, A.C., Kotha, S., & Jones, T.M. (1999). Does stakeholder orientation matter? The relationship between stakeholder management models and firm financial performance. *Academy of Management Journal*, **42**(5), 488–506.

Brass, D.J. (1995). A social network perspective on human resources management. *Research in Personnel and Human Resources Management*, **13**, 39–79.

Burnes, B. (2004). *Managing Change: A Strategic Approach to Organizational Dynamics* (4th Ed.). Harlow, UK: Pearson.

Cameron, G.T., Cropp, F., & Reber, B.H. (2001). Getting past platitudes: Factors limiting accommodation in public relations. *Journal of Communication Management*, **5**(3), 242–61.

Cancel, A.E., Cameron, G.T., Sallot, L.M., & Mitrook, M.A. (1997). A contingency theory of accommodation in public relations. *Journal of Public Relations Research*, **9**(1), 31–63.

Cancel, A.E., Mitrook, M.A., & Cameron, G.T. (1999). Testing the contingency theory of accommodation in public relations. *Public Relations Review*, 25(2), 171–97.

Cheney, G., & Christensen, L.T. (2001). Organizational identity: Linkages between internal and external communication. In F.M. Jablin & L.L. Putnam (Eds), *The New Handbook of Organizational Communication: Advances in Theory, Research, and Practice* (pp. 231–69). Thousand Oaks: Sage.

Child, J., & Faulkner, D. (1998). *Strategies of Cooperation: Managing Alliances, Networks, and Joint Ventures*. Oxford: Oxford University Press.

Christensen, L.T., Firat, A.F., & Torp, S. (2008). The organization of integrated communications: toward flexible integration. *European Journal of Marketing*, 42(3–4), 423–52.

Christensen, L.T., Morsing, M., & Cheney, G. (2008). *Corporate Communications: Convention, Complexity, and Critique*. London: Sage.

Clarkson, M. (1995). A stakeholder framework for analysing and evaluating corporate social performance. *Academy of Management Review*, 20(1), 92–117.

Coombs, W.T. (1999). *Ongoing Crisis Communication: Planning, Managing, and Responding*. Thousand Oaks: Sage.

Cooren, F., Taylor, J.R., & Van Every, E.J. (Eds). (2006). *Communication as Organizing: Empirical and Theoretical Explorations in the Dynamic of text and Conversation*. Mahwah, New Jersey: Lawrence Erlbaum Associates.

Cornelissen, J. (2008). *Corporate Communication: A Guide to Theory and Practice* (2nd Ed.). London: Sage.

Cross, R.L., Yan, A.M., & Louis, M.R. (2000). Boundary activities in 'boundaryless' organizations: A case study of a transformation to a team-based structure. *Human Relations*, 53(6), 841–68.

D'Cruz, P., & Noronha, E. (2007). Technical call centres: Beyond 'electronic sweatshops' and 'assembly lines in the head'. *Global Business Review*, 8(1), 53–67.

Daft, R.L. (2001). *Organization Theory and Design* (7th Ed.). Cincinnati, OH: South-Western College Publishing.

Deephouse, D.L., & Heugens, P. (2009). Linking social issues to organizational impact: The role of infomediaries and the onfomediary process. *Journal of Business Ethics*, 86(4), 541–53.

Deetz, S.A. (1992). *Democracy in an Age of Corporate Colonization: Developments in Communication and the Politics of Everyday Life*. Albany, NY: State University of New York Press.

Deetz, S.A., Tracy, S.J., & Simpson, J.L. (2000). *Leading Organizations through Transition: Communication and Cultural Change*. Thousand Oaks: Sage.

Dewar, S., & Boddington, P. (2004). Returning to the Alder Hey report and its reporting: addressing confusions and improving inquiries. *Journal of Medical Ethics*, 30, 463–9.

Dicken, P. (2003). *Global Shift: Reshaping the Global Economic Map in the 21st Century* (4th Ed.). London: Sage.

Donaldson, T., & Preston, L.E. (1995). The stakeholder theory of the corporation: Concepts, evidence and implications. *Academy of Management Journal*, 20, 65–91.

Dozier, D., Grunig, L.A., & Grunig, J.E. (1995). *Manager's Guide to Excellence in Public Relations and Communication Management*. Hillsdale, NJ: Lawrence Erlbaum Associates.

Drnevich, P., & Shanley, M. (2005). Multi-level issues for strategic management research: Implications for creating value and competitive advantage. In F.J. Yammarino & F. Dansereau (Eds), *Multi-Level Issues in Strategy and Methods* (Vol. 4, pp. 117–61). Stamford, CT: JAI Press.

Eden, C., & Ackerman, F. (1998). *Making Strategy: The Journey of Strategic Change.* London: Sage.

El Sawy, O.A., & Pauchant, T.C. (1988). Triggers, templates and twitches in the tracking of emerging strategic issues. *Strategic Management Journal,* **9**, 455–74.

Entman, R.M. (1991). Framing US coverage of international news: Contrasts in narratives of KAL and Iran Air incidents. *Journal of Communication,* **41**(4), 6–27.

Etzioni, A. (1964). *Modern Organizations.* Englewood Cliffs, NJ: Prentice-Hall.

Fassin, Y. (2008). Imperfections and shortcomings of the stakeholder model's graphical representation. *Journal of Business Ethics,* **80**(4), 879–88.

Ferrary, M. (2009). A stakeholder's perspective on human resource management. *Journal of Business Ethics,* **87**(1), 31–43.

Fombrun, C.J., & Rindova, V.P. (2000). The road to transparency: Reputation management at Royal Dutch/Shell. In M. Schultz, M.J. Hatch & M. Holten Larsen (Eds), *The Expressive Organization: Linking Identity, Reputation, and the Corporate Brand* (pp. 77–96). Oxford: Oxford University Press.

Freeman, R.E. (1984). *Strategic Management: A Stakeholder Approach.* London: Pitman.

Freeman, R.E. (1999). Divergent stakeholder theory – response. *Academy of Management Review,* **24**(2), 233–6.

Friedman, M. (1970), September 30. The social responsibility of business is to increase its profits. *New York Times Magazine,* September 13

Frooman, J. (1999). Stakeholder influence strategies. *Academy of Management Review,* **24**(2), 191–205.

Gerbner, G. (1956). Toward a general model of communication. *Educational Technology Research and Development,* **4**(3), 177–99.

Goodman, M.B. (2000). Corporate communication: The American picture. *Corporate Communications: An International Journal,* **6**(2), 69–74.

Gronstedt, A. (1996). Integrated communications at America's leading total quality management corporations. *Public Relations Review,* **22**(1), 25–42.

Grunig, J.E. (1992). Communication, public relations, and effective organizations: an overview of the book. In J.E. Grunig, D. Dozier, W. Ehling, L.A. Grunig, F. Repper & J. White (Eds), *Excellence in Public Relations and Communication Management* (pp. 1–28). Hillsdale, NJ: Lawrence Erlbaum Associates.

Grunig, J.E., Dozier, D., Ehling, W., Grunig, L.A., Repper, F., & White, J. (Eds). (1992). *Excellence in Public Relations and Communication Management.* Hillsdale, NJ: Lawrence Erlbaum Associates.

Grunig, J.E., & Grunig, L.A. (1992). Models of public relations and communication. In J.E. Grunig, D. Dozier, W. Ehling, L.A. Grunig, F. Repper & J. White (Eds), *Excellence in Public Relations and Communication Management* (pp. 285–326). Hillsdale, NJ: Erlbaum.

Grunig, J.E., & Huang, Y.-H. (2000). From organisational effectiveness to relationship indicators: Antecedents of relationships, public relations strategies, and relationship outcomes. In J.A. Ledingham & S.D. Bruning (Eds), *Relationship Management: A Relational Approach to Public Relations* (pp. 23–53). Mahwah, NJ: Erlbaum.

Grunig, J.E., & Hunt, T. (1984). *Managing Public Relations.* Fort Worth: Holt, Rinehart and Winston.

Grunig, L.A. (2000). Public relations research: A tripartite model. *Corporate Communications: An International Journal,* **5**, 69–74.

Grunig, L.A., Grunig, J.E., & Dozier, D. (2002). *Excellent Public Relations and Effective Organizations: A Study of Communication Management in Three Countries.* Mahwah, NJ: Lawrence Erlbaum Associates.

Hatch, M.J., & Schultz, M. (2002). The dynamics of organizational identity. *Human Relations,* **55**(8), 989–1018.

Hazen, M.A. (1993). Towards polyphonic organization. *Journal of Organizational Change Management*, 6(5), 15–26.

Heath, R.L. (1994). *Management of Corporate Communication: From Interpersonal Contact to External Affairs*. London: Lawrence Erlbaum Associates.

Heath, R.L. (2001). A rhetorical enactment rationale for public relations. In R.L. Heath (Ed.), *Handbook of Public Relations* (pp. 31–50). Thousand Oaks, CA: Sage.

Heath, R.L., & Bryant, J. (2000). *Human Communication Theory and Research: Concepts, Contexts and Challenges* (2nd Ed.). Mahwah, New Jersey: Lawrence Erlbaum Associates.

Helfat, C.E., Finkelstein, S., Mitchell, W., *et al.* (2007). *Dynamic Capabilities: Understanding Strategic Change in Organizations*. Malden, MA: Blackwell Publishing.

Jackson, P.R. (2005). Indigenous theorising in a complex world. *Asian Journal of Social Psychology*, 8, 51–64.

Jackson, P.R. (2006). Working in glass houses: Managing the complex organization. In P.R. Jackson & M. Shams (Eds), *Developments in Work and Organizational Psychology* (pp. 245–266). Oxford: Elsevier.

Jin, Y., & Cameron, G.T. (2006). Scale development for measuring stance as degree of accommodation. *Public Relations Review*, 32(4), 423–5.

Jones, T.M., & Wicks, A.C. (1999). Convergent stakeholder theory. *Academy of Management Review*, 24(2), 206–21.

Kahane, A. (2004). *Solving Tough Problems: An Open Way of Talking, Listening, and Creating New Realities*. San Francisco: Berret-Koehler Publisher, Inc.

Kauffman, S. (1993). *The Origins of Order*. Oxford: Oxford University Press.

Kiriakidou, O., & Millward, L.J. (2000). Corporate identity: External reality or internal fit? *Corporate Communications: An International Journal*, 5(1), 49–58.

Klein, K.J., & Kozlowski, S.W.J. (2000). From micro to meso: Critical steps in conceptualizing and conducting multilevel research. *Organizational Research Methods*, 3(3), 211–36.

L'Etang, J. (1996). Public relations and rhetoric. In J. L'Etang & M. Pieczka (Eds), *Critical Perspectives in Public Relations* (pp. 106–23). London: International Thompson Business Press.

Ledingham, J.A., & Bruning, S.D. (Eds). (2000). *Public Relations as Relationship Management: A Relational Approach to the Study and Practice of Public Relations*. Mahwah, New Jersey: Lawrence Erlbaum Associates.

Mitchell, R.K., Agle, B.R., & Wood, D.J. (1997). Toward a theory of stakeholder identification and salience: Defining the principle of who and what really counts. *Academy of Management Review*, 22(4), 853–86.

Monge, P.R., & Contractor, N. (2003). *Theories of Communication Networks*. New York: Oxford University Press.

Monge, P.R., & Poole, M.S. (2008). The evolution of organizational communication. *Journal of Communication*, 58(4), 679–92.

Motion, J., & Leitch, S. (2002). The technologies of corporate identity. *International Journal of Management and Organization*, 32(3), 45–64.

Murphy, P. (1991). The limits of symmetry: A game theory approach to symmetric and asymmetric public relations. *Public Relations Research Annual*, 3, 115–31.

Murphy, P. (2000). Symmetry, contingency, complexity: Accommodating uncertainty in public relations theory. *Public Relations Review*, 26(4), 447–62.

Nelson, R.R., & Winter, S.G. (1982). *The Evolutionary Theory of the Firm*. Cambridge, MA: Harvard University Press.

Neville, B.A., & Menguc, B. (2006). Stakeholder multiplicity: Toward an understanding of the interactions between stakeholders. *Journal of Business Ethics*, 66(4), 377–91.

Parker, S.K., Wall, T.D., & Jackson, P.R. (1997). "That's not my job": Developing flexible employee work orientations. *Academy of Management Journal*, 40, 899–929.

Pratt, M.G., & Foreman, P.O. (2000). Classifying managerial responses to multiple organizational identities. *Academy of Management Review*, 25(1), 18–42.

Putnam, L.L., & Fairhurst, G.T. (2001). Discourse analysis in organizations: Issues and concerns. In F.M. Jablin & L.L. Putnam (Eds), *The New Handbook of Organizational Communication: Advances in Theory, Research, and Methods* (pp. 78–136). Thousand Oaks: Sage.

Putnam, L.L., Phillips, N., & Chapman, P. (1996). Metaphors of communication and organization. In S.R. Clegg, C. Hardy & W.R. Nord (Eds), *Handbook of Organizational Studies* (pp. 375–408). London: Sage.

Reber, B.H., & Cameron, G.T. (2003). Measuring contingencies: Using scales to measure public relations practitioner limits to accommodation. *Journalism and Mass Communication Quarterly*, 80(2), 431–46.

Reddy, M.J. (1979). The conduit metaphor: a case of frame conflict in our language about language. In A. Ortony (Ed.), *Metaphor and Thought* (pp. 284–324). Cambridge: Cambridge University Press.

Rees, S.D., Gandy, O.H., & Grant, A.E. (Eds). (2001). *Framing Public Life: Perspectives on Media and Our Understanding of the Social World*. Mahwah, New Jersey: Lawrence Erlbaum Associates.

Roloff, J. (2008). Learning from multi-stakeholder networks: Issue-focussed stakeholder management. *Journal of Business Ethics*, 82(1), 233–50.

Rowley, T.J. (1997). Moving beyond dyadic ties: A network theory of stakeholder influences. *Academy of Management Review*, 22(4), 887–910.

Salancik, G., & Pfeffer, J. (1974). The bases and uses of power in organizational decision making: The case of a university. *Administrative Science Quarterly*, 19, 453–73.

Schramm, W. (1955). *The Process and Effects of Man Communication*. Illinois: University of Illinois Press.

Schultz, M., Hatch, M.J., & Larsen, M.H. (Eds). (2000). *The Expressive Organization: Linking Identity, Reputation and the Corporate Brand*. Oxford: Oxford University Press.

Shannon, C.E., & Weaver, W. (1949). *The Mathematical Theory of Communication*. Urbana, IL: University of Illinois Press.

Shin, J.-H., Cameron, G.T., & Cropp, F. (2006). Occam's razor in the contingency theory: A national survey on 86 contingent variables. *Public Relations Review*, 32, 282–6.

Siggelkow, N. (2001). Change in the presence of fit: The rise, the fall, and the renaissance of Liz Claiborne. *Academy of Management Journal*, 44(4), 838–57.

Sprigg, C.A., & Jackson, P.R. (2006). Call centers as lean service environments: Well-being and the mediating role of work design. *Journal of Occupational Health Psychology*, 11(2), 197–212.

Suchman, M.C. (1995). Managing legitimacy: Strategic and institutional approaches. *Academy of Management Review*, 20, 571–610.

Taylor, J.R., & van Every, E.J. (2000). *The Emergent Organization: Communication as Its Site and Surface*. New York: Psychology Press.

Teece, D.J. (2007). Explicating dynamic capabilities: The nature and microfoundations of (sustainable) enterprise performance. *Strategic Management Journal*, 28(13), 1319–50.

Toth, E.L. (Ed.). (2007). *The Future of Excellence in Public Relations and Communication Management: Challenges for the Next Generation*. Mahwah, New Jersey: Laurence Erlbaum Associates.

Tucker, M.L., Meyer, G.D., & Westerman, J.W. (1996). Organizational communication: development of internal strategic competitive advantage. *The Journal of Business Communication*, **33**(1), 51–69.

van Exel, A., & Fisher, S. (2005). Winning support for United's new airline. *Strategic Communication Management*, **9**(2), 22–5.

van Riel, C.B.M. (1995). *Principles of Corporate Communication*. London: Prentice Hall.

van Riel, C.B.M. (2000). Corporate communication orchestrated by a sustainable corporate story. In M. Schultz, M.J. Hatch & M.H. Larsen (Eds), *The Expressive Organization: Linking Identity, Reputation and the Corporate Brand* (pp. 157–81). Oxford: Oxford University Press.

Volberda, H.W. (1998). Toward the flexible form: How to remain vital in hypercompetitive environments. In A.Y. Ilinitch, A.Y. Lewin & R. D'Aveni (Eds), *Managing in Times of Disorder: Hypercompetitive Organizational Responses* (pp. 267–96). Thousand Oaks: Sage.

Walls, T.A. & Schafer, J.L. (Eds). (2005). *Models for Intensive Longitudinal Data*. Oxford: Oxford University Press.

Weick, K.E. (1995). *Sensemaking in Organizations*. Thousand Oaks, CA: Sage.

Wei-Skillern, J. (2004). The evolution of shell's stakeholder approach: A case study. *Business Ethics Quarterly*, **14**(4), 713–28.

Welch, M., & Jackson, P.R. (2007). Rethinking internal communication: Dimensions and definitions. *Corporate Communications: An International Journal*, **12**(2), 177–98.

Wernerfelt, B. (1984). A resource-based view of the firm. *Strategic Management Journal*, **5**(3), 171–80.

Whitley, R. (2007). *Business Systems and Organizational Capabilities*. Oxford: Oxford University Press.

Will, M. (2000). Why communications management? *Journal of Media Management*, **2**, 46–53.

Womack, J.P., & Jones, D.T. (2003). *Lean Thinking: Banish Waste and Create Wealth in Your Corporation* (2nd Ed.). New York: Free Press

Chapter 4

THE STATE OF PLAY IN COACHING TODAY: A COMPREHENSIVE REVIEW OF THE FIELD

Anthony M. Grant, Michael J. Cavanagh and Helen M. Parker
School of Psychology, University of Sydney, Australia

Jonathan Passmore
School of Psychology, University of East London, UK

Over the past decade workplace and executive coaching has grown from a relatively novel intervention to a mainstream developmental activity in organizations worldwide. The annual revenue expended on corporate coaching has been estimated to be in the region of US$1.5 billion and in 2006 it was estimated that there were approximately 30,000 professional coaches globally (International Coach Federation; ICF, 2006); the figures are probably higher today. In the US, 93% of US-based Global 100 companies use executive coaches (Bono *et al.*, 2009). In the UK 88% of organizations use coaching (Jarvis, Lane, and Fillery-Travis, 2005). In Australia 64% of business leaders and 72% of senior managers report using coaches (Leadership Management Australia, 2006). Seventy-one per cent of these Australian respondents also stated that having a coach was an important factor in their decision to stay with their organizations.

This rapid growth in organizational demand for coaching has presented both challenges and opportunities for industrial and organizational (I/O) psychologists and for the broader psychological enterprise. First, even though coaching focuses on individual and/or organizational change (a key focus of behavioural science), the majority of individuals offering coaching services to organizations are not psychologists or behavioural scientists (Grant and Zackon, 2004). The majority of coaches practicing today do not use theoretically coherent approaches and scientifically validated techniques and measures (Grant and O'Hara, 2006). Interestingly, while psychologists' training would

International Review of Industrial and Organizational Psychology, 2010, Volume 25.
Edited by G. P. Hodgkinson and J. K. Ford. Copyright © 2010 John Wiley & Sons, Ltd

appear to equip them ideally for the delivery of coaching services, psychologists have not been seen as uniquely qualified coaching practitioners – either within the coaching industry or by the purchasers of coaching services (Garman, Whiston, and Zlatoper, 2000). Nevertheless, we believe that psychologists have much to offer the field of coaching. Their training as scientist practitioners, their critical-thinking skills and understandings of validated change methodologies, coupled with a long-standing tradition of research and a sound theoretical knowledge base can bring much needed rigour to the coaching arena (for a discussion of the application of the scientist practitioner model in coaching see Cavanagh and Grant, 2006).

In this review we draw on our past scholarship in this area (Grant and Cavanagh, 2007; Grant and Cavanagh, in press; Passmore and Gibbes, 2007) to provide an extensive overview of the state of play in relation to coaching research and practice. We review the professional status of coaching and the various bodies that seek to accredit and organize coaches and the coaching industry. We highlight the development of coaching psychology as an up-and-coming psychological subdiscipline, including a review of the research into the efficacy of coaching and presentation of ideas for a future research agenda. The links between I/O psychology, positive psychology and Positive Organizational Scholarship (POS) are discussed in relation to organizational coaching and we present a model that can guide organizational coaching practice by integrating workplace engagement and well-being. In conclusion, we outline some potential lines of inquiry for future work in this emerging and exciting subfield of psychological research and practice.

UNDERSTANDING COACHING

Definitions of coaching vary but most are underpinned by a view of coaching as a collaborative relationship formed between coach and coachee for the purpose of attaining professional or personal development outcomes which are valued by the coachee (for a recent discussion, see Spence and Grant, 2007). Typically, the coaching goals are set to stretch and develop an individual's current capacity or performance. In essence the coaching process facilitates goal attainment by helping individuals to: (1) identify desired outcomes, (2) establish specific goals, (3) enhance motivation by identifying strengths and building self-efficacy, (4) identify resources and formulate specific action plans, (5) monitor and evaluate progress towards goals, and (6) modify action plans on the basis of feedback.

The 'monitor–evaluate–modify' steps of this process constitute a simple cycle of self-regulated behaviour. This is a key process in creating intentional behaviour change (Carver and Scheier, 1998). The role of the coach is to facilitate the coachee's movement through this self-regulatory cycle by helping the coachee develop specific action plans and then to monitor and evaluate progression towards those goals.

Coaching is a broadly applied human change methodology and has been applied across many areas, including: workplace stress reduction (Wright, 2007); business coaching (Clegg *et al.*, 2005); communication and leadership skills (Wilson, 2004); career development (Scandura, 1992); team building and group development (Cunha and Louro, 2000); improving sales skills and performance (Rich, 1998) and coaching to improve performance in job interviews (Maurer, Solamon, and Troxtel, 1998).

SKILLS, PERFORMANCE AND DEVELOPMENTAL COACHING

Coaching applications can be categorized under one of three main categories: skills coaching, performance coaching and developmental coaching (Witherspoon and White, 1996).

Skills' coaching focuses on developing a specific, designated skill set. The coach often models the required skills and behaviour and coaching sessions then involve a rehearsal and feedback process. For example, skills' coaching may be used for improving skills in areas such as: presentation, communication and sales skills or preparation for negotiations.

Performance coaching is concerned with improving performance over a specific timeframe; ranging from just a few weeks to several years in workplace settings. Performance coaching focuses on the processes by which the coachee sets goals, overcomes obstacles and evaluates and monitors his or her performance over a period of time. Performance coaching is somewhat more strategic than skills coaching, and in the workplace may take place following a performance review or in relation to a specific workplace project.

Developmental coaching also takes a broader strategic approach and deals with the individual's personal and professional development. Developmental coaching refers to coaching aimed at enhancing the individual's ability to meet current and future challenges more effectively via the development of increasingly complex understanding of the self, others and the systems in which the person is involved. This kind of coaching may focus on facilitating perspective taking and meaning making, enhancing emotional competencies and working more effectively with team members. Developmental coaching often involves the creation of personal reflective spaces where coachees can explore issues and options and formulate action plans in a confidential, supportive environment. The majority of leadership and executive coaching is primarily developmental in nature.

As discussed later in this chapter, the competencies and skills of effective coaches may vary somewhat across the three types of coaching. In skills coaching, the emphasis may be on the coach's ability to role model the required behaviours and provide supportive and detailed behavioural feedback to the coachee. For performance coaching, the coach may need to be more competent in root cause analysis, problem solving, action planning and goal setting skills, besides being able to manage the coachee's performance over a specific timeframe. Development coaching requires the coach to possess greater competence in the intra- and interpersonal domains, superior active listening and reflection skills and the ability to help coachees explore more personal aspects of their work or personal lives.

It is important to note that these three types of coaching are not discrete or discontinuous categories; there is considerable overlap between them. For example, a coaching intervention focusing on enhancing presentation skills for an introverted coachee would have a substantial developmental element. Conversely, a developmental coaching programme, focusing on developing leadership competencies may include some skills coaching. Nevertheless this tripartite subdivision is a useful heuristic for understanding both the nature of individual coaching sessions and whole coaching engagements.

EXECUTIVE AND WORKPLACE COACHING

Coaching in the workplace is conducted at all levels of an organization. *Executive coaching* encompasses a vast range of services and specialties, including coaching for enhanced strategic planning, presentation skills, anger and stress management, executive management team building and leadership development. Kilburg (1996) defines executive coaching as:

> A helping relationship formed between a client who has managerial authority and responsibility in an organization and a consultant who uses a wide variety of behavioural techniques and methods to help the client achieve a mutually identified set of goals to improve his or her professional performance and personal satisfaction and, consequently, to improve the effectiveness of the client's organization within a formally defined coaching agreement" (p. 138).

Executive coaching is primarily developmental interwoven with skills and performance coaching components. It is most often delivered by *external coaching* providers, that is, by professional coaches who are not part of the client organization. Typically, external coaching providers tend to offer a combination of training, consultancy and coaching, rather than just coaching services (Binstead and Grant, 2008; Clegg *et al.*, 2005). These services include coaching for workplace safety behaviours (Geller, Perdue, and French, 2004), life coaching for work–life balance (Sparrow, 2007), leadership development and executive coaching (Kilburg, 1996).

Workplace coaching includes both executive coaching and coaching that is delivered to nonexecutive employees in workplace settings. Workplace coaching may be delivered by external coaching providers or may be an internal coaching intervention, delivered by employees specially designated as occupying a coaching role (often human resources or learning and development [L&D] personnel). There is some debate as to whether the 'manager as coach' should be included within the category of formal workplace coaching. We hold that formal coaching should be distinguished from the intermittent use of coaching skills by line managers in the normal execution of their managerial duties. Hence, impromptu or 'corridor coaching' by managers is an example of the use of coaching skills in the workplace, rather than formal workplace coaching. Nevertheless the training of managers in coaching skills and their use in the workplace represents a significant contribution to rise coaching in the workplace.

Organizations tend to use a combination of both external and internal coaching approaches. One UK survey found that 51% of UK organizations used external coaches, 41% trained their own internal coaches and 79% used managers to coach employees (Kubicek, 2002). Given that coaching is currently so widely used in the workplace, what is the professional status of coaching?

THE PROFESSIONAL STATUS OF COACHING: ACCREDITATIONS AND INDUSTRY ORGANIZATIONS

When judged against the commonly accepted criteria for professional status, the coaching industry displays few of the standard hallmarks. There are no barriers to entry, no minimal or requisite educational process or specified training routes and no binding ethical or practice standards (Sherman and Freas, 2004). Anyone can claim to be a coach, or set up a coach training school and coaching practice is currently unregulated. In response, and calling for greater scientific and professional rigour in coaching, Seligman (2007, p. 266) has commented:

> People who call themselves coaches and get paid for coaching have an enormous range of academic qualifications from none at all to bachelor's degrees in almost anything, to masters degrees in counselling, education, social work, or positive psychology, to doctorates in psychology, medicine, and philosophy... Some have taken face-to-face or telecourses in coaching, but many have not. Some are "accredited" by the self-appointed International Coach Federation ... but most are not. The right to call oneself a coach is unregulated. And this is why a scientific and a theoretical backbone ... (is essential).

The accreditation of coaches is controversial. Much of the coach training industry appears to have been driven by a need for credibility and status and the demand for 'accreditation' by people who wish to work as coaches (Grant and Cavanagh, 2004). Over time, a veritable global 'coach certification' industry has developed. Indeed, some coach training organizations seem to be little more than credentialing 'mills'; that is, after a brief attendance at a training programme – in- person, online or even over the phone, (and after payment of the requisite fee), one can be awarded the title of 'Professional Certified Master Coach' or similar (Grant and O'Hara, 2006). Not surprisingly, the true worth of these certifications is decidedly questionable. This is an important issue because the general public is not well-informed about the value of bona fide psychological qualifications, let alone coaching qualifications and may rely on impressive-sounding titles to guide them in coach selection. Furthermore, naïve trainee coaches may be misled into believing that certifications awarded by an impressive-sounding 'certification board' are a guarantee of solid professional training.

However, some of the larger coaching organizations such as the European Mentoring and Coaching Council (EMCC; Brussels based, over 3,000 members) and the International Coach Federation (ICF; US based, 15,000 members in nearly 90 countries) have put significant effort into establishing credentialing processes and developing coaching competencies, both individually and collectively.

Globally, and particularly in the US and Australia, some commercial and government organizations now require as a condition of employment, that external coaches be accredited by the ICF. This development appears to represent a quest on the part of purchasers of coaching services for some security regarding the quality of offerings in an often disparate and confusing market place. Of course it may also reflect the effective lobbying of bodies such as the ICF to be seen as the official representatives of 'professional' coaching. These moves are likely to increase the tensions held by many psychologists currently coaching in the field, who consider that their training represents a superior preparation to be an organizational coach (for research on the differences between psychologist and nonpsychologist executive coaches see Bono et al., 2009).

It is noteworthy however, that government bodies are taking an active interest in the development of coaching standards. In 2008, Standards Australia (which is recognized by the Australian Government as Australia's peak standards body) began the process of consultation with key industry stakeholders, including the Australian Human Resources Institute, coaching industry bodies, Australian universities (including the Australian Graduate School of Management, the University of Sydney and Monash University), long-time purchasers of coaching services (including some of Australia's largest corporations) and coaching providers, with the aim of developing government-recognized standards for executive coaching.

Other countries have also explored the development of standards. In the US, the Graduate School Alliance for Executive Coaching (GSAEC), with institutional members from 10 universities, including University of Pennsylvania, University of Texas at Dallas and the University of Toronto, is developing a set of standards for the teaching of executive coaching at university level (see www.gsaec.org).

Unfortunately the attempt by Standards Norway (the Norwegian peak standards body) to create coaching standards for the Norwegian coaching industry collapsed in disarray after a 17-month consultative process. Standards Norway eventually stated that the industry was too immature and fragmented to develop a genuine joint standard (Ladegård, 2008).

Interestingly, the Norwegian taskforce committee was made up of several coach training schools (and their associated industry bodies) that were all vigorously competing for business in the local market. Their offerings varied greatly in quality and substance, ranging from two-day courses which awarded 'coaching certifications' to comprehensive university-level programmes. In contrast, the standards being developed by Standards Norway were comprehensive in scope; encompassing terminology, educational quality standards, practitioner competence requirements, standards for independent practitioner certification and ethical guidelines. The development of higher-level standards meant that at least some of the coach-training businesses would have to make significant changes to their training products, if they were to meet the new standards. In short, the development of a joint standard would directly impact some of the taskforce's own business products and profitability (Jensen, 2009; Ladegård, 2008). Future projects that seek to develop common standards should seek to learn from the Norwegian experience.

COACHING PROFESSIONALIZATION PARALLELS DEVELOPMENT IN OTHER FIELDS

While coaching is unlikely in the near future to achieve the status of a true profession (such as medicine or law, with their state-sanctioned monopolies of practice and clear barriers to entry), it is attempting to move towards increased professionalization. Such a move echoes the challenges experienced in the development of other related disciplines. For example, contemporary human resource management (HRM) is broadly recognized as a professional discipline; covering the recruitment, selection, training and development of employees, as well as the management of issues such as industrial relations, remuneration and working conditions (Garavan, Costine, and Heraty, 1995). As with coaching, HRM has tended to be defined by practice rather by than theory, is variously and broadly understood, and until relatively recently had not been taught at the university level (McGoldrick, Stewart, and Watson, 2001).

Those concerned with the professionalization of coaching should take note of the controversies associated with the development of HRM as a professional field. These included: issues with precisely defining HRM (Hamlin, Ellinger, and Beattie, 2009), an unclear theoretical basis, a paucity of research (McGoldrick *et al.*, 2001) and the lack of defined demarcation with related disciplines (Jacobs, 2000), leading to 'territory' disputes with areas such as L & D, change management (Worren, Ruddle, and Moore, 1999) and, albeit to a lesser extent, the broader psychological enterprise.

COACHING PSYCHOLOGY AS AN EMERGING PSYCHOLOGICAL SUBDISCIPLINE

Psychology as both an academic discipline and a professional practice has often failed to meet the demand for personal and professional development and this has left the way open for other, possibly less-qualified, individuals to dominate the market (Fox, 1996). However, the importance of psychology's role in coaching has begun to be more broadly recognized with many professional psychological societies establishing formal coaching psychology groups. These include the Australian and British Psychological Societies, the Danish Psychological Association, the Swedish Psychological Association and the Federation of Swiss Psychologists. Many other groups around the world, such as the Society for Industrial and Organizational Psychology in South Africa (SIOPSA), are developing strong interests in coaching. In April 2008, the Psychological Society of Ireland's Division of Work and Organizational Psychology established a Coaching Psychology Group to further develop coaching psychology as a psychological subdiscipline.

Now many universities worldwide offer degrees in both coaching and coaching psychology. Since the introduction of the first postgraduate degree in coaching psychology in 2000 at Sydney University, Australia, now has three universities offering masters-level coaching degrees. The UK has at least 10 degree programmes, with coaching psychology units established at the City University and the University of East London and doctoral-level mentoring and coaching programmes at Oxford Brookes and Sheffield Hallam universities. The University of Copenhagen has also established a coaching psychology unit. In Australia and the UK, there are at least nine university-accredited masters degrees in coaching psychology. In the US, at least seven universities offer coaching degree programmes, with an Institute of Coaching recently established at Harvard University. It appears that coaching is becoming increasingly accepted within academia. We anticipate that the availability of specialist university qualifications in coaching and coaching psychology will do much to raise the bar for the coaching industry.

Of course, both psychologists and nonpsychologists have much to contribute to professional coaching (Bono *et al.*, 2009). Indeed, the majority of coaching degrees are offered by faculties of business or education, rather than by schools of psychology. Psychology faces the challenge of engaging with the broader coaching industry to draw out its strengths and provide a solid foundation for professional coaching practice and training (Cavanagh and Palmer, 2006). However, regardless of whether coaching is mainly conducted by psychologists or nonpsychologists, or taught from schools of psychology or business, a solid professional foundation stems from a rigorous and coherent body of coaching-specific research (Grant and Cavanagh, 2007). We now turn to a consideration of the existing research.

COACHING RESEARCH

In reviewing the literature, the first coaching citations listed in PsycINFO are Gorby's (1937) report of senior staff coaching junior employees on how to save waste and Bigelow's (1938) article on how best to implement a sales coaching programme. Despite these early citations, contemporary research in the area of coaching is, in many ways, in its infancy. Unlike I/O and clinical psychology, where there exists a century of intensive theoretical and empirical research, the bulk of the literature on coaching is less than 10 years old.

As of May 2009, there were a total of 518 published scholarly papers and dissertations on coaching listed in PsycINFO. This figure includes life (or personal coaching) and executive and workplace coaching and excludes papers on other applications of coaching such as sports or athletic coaching, use of forensic, clinical or psychotherapeutic populations and educational coaching or coaching for faking on psychometric or educational tests.

The coaching literature has grown significantly in recent years. In the 62 years between 1937 and 1999, only 93 papers were published, whereas between 2000 and May 2009, a total of 425 papers were published. However, of the 499 papers published since 1980, 265 have been opinion papers, descriptive articles or theoretical discussions. There have also been 77 PhD dissertations and only 186 empirical studies. Many of the published empirical papers are surveys (e.g. Coutu and Kauffman, 2009) or descriptive studies into the nature of executive coaching (e.g. Bono *et al.*, 2009), surveys about different organizations' use of coaching (e.g. Douglas and McCauley, 1999; Vloeberghs, Pepermans, and Thielemans, 2005), or studies examining the characteristics of coach training schools (e.g. Grant and O'Hara, 2006). That is, most of the empirical literature to date is contextual or survey-based research about the characteristics of coaches and coachees, or about the delivery of coaching services, rather than outcome research examining the efficacy of coaching as a methodology for creating individual or organizational change.

OUTCOME STUDIES

The first-published empirical outcome study on workplace coaching in the psychology literature was Gershman's (1967) dissertation on the effects of specific factors of the supervisor–subordinate coaching climate upon improvement of attitude and performance of the subordinate. No other coaching outcome studies were published until Duffy's (1984) dissertation on the effectiveness of a feedback-coaching intervention in executive outplacement. In total, between 1980 and May 2009, as many as 156 outcome studies that have examined the effectiveness of coaching and a total of 101 case studies, 39 within-subject studies and 16 between-subject studies.

Most of the 101 case studies in the coaching literature are purely descriptive, tending to emphasize practice-related issues rather than presenting rigorous evaluations of the coaching intervention. Very few of these case studies used well established quantitative measures (one exception is Libri and Kemp, 2006). The 39 within-subject studies represent the largest single methodological approach to coaching outcome research. While within-subject studies can provide useful quantitative data and allow for the use of inferential statistics, randomized controlled studies are frequently held to represent best practice in researching the impact of specific interventions.

RANDOMIZED CONTROLLED STUDIES

Only 11 of the 16 between-subject outcome studies used a randomized controlled design (Deviney, 1994; Duijts, Kant, Van Den Brandt, and Swaen, 2008; Gattellari et al., 2005; Grant, 2002; Grant, Curtayne, and Burton, 2009; Green, Grant, and Rynsaardt, 2007; Green, Oades, and Grant, 2006; Miller et al., 2004; Spence, Cavanagh, and Grant, 2008; Spence and Grant, 2007; Taylor, 1997). Sue-Chan and Latham (2004) used random assignment to self, peer or external coaching group but did not use a no-intervention or placebo intervention control group. The 11 randomized controlled studies of coaching conducted to date indicate that coaching can improve performance in various ways. Table 4.1 presents summaries of the 16 between-subject studies.

Four of these 11 studies have been conducted in the medical or health work areas. Taylor (1997) found that solution-focused coaching fostered resilience in medical students. This study appears to be the first study reporting on the impact of solution-focused coaching. Solution-focused coaching is similar to Appreciative Inquiry (Cooperrider et al., 2000), in that it specifically focuses on the individual's strengths and goals, rather than taking a reductionist, diagnostic approach. Gattellari et al. (2005) found that peer coaching by general practitioners improved coachees' ability to make informed decisions about prostate-specific antigen screening. Miller et al. (2004) found that coaching

Table 4.1 Summary table of between-subjects studies to 2009

Study	Intervention Overview	Type of Study	Key Findings
Miller (1990)	33 employees. Some received coaching by their managers over 4 weeks	Quasi-experimental field study: (a) Coaching group (b) Control group	No significant differences pre–post for interpersonal communication skills
Deviney (1994)*	45 line supervisors at a nuclear power plant. Some received feedback and coaching from their managers over 9 weeks	Randomized controlled study: (a) Feedback plus coaching (b) Feedback with no coaching (c) Control group	No significant differences in pre–post feedback behavior
Taylor (1997)*	Participants undergoing a Medical College Admission Test preparation course	Randomized controlled study: (a) Training only (b) Coaching only (c) Training plus coaching (d) Control group	Coaching reduced stress more than training
Grant (2002)*	62 trainee accountants received group coaching over one semester	Randomized controlled study: (a) Cognitive coaching only (b) Behavioural coaching only (c) Combined cognitive and behavioural coaching (d) Control groups for each condition	Combined cognitive and behavioural coaching most effective in increasing grade point average, study skills, self-regulation and mental health. GPA gains maintained in 12-month follow-up
Miller, Yahne, Moyers, Martinez, and Pirritano (2004)*	140 licensed substance abuse professionals learnt Motivational Interviewing via a range of methods	Randomized controlled study: (a) Workshop only (b) Workshop plus feedback (c) Workshop plus coaching (d) Workshop, feedback and coaching (e) Waitlist control group	Relative to controls, the 4 trained groups had gains in proficiency. Coaching and/or feedback increased post-training proficiency

(continued)

Table 4.1 Summary table of between-subjects studies to 2009 (*Continued*)

Study	Intervention Overview	Type of Study	Key Findings
Sue-Chan and Latham (2004)	53 MBA students in two studies in Canada and Australia	Random assignment: (a) External coach (b) Peer coach (c) Self-coached	Study 1: External coaching associated with higher team playing behaviour than peer coaching Study 2: External and self coaching associated with higher grades than peer coaching
Gattellari M., N. Donnelly, *et al.* (2005)*	277 GPs in total. Some received 2 phone-based peer coaching sessions integrated with educational resources	Randomized controlled study: (a) Peer coaching and educational resources (b) Control group	Compared with controls, peer coaching increased GPs ability to make informed decisions about prostate-specific antigen screening
Gyllensten and Palmer (2005)	31 participants from UK finance organization	Quasi-experimental field study: (a) Coaching group (b) Control group	Anxiety and stress decreased more in the coaching group compared to control group
Evers, Brouwers, and Tomic (2006)	60 managers of the federal government:	Quasi-experimental field study: (a) Coaching group (b) Control group	Coaching increased outcome expectancies' and self-efficacy
Green, Oades, and Grant (2006)*	56 adults (community sample) took part in SF–CB life coaching programme	Randomized controlled study: (a) Group-based life coaching (b) Waitlist control	Coaching increased goal attainment, well-being and hope. 30-week follow-up found gains were maintained
Green, Grant, and Rynsaardt (2007)*	56 female high school students took part in SF–CB life coaching programme for 10 individual coaching sessions over 2 school terms	Randomized controlled study: (a) Coaching group (b) Waitlist control group	Coaching increased cognitive hardiness, mental health and hope.

Study	Sample	Design	Findings
Spence and Grant (2007)*	63 adults (community sample) took part in SF-CB life coaching programme	Randomized controlled study: (a) Professional coaching group (b) Peer coaching group (c) Waitlist control group	Professional coaching more effective in increasing goal commitment, goal attainment and environmental mastery
Duijts, Kant, van den Brandt, and Swaen (2008)*	Dutch employees assessed for the effectiveness of a preventive coaching programme on sickness absence due to psychosocial health complaints and on wellbeing outcomes.	Randomized controlled study: (a) 6-month course of preventive coaching (b) Control group	Significant improvements in health, life satisfaction, burnout, psychological well-being but no improvement in self-reported sickness absence
Spence, Cavanagh, and Grant (2008)	45 adults (community sample) took part in mindfulness-based health coaching over eight weeks	Randomized controlled study: (a) SF-CB coaching followed by mindfulness training (MT) (b) Mindfulness training followed by SF-CB coaching (c) Health education only control group	Goal attainment greater in coaching than in the educative/directive format. No significant differences were found for goal attainment between the two MT/CB-SF conditions
(Grant, Curtayne, and Burton, 2009)*	41 executives in a public health agency received 360-degree feedback and four SF-CB coaching sessions over ten week period	Randomized controlled study: (a) Coaching group (b) Waitlist control group	Coaching enhanced goal attainment, resilience and workplace well-being and reduced depression and stress and helped participants deal with organizational change

Asterisk denote randomized controlled study. SF–CB, solution-focused cognitive behavioural.

with feedback was superior to a training-only condition, in a programme designed to help clinicians learn motivational interviewing skills. Spence *et al.* (2008) found that goal attainment in a health-coaching programme was greater in the coaching condition when compared to an education-only intervention.

Four outcome studies have been in the life (or personal) coaching domain, with community and student samples. These have indicated that coaching can improve and indeed facilitate goal attainment, reduce anxiety and stress (Grant, 2003) and enhance psychological and subjective well-being (Green, Oades, and Grant, 2006; Spence and Grant, 2007) and resilience, while reducing depression, stress or anxiety (Green, Grant, and Rynsaardt, 2007).

There have been only two randomized controlled studies of workplace coaching. Deviney (1994) examined the efficacy of supervisors acting as internal workplace coaches, finding no changes in supervisors' feedback skills following a multiple-rater feedback intervention and coaching from their managers over nine weeks. Duijts *et al.*, (2008) examined the effectiveness of coaching as a means of reducing sickness absence owing to psychosocial health complaints. On well-being outcomes they found significant improvements in health, life satisfaction, burnout and psychological well-being but no improvement in self-reported sickness absence, showing that coaching can enhance the general well-being of employees.

There has been only one randomized controlled study of the effectiveness of executive coaching, with participants receiving 360-degree feedback followed by four sessions of executive coaching. The coaching was found to improve goal attainment, increase resilience, and reduce stress and depression (Grant *et al.*, 2009).

The paucity of randomized controlled outcome studies is perhaps the major shortcoming in the coaching literature. Some might contest the practical utility of randomized controlled studies, but they are held to be the 'gold standard' in quantitative outcome research (for discussion on this issue in relation to coaching, see Cavanagh and Grant, 2006). However, in 'real-life' field research, such as in coaching, genuine randomized allocation to intervention or control is often extremely difficult, if not impossible, to achieve. Because of this many coaching outcome studies have used single group, and 'pre-post within-subject' designs (e.g. Grant, 2003, Jones, Rafferty, and Griffn, 2006; Olivero, Bane, and Kipelman, 1997; Orenstein, 2006).

There have been some quasi-experimental studies with pre-test and post-test comparisons and nonrandomized allocation to an experimental or control group. Miller (1990) examined the impact of coaching on transfer of training skills, but the drawing of conclusions was restricted by a high participant drop-out rate: 91 participants began the study but only 33 completed the final measures. Gyllensten and Palmer (2005) found that compared with a 'no-coaching' control group, coaching was associated with lower levels of anxiety and stress. Evers, Brouwers and Tomic (2006) found that executive coaching enhanced participants' self-efficacy and their beliefs in their ability to set personal goals, but they did not measure actual goal attainment. Barrett (2007) used a quasi-experimental, modified 'post-test only' control group design. He concluded that group coaching reduced burnout but did not improve productivity.

LONGITUDINAL STUDIES

To date there have been very few longitudinal studies. Those conducted indicated that coaching can indeed produce sustained change. Grant (2002) investigated the effects of cognitive, behavioural and combined cognitive and behavioural coaching, and found that only the gains from the combined cognitive–behavioural coaching were maintained at a six-month follow-up. In a 12-month follow-up, Miller et al. (2004) found coaching with feedback was superior to a training-only condition in maintaining clinicians' interviewing skills. Green, Oades and Grant (2006) found that gains from participation in a 10-week solution-focused cognitive-behavioural life coaching were maintained at a 30-week follow-up. Libri and Kemp (2006) provide a refreshing example of a well-designed case study of cognitive-behavioural executive coaching. Using an' A–B–A–B design with an 18-month follow-up, Libri and Kemp (2006) found that cognitive–behavioural coaching enhanced sales performance and the participants' core self-evaluations.

MEASURING OUTCOMES OF COACHING

This literature review suggests that coaching outcome research, as a relatively new area of study, may be moving through the 'natural' stages of research development, that is, from case study-based research to 'within-subject' studies and on to quasi-experimental and randomized controlled 'between-subject' designs. Indeed, the 55 outcome studies conducted to date provide a useful foundation for evidence of coaching effectiveness and the number of studies is on the increase. However, the issue of variation in the outcomes measures used in the research needs to be addressed to draw meaningful comparison between studies and develop a coherent body of knowledge about the effectiveness of coaching.

For executive coaching studies, the coaching outcomes and topics vary widely and include interpersonal skills, stress management, strategic thinking, time management, dealing with conflict, leadership and management styles, delegation, staffing issues and sales or financial performance (Bono et al., 2009). Not surprisingly, the ways these study goals are measured also varies considerably. Following are some representative examples of outcome measures from the literature.

Executive Coaching Measures

In relation to executive coaching, Peterson (1993) provides a useful example of how to develop coaching assessments to suit the idiosyncratic goals of individual coaching clients. Peterson explored the effectiveness of an individualized coaching programme for managers and executives using multiple customized rating inventories and rating scales based on each coachee's individual training objectives and also drew data from several raters. Similar techniques have been reported by Orenstein (2006).

Customized surveys, completed by the coachee, their direct reports, managers and/or peers, form the largest single group of outcome measures in executive coaching outcome research. For example, Jones, Rafferty and Griffin (2006) developed a customized self-report inventory on the basis of aspects of transactional and transformational leadership (Bass and Avolio, 1994) and self-report measures of managerial flexibility. Although these measures were theoretically grounded, no reliability or validity data (beyond face validity) was reported. Gravel (2007) investigated the efficacy of executive coaching workshops with high school principals using customized surveys that assessed time spent on administrative tasks and overall job satisfaction. In a frequently cited study, Olivero, Bane and Kopelman (1997) used behavioural, task-specific outcome measures (the timely completion of patient evaluation forms), to assess the relative impact of training and coaching. They reported that a combined coaching and training programme was more effective than training alone.

Given that most executives participate in 360-degree assessments, and that such assessments are frequently used at the beginning of a coaching assignment in order to define the coaching goals (Coutu and Kauffman, 2009), it is surprising that more outcome studies do not use 360-degree assessments or validated leadership style assessments as outcome measures. Of those that did, Kampa-Kokesch (2002) used the Multifactor Leadership Questionnaire (MLQ; Bass and Avolio, 1990), a well-validated and widely used leadership assessment tool (Lowe, Kroeck, and Sivasubramaniam, 1996), to assess changes in leadership style. However, only coachees' self-ratings were taken following the coaching programme. Thach (2002) used a customized 360-degree feedback tool which drew on previously validated items to assess the impact of executive coaching collecting ratings from the coachees themselves, their mangers and their direct reports, finding that coaching increase leadership effectiveness. Thach (2002) conducted a number of additional analysis including exploring and reporting positive correlational relationships between the number of coaching sessions attended and increases in self-reported leadership effectiveness. Trathen (2008) used *CHOICES ARCHITECT*®, a research-based 360 tool designed to measure learning agility (Lominger, 2009), collecting data from both participates and their managers before and after coaching. The study found a meaningful and significant association between changes in leadership competencies and learning agility, among executive coaching participants.

Grant et al. (2009) report on a randomized controlled study of executive coaching in the health industry using the following measures: the Human Synergistics Life Styles Inventory (LSI; Lafferty, 1989) for 360-degree feedback, the Depression, Anxiety and Stress Scale (DASS; Lovibond and Lovibond, 1995), the Workplace Well-being Index (WWBI; Page, 2005) and goal attainment scaling in which participants set personal goals and rated their goal progression before and after the coaching intervention. Coaching was associated with improved outcomes on these measures.

An issue in using 360-degree assessments is the time-consuming and challenging process of data collection, as it involves coordinating employees and senior executives at multiple time points. Nevertheless, when reliable and well-validated 360 tools are used, such research is important for the advancement of coaching and we recommend that more research be conducted along these lines.

Workplace and Personal Coaching Measures

A similarly diverse pattern emerges from outcome literature on workplace coaching with nonexecutive employees. For example, Sergio (1987) evaluated a coaching intervention which aimed to modify six specific behaviours of 24 male forming-machine operators in a mid-sized fastener manufacturing organization. The outcome measures were observed behaviours, and most importantly, a reduction in actual wasted material.

Duijts, Kant, Van Den Brandt and Swaen (2008) conducted an unusual randomized controlled study into the impact of coaching on employees' sickness absence due to psychosocial health complaints and general employee well-being. Well-validated self-report measures were used including: the Short Form Health Survey (Ware and Sherbourne, 1992), the General Health Questionnaire (Koeter and Ormel, 1991), the Dutch Questionnaire on Perception and Judgment of Work (Veldhoven and Meijmen, 1994) and the Dutch version of the Maslach Burnout Inventory (Schaufeli and Dierendonck, 2000).

In a quasi-experimental study examining the impact of workplace coaching on mental health with finance industry employees, Gyllensten and Palmer (2005) used the DASS (Lovibond and Lovibond, 1995) as an outcome measure and found that levels of anxiety and stress decreased more in the coaching group compared to a control group and were also lower in the coaching group compared to the control group at the end of the study.

Evers, Brouwers and Tomic (2006) report on an executive coaching intervention with managers of the US federal government using self-report measures of self-efficacy beliefs and outcome expectancies which were linked to three central domains of functioning: setting one's own goals, acting in a balanced way and mindful living and working.

Outcome measures in coaching studies conducted in non-work settings are also varied and include: body mass index (Zandvoort, Irwin, and Morrow, 2009), personality inventories (Norlander, Bergman, and Archer, 2002), and goal self-concordance (Burke and Linley, 2007) as well as measures of mental health (Spence and Grant, 2007), well-being (Green et al., 2007), and self-refection and insight (e.g. Grant, 2008).

Of course it is important that outcome measures are purposefully aligned with individual clients' goals, and given that coaching is a highly individualized human change methodology (Kauffman and Bachkirova, 2008), it is inevitable that outcome measures will vary considerably between studies. However, over-use of idiosyncratic measures means that it is difficult for a coherent body of knowledge to develop over time. One important direction for future research will be the increased use of validated and psychometrically reliable measures (Passmore, 2008b).

Validated Measures

Given that coaching is frequently promoted as being effective as a means of en-hancing goal attainment and well-being (e.g. Levine, Kase, and Vitale, 2006; Passmore and Gibbes, 2007), it is surprising that few studies have used well-validated measures of mental health and well-being, despite the fact that there are many such measures designed for use in nonclinical populations; for ex-ample, the Depression, Anxiety and Stress Scale (Lovibond and Lovibond, 1995), the Psychological Well-being Scale (Ryff and Keyes, 1995), the Satis-faction with Life Scale (Diener et al., 1985) and the Cognitive Hardiness Scale (Nowack, 1990).

Goal attainment is an important outcome measure in coaching. However, few outcome studies have measured the impact of coaching on goal attainment. Goal Attainment Scale techniques offer a useful methodologies for measuring goal progression towards predetermined objective success benchmarks (see Fillery-Travis and Lane, 2006), and the broader use of GAS could provide a means of making comparisons between studies. Goal Attainment Scaling could also help address the serious limitations of the few studies that have examined return on investment in coaching using subjective post-coaching ratings of success (e.g. McGovern et al., 2001). For a comprehensive discussion of the use of GAS in coaching see Spence (2007).

Is Return On Investment 'the' Benchmark for Coaching Success?

Return on Investment (ROI) is often presented as the most important indicator of success in organizational coaching. ROI data, calculated using metrics such as growth in market share, profitability or sales, is frequently used by coaching and consulting organizations as a marketing tool in order to promote their coaching services. Return on investment figures of 788% (Kampa-Kokesch and Anderson, 2001) and 545% (McGovern *et al.*, 2001) are commonly reported as being '*the*' ROI for executive coaching.

In essence, return on investment is calculated by subtracting the costs of coaching from the estimated value of the outcomes of coaching and then expressing this as a percentage (estimated coaching benefits – costs of coaching / costs of coaching × 100%). There are different variations on this formula; for example, deliberately underestimating the financial return figure, thereby producing a 'conservative' estimate or including a rating of the coachee's level of confidence that all or some of the perceived benefits were in fact as a result of coaching.

However, while ROI can provide some indications about the impact of a specific coaching intervention, we argue that it has serious limitations as a key benchmark outcome measure for coaching effectiveness. Reducing the benefits of coaching to a single monetary figure may give a sense of comfort and some reassurance to the purchasers of coaching services, but does it truly measure the impact of coaching? We do not think so.

It is important to note that the ROI metric depends on two things: (1) the amount charged by the coach and the total costs of the coaching intervention and (2) the financial benefit obtained. Using an extreme example; company X employs a coach who charges US$5,000 for the coaching engagement. The coach works with an executive who is working on a project that will net US$10 million profit. The deal is completed, and the executives estimates that 50% of the result is due to the coach's input (and let us assume that this estimate is fair and accurate). In this case ROI is 99,900%. Can we now say that *the* ROI for executive coaching is in the region of 99,900%? Of course not!

The key factor in determining an ROI figure is the degree to which revenue can be attributed to the actual work of the coachee. ROI calculations tend to ignore the impact of other variables such as market context and team input. Furthermore, while organizations often seek to improve financial performance via coaching, such measures are typically not the direct focus of coaching interventions, and the estimated benefits often represent highly spurious and contextually bound variables. In addition, it is often extremely difficult to delineate specific causal relationships between a coaching intervention and improvements in organizational metrics. Moreover, while there can be reasonable certainty about the direct costs of coaching, indirect costs (e.g. opportunity costs) tend not to be included. It should be noted that these issues have not been factored into ROI studies to date.

If such factors can be accounted for, at best an ROI metric can only be indicative of a single specific coaching engagement. In order to meaningfully compare ROI across different coaching studies, all facets of the coaching engagement must be similar across the studies, including coaching costs and most importantly the opportunities that the executive has to shape the outcomes of the revenue stream. Because of these factors, we argue that the ROI metric is of very limited validity, unless such issues are specifically addressed.

It must also be noted that virtually all the ROI research that we examined was conducted by organizations that supply coaching services, or the human resources professionals that employ them to provide coaching services to their organization. Also, much of what is presented as research or case studies appeared to be more like marketing material promoting a specific proprietary coaching service than a rigorous scientific evaluation (e.g. Rock and Donde, 2008). Thus, as is often the case with unsupervized practitioner research, there may be unstated vested interests in emphasizing commercial success and reporting 'value for money'. Of course, this is not to imply deliberate misreporting of results. Rather it suggests that there may be unintended demand characteristics at play which bias participants' responses and the way that data is reported and interpreted. For example, the Rock and Donde (2008) paper claims an ROI of 17 times the organizational investment, yet beyond reporting a single 'dollarised ROI' amount (p. 79) Rock and Donde provide no details of how this figure was calculated, which is why we argue that such research should be interpreted with some caution.

A potentially positive development is that ROI research is now being conducted by coaching industry bodies such as the ICF. The ICF Global Coaching Client Survey (e.g. ICF, 2006) surveyed 2,165 clients in 64 countries on a range of issues related to coaching, including ROI. It was found that 40% of respondents indicated that they had experienced a financial change (either personally or in their business) as a result of coaching. (It should be noted that not all of the coaching was directed towards monetary gain.) The median reported ROI for organizational coaching was 700%. A distinguishing point is that the study was conducted through the International Survey Unit of PricewaterhouseCoopers (PwC) who carried out the primary fieldwork for the research. The survey did not control for individual differences in clients' abilities to generate income, or identity if ROI was indeed a focus point of the coaching intervention. Despite bodies such as the ICF having a vested interest in the outcome, the involvement of well-known independent professional services firms such as PwC has the potential to increase perceived rigour in this field.

COMPETENCIES OF EFFECTIVE COACHES AND COACHEES

Competencies have emerged as critical tools for appraisals, learning and development, and recruitment in organizations (Rodriguez, Patel, Bright, Gregory, and Gowing, 2002; Spencer and Spencer, 1993). Clearly, the identification of the key competencies of effective coaches is important for coach education and training and the coaching literature reflects this trend.

Hall, Otazo and Hollenbeck (1999) identified a range of coaching behaviours, skills and attributes that coachees found helpful. These included core empathy building skills, particularly good listening skills. Other factors contributing to the effectiveness of coaches include the coach's level of credibility and confidence (Hall *et al.*, 1999; Sue-Chan and Latham, 2004), the coach displaying authenticity and integrity and showing a willingness to probe and challenge the coachee (Gonzalez, 2004). In addition, many coachees find that the coach's ability to use their own personal career experience to inform the coaching process to be a valuable skill (Hall *et al.*, 1999). This may be particularly important for coaches acting in an executive consultancy or advisory role.

Other important factors that have been indentified include establishing clear boundaries with the client, acting to preserve confidentiality and working flexibly to meet coachees' needs (Kiel *et al.*, 1996). In addition some researchers have emphasized the importance of the coach being able to work from a psychodynamic perspective (i.e. with the client's unconscious impulses and motivations; e.g. Kilburg, 2004)

Exploring senior executives' view on what makes executive coaching effective Passmore (2008a) found that executives hold strong opinions about what works in coaching. The factors identified included the coach's ability to manage emotions, their flexibility in moving between being challenging and supporting, being able to stimulate reflection and problem solving, setting between-session client action steps (sometimes known as homework) and helping the coachee develop alternative points of view.

There have been a number of attempts to place these behaviours, skills and attributes within a competency model. Ahern (2003) outlined a competency model for use by executive coaches based on a quadrate matrix, with business competence (high and low) and coaching competence (high and low) forming the two dimensions. What is interesting about Ahern's model in relation to coaching is its emphasis on the coach having high levels of business competence in the form of business sector knowledge and commercial awareness. This stands in contrast to the approaches to coaching that argue that the coachee, should be the expert and the coach should play the role of a facilitator rather than advice-giver (Whitmore, 1992).

Although the above work on competencies is very useful, apart from Ahern's model, most of this work treats coaching as a monolithic or unidimensional change methodology. In reality there are many different applications of coaching, and these different applications demand different skills sets of the coach. Yet it is difficult to find truly comprehensive work that links specific coaching applications (e.g. skills, performance or development coaching) to specific

Table 4.2 European Mentoring and Coaching Council competency cluster framework

Self	The processes of coaching
Self belief	Building the relationship
Self awareness	Maintaining the relationship
Self development	Session management
Self management	Evaluating process
Values and coaching approach	Evaluating outcome
Belief in others	Contracting and record keeping
Integrity	Review process
Valuing diversity	Transfer of learning
Political awareness	Development planning
Flexible approach	Terminating the relationship
	Evaluating practice
Cognitive skills	**Communication skills**
Problem solving	Listening skills and empathy
Systems thinking	Promoting understanding
Assessment skills	Asking questions and giving feedback
Knowledge base integration	Communication style
Domain-specific knowledge, expertise and focus	**Facilitating**
Therapeutic approaches	Goal focused and achievement
Corporate knowledge	Supporting independence
Psychological models	Working with attitudes
Management expertise	Developing internal motivation
Leadership expertise	Advice and advocacy
Organization development	Professionalism and building a practice
Learning theory	Professional practice
Artistic skills	Continuing professional development
Business focus	Business development and professional discipline

Source: EMCC. (2005). *Competency Research Project: Phase 2 Output*. London: EMCC. © 2005 EMCC. Reproduced with permission.

competency sets and it is important for the development of the field that such work be undertaken.

The professional coaching bodies have also engaged with the competency issue to set standards for coaching. Perhaps the most comprehensive perspective to date is the EMCC coaching competencies (EMCC, 2005) which were developed through an extensive Europe-wide consultative process, drawing on both expert and practitioners' experiences (see Table 4.2 for a summary). The development of standards for coaching by the EMCC is an ongoing project, with future competencies to be published which will reflect industry developments.

The British Psychological Society Special Group in Coaching Psychology (BPS SGCP, 2006) has also undertaken work on coaching competencies, as part of a wider project to establish clear accreditation standards for UK coaching psychologists. This work has been expert led and based on a meta-analysis of previous research and personal experience. The BPS SGCP model divides coaching competencies into four broad clusters:

- Professional autonomy and accountability of the coaching psychologist;
- The application of coaching psychology practice in enhancing well being and performance;
- The knowledge, understanding and skills that underpin the education and training of coaching psychologists;
- Effectiveness of the coach–client relationship.

Reflecting past work in the psychotherapeutic arena (e.g. Horvath and Symonds, 1991), aspects of coach–coachee relationship or working alliance have also been examined. Key factors related to successful coaching outcomes indentified thus far include a collaborative style of working, being friendly without becoming a friend, maintaining coachee confidences (Jones and Spooner, 2006), providing candid feedback and fostering self-awareness in the coachee (Luebbe, 2005), and ensuring that the coaching conversation focuses completely on the coachee's needs (Hall et al, 1999; Jones and Spooner, 2006). Additionally, Bush (2005) highlighted the importance of the coachee's commitment to the process. Along similar lines, Marshall (2007) in a critical incident study based on a sample of over 100 coaches, suggested that key factors in the coaching relationship which contributed to successful outcomes were a connection between the coach and client, unconditional positive regard, the coach selection process, client accountability, openness and motivation on the part of both parties and the tacit knowledge of the coach.

More recently the role of personality in coaching has been examined. Stewart et al. (2008) found that conscientiousness, openness to experience and emotional stability were related to the transfer of developmental insights from coaching into the workplace and suggested that personality measures may have value as a means of identifying coachees who may require support in order to make manifest the learnings developed in the coaching session. For additional discussion of the central importance of the coaching relationship for ensuring positive outcomes, see Gyllensten and Palmer (2005).

The aforementioned work on competencies has yet to coherently inform the teaching of coaching and coaching psychology at university level; there are a wide variety of competency frameworks underpinning university degrees. For example, the University of Sydney courses make reference to both the ICF and the BPS SGPC competency frameworks. The courses offered at the University of East London's Coaching Psychology Unit also draw on the BPS SGPC competency framework. The programmes taught at Oxford Brookes University draw on the EMCC competency model, and the Master of Business Coaching taught at the University of Wollongong places significant emphasis on a generic ethical business practice and competency framework rather than a set of EMCC or ICF coach-specific competencies.

Of course, in part this is a result of variance in the taught content of the courses. The courses at the University of Sydney and the University of East London emphasize the psychology of coaching, the Oxford Brookes University programmes are grounded in models of adult learning and mentoring and the University of Wollongong programme is specifically designed to produce business coaches and consultants. However, this lack of a common underpinning competency framework is also indicative of the relative infancy of the field.

One sign of maturation in the field will be the development and adoption of common educational standards and competencies in university level education. The work on developing a common set of teaching standards and competencies for executive coaching being done by the GSAEC in the US, is an important indication of how coach education at university level can be further developed.

RESEARCH DIRECTIONS

Two questions about the future of coaching emerge from this review: What are the main foci of organizational coaching research? What are trends that will shape the future of coaching in organizations?

The answer to the first question is wide open. While coaching, and particularly coaching psychology, is connected to more than a century of psychological theory, research and development, the coaching field is still in its infancy and the potential research agenda is vast. Nevertheless, we argue that three basic areas of research focus are needed and are emerging.

First, there is a clear need to focus on conducting well-designed outcome studies. These should include large-scale efficacy studies of both internal and external coaching in the enhancement of goal attainment and performance. Multiple studies using randomized controlled methodologies are required to assess the effects of numerous contextual variables, and establish what kinds of coaching interventions work best in specific organizational settings.

However, while these methodologies would certainly contribute to the knowledge-base, it is also important that researchers embrace a range of investigative paradigms. In many coaching contexts, randomized controlled methodologies are simply not feasible. Indeed, such approaches may well not be suitable for coaching populations where coachees are working on attaining highly personal and individualistic goals. By taking coaching research further into the laboratory we may well overly 'sanitize' the research process, losing the very data we seek to examine. Thus, in some situations well-designed single cases studies using relevant pre- and post-measures may be more appropriate, and we would certainly encourage research along these lines.

Boundary Issues

The second focus for research is the boundary between coaching and other forms of organizational and psychological intervention. This includes the boundaries between coaching and organizational development and research into the differential effectiveness of coaching compared to training. The most often quoted study on the relative impact of coaching and training is that by Olivero, Bane, and Kopelman (1997). Using a quasi-experimental design they found training increased productivity by 22.4%, whereas training followed by eight weeks of one-on-one coaching enhanced increased productivity by 88%. Little rigorous research has been conducted since, to assess more fully the value of coaching over and above training.

As mentioned, an area that requires conceptual and empirical clarification is the boundary between the work of professional coaches who coach in organizational contexts, and the work of Organizational Development (OD) and Human Resource Development (HRD) professionals who use coaching as a means of facilitating organizational change (Hamlin, Ellinger, and Beattie, 2008). In fact, differentiating between the work conducted by professional coaches in an organizational context and the work of OD and HRD professionals is extremely difficult (Hamlin, Ellinger, and Beattie, 2009).

First, this is because many definitions of HRD have a high degree of convergence with definitions of coaching. For example, Hamlin (cited in Hamlin *et al.*, 2009; p. 20) defines HRD as

> planned activities and processes designed to enhance organizational and individual learning, develop human potential, maximize organizational effectiveness and performance, and bring about effective and beneficial change within and beyond the boundaries of organizations.

This definition aligns quite closely with the ICF's definition of coaching (ICF, 2009b) as

> partnering with clients in a thought-providing and creative process that inspires them to maximise their personal potential. It is an ongoing relationship which focuses clients on taking action towards the realisation of their visions, goals or desires.

Second, the actual practice of professional coaches in organizational contexts and the practice of OD and HRD professional are very similar, and in some cases, may in fact be identical. The potential overlap between professional coaching and OD and HRD professionals is exemplified in Schein's (1969) notion of process consulting.

Brown and Harvey (2006) estimate that 80% of OD practitioners use Schein process consulting methodologies and that process consulting is the most often-used OD skill set. The central emphasis in process consulting is on facilitating the self-directed learning and growth of the client, and this emphasis is echoed in the majority of coaching philosophies (Whitmore, 1992).

Process consulting is based on the notion that the primary role of the process consultant is to 'help the human system to help itself', and this can be contrasted with more directive approaches such as the consultant as 'expert' (the selling and telling model) and the consultant as 'diagnostician' (the doctor – patient model). In process consulting these are not discontinuous approaches, and interventions generally start with the development of the helping relationship, then proceed into a joint diagnosis phase (consultant and client) and then into various specific interventions.

The majority of interventions in process consulting are conducted in group settings, and Schein refers to these group processes as 'facilitation'. Process consultants also conduct interventions on an individual level, and Schein refers to these individual processes as 'coaching'. In fact, Schein specifically defines coaching as working with individuals and sees coaching very much as a subset of process consulting, with the coach moving between the same three stages, expert, diagnostician and process consultant as required (for a discussion on how this relates to the role of the executive coach see Chapman, Best, and Van Casteren, 2003).

Schein views the role of coaching as establishing behaviours that helps the client to develop new ways of seeing, feeling and behaving in problematic situations. Schein's approach is to coach the individual who is then able to influence the broader organizational system (for discussion on the similarities and differences between group facilitation and group coaching, see Brown and Grant, in press).

Thus one key distinction between understandings of OD and HRD and professional coaching in organizational contexts may well be that professional coaching tends to be focused at the individual level, where the work of OD and HRD professionals tends to be more aligned with organizational-level change.

Most importantly, distinctions between the work of OD and HRD professionals and professional coaches will also depend to a great extent on which type of coaching is being referred to, as well as whether the coaching is primarily aimed at systems- or individual-level changes. For example, developmental executive coaching with a coachee who is at risk of derailment owing to an over-controlling leadership style, may well require a specialized skill set that does not fall within the training afforded to OD and HRD professionals. In addition, workplace coaching which draws on domain-specific knowledge (such as sales skills coaching) may well fall outside the OD and HRD professional's remit. One example here is the kind of coaching that is conducted in the field by sales managers with sales representatives during customer service calls.

Of course, if coaching is conducted completely outside of the organizational or workplace context and focuses on non-work-related issues, it becomes far easier to distinguish between the work of professional coaches and that of OD and HRD professionals; thus, there are several differences between these modalities. However, it is clear that far more work needs to be conducted in relation to clarifying the boundaries between the role of the OD and HRD professional and the professional coach, and this will be important in further developing theoretical and practice frameworks for coaching, as well as better meeting clients' needs.

Of particular importance for future research is boundary between coaching and therapy. This issue came to the fore following the publication of Berglas's (2002) often-cited article on the potential dangers of psychologically untrained executive coaches inadvertently reinforcing unhealthy behaviours patterns in those they coach.

However, while this issue is often mentioned in the coaching literature, very little empirical research has examined the prevalence of mental health issues in coaching clients. There has been some mental health–related data published in relation to studies of life coaching clients. Green, Oades and Grant (2006) and Spence and Grant (2007) found clinically significant levels of mental distress in 52% and 26% of participants seeking life coaching in their studies, respectively.

It is probable that those presenting for executive and workplace coaching will have a different mental health profile than people presenting for free life coaching as part of a research study, but little specific research has been conducted into the mental health of executive and workplace coaching clients. Our experience makes us believe that mental health issues are indeed an important consideration in coaching and that coaches therefore need to be able to identify potential mental health issues and make sound judgements as to when the a coachee should be referred for specialist mental health care. Hence coaches need to be aware of the features and presentation style of both mood and personality disorders in coaching settings (Cavanagh, 2005). Currently, research into the prevalence and presentation of the full range of mood disorders and personality disorders in coaching is sorely needed.

Impact in Organizations

The third focus for research is into the impact of coaching on organizations. We suggest that this should go well beyond merely examining the ROI for coaching programmes and into the way that organizational coaching interventions affect a wide range of variables including workplace well-being, organizational performance, intrapersonal communication styles and organizational culture itself. Thus such research should span the impact of coaching interventions not just on the individuals, but on different groups and workplace teams, whole organizations as well as the wider community. In this way, coaching can be assessed as a developmental methodology to see if it has the potential to create stronger, more resilient individuals, organizations and communities.

With regard to the second question on which trends will shape the future of coaching in organizations, we anticipate that research into the use of coaching as a methodology for facilitating organizational change will continue. We expect that the use of both executive and workplace coaching will increase, with an emphasis on developing internal coaches and that coaching will become increasingly used as a means of facilitating organization-wide change with a new emphasis on driving cultural change. Indeed, such interventions are being reported in the professional and trade media (e.g. Anderson, Anderson, and Mayo, 2008) (for further discussion on an agenda for coaching research, see Bennett, 2006).

The needs of organizational performance and organizational cultural change will continue to shape the type of research conducted in executive and workplace coaching. Hence aside from research into ROI and general individual and organizational performance measures, we expect that there will be greater levels of research into the interplay between complex systems dynamics and coaching. The use of complexity theory in relation to organizations is well established (e.g. see Stacey, 2000; Waldrop, 1992; Wheatley, 1999), but its application to coaching is more recent (Cavanagh, 2006).

Networking theory is an emerging science that has great potential and clear application to coaching in organizational contexts. This area of theoretical development focuses on the dynamics which shape connectivity in complex natural networks such as cells, organs and ecosystems and social networks such as organizations, professional networks, the Internet and even terrorist groups (Kilduff et al., 2009). The application of both complexity and network theories would seem to be a fertile avenue of research for coaching, given that one of the major foci of coaching interventions is the enhancement of communications within and across social and organizational networks.

How could the impact of coaching interventions in organizational settings be measured within these approaches? One answer may be to adapt the social-network analysis methodologies used by Cross, Baker and Parker (2003) who explored the 'energy networks', which are the extent to which relationships and interactions were perceived as being energizing or de-energizing.

Cross et al. (2003) used a case-based approach informed by perspectives from social-network analysis, charismatic leadership, motivation, role theory and goal-setting theory, conducting interviews with members of the social and organizational networks with each member rating others whom they perceived to be energizing or de-energizing (using a simple 1 to 5 rating scale). Their aim was to examine if the levels of positive energy in networks are truly related to organizational performance and learning and to explore the way energy is created and transferred in groups. The semi-structured interviews allowed them to create an 'energy map' of the social and organizational networks, and then to relate the perceived levels of energy to actual performance indicators. Some of their key findings were that high energizers were themselves high performers, high energizers facilitated high performance in others, and not surprisingly, high energizers got more effort and commitment from those around them.

This methodology could be used in coaching by surveying organizational networks and collecting data on a range of variables before and after a coaching intervention. In this way it might be possible to develop representations of how the communication, relationship and energy dynamics change following individual or group coaching.

New Directions

The past two decades have seen renewed interest in areas of psychological research which were previously viewed as being scientifically marginal. For example, there has been increasing interest in both the clinical and positive psychology literature in mindfulness meditation and the intentional use of attention (e.g. Shapiro, 2009). We expect that the use of mindfulness and other metacognitive techniques in coaching will become an increasing focus of research (for exploration of the use of metacognition and mindfulness in coaching, see Collard and Walsh, 2008; Passmore and Marianetti, 2007; Spence *et al.*, 2008).

Coaching is also increasingly being viewed as an applied arm of the positive psychology movement (Grant and Cavanagh, 2007). As both coaching and positive psychology develop, we anticipate that there will be a greater cross-pollination of ideas, models of practice and research between them and that such interactions will be of benefit to both psychological subdisciplines. Indeed, both Seligman (2007) and Kauffman (2006) argue that positive psychology research can help to scientifically ground the field of coaching, proposing that that "positive psychology theory and research will provide the scientific legs upon which the field of coaching can firmly stand" (Kauffman, 2006; p.221).

A POSITIVE FUTURE?

The focal point of I/O psychology is the role of psychological theory and practice in the service of organizational goals. Organizational psychologists seek to 'enhance organizational effectiveness, productivity and individual wellbeing... [by applying] psychological principles and methods to understand and influence work behaviour and attitudes, and organizational structures' (APS, 2008). The occupational psychology division of the BPS is concerned with 'the performance of people at work and in training, with developing an understanding of how organizations function and how individuals and groups behave at work. (We) aim...to increase effectiveness, efficiency and satisfaction at work' (BPS, 2009). Such a stance clearly resonates with the emerging positive psychology agenda. This agenda focuses on the scientific study of optimal human functioning, with the aim of discovering the factors that allow individuals, organizations, communities and societies to thrive and flourish (Keyes and Haidt, 2003; Seligman and Csikszentmihalyi, 2000).

A recent related development is the emerging Positive Organizational Scholarship (POS) movement (Cameron, Dutton, and Quinn, 2003). The aims of POS are to understand the organizational dynamics and factors that foster strengths, resilience and well-being and to explore ways of facilitating the emergence of excellence and positive human change in organizational settings (see Cameron and Caza, 2004). Thus, the focus on well-being, functionality and performance that are central to the I/O agenda receives even greater explicit emphasis within POS. We anticipate that a conjunction of POS and I/O will provide an important framework for coaching in organizational settings. Indeed, a number of authors have already explored this issue (e.g. Boyatzis, Smith, and Blaize, 2006; Luthans and Youssef, 2007).

However, as in much of the positive psychology literature, the POS literature tends to report theoretical, cross-sectional or correlational research rather than research based on interventions specifically designed to enhance workplace well-being and individual or organizational performance (e.g. Luthans, 2002; Muse et al., 2008; Spreitzer et al., 2005; Wright, 2003; Zhong, 2007). We think that evidence-based approaches to coaching will prove to be an important methodology for applying the insights developed in such cross-sectional or correlational research.

A WELL-BEING AND ENGAGEMENT FRAMEWORK FOR ORGANIZATIONAL COACHING

How can we draw on the present literature with the aim of using organizational coaching as applied positive psychology for enhancing performance and well-being in the workplace? The work engagement literature (e.g. Llorens et al., 2007; Schaufeli and Bakker, 2003) and recent work by Keyes (2003) on languishing and flourishing holds promise for a framework for organizational coaching.

According to Keyes (2003) mental health is far more than the mere absence of mental illness symptoms. It is represented by high levels of psychological wellbeing, including self-acceptance, purpose in life, positive relations with others, environmental mastery and autonomy (Ryff and Keyes, 1995). Individuals high in mental health are designated as flourishing in life, whereas those low in mental health symptoms are designated as languishing.

Workplace or employee engagement is another important concept for organizational coaching that has emerged from I/O research. Conceived as the positive opposite of job burnout, workplace engagement can be understood as a state of high energy, strong involvement and strong sense of commitment to the performance of work functions (Maslach and Goldberg, 1998).

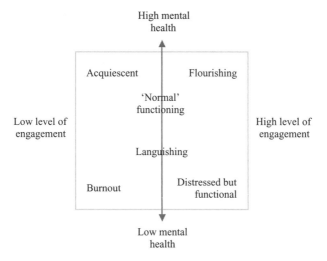

Figure 4.1 A well-being and engagement framework for organizational coaching.

The dimensional model outlined above is based on an assumption that organizational performance is closely related to the degree to which employees can be considering as flourishing or languishing in life (Wright and Cropanzano, 2004). As can be seen in Figure 4.1, the model has two dimensions: a *mental health* dimension (high and low) and a *workplace engagement* dimension (high and low).

It should be noted that the areas within this diagram are qualitatively representative only and are not meant to reflect the quantitative distribution of individuals across the various quadrants.

Area of Flourishing

The area of flourishing is located in the upper right area of Figure 4.1, where individuals experience elevated mental health and high levels of engagement. For many this area is likely to represent the ideal (or target) state. One would expect individuals in this area to be highly involved with and absorbed in their work, have a well-developed sense of work-related meaning and purpose and enjoy positive relations with work colleagues. The concept of goal self-concordance is particularly relevant in this quadrant.

Self-concordance refers to degree to which individuals' goals are aligned with their developing interests and core values (Sheldon and Elliot, 1999). When people set goals that are self-concordant, they feel a greater sense of ownership over these goals. Not surprisingly, this sense of ownership is associated with higher levels of goal striving and greater levels of well-being upon goal attainment (Sheldon and Elliot, 1998). We could therefore expect that, for individuals in this quadrant, work-related goals will be more self-concordant for individuals in this quadrant than for those in other quadrants, and such self-concordance will be related to commitment to the organization (see Bono and Judge, 2003).

Area of Acquiescence

The upper-left area of Figure 4.1 reflects the experience of individuals who have good mental health but relatively low levels of workplace engagement. The notion that individuals can have good levels of mental health and not be intentionally engaged with their workplace may sound somewhat incongruous. In the workplace, employees who acquiesce can be described as 'happy but disengaged', in the sense that they might be physically and emotionally present but not actively engaged with the goals and day-to-day work of the organization. Although some individuals may well seek out work that does not demand such engagement, it may also happen that individuals in this quadrant may become increasingly cynical about their work over time, and thereby drift into a state of languishing.

Area of Languishing

The area of languishing represents individuals with low levels of well-being without elevated levels of depression, anxiety and/or stress and with moderate levels of workplace engagement. Whilst individuals who are languishing may be trying to become more engaged and involved with their work (possibly with the assistance of a coach), in general, their working lives are devoid of the energy, vigour and resilience usually associated with high levels of workplace engagement and flourishing (Maslach and Goldberg, 1998).

Area of the Distressed but Functional

The lower-right area is the area of distressed but functional individuals who have relatively high levels of workplace engagement. This means that while these individuals may be highly functional in terms of work performance, they may also be dysthymic (a chronic form of depression which is less severe than major depression), highly anxious or chronically stressed. Issues of mental health or mental illness here can range from moderately dysthymic or distressed to quite high levels of distress. This area represents an area of significant challenge for coaches who do not have clinical or counselling training (Cavanagh, 2005) because, contrary to popular belief, it is not always easy to identity depression or anxiety disorders particularly for those who are untrained in psychopathological diagnostics. In fact coachees in this area may not even be aware that they have such mental health problems and are unlikely to request or seek out treatment. Rather, the coachee is more likely to present with issues related to motivation, time management, staff retention or interpersonal communication difficulties; in other words, issues that appear on the surface to be appropriate to the coaching context.

Area of Major Psychopathology

The lower left area in the model is the area of major psychopathology. Here we find individuals with high levels of mental illness, which might include illness such as major depression, major anxiety disorders, serious chemical dependencies, self-defeating behaviour patterns or major personality disorders. In addition, clients in this area have very low levels of workplace engagement (i.e. they experience major symptoms of job burnout, including feelings of cynicism, low efficacy and exhaustion).

Although it may be argued that individuals in this area are not be suitable candidates for workplace coaching, some commentators have suggested that coaching might be a more acceptable alternative to therapy, especially for those who are resistant to therapy (Filippi, 1968; McKelley and Rochlen, 2007). Clearly, the boundaries between workplace coaching and therapy become dangerously blurred in this quadrant. Whilst a solid argument can be made in favour of trained mental health professionals using coaching methods to treat some forms of psychological disorder (e.g. schizophrenia or depression), this would be ethically inappropriate for coaches or organizational psychologists who are not trained mental health professionals (Spence, Cavanagh, and Grant, 2006). With this caveat, we believe workplace coaching has great future potential as a methodology to enhance workplace engagement and well-being, and increase the performance and working environment of the contemporary workplace.

Research and Practice Using the Well-being and Engagement Framework

The Well-being and Engagement Framework (WEBF) presented earlier may prove to be a useful framework for future research (see Fig. 4.1) . As regards potential research, a number of interesting (although somewhat speculative) hypotheses flow from the framework. For example, individuals who are in the area of flourishing should have higher levels of self-concordance for work-related goals than those in the distressed but functional area. Individuals who are in the area of flourishing should also be more productive than those in the other three quadrants. We could also expect teams led by team leaders in the flourishing area will tend to be more productive and cohesive than those led by team leaders in the distressed but functional, or the acquiescent areas.

As regards implications for practice, at an organizational level, by using aggregate well-being and engagement metrics the WEBF might provide a useful heuristic from which to categorize work groups, managerial teams and even whole organizations, benchmarking the extent to which an organization is flourishing, languishing or in a collective state of psychological distress. At an individual level, the WEBF could provide a useful diagnostic tool to help determine whether individuals would benefit from counselling or coaching and to help determine the focus of the coaching intervention; that is. if the coach should be primarily aimed at reliving stress, increasing well-being or enhancing engagement through the pursuit of workplace goals that are meaningful and poignant for the individual.

As yet there have been very few attempts to develop frameworks for organizational coaching that integrate goal striving, workplace engagement and well-being. We hope the ideas presented above stimulate thought, research and practice and help organizational coaching further develop.

COACHING AND COACHING PSYCHOLOGY: A SHARED PATH FORWARD?

This review positions coaching as an academically immature yet emerging discipline. This is true of both the wider coaching industry and coaching psychology. Many of the challenges facing coaching are a function of its youth. As with all emerging areas of professional expertise, practice tends to precede the establishment of a sound theoretical and empirical foundation. Indeed, coaching practice has been largely disconnected from the peer reviewed literature. Until very recently, the literature on coaching has been spread thinly throughout the wider psychological and business journals. One of the challenges for researchers and theoreticians in coaching has been to establish effective platforms to facilitate the sharing of ideas and research. The journals emerging as key in the field find their foundations in a range of disciplines, including psychology, education and business. Such specialist journals include the *International Coaching Psychology Review, Coaching: An International Journal of Theory Research and Practice* and the *International Journal of Evidence-based Coaching and Mentoring*.

In coaching there is a large body of practitioner expertise and experience which is only now beginning to be reflected in this peer reviewed press. The future of coaching in moving from an industry toward a profession will be largely tied to the development of its theory and research base and its ability to integrate theory are research from a range of disciplines relevant areas to human development, well-being and productivity.

The boundaries between coaching as an emerging discipline of practice, and coaching psychology as a subdiscipline of psychology are unclear, and the place of psychology in the coaching market remains uncertain. It is becoming increasingly clear however, that there is a high degree of interdependence between psychology and coaching, both in the marketplace and in practice development. The future for coaching psychologists and coaches is likely to be intertwined. At the heart of any future is the quality of the knowledge base that is produced.

The imperative to develop a clear knowledge base and shared frameworks of practice, education and professional standards has not been lost on the wider coaching industry. There are many initiatives currently afoot to increase common points of reference. For example, the ICF and the EMCC are attempting to develop common codes of ethics. In July 2008, representatives and leaders of many of the major coaching bodies around the world (e.g., the ICF, EMCC and many psychological bodies) met to discuss the establishment of common frameworks of ethics, education, research and practice. This gathering, the Global Convention of Coaching (GCC), produced the Dublin Declaration on Coaching and an ongoing dialogue about the future of coaching. Like coaching itself, these conversations are in their early stages and what they will produce into the future is unclear. Nevertheless, a flavour of these conversations can be gleaned in the first two articles of the Dublin Declaration on Coaching. The delegates sought to foster a global dialogue to:

1. Establish a common understanding of the profession through creation of a shared core code of ethics, standards of practice, and educational guidelines that ensure the quality and integrity of the competencies that lie at the heart of our practice;
2. Acknowledge and affirm the multidisciplinary roots and nature of coaching as a unique synthesis of a range of disciplines that creates a new and distinctive value to individuals, organizations and society. To accomplish this we need to add to the body of coaching knowledge by conducting rigorous research into the processes, practices, and outcomes of coaching, in order to strengthen its practical impact and theoretical underpinnings. (Global Coaching Community, 2008),

As the practice of coaching matures it is well positioned to draw together existing psychological approaches including I/O psychology, clinical and developmental psychology, positive psychology and POS.Coaching has the very real potential to make significant contributions to the further development of evidence-based approaches to the enhancement of individual and organizational well-being and performance. Coaching psychology itself is a growing psychological subdiscipline and represents a welcome evidence-based approach to coaching, one which draws on a wide range of extant and emerging knowledge bases. We look forward to the future developments with anticipation and interest.

REFERENCES

Ahern, G. (2003). Designing and implementing coaching/mentoring competencies: a case study. *Counselling Psychology Quarterly*, 16(4), 373–83.

Anderson, M.C., Anderson, D.L., & Mayo, W.D. (2008). Team coaching helps a leadership team drive cultural change at Caterpillar. *Global Business and Organizational Excellence*, 27(4), 40–50.

APS. (2008). Organisational Psychologists. Retrieved May 17, 2009, from http://www.psychology.org.au/community/specialist/organisational/.

Barrett, P.T. (2007). The effects of group coaching on executive health and team effectiveness: A quasi-experimental field study. *Dissertation Abstracts International Section A: Humanities and Social Science*, 67, 26–40.

Bass, B.M., & Avolio, B.J. (1990). *Transformational Leadership Development: Manual for the Multifactor Leadership Questionnaire*. Palo Alto, CA: Consulting Psychologists Press.

Bass, B.M., & Avolio, B.J. (1994). *Improving Organisational Effectiveness through Transformational Leadership*. London: Sage.

Bennett, J.L. (2006). An agenda for coaching-related research a challenge for researchers. *Consulting Psychology Journal: Practice & Research*. 58(4), 240–249.

Berglas, S. (2002). The very real dangers of executive coaching. *Harvard Business Review*, June, 87–92.

Bigelow, B. (1938). Building an effective training program for field salesmen. *Personnel*, 14, 142–50.

Binstead, T., & Grant, A.M. (2008). An exploratory study of Australian executive coaches. *International Coaching Psychology Review*, 3(1), 41–54.

Bono, J.E., & Judge, T.A. (2003). Self-Concordance at Work: Toward Understanding the Motivational Effects of Transformational Leaders. *Academy of Management Journal*, 46(5), 554–71.

Bono, J.E., Purvanova, R.K., Towler, A.J., & Peterson, D.B. (2009). A survey of executive coaching practices. *Personnel Psychology*, 62(2), 361–404.

Boyatzis, R.E., Smith, M., L., & Blaize, N. (2006). Developing sustainable leaders through coaching and compassion. *Academy of Management Learning and Education*, 5(1), 8–24.

BPS. (2009). Occupational psychology. Retrieved May 17, 2009, from http://www.bps.org.uk/dop/about-the-division/about-the-division_home.cfm

BPS SGCP. (2006). Coaching Subject benchmarks. Retrieved December 3, 2009, from http://tinyurl.com/y9dq4of on

Brown, D., & Harvey, D. (2006). *An Experiential Approach to Organization Development* (7th Ed.). New Jersey: Pearson Education.

Brown, S.W., & Grant, A.M. (in press) From GROW TO GROUP: A practitioner's view of group coaching and a practical model for organizational coaching practice. *Coaching: An International Journal of Theory, Research and Practice*

Burke, D., & Linley, P. (2007). Enhancing goal self-concordance through coaching. *International Coaching Psychology Review*, 2(1), 62–9.

Bush, M.W. (2005). Client perception of effectiveness in coaching. *Dissertation Abstract International Section A: Humanities & Social Science*, 66, 1417.

Cameron, K.S., & Caza, A. (2004). Contributions to the Discipline of Positive Organizational Scholarship. *American Behavioral Scientist*, 47(6), 731–9.

Cameron, K.S., Dutton, J.E., & Quinn, R.E. (Eds). (2003). *Positive Organizational Scholarship: Foundations of a New Discipline*. San Francisco: Berrett-Koehler.

Carver, C.S., & Scheier, M.F. (1998). *On the Self-Regulation of Behavior*. Cambridge, UK: Cambridge University Press.

Cavanagh, M. (2005). Mental-health issues and challenging clients in executive coaching. In M. Cavanagh, A.M. Grant & T. Kemp (Eds), *Evidence-Based Coaching (Vol 1): Contributions from the Behavioural Sciences* (pp. 21–36). Bowen Hills, Queensland: Australian Academic Press.

Cavanagh, M. (2006). Coaching from a systemic perspective: A complex adaptive conversation. In D. Stober & A.M. Grant (Eds.), *Evidence-Based Coaching Handbook* (pp. 313–54). New Jersey: Wiley.

Cavanagh, M., & Grant, A.M. (2006). Coaching psychology and the scientist-practioner model. In S. Corrie & D. Lane (Eds), *The Modern Scientist Practitioner* (pp. 146–57). New York: Routledge.

Cavanagh, M., & Palmer, S. (2006). The theory, practice and research base of coaching psychology is developing at a fast pace. *International Coaching Psychology Review*, 1(2), 5–7.

Chapman, T., Best, B., & Van Casteren, P. (2003). *Executive Coaching: Exploding the Myths*. New York: Palgrave MacMillan.

Clegg, S., Rhodes, C., Kornberger, M., & Stilin, R. (2005). Business coaching: Challenges for an emerging industry. *Industrial and Commercial Training*, 37(5), 218–23

Collard, P., & Walsh, J. (2008). Sensory awareness mindfulness training in coaching: Accepting life's challenges. *Journal of Rational-Emotive and Cognitive Behavior Therapy*, 26(1), 30–7.

Cooperrider, D.L., Sorensen, P.F., Whitney, D., & Yaeger, T.F. (2000). *Appreciative Inquiry: Rethinking Human Organization Toward a Positive Theory of Change*. Champaign, IL: Stipes Publishing.

Coutu, D., & Kauffman, C. (2009). *The Realities of Executive Coaching: Harvard Research Report*. Cambridge, MA: Harvard Business Review

Cross, R., Baker, W., & Parker, A. (2003). What creates energy in organisations? *MIT Sloan Management Review, Summer*, Summer, 51–6.

Cunha, P.V., & Louro, M.J. (2000). Building teams that learn. [Article]. *Academy of Management Executive*, 14(1), 152.

Deviney, D.E. (1994). the effects of coaching using multiple rater feedback to change supervisor behavior. *Dissertation Abstracts International Section A: Humanities and Social Science*, 55, 114.

Diener, E., Emmons, R.A., Larsen, R.J., & Griffin, S. (1985). The Satisfaction with Life Scale. *Journal of Personality Assessment*, 49(1), 71–5.

Douglas, C.A., & McCauley, C.D. (1999). Formal Developmental Relationships: A Survey of Organizational Practices. *Human Development Quarterly*, 10(3), 203–20.

Duffy, E.M. (1984). A feedback-coaching intervention and selected predictors in outplacement. *Dissertation Abstracts International Section B: The Sciences and Engineering*, 45(5-B), 1611.

Duijts, S.F.A.P., Kant, I.P., Van Den Brandt, P.A.P., & Swaen, G.M.H.P. (2008). Effectiveness of a preventive coaching intervention for employees at risk for sickness absence due to psychosocial health complaints: Results of a randomized controlled trial. *Journal of Occupational and Environmental Medicine*, 50(7), 765–76.

EMCC. (2005). *Competency Research Project: Phase 2 Output*. London: EMCC.

Evers, W.J., Brouwers, A., & Tomic, W. (2006). A quasi-experimental study on management coaching effectiveness. *Consulting Psychology Journal: Practice and Research*, 58, 174–82.

Filippi, R. (1968). Coaching: A therapy for people who do not seek help. [Article]. *Zeitschrift Fuer Psychotherapie und Medizinische Psychologie*, 18(6), 225–9.

Fillery-Travis, A., & Lane, D. (2006). Does coaching work or are we asking the wrong question? *International Coaching Psychology Review*, 1(1), 23–35.

Fox, R.E. (1996). Charlatanism, scientism, and psychology's social contract. *American Psychologist*, 51(8), 777–84.

Garavan, T.N., Costine, P., & Heraty, N. (1995). The emergence of strategic human resource development. *Journal of European Industrial Training*, 19(10), 4–10.

Garman, A.N., Whiston, D.L., & Zlatoper, K.W. (2000). Media perceptions of executive coaching and the formal preparation of coaches. *Consulting Psychology Journal: Practice and Research*, 52(3), 201–5.

Gattellari, M., Donnelly, N., Taylor, N., Meerkin, M., Hirst, G., & Ward, J. (2005). Does 'peer coaching' increase GP capacity to promote informed decision making about PSA screening? A cluster randomised trial. *Family Practice*, 22(3), 253–65.

Geller, E.S., Perdue, S.R., & French, A. (2004). Behavior-based safety coaching. *Professional Safety*, July, 42–9.

Gershman, L. (1967). The effects of specific factors of the supervisor-subordinate coaching climate upon improvement of attitude and performance of the subordinate. *Dissertation Abstracts International Section B: The Sciences and Engineering*, 28, 2122.

Global Coaching Community (2008). The Dublin Deceleration on Coaching. Retrieved May 23, 2009 from http://www.pdf.net/Files/Dublin%20Declaration%20on%20Coaching.pdf

Gonzalez, A.L. (2004). Transforming conversations: Executive coaches and business leaders in dialogical collaboration for growth. *Dissertation Abstract International Section A: Humanities and Social Science*, 65, 1023.

Gorby, C.B. (1937). Everyone gets a share of the profits. *Factory Management and Maintenance*, 95, 82–3.

Grant, A.M. (2002). Towards a psychology of coaching: The impact of coaching on metacognition, mental health and goal attainment. *Dissertation Abstracts International Section A: Humanities and Social Sciences*, June, 63(12), 6094.

Grant, A.M. (2003). The impact of life coaching on goal attainment, metacognition and mental health. *Social Behavior and Personality: An International Journal*, 31(3), 253–64.

Grant, A.M. (2008). Personal life coaching for coaches-in-training enhances goal attainment, insight and learning. *Coaching: An International Journal of Theory, Research and Practice*, 1(1), 54–70.

Grant, A.M., & Cavanagh, M. (2007). Evidence-based coaching: Flourishing or languishing? *Australian Psychologist*, 42(4), 239–54.

Grant, A.M., & Cavanagh, M. (in press). Coaching and positive psychology. In K.M. Sheldon, T.B. Kashdan & M.F. Steger (Eds), *Designing the Future of Positive Psychology*. Oxford: Oxford University Press.

Grant, A.M., & Cavanagh, M.J. (2004). Toward a profession of coaching: Sixty-five years of progress and challenges for the future. *International Journal of Evidence Based Coaching and Mentoring*, 2(1), 1–16.

Grant, A.M., Curtayne, L., & Burton, G. (2009). Executive coaching enhances goal attainment, resilience and workplace well-being: A randomised controlled study. *Journal of Positive Psychology*, 4(5) 396–407.

Grant, A.M., & O'Hara, B. (2006). The self-presentation of commercial Australian life coaching schools: Cause for concern? *International Coaching Psychology Review*, 1(2), 20–32.

Grant, A.M., & Zackon, R. (2004). Executive, workplace and life coaching: Findings from a large-scale survey of International Coach Federation members. *International Journal of Evidence-based Coaching and Mentoring*, 2(2), 1–15.

Gravel, T.M. (2007). Principal time commitment and job satisfaction before and after an executive coaching workshop. *Dissertation Abstracts International Section A: Humanities and Social Sciences*, 68(4-A), 1247.

Green, L., Oades, L., & Grant, A. (2006). Cognitive-behavioral, solution-focused life coaching: Enhancing goal striving, well-being, and hope. *The Journal of Positive Psychology*, **1**(3), 142–9.

Green, L.S., Grant, A.M., & Rynsaardt, J. (2007). Evidence-based life coaching for senior high school students: Building hardiness and hope. *International Coaching Psychology Review*, **2**(1), 24–32.

Gyllensten, K., & Palmer, S. (2005). Can coaching reduce workplace stress: A quasi-experimental study. *International Journal of Evidence Based Coaching and Mentoring*, **3**(2), 75–85.

Hall, D.T., Otazo, K.L., & Hollenbeck, G.P. (1999). Behind closed doors: what really happens in executive coaching. *Organizational Dynamics*, **27**(3), 39–53.

Hamlin, R., Ellinger, A.D., & Beattie, R. (2009). Toward a profession of coaching? A definitional examination of 'coaching,' 'organization development,' and 'human resource development' *International Journal of Evidence Based Coaching and Mentoring*, **7**(7), 13–38.

Hamlin, R.G., Ellinger, A.D., & Beattie, R.S. (2008). The emergent 'coaching industry': a wake-up call for HRD professionals. *Human Resource Development International*, **11**(3), 287–305.

Horvath, A.O., & Symonds, B. (1991). Relation between working alliance and outcome in psychotherapy: A meta-analysis. *Journal of Counseling Psychology*, **38**(2), 139–49.

International Coach Federation. (2006). Global coaching study. Retrieved October 20, 2008, from http://www.coachfederation.org/research-education/icf-research-portal/research-portal–reports/

International Coach Federation. (2009a). *ICF Global Coaching Client Survey 2009*. Lexington, KY: International Coach Federation.

International Coach Federation. (2009b). What is Coaching? Retrieved May 17, 2009, from http://www.coachfederation.org/find-a-coach/what-is-coaching/

Jacobs, R.L. (2000). Developing the boundaries of HRDQ and HRD. *Journal of Management Studies*, **11**(2).

Jarvis, J., Lane, D., & Fillery-Travis, A. (2005). *Making the Case for Coaching: Does it Work*. London: Chartered Institute of Personnel and Development.

Jensen, I. (2009). Can we have a joint coaching standard? A discussion of practical and ethical issues in the Norwegian coaching industry *Unpublished report, Coaching Psychology Unit, University of Sydney, Sydney, Australia*.

Jones, G., & Spooner, K. (2006). Coaching high achievers. *Consulting Psychology Journal: Practice and Research*, **58**(1), 40–50.

Jones, R.A., Rafferty, A.E., & Griffin, M.A. (2006). The executive coaching trend: Towards more flexible executives. *Leadership & Organization Development Journal*, **27**, 584–96.

Kampa-Kokesch, S. (2002). Executive coaching as an individually tailored consultation intervention: Does it increase leadership? [Empirical, PhD, WS, outcome]. *Dissertation Abstracts International: Section B: the Sciences & Engineering*, **62**(7-B), 3408.

Kampa-Kokesch, S., & Anderson, M.Z. (2001). Executive coaching: A comprehensive review of the literature. *Consulting Psychology Journal: Practice and Research*, **53**(4), 205–28.

Kauffman, C. (2006). Positive Psychology: The Science at the Heart of Coaching. In D.R. Stober & A.M. Grant (Eds), *Evidence Based Coaching Handbook: Putting Best Practices to Work for Your Clients* (pp. 219–53). Hoboken, NJ: Wiley.

Kauffman, C., & Bachkirova, T. (2008). Coaching is the ultimate customizable solution: an interview with David Peterson. *Coaching: An International Journal of Theory, Research and Practice*, **1**(2), 114–9.

Keyes, C.L.M. (2003). Complete mental health: An agenda for the 21st century. In C.L.M. Keyes & J. Haidt (Eds), *Flourishing: Positive Psychology and the Life Well-lived* (pp. 293–0). Washington DC: American Psychological Association.

Keyes, C.L.M., & Haidt, J. (Eds). (2003). *Flourishing: Positive Psychology and the Life Well-lived.* Washington DC: American Psychological Association.

Kiel, F., Rimmer, E., Williams, K., & Doyle, M. (1996). Coaching at the top. *Consulting Psychology Journal: Practice and Research,* **48**(2), 67–77.

Kilburg, R.R. (1996). Toward a conceptual understanding and definition of executive coaching. *Consulting Psychology Journal: Practice and Research,* **48**(2), 134–44.

Kilburg, R.R. (2004). When Shadows Fall: Using Psychodynamic Approaches in Executive Coaching. *Consulting Psychology Journal: Practice and Research,* **56**(4), 246–68.

Kilduff, M., Crossland, C., Tsai, W., & Krackhardt, D. (2009). Organizational network perceptions versus reality: A small world after all? *Organizational Behavior and Human Decision Processes,* **107**, 15–28.

Koeter, M.W.J., & Ormel, J. (1991). *General Health Questionnaire Manual, Dutch Version.* Lisse: Swete and Zeitlinger.

Kubicek, M. (2002). Is coaching being abused? *Training, May,* 12–4.

Ladegård, G. (2008). *Coaching in Norwegian businesses.* Oslo, Norway: The Department of Economics and Resource Management, Norwegian University of Life Sciences, Department of Economics and Resource Management.

Lafferty, J.C. (1989). *Life Style Inventory LSI 1: Self-development guide.* Plymouth, MI: Human Synergistics.

Leadership Management Australia. (2006). *The L.E.A.D. Survey 2005/6.* Melbourne: Leadership Management Australia

Levine, T., Kase, L., & Vitale, J. (2006). *The Successful Coach: Insider Secrets to Becoming a Top Coach.* New York, NY: Wiley.

Libri, V., & Kemp, T. (2006). Assessing the efficacy of a cognitive behavioural executive coaching programme. *International Coaching Psychology Review,* **1**(2), 9–18.

Llorens, S., Schaufeli, W., Bakker, A., & Salanova, M. (2007). Does a positive gain spiral of resources, efficacy beliefs and engagement exist? *Computers in Human Behavior,* **23**(1), 825–41.

Lominger. (2009). *CHOICES ARCHITECT®.* Minneapolis, MN: Lominger International.

Lovibond, S.H., & Lovibond, P.F. (1995). *Manual for the Depression Anxiety Stress Scales.* Sydney: Psychology Foundation of Australia.

Lowe, K.B., Kroeck, K.G., & Sivasubramaniam, N. (1996). Effectiveness correlates of transformation and transactional leadership: A meta-analytic review of the MLQ literature. *Leadership Quarterly,* **7**(3), 385–425.

Luebbe, D.M. (2005). The three way mirror of executive coaching. *Dissertation Abstracts International: Section B: The Sciences and Engineering,* **66**(3), 1771.

Luthans, F. (2002). The need for and meaning of positive organization behavior. *Journal of Organizational Behavior,* **23**(6), 695–706.

Luthans, F., & Youssef, C.M. (2007). Emerging positive organizational behavior. *Journal of Management,* **33**(3), 321–49.

Marshall, M.K. (2007). The critical factors of coaching practice leading to successful coaching outcomes. *Dissertation Abstracts International: Section B: The Sciences and Engineering,* **67**, 4092.

Maslach, C., & Goldberg, J. (1998). Prevention of burnout: New perspectives. *Applied and Preventive Psychology,* **7**(1), 63–74.

Maurer, T., Solamon, J., & Troxtel, D. (1998). Relationship of coaching performance with performance in situational employment interviews. *Journal of Applied Psychology,* **83**(1), 128–36.

McGoldrick, J., Stewart, J., & Watson, S. (2001). Theorizing human resource development. *Human Resource Development International*, 4(3), 343–56.

McGovern, J., Lindermann, M., Vergara, M.A., Murphy, S., Barker, L., & Warrenfelz, R. (2001). Maximizing the impact of executive coaching: Behavioral change, organizational outcomes and return on investment. *The Manchester Review*, 6(1), 1–9.

McKelley, R.A., & Rochlen, A.B. (2007). The practice of coaching: Exploring alternatives to therapy for counseling-resistant men. *Psychology of Men and Masculinity*, 8(1), 53–65.

Miller, D.J. (1990). The effect of managerial coaching on transfer of training. *Dissertation Abstracts International Section B: The Sciences and Engineering*, 50(2435).

Miller, W.R., Yahne, C.E., Moyers, T.B., Martinez, J., & Pirritano, M. (2004). A randomized trial of methods to help clinicians learn Motivational Interviewing. *Journal of Consulting and Clinical Psychology*, 72(6), 1050–62.

Muse, L., Harris, S.G., Giles, W.F., & Feild, H.S. (2008). Work-life benefits and positive organizational behavior: Is there a connection. *Journal of Organizational Behavior*, 29, 171–92.

Norlander, T., Bergman, H., & Archer (2002). Relative constancy of personality characteristics and efficacy of a 12-month training program in facilitating coping strategies. *Social Behavior and Personality*, 30(8), 773–83.

Nowack, K.M. (1990). Initial development of an inventory to assess stress and health *American Journal of Health Promotion*, 4, 173–80.

Olivero, G., Bane, K., & Kopelman, R.E. (1997). Executive coaching as a transfer of training tool: Effects on productivity in a public agency. *Public Personnel Management*, 26(4), 461–9.

Orenstein, R.L. (2006). Measuring executive coaching efficacy? The answer was right here all the time. *Consulting Psychology Journal: Practice & Research*, 58 (106–16).

Page, K. (2005). *Subjective Wellbeing in the Workplace*. Unpublished honours thesis, Deakin University, Melbourne, Australia.

Passmore, J. (2008a). *The Character of Workplace Coaching: The Implications for Coaching Training and Practice*. Stratford: University of East London.

Passmore, J. (Ed.). (2008b). *Psychometrics in Coaching*. London: Kogan Page.

Passmore, J., & Gibbes, C. (2007). The state of executive coaching research: What does the current literature tell us and what's next for coaching research? *International Coaching Psychological Review*, 2(2), 116–28.

Passmore, J., & Marianetti, O. (2007). The role of mindfulness in coaching. *The Coaching Psychologist*, 3(3), 130–6.

Peterson, D. B. (1993, September). Skill learning and behavior change in an individually tailored management coaching and training program. *Dissertation Abstracts International Section B: The Sciences and Engineering*, 54/30, 7071.

Rich, G.A. (1998). Selling and sales management in action: The constructs of sales coaching: Supervisory feedback, role modelling and trust. *Journal of Personal Selling & Sales Management*, 18(1), 53–63.

Rock, D., & Donde, R. (2008). Driving organisational change with internal coaching programmes: part two *Industrial and Commercial Training*, 40(2), 75–80.

Rodriguez, D., Patel, R., Bright, A., Gregory, D., & Gowing, M.K. (2002). Developing competency models to promote integrated human resource practices. *Human Resource Management*, 41(3), 309–24.

Ryff, C.D., & Keyes, C.L.M. (1995). The structure of psychological well-being revisited. *Journal of Personality and Social Psychology*, 69(4), 719–27.

Scandura, T. (1992). Mentoring and career mobility: An empirical investigation. *Journal of Organizational Behavior*, 13(2), 169–74.

Schaufeli, W.B., & Bakker, A.B. (2003). *Test Manual for the Utrecht Work Engagement Scale.* Utrecht, The Netherlands: Utrecht University, Department of Psychology.

Schaufeli, W.B., & Dierendonck, D. (2000). *UBOS, Utrechtse Bournout Schaal, Handeiding.* Lisse: Swets Test Publishers.

Schein, E.H. (1969). *Process Consultation: Its Role in Organizational Development.* London: Wesley.

Seligman, M.E. (2007). Coaching and positive psychology. *Australian Psychologist,* 42(4), 266–7.

Seligman, M.E., & Csikszentmihalyi, M. (2000). Positive psychology: An introduction. *American Psychologist,* 55(1), 5–14.

Sergio, J.P. (1987). Behavioral coaching as an intervention to reduce production costs through a decrease in output defects. *Dissertation Abstracts International,* 47(8-B), 3566–7.

Shapiro, S.L. (2009). The integration of mindfulness and psychology. *Journal of Clinical Psychology,* 65(6), 555–60.

Sheldon, K.M., & Elliot, A.J. (1998). Not all personal goals are personal: Comparing autonomous and controlled reasons for goals as predictors of effort and attainment. *Personality and Social Psychology Bulletin,* 24(5), 546–57.

Sheldon, K.M., & Elliot, A.J. (1999). Goal striving, need satisfaction, and longitudinal well-being: The self-concordance model. *Journal of Personality and Social Psychology,* 76(3), 482–97.

Sherman, S., & Freas, A. (2004). The Wild West of executive coaching. [Article]. *Harvard Business Review,* 82(11), 82–90.

Sparrow, J. (2007). Life coaching in the workplace. *International Coaching Psychology Review,* 2(3), 277–91.

Spence, G.B. (2007). GAS powered coaching: Goal Attainment Scaling and its use in coaching research and practice. *International Coaching Psychology Review,* 2, 155–67.

Spence, G.B., Cavanagh, M., & Grant, A.M. (2006). Duty of care in an unregulated industry: Initial findings on the diversity and practice of Australian coaches. *International Coaching Psychology Review,* 1(1), 71–85.

Spence, G.B., Cavanagh, M.J., & Grant, A.M. (2008). The integration of mindfulness training and health coaching: an exploratory study. *Coaching: An International Journal of Theory, Research and Practice,* 1(2), 145–63.

Spence, G.B., & Grant, A. (2007). Professional and peer life coaching and the enhancement of goal striving and well-being: An exploratory study. *The Journal of Positive Psychology,* 2, 185–94.

Spencer, L.M., & Spencer, S.M. (1993). *Competence at Work: Models for Superior Performance.* New York: John Wiley

Spreitzer, G., Sutcliffe, K., Dutton, J., Sonenshein, S., & Grant, A.M. (2005). A socially embedded model of thriving at work. *Organization Science,* 16(5), 537–49.

Stacey, R.D. (2000). *Strategic Management and Organizational Dynamics* (3rd Ed.). Harlow, UK: Pearson Education.

Stewart, L.J., Palmer, S., Wilkin, H., & Kerrin, M. (2008). The influence of character: Does personality impact coaching success? *International Journal of Evidence Based Coaching and Mentoring,* 6(1), 32–42.

Sue-Chan, C., & Latham, G.P. (2004). The relative effectiveness of expert, peer and self coaches. *Applied Psychology,* 53(2), 260–78.

Taylor, L.M. (1997, November). The relation between resilience, coaching, coping skills training, and perceived stress during a career-threatening milestone. [Empirical, PhD, WS]. *Dissertation Abstracts International Section B: The Sciences and Engineering* 58/50, 8372.

Thach, L.C. (2002). The impact of executive coaching and 360 feedback on leadership effectiveness. [Empirical,, WS, action research]. *Leadership and Organization Development Journal*, **23**(4), 205–14.

Trathen, S.A. (2008). Executive coaching, changes in leadership competencies and learning agility amongst Microsoft senior executives. *Dissertation Abstracts International: Section B: The Sciences and Engineering*, **69**(1-B), 727.

Veldhoven, M., & Meijmen, T. (1994). *Questionnaire on Perception and Judgment of Work.* Amsterdam: NIA.

Vloeberghs, D., Pepermans, R., & Thielemans, K. (2005). High-potential development policies: An empirical study among Belgian companies. *Journal of Management Development*, **24**(6), 546–58.

Waldrop, M. (1992). *Complexity: The Emerging Science at the Edge of Order and Chaos.* New York: Simon & Schuster.

Ware, J.E., & Sherbourne, C.D. (1992). The MOS 36-item short-form health survey (SF-36): Conceptual framework and item selection. *Medical Care*, **30**, 473–83.

Wheatley, M. (1999). *Leadership and the New Science: Discovering Order in a Chaotic World.* San Francisco: Berrett-Koehler.

Whitmore, J. (1992). *Coaching for Performance.* London: Nicholas Brealey.

Wilson, C. (2004). Coaching and coach training in the workplace. *Industrial and Commercial Training*, **36**(3), 96–8.

Witherspoon, R., & White, R.P. (1996). Executive coaching: A continuum of roles. *Consulting Psychology Journal: Practice and Research*, **48**(2), 124–33.

Worren, N.A.M., Ruddle, K., & Moore, K. (1999). From organizational development to change management: The emergence of a new profession. *Journal of Applied Behavioral Science*, **35**(3), 273–86.

Wright, J. (2007). Stress in the workplace: A coaching approach. *Work: Journal of Prevention, Assessment and Rehabilitation*, **28**, 279–84.

Wright, T.A. (2003). Positive organizational behavior: An idea whose time has truly come. *Journal of Organizational Behavior*, **24**(4), 437–42.

Wright, T.A., & Cropanzano, R. (2004). The role of psychological welling in job performance. *Organisational Dynamics*, **334**, 338–51.

Zandvoort, M.V., Irwin, J. D., & Morrow, D. (2009). The impact of co-active life coaching on female university students with obesity. *International Journal of Evidence Based Coaching and Mentoring*, **7**(1), 104–8.

Zhong, L. (2007). Effects of psychological capital on employees' job performance, organizational commitment, and organizational citizenship behavior. *Acta Psychologica Sinica*, **39**(2), 328–34.

Chapter 5

EMPLOYEE SELECTION IN TIMES OF CHANGE[1]

Chockalingam Viswesvaran
Department of Psychology, Florida International University, Miami, FL, USA

Deniz S. Ones
Department of Psychology, University of Minnesota, Minneapolis, MN, USA

We write this chapter at a time when individuals, organizations, nations, and our world are faced with monumental challenges. Economies around the world are in the throes of a global recession: financial and employment markets are the worst since the Great Depression. Our planet is under assault from human activities, and its resources to sustain life are being irreversibly taxed. Resources that have traditionally fueled economic development are being depleted with reverberating economic and geopolitical repercussions. Against these calamities, humanity is being exalted to new heights through scientific and technological advances, but especially through increased communication and data storage, management, and utilization capabilities. Many of these advances, unprecedented in their reach, have rendered our world a truly global village. Organizations and employees of today must adapt and function against this backdrop. Challenges of environmental and economic sustainability, transformational forces of technological and demographic change, and concomitant globalization of markets and the workplace, are already having a dramatic impact on research and practice of personnel selection. For the science of personnel selection to retain its relevance to organizational and societal needs, the monumental changes of our times need to be incorporated into our models.

---

[1] Both authors contributed equally to this chapter.

International Review of Industrial and Organizational Psychology, 2010, Volume 25.
Edited by G. P. Hodgkinson and J. K. Ford. Copyright © 2010 John Wiley & Sons, Ltd

Personnel selection has been a central function in organizational sciences in general and in industrial, work, and organizational (IWO) psychology in particular (Guion, 1998; Schmitt and Chan, 1998; Salgado, Viswesvaran, and Ones, 2001). Personnel selection is one way of ensuring that employees have the requisite characteristics, knowledge and skills to perform the work they are hired to do. Furthermore, people make the place (Schneider, 1987) and personnel selection plays the important role of ensuring what types of people make an organization.

Personnel selection research has evolved over the past century from the need to demonstrate its practical utility to a scientific understanding of the processes motivating performance, individual differences in capacity, and willingness to perform work behaviors (Schmidt and Kaplan, 1971). Over the years, despite minor variations, a model of personnel selection has evolved.

We begin this chapter by describing the main tenets of this model. We then highlight in the second section, the environmental changes and challenges currently buffeting the implementation of this model. This framing is hoped to provide the necessary background to interpret the new research and developments in employee selection.

Following these two sections, we organize our review around the several themes currently garnering research attention. First, we provide a review of the research on attracting a pool of qualified applicants. We discuss the role of organizational reputation and personality on organizational attractiveness, as well as the general role of the Internet in recruitment activities. The emerging literature on the importance of applicant reactions as well as the different theoretical perspectives offered for their understanding is also covered as part of this section. Then, we selectively summarize research on predictor variables used in employee selection, both traditional (e.g., cognitive ability and personality) as well as new and emerging (e.g., emotional, social, tacit, cultural, and/or practical intelligence). The following section focuses specifically on the issue of accuracy in employee assessment and various barriers to accurate assessment (e.g., cheating or faking). In particular, we discuss response distortion in using noncognitive measures for selection. In the following section, we review research on group differences (e.g., gender or race) on predictors and implications of these differences for selection system design. Throughout each of the above outlined sections, we highlight the influence of current challenges and changes (e.g., technological advances [Viswesvaran, 2003]).

SETTING THE STAGE: THE PREDOMINANT (?) SELECTION MODEL

We begin our review by presenting what in our view is a scientifically based model of personnel selection. We admit there are many variations of the model that are science-based, and it is with some trepidation that we present this model as the predominant or general model (albeit with a question mark after the claim, predominant). Doing so enables us to map out the issues and lay some ground rules for identifying particular areas of selection research that the rest of this chapter addresses.

Personnel selection involves the decision of which individuals among the pool of applicants possess the needed knowledge, skills, abilities, and other characteristics to successfully perform a job and then accordingly select them. The first and critical step to personnel selection is to ensure that there is a pool of applicants with the required knowledge, skills, abilities, and other characteristics. Selection can only work if the decision-making process is selective. Ensuring a sufficient applicant pool can be accomplished through recruitment efforts, and there is much research investigating several factors influencing the quality of applicant pools (e.g., Barber, 1998; Breaugh and Starke, 2000). Applicant reactions to the selection process, including the assessments used, are also relevant to the extent that they have the potential to influence the quality of the applicant pools available to organizations.

Deciding whom to hire from the pool of applicants involves identifying constructs reflecting the knowledge, skills, abilities, and other characteristics on which there are individual differences among the applicants that are related to job performance and other key behaviors and outcomes on the job. Traditional constructs used in personnel selection include general mental ability (GMA), personality, and integrity. Determining the standing of applicants on desired constructs requires measurements that then form the basis of selection decisions. Several methods (e.g., tests and interviews) can be used for making these measurements (Schmitt and Chan, 1998). The combinations of constructs and methods used for forecasting future work behaviors in employee selection are referred to as predictors (see also Salgado et al., 2001). At the heart of the personnel selection process is the use of applicants' scores on predictors so as to select applicants who are likely to be the best candidates for later performance. Thus, the predominant model of personnel selection outlined here involves (1) identifying the requisite tasks and domains of behaviors to be exhibited, (2) identifying the knowledge skills, abilities (KSAs), and other characteristics needed to accomplish those tasks and behave in ways that facilitate the organization's goals, (3) generating a pool of applicants for the job, (4) developing predictor measures to assess individual differences in the requisite KSAs and other characteristics among the applicants, (5) administering the predictor measures to the applicants, and (6) choosing, on the basis of their predictor scores, those applicants most likely to succeed as employees.

How do we know that in a given organization the employee selection system works? For successful selection decisions, the predictor scores used for the decisions ought to be reliable (Schmidt and Hunter, 1996) and valid (Schmidt, Viswesvaran, and Ones, 2000). Predictors used in employee selection decisions should show consistency of measurement (i.e., be reliable), both across items (or raters) used in measurement and over time (Schmidt and Hunter, 1999; Thorndike, 1949). Thus, establishing different forms of reliability for predictor scores is important for both predictive accuracy (i.e., reliability sets a ceiling on validity) and for knowing the degree of imprecision associated with scores (i.e., standard error of measurement).

A critical issue in assessing the appropriateness of a predictor for personnel selection is evidence of criterion-related validity. Criterion-related validities can be based on either employee or applicant samples, have the criterion measured with the predictor either concurrently or later, and there may or may not be selection on the predictor scores. For personnel selection, the criterion-related validity is best estimated with applicant samples, without prior selection, with a time interval between the assessment of predictor and criterion scores. All other validities are useful only as approximations of this estimate (Barrett, Phillips, and Alexander, 1981).

Furthermore, in assessing the criterion-related validity, the magnitude of the correlation is affected by several artifacts; most notably range restriction and measurement error in criterion scores (Hunter and Schmidt, 2004; Schmidt and Hunter, 1977). To assess how predictive the scores are of the criterion of interest (i.e., job performance) in personnel selection, the observed correlation should be corrected for range restriction and criterion unreliability. Typically, meta-analytic methods (Callender and Osburn, 1980; Cooper and Hedges, 1994; Hunter and Schmidt, 2004) are used to estimate the criterion-related validity of the predictors used in personnel selection. Such meta-analyses also test whether validities generalize across jobs and settings and are therefore also referred to as validity generalization studies. Given the potential for statistical artifacts to cloud empirical findings in individual studies (Hunter and Schmidt, 2004; Schmidt, 1992), we rely on meta-analytic cumulations of individual studies in evaluating the usefulness of predictors we review in this chapter.

The model of personnel selection sketched previously is not the only model, and even within this general model, several variants exist. The model outlined earlier in the chapter probably suits large organizations with well-defined job clusters, lines of career transitions, and facing relatively stable external environments. When the number of potential applicants and the number of positions are small, as in executive selection, this model may not be suitable (Day, 2009). Variants of this model in which a clinical psychologist employs a personality-oriented interview-based approach or in which consulting firms benchmark individuals to industry standards (Bank et al., 2009) have also been proposed. Such variants focus on or redefine job clusters/industries and even relevant samples for constituting applicant pools or build "change" considerations into selection processes.

In preindustrial, agricultural societies, selection was mostly approached with concerns to family ties (Howard, 1996), and such relational ties may play a role in more collectivistic cultures in modern times also. For example, hiring decisions in many parts of the world, but particularly in collectivistic cultures, still rely on personal ties. Nepotism is a major, persisting global concern.

In postindustrial information-based economies, we have the situation where it is crucial for organizations to staff technological experts from a pool of highly qualified experts with known reputations for short-time rapidly changing projects (Casper, 2007). The staffing of organizations in the Silicon Valley industries (Whitley, 2006) is an example. However, our contention in this chapter is that even for these variants the underlying logic and the parameters of evaluation of the selection efforts are likely to be the same. The requirements of reliability, validity, and the absence of bias are fundamental considerations in any selection model. In the following section, we discuss how various environmental factors influence the selection model—a discussion that facilitates an understanding of, and provides a context for, the topical research in personnel selection.

FORCES OF CHANGE INFLUENCING PERSONNEL SELECTION IN ORGANIZATIONS

The model of personnel selection sketched in the last section evolved in the early 1900s as economies moved from an agricultural to an industrial era (Howard, 1996). Cappelli (2009) describes the prototypical form of organization at that time as one characterized by formal structures based on hierarchical command, with large-scale production operations predicated upon mass-production principles. During this period of early industrialization, organizations faced relatively stable environments and deployed relatively fixed technologies. The majority of firms did not have a global focus. In the first decade of the twenty-first century, work activities and conditions around the world are dramatically different from those encountered a century ago.

As briefly mentioned in the opening paragraph of this chapter, today we must contend with monumental environmental changes and trends. The four major trends currently defining the environment of all human resources practices including employee selection are: challenges that relate to our physical environment (e.g., depletion of resources, energy generation and consumption, environmental sustainability, population growth, and disappearance of biodiversity), creation of new technologies and new innovations (especially in the domain of data management and communication), globalization of employment activities, and changing characteristics of work forces around the world. Coupled with these mega trends, there are also the bleak economic conditions that affect personnel selection. Table 5.1 presents an overview of these environmental challenges and presents examples of how each challenge has had an influence on recruitment, applicant attraction, and applicant reactions to employee selection practices as well as on predictors used in employee

Table 5.1 Effect of environmental changes and challenges on key employee selection topics: illustrative examples

	Attracting Applicants		Predictors		Some Challenges		
	Recruitment	Applicant Reactions	Traditional Predictors	New Predictors	Accuracy of Assessment: Response Distortion	Diversity Issues: Group Differences	Comparability of Scores: Equating
Developments in Technology & Innovation							
Examples:							
- Advances in manufacturing	Use of Internet in recruiting	Applicant reactions to technology use	Computer adaptive measures; on-line testing	Measures of technological savvy	Response latencies to assess distortion	Internet access differences among groups	Equivalence of computerized vs traditional test forms
- Advances in communication							
- Data mining							
Environmental challenges							
Examples:							
- Population growth	Increase in desire to recruit green collar employees		Sustainability involvement built into biodata inventories				N/A
- Energy							N/A
- Sustainability							N/A
Globalization							
Examples:							
-International movements	Global talent pools	Applicant reactions to globalization of selection practices and procedures	Culture fair measurement	Cultural Intelligence	Cross-cultural differences in social desirability	Cultural differences on predictors	Establishing test equivalence for cultural groups
- Employees							
- Jobs							

Changing workforce characteristics

Examples:

	Greater tendency for applicant movements	Evolving applicant reactions as educational levels rise	Need to assess ability with greater precision at higher end of spectrum	Specific ability assessment owing to lower intercorrelations among high ability test takers	Contamination of cognitive ability in non-cognitive assessments	International differences in workforce characteristics	Establishing equivalence of measures for highly educated, intelligent applicants
-Higher degree of education							
-Increasing ability levels							
-Changing demographics							

Changing economic conditions

Examples:

	Larger applicant pools	Greater tolerance among applicants for testing	Expanded role for traditional predictors	Increased capability to select using "new" predictors	Potential for increased response distortion among applicants	Variability in selection ratios internationally	N/A
- Global recession							
- Collapse of financial markets							
- Increasing unemployment							

175

selection, including constructs assessed, specific measurement approaches used, accuracy with which we can measure applicant attributes, and workforce diversity. There are clear implications of changing environmental conditions for employee selection.

Consider the challenges that relate to our physical environment. Clearly our world has suffered from the explosion of economic activity that started with the Industrial Revolution. Its resources are being depleted, and its hospitability for life is being critically affected. Global warming, declining biodiversity, diminishing critical resources (e.g., energy sources such as oil, gas), and unprecedented size of human population to be sustained all point to a Malthusian nightmare. Businesses are now aware of the calamities that will befall our collective fate unless business alters the way that economic activity is undertaken. Employees engage in economic activity, and therefore, how work is accomplished must be in ways that promote environmental sustainability. Enhancing environmentally conscious employee behaviors requires human resources interventions that predict and target such behaviors. Hence, new approaches to employee selection must include components that promote green work behaviors (Ones, 2009).

Now consider another fast moving frontier: technology and innovation. Personnel selection research and practices are undoubtedly influenced by unparalleled technological advances (Viswesvaran, 2003). Indeed, starting with attracting a qualified pool of applicants, technology has revolutionized personnel selection practices. Databases such as O*Net (for extensive job descriptions) have revolutionized how job analyses are conducted and how jobs are described. Voskuijl (2005)summarizes how future-oriented, strategic job analysis has changed the identification of predictors and selection practices in organizations. Internet and online job bulletin boards have changed how organizations reach out to applicants, which in turn is having profound effects on applicants' reactions. Even variables such as Web page design features have been found to affect organizational attractiveness (Cober et al., 2003). Technology has also changed how selection tools like cognitive ability tests are designed and utilized. Computer adaptive testing has become more popular (Tippins, 2009), spawning issues such as cheating on unproctored online tests (Bartram, 2009). Technology has given us the ability to design new types of more realistic items (mirroring real-world work conditions) and be able to accommodate individual needs in testing (e.g., disabilities) but has raised issues of standardization. Technology has also equipped us with the ability to design new items to assess potentially novel constructs (Vispoel, 1999) and even detect potential response distortion (e.g., using calibrated response latencies). In general then, technological innovations are revolutionizing the way employee selection is undertaken, and novel research follows these practice trends.

In another domain, change has been more gradual, nonetheless as profound, in its impact on employee selection. Consider the pervasive influence of globalization (Lievens, 2008). Despite the existence of national borders and barriers to cross-national employment, labor markets of the world are mostly global. Only a small proportion of *workers* move for long periods of time to overseas locales as expatriates (Foldes, Ones, and Sinangil, 2006), but interestingly *jobs* move across borders with much greater ease. In fact, jobs at all levels of complexity get imported and exported by organizations. Thus, large cadres of employees around the world work for multinationals or for foreign companies (Reich, 1991). Given these developments, recruitment has taken a global outreach. Expatriate selection has become a much-researched topic (Sinangil and Ones, 2001). The role of national and cultural variables in affecting personnel selection system design has been noted (Hodgkinson and Payne, 1998; Shackleton and Newell, 1991, 1994). The relative importance placed on different predictors for local versus global selection has been studied (Dunn *et al.*, 1995; Ones and Viswesvaran, 1999). Even new predictors such as global mindset and cultural intelligence have been proposed as being critical for success in a global economy (Bernardin, 2007). Globalization and internationalization, especially enabled by technological innovations, is changing the applied face of employee selection practices.

Changes are occurring also at more localized levels, yet are observable in multiple countries around the world. Consider the changing nature of workforces. The workers of today are brighter (thanks to the Flynn effect, for details, see Neisser, 1998), generally more educated, and are likely to be working in teams with peers of different backgrounds (Adair, Okumura, and Brett, 2001). In diverse, more educated, intelligent workplaces of today, constructs such as organizational justice have to be attended to with greater care (Greenberg, 2009). Research in personnel selection has started to attend to these issues as well. For example, Truxillo, Bauer, and Campion (2009) show how interventions can be designed to enhance the effectiveness of selection systems for a generation of applicants sensitized to justice perceptions. The psychological contract between employees and organizations has changed in a way that employees expect frequent changes in their employment (Rousseau, 1990). This affects the predictors used and the utility of selection system in general (Vinson, Connelly, and Ones, 2007).

Coupled with these sweeping social, economic, and technological changes influencing the way employees are or ought to be selected, there are also some shorter-term changes that affect employee selection. Consider the effects of global recession and rising unemployment rates. Undoubtedly, selection ratios of most organizations can become more stringent as greater pools of qualified talent search for jobs. Stiffer competition among applicants can mean that individuals go to greater lengths to get hired (e.g., distorting responses on noncognitive measures). The changing economic environment of business necessitates a better understanding of how variables such as unemployment and greater competition among applicants affect employee selection. Yet, economic downturns, however severe, are never permanent; rather, they are cyclical. Research is therefore needed to understand how different economic conditions come to influence personnel selection practices. Yet, selection science needs to be applicable to a variety of economic conditions.

In the dynamic context of constant change, the need for selecting the right people is a source of sustainable competitive advantage (Fernandez-Araoz, 2007; Pfeffer, 1994). We highlight and interpret the research on personnel selection in view of these forces affecting personnel selection. It is vital that researchers address these dynamic changes without losing sight of fundamental psychometric principles (e.g., reliability, criterion-related validity, or bias) that have distinguished our contribution as a profession.

ATTRACTING A QUALIFIED POOL OF APPLICANTS

Recruitment

Recruitment has been broadly defined as all organizational activities designed to generate a qualified pool of applicants (Barber, 1998). Research in personnel selection has investigated issues such as effectiveness of recruitment media, content of recruitment materials and recruiter behaviors associated with good recruitment practices (Breaugh, 1992). These three have been referred to as the 3Rs of recruitment (Saks, 2005). Barber (1998) has organized this voluminous literature in terms of actors (individual or applicant, organization, organizational agents, and outsiders), activities (defining the target population, choice of recruiting medium/source, message delivery, closing the deal, and administrative process), outcomes (attraction, posthire attitudes, organizational performance, etc.), context (internal or external), and phases (generating applicants, maintaining applicant status, and job choice).

Of the various environmental changes impacting on current employee selection practices discussed earlier, technological innovations have had the greatest effect on the recruitment of candidates. Two issues in particular, the role of Internet in recruitment and the antecedents of organizational attraction, are generating exciting new lines of inquiry that look promising as a basis for addressing some of the most pressing recruitment problems confronting organizations in these challenging times.

The use of the Internet has changed how positions are advertised (Chapman and Webster, 2003). Organizations can reach an expanded pool of applicants in a shorter time frame. Initial screening of applicants can be automated to key search words in the submitted applications. Increasingly, standardized applications and interactive voice response systems are being widely used for initial screening of applicants.

Organizational Web sites have been utilized to attract applicants—an organization's culture, development opportunities, compensation, and so forth, can be conveyed through its Web site. Cober et al. (2003) present data on the Web site features that are useful in recruitment. Extrapolating from the marketing literature, Cober *et al.* argue that Web site content and style influence organizational attractiveness. Dineen, Ash, and Noe (2002) found that applicant attraction is influenced by the aesthetic characteristics of Web pages. Interactivity, vividness and ease of navigation have been found in the marketing literature to affect quality ratings of Web pages (Coyle and Thorson, 2001). As argued by Anderson (2003), organizations and researchers alike need to invest more resources to gain a better understanding of the influence and potential of the Internet in recruitment. Not least, there is an urgent need for research that addresses the digital divide that likely exists across various ethnic groups (as well as groups differentiated by age and sex), which poses considerable challenges for diversity management in organizations, especially the eradication of bias in selection decisions.

Recent recruitment research (e.g., Slaughter and Greguras, 2009) has also focused on initial organizational attraction. This research explores the antecedents that influence an individual to move from the general population to being an applicant. Lievens and Highhouse (2003) reported that on the basis of the information available, individuals form opinions about the symbolic and instrumental attributes of an organization. These attributions affect perceptions of fit and influence applicants' attraction to the organization. Slaughter *et al.* (2004) suggest that individuals form personality trait inferences about organizations, which in turn influence their decisions regarding whether or not to pursue particular employment opportunities. Slaughter *et al.* (2004) developed their scales of organizational personality by drawing on Aaker's (1997) work in the field of marketing, together with more recent personality theory and research on personnel selection (e.g., Hough and Dilchert, in press; Hough and Oswald, 2000; Ones, Dilchert, and Viswesvaran, 2005b). Organizational personality has been described in terms of five dimensions: boy scout (e.g., honest), innovativeness, dominance (organizational size), thrift, and style (trendy). Individual personality has been found to interact with organizational (perceived) personality in determining intentions to apply and pursue job offers with an organization (Judge and Cable, 1997; Slaughter and Greguras, 2009). We expect that future research in the coming years in this area will yield refinements in the conceptualization of pertinent constructs, with accompanying advances in measurement, including the enhancement of established scales. Innovations in profile-matching approaches can also be especially helpful in this domain (e.g., Davison and Davenport, 2002)

The use of emails, bulletin boards, and the Internet has definitely shortened the time needed to fill positions. In addition to the gain in time, Internet searches facilitate reaching a wider audience which has also the disadvantage of having to manage a larger database—Chapman and Webster (2003) provide the example of a company that received over 40,000 applications in a four-month period. Technology also affects how the initial screening of candidates is conducted, including keyword searches of resumes, computer-based scoring of application blanks, among others. Automated initial screening has the advantage of overcoming rater bias in such assessments (Dipboye, Fontenelle, and Garner, 1984) but has the disadvantage of being incapable of evaluating unique characteristics. The multitude of applicant tracking systems offer practical and useful solutions to the unprecedented applicant management requirements placed on organizations of today. However, we caution that such systems can benefit from the science of personnel selection.

A related technological trend in recruitment is the increasing use of online recruiting sites such as Monster.com and hotjobs.com (Jones, 2001). Organizations are also placing more emphasis on the recruitment sections of their corporate Web pages—Lievens and Harris (2003) reported that 88% of Global 500 companies had recruitment sections in their company Web sites, while Maher and Silverman (2002) reported that large organizations aim to recruit a substantial number of employees through Internet recruitment sites. As observed earlier, the characteristics of corporate Web sites affect applicant perceptions and subsequent organizational attraction (see also Cober et al., 2003). McManus and Ferguson (2003) found mean score difference between Internet and traditional source applicants in personality traits of achievement drive, energy, initiative and persistence, and persuasion in a sample of 19,758 applicants in the financial sector.

As noted by Anderson (2003), most of the research on the effects of new technology on recruitment has been atheoretical. Anderson suggests that theoretical frameworks from the innovation and creativity literatures, reviewed in King and Anderson (2000), might prove useful in developing this line of work. In addition, organizational justice theories (e.g., Gilliland, 1993) could be employed to study the reactions to and acceptance of technological changes in selection. Justice theories suggest that behavior is affected not only by perceptions of the outcomes of selection decisions (i.e., distributive justice), but also by perceptions of the checks and balances offered in the decision-making process (i.e., procedural justice). Theories of communication (e.g., Short, Williams, and Christie, 1976) could also be used as the richness of communication varies by technology and is likely to affect the adoption, use, and reactions to new technology. Human capital theory could also be invoked to explain why individuals differ in their willingness to accept new technology (Perry et al., 2003). Finally, as mentioned earlier, research should also consider the potential for adverse impact across demographic groups given the differences in access to and familiarity with technology across different groups.

Applicant Reactions

The last three decades have seen an increasing emphasis on studying applicant reactions to selection systems. Earlier research on this topic has taken an organizational perspective in that negative applicant reactions have been hypothesized to reduce the utility of the selection system with top choices declining job offers (Murphy, 1986). The potential for litigation initiated by negative applicant reactions as well as applicants removing themselves from the selection process (Guion, 1998) have been advanced as reasons for improving applicant reactions. Applicant reactions can and, likely, do influence recruitment efforts. However, recent research has stressed the need to study applicant reactions from an applicant perspective—to avoid negative psychological effects on the applicants (Anderson, 2004). Similarly early research had explored applicant reactions to several predictors and a meta-analytic cumulation of this literature exists (Hausknecht, Day and Thomas, 2004). Hausknecht *et al.* (2004) found that applicant justice perceptions (procedural and distributive) were related to both face validity and perceived predictive validity. However, the magnitudes of the relationships found varied by actual versus hypothetical selection contexts contributing to the meta-analysis (about half of the contributing samples who were not actual job applicants). Nonetheless, the findings from the meta-analysis echo several individual studies in which applicants had more favorable reactions to predictors that are job relevant, face valid, and provide opportunities for candidates to demonstrate their suitability (for a review see Ployhart and Ryan, 1997). In a similar vein, applicant reactions to noncognitive measures appear to suffer because of perceived reduced predictive validity as a result of potential distortion by job applicants. Specifically, despite the strong empirical support that response distortion is not a major threat to the validity of the self-assessments on noncognitive characteristics, there appears to be a uniform negative perception about the prevalence and deleterious effects of response distortion (Alliger, Lilienfeld, and Mitchell, 1996).

Fairness reactions to different selection predictors have not only been assessed with US samples (e.g., Kluger and Rothstein, 1993) but also in other countries and cultures. For example, Steiner and Gilliland (1996) reported fairness reactions in French samples and compared them to the results found in the US samples. Anderson and Witvliet (2008) compared the reaction of a Dutch sample of respondents to different selection methods. Bertolino and Steiner (2007) reported applicant reactions to different selection predictors from an Italian sample, whereas Nikolaou and Judge (2007) presented data on fairness reactions to different selection predictors from a Greek sample. Moscoso and Salgado (2004) presented data from Spanish and Portuguese respondents. Phillips and Gully (2002) compared the reactions of respondents from Singapore to US samples. These studies underscore pervasive global interest in how applicants react to personnel selection systems and their characteristics. Across these studies, although there appear similar determinants of applicant reactions to selection system characteristics, the relative importance and criticality of these appears to vary by culture. However, the data to date are too scant to fully understand and model intercultural variability in job applicant reactions especially in actual selection situations.

In studying applicant reactions to selection methods, international comparisons have been facilitated by the development of comprehensive models of selection fairness. Research on applicant reactions has moved away from a simplistic overall evaluation of different predictors (and comparing the overall evaluation) to investigations of models of fairness. Early on, Gilliland (1993) presented a model based on organizational justice principles to explain applicant reactions. Herriot (1989) presented a model of selection as a socialization process where applicant reactions play an integral role in the overall system success. The role of self-serving bias and other mechanisms in determining these reactions to different predictors have been investigated (Schmitt *et al.*, 2004).

Arvey and Sackett (1993) also presented a model of the determinants of applicant reactions to selection systems where 22 antecedents are grouped into five categories: selection system content (e.g., use of merit-based variables), selection system development (e.g., adequacy of job analysis), selection system process (e.g., consistency of administration across candidates), system context (e.g., company history of discrimination), and selection system outcomes (e.g., maximize representativeness). Similar to the Arvey and Sackett model of fairness that takes into account contextual factors, Anderson, Born, and Cunningham-Snell (2001) also presented a model that takes into account cultural factors in determining applicant reactions. Schuler (1993) presented the concept of social validity to incorporate the importance of integrating applicant reactions in evaluating a personnel selection system. Chan and Schmitt (2004) stressed the need for collecting data on applicant reactions over time (as candidates move through initial application to accepting a job offer and reporting to work) as well as the need to study the dimensions of applicant reactions (not a overall evaluation to particular selection techniques). The models highlighted earlier can provide the frameworks necessary to begin these investigations. The specific dimensions will depend on the theoretical framework employed—face validity, perceptions of predictive validity, and consistency of application across applicants are dimensions incorporated within justice theory conceptions of applicant reactions to the selection process (Ryan and Ployhart, 2000). Questions of negative psychological effects arise when a different lens (e.g., a health perspective) is employed (Anderson, 2004). In fact, theoretically based measures of applicant fairness perceptions have been constructed (e.g., Bauer *et al.*, 2001; Schreurs *et al.*, 2008). Future research is likely to consider applicant reactions to the fairness of the overall decision-making in selection systems in addition to specific procedures (Born and Scholarios, 2005). To this, we add the needs to emphasize psychological fidelity of application situations in research and the cross-cultural sensitivities needed to draw generalizable conclusions while maintaining flexibility in global practice.

In our changing times, the impact of technology and innovation is most immediately salient to applicant reactions. Applicant reactions to the use of new technology in recruitment has been found to be favorable as that for traditional recruitment sources (Van Rooy, Alonso, and Fairchild, 2003; Zusman and Landis, 2002). Research has also investigated applicant reactions to the use of new technology in selection procedures. Even early on, several studies reported positive reactions to computer-administered ability tests (e.g., Burke, Normand, and Raju, 1987). Baron and Austin (2000) reported more positive reactions to a cognitive ability test administered through the Internet (compared to traditional paper-and-pencil tests). Buchanan and Smith (1999) reported positive applicant attitudes to computerized assessments of personality. Similar results were also reported by Reynolds, Sinar, and McClough (2000). Straus, Miles, and Levesque (2001) found that college students reacted more favorably to a videoconference-based interviews than traditional face-to-face interviews. However, Bauer, Truxillo, and Paronto (2003) found that applicants had more positive reactions to a situational judgment test when it was delivered face-to-face than via telephone.

The influence of *other* prominent environmental changes on applicant reactions has not been studied. For example, how do job applicants who are concerned about the environment react to the various recruitment and employee selection system features? How do applicant reactions vary as a function of likely applicant pool composition both in terms of cross-national representation and a variety of diversity considerations within a culture? Do brighter, more educated applicants react differently to selection system characteristics than labor forces that are less educated and lower on the skill totem pole? How do applicant reactions vary as economic conditions vary? These are a small sampling of the questions that await research-based answers.

PREDICTORS USED IN EMPLOYEE SELECTION

In this chapter, our focus is on employee selection and therefore an integral part of our review must be devoted to predictors used in making hiring decisions. We first focus on traditional predictors encountered in employee selection, followed by a discussion of "new" or emerging predictors. The choice of predictors with the potential to be used in employee selection is far greater than is possible to discuss in the limited space we have; however, our aim is to cover the key traditional and emerging approaches here. We then turn our attention to three specific areas that are receiving a great deal of attention from the research community perhaps in reaction to pressing challenges we have already identified: response distortion on noncognitive self report measures, group differences, and score equivalence.

Traditional Predictors

Several predictors have been used in personnel selection (cf. Guion, 1998; Schmidt and Hunter, 1998), and we begin this section with a very brief summary of meta-analytic findings concerning the criterion-related validity of the different predictors. Along with a discussion of the criterion-related validity, we also present some recent research on each of the predictors and issues that are likely to engage our professional attention in the coming years. Our discussion of the predictors will start with background characteristics and move to individual differences constructs such as cognitive ability and personality.

One of the most traditional approaches that organizations employ to shortlist candidates from among the wider pool of applicants is the application form. Sophisticated versions of application forms have been extensively researched in the selection literature (Carlson et al., 1999). Weighted application blanks (WAB) have been generated to compare applicant past experiences in a structured manner. The goal is to relate the specific past experiences of the applicants to potential for job performance. In addition to WAB, selection researchers have employed biographical inventories, behavioral consistency instruments, and measures of work experiences. These instruments assess relevant experiences and accomplishments from the applicants' background (i.e., biodata). The validity of biodata has been extensively studied (cf. Rothstein et al., 1990; Russell et al., 1990) and research supports the inference that biodata keys can generalize across organizations. Biodata responses can also be used to infer personality and ability differences among applicants. Hunter and Hunter (1984) found validities of 0.25, 0.26, 0.30 and 0.37, respectively, for predicting turnover, promotion, training performance, and supervisory ratings of job performance. These levels of criterion-related validity are somewhat lower than those reported for biodata inventories to be used for special occupational groups, built with the explicit goal of validity generalization (e.g., Carlson et al., 1999).

Researchers have also investigated the predictive and explanatory value of prior work experience for overall job performance (e.g., Schmidt, Hunter, and Outerbridge, 1986). Quinones, Ford, and Teachout (1995) reported a meta-analysis of the validity of job experience. They found that experience can be measured either as the amount of work experience or as time spent or as type of experience. Amount of experience correlated 0.43 with measures of job performance compared to lower validity of 0.27 for time measures. Similarly, experience could also be classified as experience in tasks or job or in an organization. Quinones et al. reported that task level measures of experience had the highest validity (0.41 compared to job-level measures with a validity of 0.27). However, the effects of amount of experience and type of experience could not be unconfounded in the Quinones et al.'s meta-analysis owing to lack of sufficient studies. In over a decade following Quinones et al., little attention has been devoted to job or work experience as a focal predictor construct in employee selection. Arguably experience assessments can be important for some key domains that are influencing or will impact employee selection: experience with various technologies, experience innovating, experience in environmental sustainability at work, and experience with diversity (e.g., working as part of diverse work teams, in ethnically diverse organizations, and in cross-cultural environments.)

Background checks and reference letters have also been employed as predictors in personnel selection. Their validity is reported in the 0.10s (Schmidt and Hunter, 1998) and recent studies have focused on specific forms of background checks—credit checks. In the face of economic challenges faced in economies worldwide, it is not unusual to find great variability in the financial affairs of job applicants. Credit checks systematically capture financial health indicators for individuals. In the first study of its kind, Oppler *et al.* (2008) reported a correlation of 0.13 between financial history and counterproductive behaviors in a sample of 2,519 government employees. Individuals who were in financial dire straits were more likely to engage in counterproductive work behaviors.

We now turn our attention from background-oriented predictors such as application forms, background checks, and reference letters to psychological construct–based predictors assessed by psychological tests. In employee selection, psychological tests are typically used to assess cognitive abilities or noncognitive traits. The list of cognitive and noncognitive constructs that have been employed for selection is long (Salgado *et al.*, 2001), and in this section we discuss the validity of cognitive ability, physical ability, perceptual ability, and Big Five dimensions of personality. Other cognitively based predictors such as job knowledge and skill tests can be viewed as cognitive abilities invested in specific domains. As may be expected, measures of job knowledge demonstrate excellent psychometric properties, including reliability and validity (Schmidt and Hunter, 1998; Ones and Viswesvaran, 2007a, 2007b). However, knowledge and skill measures have to be customized to specific jobs and/or settings, making them costly to develop and deploy. Furthermore, in the age of knowledge-based revolutions, developing knowledge tests for use in employee selection is a short-term enterprise: knowledge gets outdated faster than any previous time in history.

Cognitive ability has been found to be one of the best predictors of employee performance. Both specific abilities (e.g., verbal comprehension or analytic ability) and GMA have been found to be predictive of job performance across organizations and occupations (Ones *et al.*, in press). Criterion-related validities for predicting overall job performance are impressive. In fact, Ones, Viswesvaran, and Dilchert (2005a) comprehensively summarized the multiple meta-analyses that have, without exception, found high validities for GMA. Viswesvaran and Ones (2002) stress that if organizations have access to only one piece of applicant information for making selection decisions, they should assess GMA. GMA reflects the information processing speed of individuals, and in a dynamic global economy will be an important predictor in selection (Gottfredson, 2002). In light of increasing globalization of work, it is important to note that validities of cognitive ability tests are substantial and generalizable regardless of the culture examined (see, e.g., Salgado *et al.*, 2003 for a comprehensive overview of findings in respect of the European Community). In recognition of intelligence as a key determinant of work success at all levels of the organization, global selection systems of multinationals have started to rely on standardized cognitive ability tests administered via the Internet (see Ones *et al.*, in press, for an example).

In contrast to cognitive abilities that have been found to be predictive of performance in all jobs, physical ability has been found to be predictive in jobs found in building trades and manufacturing. Police and firefighter jobs have also considered physical abilities critical for job performance. The trend in the workplace, however, is a move away from an emphasis on physical abilities to cognitive abilities (Hodgkinson and Healey, 2008; Howard, 1996). Technological innovations more easily compensate for deficiencies in physical ability than deficiencies in other ability domains such as cognitive ability. Nevertheless, professionally well-developed tests of physical abilities have been found to be useful predictors when jobs call for them (Hogan, 1991). Similarly, perceptual abilities have been found to be predictive in jobs requiring constant vigil and extended attention spans (e.g., Campbell and Catano, 2004; Chung-Yan, Hausdorf, and Cronshaw (2005); Mount, Oh, and Burns, 2008) The use of personality tests for selection has received a boost in the last two decades, following a hiatus in the 1970s and 1980s (Hough and Oswald, 2000; Ones and Dilchert, 2009a, 2009b). Whereas earlier research suffered in terms of classifying the different personality variables into a coherent framework (Hough, 1998; Hough and Ones, 2001), developments in personality research such as the refinements of the Big Five personality factors have helped the personality renaissance in personnel selection (and in organizational sciences in general). Despite the occasional critics (e.g., Morgeson *et al.*, 2007; Murphy and Dzieweczynski, 2005) who allege low validities associated with self-report measures, most researchers, on the basis of voluminous empirical data, accept personality variables, especially the Big Five, as important predictors of job performance.

Starting with the classic meta-analysis of Barrick and Mount (1991) who cumulated the validities of the Big Five personality factors and found the conscientiousness factor to be predictive across samples, personality variables have been the focus of over 20 meta-analytic investigations for a variety of organizational behaviors and outcomes (see Ones *et al.*, 2007 for a summary of these meta-analyses documenting the validity of personality not only for the criterion of performance but for many additional organizationally important criteria). Overall job performance is perhaps the most important criterion for which validities have been cumulated. Barrick, Mount, and Judge (2001) summarized the results from different meta-analyses for the criterion of overall job performance both across jobs and for particular occupational categories—all unanimous in their support for the predictive validity of personality variables. In particular, conscientiousness predicts performance regardless of job or setting. The global (validity) generalization of these findings has come in the form of multiple individual studies as well as large scale, comprehensive meta-analyses. For example, Salgado (1997) cumulated the validity evidence from European samples and found conscientiousness and emotional stability to be generalizable predictors across organizations and situations. Operational validities for conscientiousness in predicting overall job performance were similar to those found in the US. In addition to such meta-analyses, evidence for cross-cultural validity of personality variables comes from multiple primary studies. For example, Smithikrai (2007) reported multiple studies demonstrating the validity of personality variables in Thai samples.

In addition to the Big Five personality factors, personnel selection research has considered compound or emergent traits that combine aspects of multiple Big Five dimensions. Ones and Viswesvaran (2001) note that most personality inventories and scales were developed to assess general personality of individuals and not necessarily to assess personality relevant to work. However, recent years have seen the development of personality scales focused on assessment in the workplace. Gill and Hodgkinson (2007), for example, reported the development of the Five Factor Model Questionnaire (FFMQ), an inventory designed specifically to assess the Big Five in occupational settings. More generally, Ones and Viswesvaran (2001) refer to such workplace personality instruments as occupational personality scales (OPS) and further distinguish between scales as job-or occupation focused OPS (JOPS) and criterion-focused OPS (COPS). Job- (or occupation-) focused OPS include scales to predict managerial potential, leadership, sales potential, and clerical potential among others. Hough, Ones, and Viswesvaran (1998) reported a meta-analytic cumulation supporting substantial validity of managerial potential scales for overall job performance and Vinchur et al. (1998) found sales potential as a valid predictor of sales performance. It is noteworthy that the operational validities JOPS tend to be much higher than those reported for any of the Big Five factors or their optimally weighted composite for predicting overall job performance.

In comparsion to JOPS, there is a vast amount of research devoted to criterion-focused OPS. Such tests assess employee integrity, customer service orientation, violence potential, and stress tolerance among others. The meta-analysis of 665 integrity test validities conducted by Ones, Viswesvaran and Schmidt (1993) is the largest scale meta-analysis devoted to estimating the validity of a single personality construct to date. Ones et al.'s meta-analysis established the predictive validity of integrity tests for overall job performance in addition to counterproductive behaviors such as absenteeism, theft, and violence on the job (true predictive validities were meta-analyzed for integrity tests; a rarity for personality tests in the employee selection literature). Although the data on other COPS are more modest, similarly robust operational validities have been reported for customer service scales, and stress tolerance scales, among others (Ones and Viswesvaran, 2001). An interesting finding when the different COPS have been correlated with the Big Five personality factors is that all COPS correlate with conscientiousness, agreeableness, and emotional stability (but not with extraversion and openness to experience) albeit with different levels of magnitude. For example, integrity scales correlate highest with conscientiousness (and then agreeableness and emotional stability), while customer service scales correlate highest with agreeableness and stress tolerance scales with emotional stability. In sum, these three of the Big Five personality factors seem to cluster into a functional personality trait and should be the focus of future personnel selection research and practice-based interventions (Ones and Viswesvaran, 2001). Salgado and De Fruyt (2005) summarized the evidence for the potential of these compound traits for incremental validity over GMA. Compared to the Big Five personality dimensions, the operational validities of COPS for overall job performance are higher and their potential for incremental validity over cognitive ability tests is greater.

Thus far, we have discussed both background variables and psychological constructs that are typically assessed as part of a battery of predictors used in selecting employees. However, there are a number of popular predictor methods that can be used to assess many constructs of interest. These include interviews, assessment centers, and situational judgment tests. Here because of space constraints, we focus only on interviews (the most popular approach) and assessment centers (historically the starting point for most simulation-based assessments). The interested reader is referred to Weekley and Ployhart's (2006) edited volume for current research and issues on situational judgment tests (later in this chapter, we discuss cognitive ability assessment using a situational judgment format, when we review the psychometric evidence concerning practical intelligence [PI] tests).

Interviews have been researched for many decades (Wagner, 1949) and an impressive body of validity evidence is available (Schmidt and Hunter, 1998). The key questions about the validity of interviews appear to have been answered by a series of meta-analyses published through mid-1990s to 2000s (e.g., McDaniel et al., 1994; Salgado and Moscoso, 2002). There are several moderators that influence the operational validity of interviews. Chief among these is the degree of structure. A robust finding in the interview research is that the structure of interviews enhances the validity of scores for predicting job performance (Campion, Palmer, and Campion, 1997). Yet, Schmidt and Zimmerman (2004) present a counterintuitive hypothesis on the validity-enhancing property of interview structure, suggesting the need for more context and theory-driven research to disentangle the effects of interview struc-ture. Considering the role of technology on interview validities, Schmidt and Rader (1999) reported that interviews conducted over the phone also yielded substantial validities, confirming that medium does not necessarily hamper the predictive value of interviews. Although research on this most widely utilized employee selection method has burgeoned, we observe that the database on which the interview literature is predicated represents the better side of prac-tice. Typical everyday interviews, in which no scoring rubrics are applied (a requirement for being able to relate "interview scores" to any other variable), are likely to yield lower validities than the operational validities estimated in meta-analytic research.

Assessment centers have been used for managerial selection. There have been two meta-analyses that have focused on the validity of overall assess-ment center ratings. Both Gaugler et al. (1987) and Hermelin, Lievens, and Robertson (2007) established the validity of overall assessment center ratings in the upper 0.20s and mid 0.30s for performance criteria. Relationships with promotion criteria tend to be higher. Interestingly, another meta-analysis has estimated the validity of construct based single assessment dimensions to have operational validities in the same range (Arthur et al., 2003). A major criti-cism of assessment centers is the finding replicated in many empirical studies showing that the dimension scores correlate more highly with scores on other dimensions within an exercise compared to scores on the same dimension from different exercises (Bycio, Alvares, and Hahn, 1987; Robertson et al., 1987; Sackett and Dreher, 1984). Consistent and pervasive replication of this find-ing has led to the recent argument that assessment center exercises function as mini work simulations and especially given construct validity related problems encountered in assessment center research (Lievens, Dilchert, and Ones, in press), the predictive focus of assessment centers should be exercises rather than constituent dimensions (Lance, 2008). Yet, we note that at the present time there is far too scant exercise criterion-related validity evidence offered for predicting job performance (Connelly et al., 2008).

The question of incremental validity of assessment center ratings over per-sonality variables and cognitive ability has been explored. Meta-analytic find-ings and large-scale primary studies both suggest that construct-based AC dimensions add incremental validity over tests of personality and cognitive ability, while overall assessment center ratings do not. Similar investigations for assessment center exercises are lacking for the criterion of overall job per-formance (Dilchert and Ones, 2009).

Emerging Predictors in Personnel Selection

Perhaps in response to changes in the environment in which businesses oper-ate, there have been a variety of new predictors introduced for use in employee selection. The desire of organizations to better predict performance as well as to have more diverse workforces has resulted in at least three "new intelligence" constructs being proposed: emotional intelligence, practical intelligence, and cultural intelligence (Van Rooy et al., 2006). In this section, we consider each of these constructs in turn. We also note that in evaluating these constructs as a basis for forming new predictors, in addition to the psychometric properties outlined in our description of the predominant model of selection (e.g., reliability, criterion-related validity), we should also investigate whether these constructs add predictive value distinct from the traditional individual differences variables already being utilized in employee selection, particularly cognitive ability and personality variables. Thus, the incremental validity of these new variables over and above traditional predictor constructs needs to be established.

Emotional intelligence (EI) was introduced as a predictor in the 1990s (Bar-On, 1997; Davies, Stankov, and Roberts, 1998; Matthews, Zeidner, Roberts, 2002; Mayer, Caruso, and Salovey, 1999; Salovey and Mayer, 1990) and rose to prominence following the publication of popular books by Goleman (1995, 1998). EI has been broadly defined as the ability to discern and manage emotions. Some researchers (e.g., Salovey and Mayer, 1990) have conceptualized EI as a specific ability and have argued that self-reports are not appropriate methods of assessment. In this specific-ability conceptualization of EI, EI should correlate moderately with GMA, be uncorrelated with personality variables, and should show developmental age differences. Others have conceptualized EI as incorporating the components of the ability model in addition to noncognitive components such as empathy, well-being, and related personality characteristics (Bar-On, 1997; Petrides and Furnham, 2001). Both ability-based and mixed-model (trait) conceptualizations of EI can be useful in personnel selection, and in fact a meta-analyses of the criterion-related validities of the EI measures showed substantial validities for both conceptualizations (Van Rooy and Viswesvaran, 2004).

Van Rooy, Viswesvaran, and Pluta (2005) found that measures based on the ability conceptualization of EI correlated only 0.14 with measures of EI based on the alternate conceptualization (across 13 samples, involving a combined total of 2,442 respondents). The pattern of correlations with the Big Five personality factors and GMA was also distinct between the two different conceptualizations. Mixed model measures of EI exhibited greater overlap with personality than ability-based EI measures. Conversely, ability-based EI measures demonstrated a higher correlation with cognitive ability than mixed measures (0.34 vs 0.13).

The factor structure of the different measures of EI has been analyzed and a four-dimensional structure has been proposed (Petrides and Furnham, 2001). A second-order hierarchical model of EI with the four factors at the first level has been supported (Whitman et al., 2009). However, neither the ability-based model of EI nor the mixed (trait-based) model of EI demonstrated substantial incremental validity over the Big Five personality factors and GMA (see also Schulte, Ree, and Carretta, 2004), calling into question whether there exists a distinct EI construct separate from the traditional predictors.

Another predictor that has been introduced for use in personnel selection is PI. Hedlund and Sternberg (2000) proposed that PI is distinct from EI and GMA. In fact, the proposed justification for both EI and PI comes from the writings of Thorndike (1920) who argued: "No man is equally intelligent for all sorts of problems" (p. 228). Thorndike divided intelligence into three components: abstract, mechanical, and social intelligence (see also Roberts, Zeidner, and Matthews, 2001). Thorndike defined social intelligence as "the ability to understand and manage men and women, boys and girls – to act wisely in human relations" (p. 228). Social intelligence is often regarded as being the construct origin of emotional as well as PI (Roberts *et al.*, 2001). Indeed, Fox and Spector (2000) stated that EI can be considered as a subset of PI.

Supporting Fox and Spector's point of view, Hedlund and Sternberg (2000) have argued that PI is not limited to solving problems of social nature. Correlations between EI and PI have ranged between 0.13 and 0.38. Sternberg *et al.* (2000) define PI as the ability to solve problems of everyday nature with a certain amount of practical (as opposed to academic or scholastic) skills. PI is akin to the everyday notion of common sense. PI is typically assessed using situational judgment tests. Despite claims for the orthogonality of PI and GMA by proponents of the former, a recent meta-analytic study found the two constructs to be reasonably strongly correlated, with a mean correlation coefficient of 0.58 (Dilchert and Ones, 2004). Furthermore, in primary studies reported by proponents of PI, incremental validity evidence is scant and PI does not correlate with the criterion higher than measures of GMA (Grigorenko and Sternberg, 2001; Sternberg and Hedlund, 2002). Although, the meta-analytically estimated operational validity of PI measures is in the 0.30s, the underlying meta-analytic evidence suggests that there is little incremental validity of PI over measures of general cognitive ability (Dilchert and Ones, 2004).

A final new emerging predictor we consider in this review is "global mindset." As organizations expand their operations to different countries (Aycan, 2001; Bernardin, 2007), employee selection needs to consider individual differences in potential for success in international assignments as well as being able to integrate the globalization into daily performance of employees (cf. Sparrow, 2006). As such, two questions arise. First, are there predictors distinct from those already discussed that are valid predictors of success in international or expatriate assignments? Second, are there individual differences variables that are predictive of performance in a global economy (not just for expatriates but all employees)? Researchers and organizations have explored the first question, and several taxonomies of skills needed for expatriate success have been proposed (e.g., Arthur and Bennett, 1995; Spreitzer, McCall, and Mahoney, 1997). A perusal of these taxonomies suggests that most predictors are within the framework of GMA, life experiences, and Big Five personality factors (Caligiuiri, 2000; Ones and Viswesvaran, 1997).

With respect to the possibility of individual differences variables that predict performance in the global economy (not just important for expatriates but for all employees), the recent popular literature has argued for the idea of a global mindset (e.g., Jeannet, 2000). Global mindset has been defined as capturing cross-cultural skills (i.e., competence in effectively interacting with managers from different cultures, foreign language skills). Successful employees need to have a global vision that incorporates the cultural, legal, and political ramifications of work (Goldsmith and Walt, 2000). The ability to develop and convey a shared vision (Marquardt and Berger, 2000) depends on the extent to which an individual has interests in other cultures, is sociable, and has an individual identity as a global citizen (Odenwald, 1996; Stahl, 2001). However, empirical research on these constructs is scarce and future research is needed to assess the incremental validity of these predictors over traditional predictors.

We have discussed how the nature of work has changed over the decades and how these changes have affected personnel selection. In the following sections, we turn our attention to three areas of employee research that are receiving attention largely because of the influences of the environmental changes and challenges we identified at the outset of this chapter, namely, response distortion in psychological measurement, group differences, and establishing equivalence of test scores.

A TRENDING CONCERN IN EMPLOYEE SELECTION: RESPONSE DISTORTION IN PSYCHOLOGICAL MEASUREMENT

The recent years have seen an increase in the use of noncognitive measures as predictors in selection (Schmidt and Hunter, 1998). There are two potential causes fueling this trend: increasing interpersonal interactions in work environments and a desire to attain racially diverse workforces. First, the increasing number of workers employed in the service industry (as compared to the agricultural and manufacturing sectors) has definitely played a role in this enhanced emphasis in the noncognitive measures (Howard, 1996). For example, in the early 1900s 42% of the workforce in the United States was in the agricultural sector, while 28% were in the goods-production sector with the remaining 30% in the service sector (U.S. Bureau of Census, 1975). In the 1990s only 2.3% were in the agricultural sector with more than 50% in the service sector (Howard, 1996). Other changes like the increasing use of teams and rapid changes in technology have each played a role in the upsurge of noncognitive measures, as interactions among individuals have become important for successful performance in the workplace. Similar trends are reverberating across the globe as interconnectivity within and between organizations, crossing organizational and national cultures increases.

The second impetus for the increased use of noncognitively based predictors is a growing recognition of some legitimate drawbacks of cognitively based predictors, chief among them being large racial and ethnic group differences leading to a disproportionate hiring of job applicants from different sections of society.

Among noncognitive predictors, vast validity data support personality variables to be predictive of a variety of organizational and individual outcomes (Barrick *et al.*, 2001; Ones *et al.*, 2007). However, the increasing use of personality variables in employee selection has raised concerns about the potential for response distortion by respondents (Hough and Oswald, 2000). Several terms such as *faking, lying, impression management, socially desirable responding, self-deception,* and *other-deception* have been used to describe the behavior of respondents seeking to enhance their observed score compared to their true score on the construct dimensions being measured (Mesmer-Magnus and Viswesvaran, 2006; Viswesvaran and Ones, 1999). Given the inordinate amount of research attention directed at examining response distortion on personality-based measures when decisions are based on such noncognitive assessments, in this section we are compelled to briefly review the findings of this research.

Although terms such as impression management and faking have rather different connotations, for present purposes it is convenient to adopt the generic term of *response distortion* as an overarching phenomenon. First, we need to make clear that this issue of response distortion is not unique for the use of personality tests, but arises whenever noncognitive measures (i.e., measures without an objective correct answer) are employed. Second, the issues described here are not confined to self-report paper-and-pencil measures. Impression management can occur in interviews as well as in simulations, where traits without an objectively "correct" answer are involved or where such traits are perceived and assessed by others.

Discussions of response distortion have revolved around the following questions: (1) Can respondents distort their responses if motivated to do so? (2) To what extent and in what ways do they distort in personnel selection contexts? (3) What is the effect of such distortion on criterion-related validity, construct validity, and the perceived fairness of selection decisions? (4) What are some strategies that can be used to reduce the levels of and/or mitigate the effects of such response distortion? (5) Which process models best explain response distortion?

Can Respondents Distort Their Responses on Noncognitive Measures?

Empirical evidence to address this question comes from studies using instructional sets, whereby respondents are assessed under different instructions. Fake-good, fake-bad, respond honestly, respond as an applicant, and so forth, are some of the different instructions used (Mesmer-Magnus and Viswesvaran, 2006), and the scores from groups of respondents with particular instructional sets are compared to the scores from a group of respondents without any such instructions. Both within-subjects and between-subjects designs have been used as well as more complex designs such as the Solomon 4-group design to tease out testing effects and interactions (e.g., Whitman *et al.*, 2008). Mean scores from the different instructional sets are compared—indexed as a standardized effect size (Cohen, 1977). The standardized effect size is computed as the difference in the mean scores divided by the pooled (between-groups) standard deviation (SD) and is equivalent to the point–biserial correlation, where the predictor scores are correlated with group membership. Meta-analytic cumulation of these effect sizes clearly shows that respondents can successfully distort their responses to noncognitive measures by more than half a standard deviation if instructed to fake-good (Viswesvaran and Ones, 1999). The increase in scores is higher for studies using a within-subjects design than for studies using a between-subjects design. Within-subjects designs can potentially take into account individual differences in ability and motivation to fake—a topic we return to at the end of this section when we discuss models of response distortion that have been advanced in the literature to understand the process of response distortion (e.g., McFarland and Ryan, 2000).

One concern with the faking studies discussed earlier is that they rely on experimental designs that can only demonstrate if an effect (i.e., response distortion) is possible (Mook, 1983). Many of them have used student samples, although some (e.g., Viswesvaran and Ones, 1999) have used incumbent employees. Merely, demonstrating that experimental demand can yield large shifts in scale scores tells us little about the degree of response distortion in field settings and more importantly whether such distortion destroys psychometric properties measures utilized (Dilchert *et al.*, 2006). Fortunately, however, as we shall see, there are several alternative approaches to address the question of whether respondents can and do distort their responses in field settings.

Do Respondents Distort Their Responses in Personnel Selection Settings?

To answer the question of whether respondents distort their responses in a personnel selection context, several lines of evidence have been presented. The first approach to address whether response distortion occurs in personnel selection contexts is to compare the responses from applicants and incumbents.

In this approach, within-subject designs are more convincing than comparing applicant scores with another group of incumbents (a between subjects design) (Ellingson, Sackett, and Connelly, 2007). However, we note that even when a group of applicants are tracked over time, with later assessments following the selection decision when they are employees (i.e., a within-subjects design), it is not possible to unequivocally attribute the differences to response distortion under selection. All applicant/incumbent comparisons are necessarily confounded by several nonresponse distortion related differences. For example, applicant scores are subject to occupational gravitation/attraction forces. Employee scores are subject to attraction as well as selection and attrition influences (Schneider, 1987). Furthermore, personality could change as a function of developmental processes or job experience, motivation to take the assessment seriously may differ across the two assessments, and/or greater range restriction of scores at time 2 could explain the differences between the two assessments (in addition to the response distortion explanation). Neither can obtaining data from the applicants twice before they are informed of the selection outcome, a research strategy adopted by Griffith and McDaniel (2006), unambiguously assesses the level of response distortion in selection contexts. Mean score differences aside, Bradley and Hauenstein (2006) reported a meta-analytic cumulation that suggests that the score differences between the applicant and incumbent samples may not be unequivocal when the focus is on the construct-validity of personality measures utilized.

Another line of evidence presented to support the argument that response distortion occurs in personnel selection contexts is to show differences between face-to-face assessments and computerized assessments (Potosky and Bobko, 1997). The thesis here is that response distortion is more likely to occur in face-to-face assessments. Richman et al. (1999) meta-analytically cumulated the differences between the two administration modes and found a "near-zero" overall effect size between the two modes of administration. When moderators were considered, scores on the computerized assessments were higher for personality scales and lower for social desirability scales. Again, there is other research showing the equivalence of the two modes of administration (Bartram and Brown, 2004; Lievens and Harris, 2003). Hence, it is not possible to accept mean differences per se, as prima facie evidence of faking.

Researchers (Dwight and Donovan, 2003) have suggested comparing anonymous and nonanonymous responses as evidence of response distortion in field settings. The random response technique has been advanced as a survey approach to assess the percentage of applicants engaging in response distortion in selection assessments (Donovan, Dwight and Hurtz, 2003). In this technique, the participants are asked to flip a coin and respond "yes" if either comes up or they had fake in the selection assessment. Knowing that an unbiased coin will come with heads on 50% of occasions, the total number of respondents, the number indicating "yes," researchers can estimate the percentage of fakers (see also Ahart and Sackett, 2004 for a related approach, the Un-matched Count technique). Such designs, although interesting and potentially relevant in determining base rates for response distortion at the group level, yield little information about the magnitude of potential response distortion on personality scales and yield little understanding about response distortion at the individual level.

Perhaps the most vociferous assertion that applicants distort their responses in selection comes from the popular literature (e.g., Song, 2005). Rees and Metcalfe (2003) reported that most managers believed that more than half of applicants distort their responses. Hoffman (2000) published a popular book entitled *Ace the Corporate Personality Test*. While it is incumbent on researchers to investigate common conceptions held by the public, it is also necessary to critically evaluate these commonsense perceptions with unequivocal empirical data (Bernardin, 2007; Siegfried, 1994). When unequivocal data are not feasible, arguing that several lines of evidence "suggest" distortion takes place in selection and, therefore, applicants fake, is a difficult position to hold scientifically. We now turn to the next question of the potential effects of response distortion in noncognitive scores.

Potential Effects of Response Distortion

The effects of response distortion by respondents have been extensively studied in terms of their effects on the criterion-related validity and construct validity of noncognitive measures (Salgado *et al.*, 2001). This is especially true for personality variables, as observed by Dilchert *et al.* (2006). Criterion-related validity is established when a correlation is observed between a predictor and the criterion scores (Guion, 1998), while construct validity is established by observing the overall pattern of correlations among a range of measures, known as a nomological net (Cronbach and Meehl, 1955). Correlations are affected by response distortion in predictors only if there are individual differences in the levels of response distortion. That is, if all applicants distort to the same extent, it will only add a constant score to all applicants with no effect on either the criterion-related validity or who gets selected (unless there is a ceiling effect or a cut-score is used for selection). This reality has produced the twofold strategy of first assessing individual differences in levels of distortion and then using this measure of individual differences to assess the criterion-related validity, after partialing out the individual differences in response distortion.

Several scales have been constructed to assess individual differences in levels of response distortion and popular personality inventories have embedded scales for this assessment (Goffin and Christiansen, 2003). These scales are commonly referred to as social desirability scales (Crowne and Marlowe, 1960; Edwards, 1957). Empirical studies have repeatedly found that partialing out social desirability scale scores affects neither the criterion-related validity (e.g.,

Christiansen *et al.*, 1994) nor the construct validity (e.g., Ellingson, Sackett, and Hough, 1999; Ellingson, Smith, and Sackett, 2001). Meta-analytic cumulation of these studies confirmed these findings. Ones, Viswesvaran, and Reiss (1996) found that partialing out social desirability scores from the criterion-related validities of personality variables (grouped into the Big Five factors) neither improved nor lowered predictive validity. Ones and Viswesvaran (1998) also found that the intercorrelation among the five factors did not change when social desirability scores were partialed out. Li and Bagger (2006) meta-analytically confirmed these findings when social desirability scale components of self deception and impression management were separately assessed.

A more direct approach to examining whether response distortion affects criterion and construct validity of personality measures comes from studies examining actual job applicants undergoing selection. Such an approach does not rely on social desirability or impression management scales, which have been demonstrated to reflect true trait variance from emotional stability and conscientiousness (McFarland and Ryan, 2000; Ones *et al.*, 1996). Bradley and Hauenstein (2006) meta-analyzed the correlations between the Big Five factors from applicant and incumbent samples and found the same factor-structure supported in both types of samples. Perhaps the most compelling evidence for the operational criterion-related validity of personality measures comes from predictive validation studies conducted on actual job applicants. The only meta-analytic investigation of such studies to date demonstrated that integrity test validities are substantial in job applicant samples under predictive validation designs for both the criterion of overall job performance and counterproductive work behaviors (Ones, Viswesvaran, and Schmidt, 1993; see also Ones, Dilchert, and Viswesvaran, 2005b). Finally, in a very unique and novel primary study, Hogan, Barrett, and Hogan (2007) examined over 5,000 job applicants who had been rejected on the basis of a personality measure. Over six months later, the same applicants reapplied for the same job. This allowed for a comparison of scores between two administrations of the test, with rising pressure to do considerably better the second time round. Only three candidates improved their scores significantly (beyond a 95% confidence interval). The factor structure of the personality measure was similar between the two test administrations. The authors concluded "Results suggest that faking on personality measures is not a significant problem in real-world selection settings." (Hogan *et al.*, 2007, p. 1270).

Strategies to Reduce Response Distortion

Several strategies have been proposed to deal with response distortion, which Dilchert *et al.* (2006) classified into three categories: (1) strategies to discourage applicants from distortion, (2) hurdle strategies, and (3) detection and correction strategies. Detection and correction strategies, involving social desirability scales, have already been discussed earlier. As we have seen, they do not improve construct or criterion-related validity of personality measures. Strategies to discourage distortion involve warning applicants that distortion can be detected and will result in negative consequences. Dwight and Donovan (2003) in a meta-analytic cumulation found that such warnings reduce the mean scores, suggesting that they are effective in mitigating score inflation potentially because of socially desirable responding (although the impact of warnings on the construct validity of measures utilized is unknown). However, warnings candidates could generate negative applicant reactions (McFarland, 2003). For this reason, Pace et al. (2005) proposed the use of different types of warning instructions that stress applicant interests. For example, a warning could be given to applicants about the undesirable consequences of getting a job without a personality fit or a warning based on an appeal to moral convictions against faking. Seiler and Kuncel (2005) reported that moral convictions were negatively correlated with intentions to distort. Increasing the self-efficacy of applicants reduces distortion to the extent applicants feel compelled to fake as well as change their goals from obtaining a job at any cost to obtaining a job with adequate fit (Pace and Borman, 2006).

The second type of strategies to reduce response distortion is to design the predictor instrument to make distortions difficult. The use of subtle items (Alliger et al., 1996; Holden and Jackson, 1981) has been proposed as one hurdle to distortion. McFarland, Ryan and Ellis (2002) have proposed scattering items of one construct throughout the entire inventory to reduce the ease of distortion. Other researchers have suggested that asking respondents to elaborate their answers poses another hurdle to response distortion (Heggestad et al., 2006; Schmitt et al., 2003). Forced-choice measures, where the choices are matched on social desirability (Waters, 1965), have been proposed as yet another approach to reduce response distortion (Bartram, 2007). However, there are challenges with the latter. Psychometric properties of scale scores such as reliability, factor structure, and validity are adversely affected by pure ipsativity. A key question is how to recover reliable and criterion-related (valid) normative scores from fundamentally ipsative forced-choice measures.

The efficacy of the different hurdle strategies is not clear. Some studies have found that these strategies may alter the correlation between the noncognitive constructs under focus and GMA (Vasilopoulos, Cucina, and McElreath, 2005). Social psychology research has explored the processes underlying responses to a given question. The hurdle strategies have the potential to affect these mechanisms. For example, Ortner (2008) found that changing the item order affected the obtained scores on personality measures.

Many researchers have proposed that item response theory (IRT) models can be used to flag potential distorters as well as conduct the analyses at the item level (e.g., Zickar and Drasgow, 1996; Zickar and Robie, 1999). However, an effect known as the item order effect, whereby the answer to a given item depends on the answers to preceding items, is a reason for cautioning against the use of IRT for assessing the effects of response distortion in noncognitive measures. In order to examine whether personality items function similarly for individuals who may be distorting responses versus those who may have lower motivation to distort, Stark Chernyshenko et al. (2001) tested for differential item functioning on personality items between a group of 1,135 applicants and a group of 1,023 nonapplicant responses. Such analyses presume all differences between responses of applicants and incumbents are a result of distortion effects. In addition, given the possibility of context effects, care is needed in interpreting the findings, and only future research can address whether computer-adaptive personality testing can yield criterion-related validities for personality constructs that are superior to traditional paper-and-pencil personality measures.

Process Models to Explain Response Distortion

The question of response distortion needs fresh perspectives. We know that (1) respondents can distort, (2) do not know unequivocally that they do distort their responses in personnel selection contexts, (3) the various strategies designed in an attempt to reduce the occurrence of such distortion have advantages and disadvantages, and (4) the effect of such response distortion is not devastating on the criterion- and construct validity of the scores for predicting performance. We also know that practicing managers and lay persons consider it a serious issue. One response to such concerns is to assert that in light of the overwhelming evidence of validity for the effectiveness of various selection practices, to use them in selection decisions, and to address laypersons' concerns regarding response distortion through more effective educational marketing (Salgado and De Fruyt, 2005). The assumption is that this is one area where robust research has failed to influence practice (Anderson, 2005).

We should better attempt to understand the process by which responses are generated (Hogan, 2005), perhaps casting doubt on the notion that self-presentations are necessarily distortions reflective of faked responses. A useful theoretical perspective on response distortion comes in the form of a socio-analytic theory of item responses (Hogan, 1983, 2005; Hogan et al., 2007). According to this theory, item responses should be construed as an effort by the respondent to negotiate a reputation, and this effort is what gets assessed by personality items.

Tourangeau (1987) has proposed that when individuals are confronted with providing a response to an item, they (1) understand the question; (2) recall relevant beliefs, feelings, and opinions; (3) form a judgment; and (4) choose a response. This model can also provide insights into when the motivation to distort can occur and what effects will manifest.

Recent research on response distortion has made implicit use of this latter model. For example, with a focus on judgment formation and response choices, Kuncel and Borneman (2007) present a new approach to model the deliberate faking of responses at the response option level, rather than at the scale or even item level.

In general, investigating how responses are generated can increase our understanding of the links between underlying personality constructs and their manifest measurements and can offer clues about how to advance our assessments. Modeling response distortion can also help improve our understanding of the phenomenon as well as identifying potential palliatives. McFarland and Ryan (2000) present a model of faking, where response distortion is postulated as predicated by three sets of variables: motivation to fake, ability to fake, and situational constraints. Motivation to fake is affected by beliefs toward faking and the extent to which individuals desire the job, whereas the ability to fake depends on the individual's cognitive ability, knowledge of the desired job characteristics, and the transparency of the items. This model of faking provides a framework to classify and study the different variables affecting response distortion; however, applications of the model to design and implement interventions to address response distortion are yet to be realized.

A final point to consider is that personnel selection decisions are made with data from several predictors. Thus, response distortion in one predictor can only tangentially affect personnel selection decisions. In an examination of this idea, Converse, Peterson, and Griffith (2009) report the effects of a simulation of selection decision quality when two predictors—response distortion in one but not the other—are combined. The outcome of such personnel decisions will depend on the relative levels of distortion in the different predictors combined, the intercorrelation among them, and the selection ratio as well as the validity of the different predictors.

DOCUMENTING AND ADDRESSING DIVERSITY CHALLENGES IN EMPLOYEE SELECTION: GROUP DIFFERENCES IN PREDICTOR SCORES

We have thus far reviewed the different predictors proposed for use in personnel selection and the empirical research on their validity. Although criterion-related validity is an important issue, organizations may have multiple goals of obtaining a demographically diverse workforce in addition to the goal of selecting employees with good chances of successful performance (De Corte, Lievens, and Sackett, 2008; Maxwell and Arvey, 1993). When there are substantial and significant differences between demographic groups in predictor scores, there is the possibility of the low-scoring group not being selected as often as the members of the high-scoring group. It is to this issue of group differences in predictors that we turn to in this section. The challenges, posed by increasingly diverse populations within and across national borders, in part a reflection of global labor movements, for ensuring fairness in selection decisions are particularly salient at this juncture. First, however, we would like to clarify the meaning of several key terms—group differences, adverse impact, culture-free assessment, differential item functioning, predictive bias, measurement bias, single-group validity, and differential validity—to prevent any misunderstandings or misinterpretations of pertinent findings in the relevant scientific and professional literatures that have a bearing on the detection, correction, and prevention of unfairness in selection and assessment practices.

Group differences refer to mean score differences across groups of interest (e.g., groups defined by race, ethnicity, and sex) and is usually expressed in standard deviation units (the difference in mean scores divided by the pooled standard deviation). A group difference of one standard deviation means that the average score of the member belonging to the higher-scoring group is at the 84th percentile of the lower-scoring group.

Adverse impact refers to the fact that members of one group are selected a lower rate (i.e., adversely affected) compared to members of other groups. Group differences may or may not cause adverse impact, depending on how large the group differences are and the extent to which the organization is selective (Sackett and Ellingson, 1997). In fact, there could be adverse impact in the absence of group difference owing to the selection criteria used. In the United States, adverse impact is usually assessed by the four-fifths rule (an administrative rule promulgated by the Equal Employment Opportunity Commission). According to the four-fifths rule, there is adverse impact when the selection rate for one group is less than 80% of the more successful group. Dunleavy *et al.* (2008) point out how in the age of online applications and automated personnel systems, adverse impact computations are skewed by frequent applicants (i.e., applicants who apply for multiple positions or the same position on multiple occasions). Adverse impact can also be inferred by comparing the hiring rates for a particular group within an organization with the hiring rates for that group within the relevant industry as a whole. Alternatively, the hiring rates of the group within the organization of interest can be compared with the numbers that might be expected to be hired on the basis of population percentages. Finally, the hiring rates associated with a given group can be benchmarked against the hiring rates of that group by salient competitors. Adverse impact has also been assessed by testing the statistical significance of the difference between hiring rates for multiple groups (Morris and Lobsenz, 2000). However, as Collins and Morris (2008) point out in their review and assessment of several approaches for assessing adverse impact when sample sizes are small, statistical significance tests have low power and are suboptimal for studying or documenting adverse impact.

After group differences and adverse impact assessments, the most important issue pertaining to the efficacy of the various predictors in use is the question of bias. Bias is the systematic over- or underprediction based on group membership (Schmidt, 2002) and is usually investigated as a test of equality of the regression lines for the two groups (Cleary, 1969). Predictive bias pertains to bias in predicting criterion scores with predictor scores, whereas measurement bias pertains to bias in the assessment of an underlying or latent construct with observed scores (Jensen, 1980, 1998). Although it is possible to have measurement or construct bias in the absence of predictive bias, we focus our discussion on predictive bias. In the context of selection decisions, predictive bias manifests as the systematic over- or underprediction of criterion scores on the basis of group membership (Schmidt, 2002) and is usually investigated as a test of equality of the regression lines for the groups of interest (Cleary, 1969). Such bias can occur with or without group differences and/or adverse impact.

Single-group validity refers to the predictor in question being a valid predictor of the criterion of interest (i.e., the correlation between the predictor and criterion is non-zero) for one group but not for others, whereas differential validity refers to the predictor being statistically significant predictor for all groups but the magnitude differing across the groups. In conclusions of single-group validity one should ensure that the sample sizes are approximately equal across the groups. In fact, testing for the equality of regression lines (i.e., predictive bias) will ensure the absence of differential or single group validity; therefore, we do not discuss these two terms further.

Finally, researchers have explored the possibility of differential item functioning (DIF), a potential source of measurement bias (e.g., Holland and Wainer, 1993). The essential strategy for detecting such bias is to equate individuals from the different groups of interest on the construct being measured and test whether the percentage of individuals falling within each response category differs significantly across the various groups. Several statistical procedures have been developed to test the presence of DIF but in the absence of bias at the test level, it is not clear how DIF is to be interpreted. DIF will be useful in test construction, but in evaluating predictors for the purposes of personnel selection, we focus our discussion on empirical studies that have variously assessed group differences in mean scores and predictive bias. We conclude this section by presenting some strategies advanced in the literature for organizations to design selection systems when faced with valid and unbiased predictors in which there are group differences (e.g., cognitive ability).

Group Differences

Group differences in cognitive ability tests have been extensively studied and sex differences in the general factor of intelligence have been found to be small (Hyde, 2005; Sackett and Wilk, 1994). However, ethnic group differences have been found between whites and blacks in several empirical studies. A meta-analytic cumulation of these studies found a mean difference of 1.1 standard deviations (Roth *et al.*, 2001). The difference between whites and Hispanics was estimated at 0.72 SD. Lynn and Vanhanen (2006) cumulated results across 21 studies and found a difference of slightly less than 1.0 SD between whites and Native Americans. In a study comparing Canadian First Nation (American Indian) with white recruits for military, Vanderpool and Catano (2008) reported a 1.0 SD difference in mean scores. Thus, ethnic differences in cognitive ability scores are substantial (Gottfredson, 2002; Herrnstein and Murray, 1994) and these differences do not favor minorities.

Ethnic differences in personality variables have not been explored as extensively as they have been with cognitive ability (Sackett and Wilk, 1994). Ones and Viswesvaran (1998) using four large samples found that gender differences slightly favored women in integrity assessments. Feingold's (1994) meta-analysis indicated that most gender differences on personality variables were small to moderate with only facets of agreeableness indicating larger differences (e.g., tender-mindedness, aggression). Hough, Oswald, and Ployhart (2001) summarized the gender and ethnic differences in personality variables—most differences were in favor of women and minorities and thus are unlikely to cause litigation concerns with their use in personnel selection (Guttman, 2000). Across 11 personality inventories, Hough (1998) reported negligible race differences in personality. There were some notable exceptions: Hispanic Americans scored higher than whites in response distortion scales (0.60 SD units) and whites scored 0.30 SD units higher than blacks (Hough, 1998). Goldberg *et al.* (1998) obtained data on American adults using two Big Five measures and found small race differences. A large scale meta-analysis of race and ethnic group differences on Big Five personality factors as well as their facets showed that although differences at the factor level were negligible to small, differences at the facet level tended to be larger in the moderate range (this finding varied by Big Five dimension studied) (Foldes, Duehr, and Ones, 2008).

On other predictors used in employee selection, the magnitudes of group differences appear to follow the pattern of findings found for cognitive ability tests or personality measures, depending on the cognitive loading of the predictor examined. Here we briefly mention key findings to illustrate the magnitudes of group differences that can be anticipated when various predictors are used. Gender differences of the order of 0.10 to 0.20 SD units have been found in EI favoring women (Mayer *et al.*, 1999; Schutte *et al.*, 1998). Van Rooy, Alonso, and Viswesvaran (2005) reported Hispanic–white differences on EI where Hispanics scored a half standard deviation above whites. Blacks scored one-third of a standard deviation above whites but almost one-fifth lower than Hispanics. VanRooy *et al.* also reported a difference of 0.20 SD units favoring women in EI and a correlation of 0.17 between age and EI scores (older respondents scored higher on EI). Gandy, Dye, and MacLane (1994) found on a sample of 5,758 individuals black–white differences of 0.35 SD units, whereas Pulakos and Schmitt (1996) in a smaller sample ($N = 357$) found a differences of 0.05 SD units favoring blacks. Gender differences have been small in assessment center scores (Moses and Boehm, 1975) but Schmitt (1993) reported mean score differences of 0.40 SD units between Caucasian and non-Caucasian applicants. Hogan (1991) summarized the results across 14 studies comparing men and women in physical-ability assessments. Hogan found that in endurance assessments men outperformed women by 1.27 SD units (across 12 studies), whereas the gender differences were smaller in measures of balance and coordination (about half a standard deviation favoring males). Schmitt, Clause, and Pulakos (1996) found differences between blacks and Caucasians (0.66 SD units) in spatial ability. Schmitt et al. found a difference of 0.38 SD units when blacks and whites were compared on work sample tests but virtually no differences between Hispanics and whites. Women had higher scores on work sample tests (Schmitt et al., 1996). Huffcutt and Roth (1998) also report little negative impact for minorities in structured interview scores. As we noted earlier though, documentation of group differences can provide an understanding of likely adverse impact that can result from using various predictors in personnel selection. Yet, mean group differences do not lead to an inference of predictive bias, a topic we turn to next.

Predictive Bias

Predictive bias has been extensively studied with respect to cognitive ability, and in a meta-analytic cumulation of this literature, Hunter, Schmidt, and Hunter (1979) found that differential validity occurs only at chance levels across the multitude of studies reviewed. Very little research has addressed predictive bias on other predictors. Perhaps this is a result of the empirical finding that minorities and women score higher in other noncognitive predictors or at least the differences are not substantial.

Limited research has, nevertheless, addressed the potential for predictive bias in noncognitive predictors. In fact, if we put aside the voluminous empirical literature on the predictive bias in cognitive ability, the majority of studies on predictive bias have been conducted in lab studies, often relying on students as participants. The primary focus of investigation in these studies has been the potential bias in interview evaluations. There are serious limitations of such studies especially with respect to their real-world applications (Landy, 2008).

Bliesener (1996) conducted a meta-analysis and found that the criterion-related validity of biodata (for the criterion of overall job performance) was 0.51 for female samples but only 0.27 in male samples. Saad and Sackett

(2002) examined predictive bias for men and women on personality measures and found little evidence of slope and intercept differences. In general, the employee selection literature on predictive bias remains impoverished. For many racial, ethnic groups, men and women, predictive bias (i.e., slope and intercept differences between various groups of interest) in various predictors for predicting various criteria is yet to be examined. Predictive bias should be examined for the multitude of predictor–criterion combinations organizations and researchers are interested in. In addition, the legal and cultural environment of personnel selection in a given country affects the groups of interest for which predictive bias analyses need to be conducted. In sum then, predictive bias analyses for various predictors (construct by method), in predicting different criteria (e.g., job performance, counterproductive work behaviors) need to be examined for diverse groups of interest.

Nonetheless, we are left with the empirical finding that predictive bias is not a major concern for cognitive ability tests despite large group differences on these tests favouring whites. More importantly, cognitive ability is the best individual differences predictor available for the prediction of overall job performance among employees (Ones et al., 2005a, in press; Salgado et al., 2001; Schmidt, 2002). These empirical facts pose a dilemma for organizations seeking to use the most valid predictors without doing so at the expense of diversity considerations. Several strategies have been proposed for addressing this dilemma and evaluated (see Ryan and Tippins, 2004 for an elaboration of the different strategies).

Organizational Strategies to Address Group Differences

The most straightforward and simple strategy is to eliminate or de-emphasize the role of cognitive ability in selection (Outtz, 2002); however, this strategy affects the overall usefulness (i.e., utility) that can be derived from selection systems (Schmidt and Hunter, 1998). The use of low cut-scores also compromises the utility of selection systems as the ability–performance link has been found to be linear (Coward and Sackett, 1990). The use of alternate predictors, even with equal validity, is likely to result in a different set of employees (Kehoe, 2002), and it is unclear whether organizations will profit from de-emphasizing cognitive ability in a global economy with dynamic changes and technological innovations. The changes outlined earlier (e.g., rapid technology changes, globalization) are bound to increase the importance of cognitive ability for successful training and job performance. The value of general cognitive ability is expected to increase during the times of rapid change we are experiencing across different domains: there is new and changing knowledge to be acquired; there are innovations to be made; there are seemingly insurmountable global problems that need to be solved; and there is time pressure to reach good decisions in short amounts of time. Many of the environmental changes and challenges we reviewed above call for an increasing role and value of assessing cognitive ability in hiring. Unfortunately, cognitive assessments also bring with them the price of greater racial and ethnic homogeneity among hired employees. Diversity suffers. Furthermore, as Reeve and Bonaccio (2009) reconfirmed, group differences become more pronounced as the g loading of the test increases. Thus, the more effective a test is in assessing cognitive ability, the greater are the group differences. What can be done to alleviate this problem? Alternate predictors can be supplements, not substitutes, for cognitive ability in selection (Ones et al., in press; Viswesvaran and Ones, 2002). Combining cognitive ability test results with noncognitive measures that typically show lower levels of racial and ethnic group differences (Foldes et al., 2008) may not be a solution either. Ryan, Ployhart, and Friedel (1998) noted that adding personality to a selection system did not reduce potential adverse impact for minorities; Sackett and Ellingson (1997) demonstrated the manner in which the addition of multiple predictors affects adverse impact of the overall system. The effectiveness of composites in reducing adverse impact will depend on the predictor intercorrelations as well as on how the selection system is designed (Potosky, Bobko, and Roth, 2005; Roth, Bobko, and Switzer, 2006; Schmitt et al., 1997).

It has been proposed that changing the mode of presentation on cognitive measures has the potential to reduce group differences (e.g., Chan and Schmitt, 1997). The general idea is that as the items are made more context-specific (i.e., real world), differences are reduced across groups; however, evidence to support this strategy is scarce and has failed to take into account reliability differences in the different modes of presentation. Further, there is the troubling question of how one affects reduction in group differences in an unbiased test without introducing bias in favor of the low-scoring groups.

In the last two decades, some researchers have proposed the use of score banding as a means to address group differences in cognitive ability tests (e.g., Aguinis, 2004). Banding of scores has been used for administrative purposes in selection (Guion, 1998) but the thrust here is to use information pertaining to the statistical significance of score differences as the basis for banding (Cascio et al., 1991). The proposal argues that scores that are not statistically significantly different are to be banded together, but in reality, the scores not different from the top score are banded together. Several issues such as the reliability of the tests, the level of significance, among others, will affect the width of the band constructed and different methods can be used for selection within the bands (random, alternate predictors or preferential hiring). The logical argument of Schmidt (1991) is still valid: there is inherent contradiction in equating an individual score with the top score (because it is not statistically different but not considering scores lower than this score that are not statistically different from it). Campion, et al. (2001) present a lively debate of these issues. We refer the interested reader to an edited volume by Aguinis (2004) in which various perspectives on banding are presented and discussed in greater detail than is possible within the confines of this chapter.

Expanding the criterion domain for selection has been proposed as a further approach for organizations dealing with group differences in cognitive ability (Borman and Motowidlo, 2007). The hope is that when organizations take into account all facets of performance (not just task performance), group differences in cognitive ability (a predictor of task performance) will result in lower adverse impact. This strategy assumes: (1) organizations are interested in many dimensions of performance (probably true), (2) different predictors predict the other dimensions better than cognitive ability, and as such (3) placing more weight on the other predictors will reduce adverse impact (Hattrup and Rock, 2002). Unfortunately, the research on predictor combinations and resulting group differences does not lend much support to this strategy (Sackett and Ellingson, 1997). Finally, recognizing that organizations have to make trade-offs between diversity and productivity goals, De Corte et al. (2008) present approaches to assess pareto-optimal solutions for optimizing such choices. Kehoe (2008) as well as Potosky, Bobko, and Roth (2008) caution, however, that such trade-offs come with steep costs for organizations. As diversity goals go global, we expect much more debate and research on these issues.

A CHALLENGE ROOTED IN TECHNOLOGICAL AND GLOBALIZATION TRENDS: EQUIVALENCE OF SCORES

Technological innovations in the way that tests are administered have created the need to evaluate whether computerized versus traditional versions of the same instrument produce equivalent scale scores. Early on, Mead and Drasgow (1993) presented a meta-analytic cumulation that supported the equivalence of scores between computerized and traditional versions of cognitive ability tests. However, equivalence was lower in speeded tests compared to power tests. Finger and Ones (1999) reported similar meta-analytic results for personality tests. Although telephone interviews have been found to be predictive (Schmidt and Rader, 1999), demonstrating the equivalence of telephone interview scores to traditional interviews has been elusive (Silvester et al., 2000).

Recently, researchers have explored the equivalence of scores obtained from unproctored online tests to traditional proctored administrations (for a review, see Tippins, 2009). Nye et al. (2008) found that scores on unproctored tests were actually lower than those obtained in a subsequent proctored retesting, suggesting that cheating may not be a major issue. Test publishers present several steps that can be taken to ensure more honest responding (see Tippins, et al., 2006 for details). Professional associations have presented guidelines for effective testing on the Internet (for representative examples, see Bartram,

2006; Harris, 2000) but several unanswered questions remain. Future research is needed urgently to assess several issues such as the extent of cheating, the effectiveness of risk mitigation strategies, impact on validity, and meaning of test scores.

Another trend in the environment, globalization, also calls for equating of test scores for different groups of test takers. As multinational organizations aim to select their diverse workforces around the world, different language versions of the same test are being increasingly used, raising the thorny issue of the equivalence of the assessment processes and outcomes across linguistic and cultural settings. There is a voluminous literature that has developed concerning the equivalence of ability and achievement tests in diverse educational settings (see Hambleton, Merenda, Spielberger, 2005; Geisinger, 1994 for overview discussions). It is rather disconcerting, if not disheartening, that comparatively little research effort has gone into addressing the question of the equivalence of employment tests and organizational assessment practices more widely when used cross-culturally. The increasing movement of employees and jobs across borders demands that our field urgently redresses this imbalance.

CONCLUSIONS

In this chapter, we surveyed the vast literature in the area of employee selection. Obviously there are many more studies than we could even mention in a review of this nature. In deciding what to highlight, we took our cue from fundamental changes that are affecting or ought to be affecting the science and practice of employee selection. Juxtaposing environmental changes and challenges with main topics covered in this chapter has yielded some unique insights. For example, it is quite obvious from Table 5.1 that whereas the impact and role of technological innovations in employee selection are being widely researched, the much broader impact of environmental challenges, such as population growth, energy depletion, and sustainability, on the way that employee behavior must change and adapt has been virtually ignored in selection research. Clearly, this is a major area that requires the attention of IWO psychologists. Table 5.1 also reveals that although diversity concerns within national borders have been attended to, there is a dearth of research on globally relevant and usable predictor measures. Finally, it appears that we know little about how many of the findings pertaining to the psychometric efficacy of the various tools and techniques investigated painstakingly in primary studies over many years and summarized in meta-analyses are affected by changing economic conditions. Examinations of historic trends in validity data may reveal important and interesting findings.

Also, several mainstream issues remain to be addressed as to the combination of the different predictors, the methods of combination, and how decisions are made using those combinations. We need research on the interactive effects of validity, bias, reactions, response distortion of each predictor, and for combinations of predictors. Predictor intercorrelations should be systematically assessed and theory-driven research is needed to assess team-level selection. Currently, we have more information on individual traits that make for successful teamwork (Lievens, 2008) but not much on team composition of required skills (Barrick et al., 1998). Staffing for team-level effectiveness (Ployhart and Schneider, 2005) is in need of new theories, models, and methods of multilevel selection. We thus look forward to the coming decades for fruitful developments in the science and practice of personnel selection.

In a global economy with rapid changes in so many different areas, personnel selection techniques and models are likely to change over the years. Our profession needs to find effective means to translate research findings for the world of practice (cf. Anderson, Herriot, and Hodgkinson, 2001). Rynes, Brown, and Colbert (2002) discuss some common misconceptions about selection practices among practitioners and ways to address the scientist–practitioner divide (see also Anderson, 2007; Gelade, 2006; Hodgkinson, 2006; Hodgkinson and Rousseau, 2009; van de Ven, 2007; Wall, 2006). Several ethical codes govern the practice of personnel selection, and as we sail into more complex areas of global selection, such guidelines are going to be more valuable in guiding practice (Voskuijl, Evers, and Geerlings, 2005).

Employee selection is an applied venture with high stakes for organizations and individuals alike. There is much work to be done as our field tackles issues of science and practice in these challenging, but also exciting, times of change.

REFERENCES

Aaker, J. L. (1997). Dimensions of brand personality. *Journal of Marketing Research*, **34**, 347–56.

Adair, W. L., Okumura, T., Brett, J. M. (2001). Negotiation behavior when cultures collide: The United States and Japan. *Journal of Applied Psychology*, **86**, 371–85.

Aguinis, H. (2004). *Test-Score Banding in Human Resource Selection: Technical, Legal, and Societal Issues*. Westport, CT: Greenwood.

Ahart, A. M., & Sackett, P. R. (2004). A new method of examining relationships between individual difference measures and sensitive behavior criteria: Evaluating the unmatched count technique. *Organizational Research Methods*, 7, 101–14.

Alliger, G. M., Lilienfeld, S. O., & Mitchell, K. E. (1996). The susceptibility of overt and covert integrity tests to coaching and faking. *Psychological Science*, 7, 32–9.

Anderson, N. (2003). Applicant and recruiter reactions to new technology in selection: A critical review and agenda for future research. *International Journal of Selection and Assessment*, 11, 121–36.

Anderson, N. (2004). Editorial—The dark side of the moon: Applicant perspectives, negative psychological effects (NPEs), and candidate decision making in selection. *International Journal of Selection and Assessment*, 12, 1–8.

Anderson, N. (2005). Relationships between practice and research in personnel selection: Does the left hand know what the right is doing? In A. Evers, N. Anderson & O. Voskuijl (Eds), *The Blackwell Handbook of Personnel Selection* (pp. 1–24). Oxford, UK: Blackwell.

Anderson, N. (2007). The practitioner-researcher divide revisited: Strategic-level bridges and the roles of IWO psychologists: Rejoinder. *Journal of Occupational and Organizational Psychology*, 80, 175–83.

Anderson, N., Born, M., & Cunningham-Snell, N. (2001). Recruitment and selection: Applicant perspectives and outcomes. In N. Anderson, D. S. Ones, H. K. Sinangil & C. Viswesvaran (Eds), *Handbook of Industrial Work and Organizational Psychology*, Vol. 1 (pp. 200–18). London: Sage.

Anderson, N., Herriot, P., & Hodgkinson, G. P. (2001). The practitioner-researcher divide in Industrial, Work, and Organizational (IWO) psychology: Where are we now, and where do we go from here? *Journal of Occupational and Organizational Psychology*, 74, 391–411.

Anderson, N., & Witvliet, C. (2008). Fairness reactions to personnel selection methods: An international comparison between the Netherlands, the United States, France, Spain, Portugal and Singapore. *International Journal of Selection and Assessment*, 16, 1–13.

Arthur, W., & Bennett, W., Jr. (1995). The international assignee: The relative importance of factors perceived to contribute to success. *Personnel Psychology*, 48, 99–114.

Arthur, W., Day, E. A., McNelly, T. L., & Edens, P. S. (2003). A meta-analysis of the criterion-related validity of assessment center dimensions. *Personnel Psychology*, 56, 125–54.

Arvey, R. D., & Murphy, K. R. (1998). Performance evaluation in work settings. *Annual Review of Psychology*, 49, 141–68.

Arvey, R. D., & Sackett, P. R. (1993). Fairness in selection: Current developments and perspective. In N. Schmitt & W. Borman (Eds), *Personnel Selection in Organizations* (pp. 171–202). San Francisco: Jossey-Bass.

Aycan, Z. (2001). Expatriation: A critical step toward developing global leaders. In M. E. Mendenhall, T. M. Kühlmann & G. K. Stahl (Eds), *Developing Global Business Leaders: Policies, Processes, and Innovations* (pp. 119–35). Westport, CT: Greenwood.

Bank, J., Crandell, S., Goff, M., Ramesh, A., & Sokol, M. (2009). Executive selection: Yes, we can do better. *Industrial and Organizational Psychology: Perspectives on Science and Practice*, 2, 151–4.

Barber, A. E. (1998). *Recruiting Employees: Individual and Organizational Perspectives*. Thousand Oaks, CA: Sage.

Baron, H., & Austin, J. (2000). *Measuring ability via the internet: Opportunities and issues*. Paper presented at the Annual Conference of the Society for Industrial and Organizational Psychology, New Orleans, LA.

Bar-On, R. (1997). *Bar-On Emotional Quotient Inventory: Technical manual*. Toronto: Multihealth Systems.

Barrett, G. V., Phillips, J. S., & Alexander, R. A. (1981). Concurrent and predictive validity designs: A critical analysis. *Journal of Applied Psychology*, 66, 1–6.

Barrick, M. R., & Mount, M. K. (1991). The Big Five personality dimensions and job performance. *Personnel Psychology*, 44, 1–26.

Barrick, M. R., & Mount, M. K. (1996). Effects of impression management and self-deception on the predictive validity of personality constructs. *Journal of Applied Psychology*, 81, 261–72.

Barrick, M. R., Mount, M. K., & Judge, T. A. (2001). Personality and performance at the beginning of the new millennium: What do we know and where do we go next? *International Journal of Selection and Assessment*, 9, 9–30.

Barrick, M. R., Stewart, G. L., Neubert, M. J., & Mount, M. K. (1998). Relating member ability and personality to work-team processes and team effectiveness. *Journal of Applied Psychology*, **83**, 377–91.

Bartram, D. (2006). Testing on the Internet: Issues, challenges and opportunities in the field of occupational assessment. In D. Bartram & R. K. Hambleton (Eds), *Computer-Based Testing and the Internet: Issues and Advances*. London: Wiley.

Bartram, D. (2007). Increasing validity with forced-choice criterion measurement formats. *International Journal of Selection and Assessment*, **15**, 263–72.

Bartram, D. (2009). The International Test Commission guidelines on computer-based and internet-delivered testing. *Industrial and Organizational Psychology: Perspectives on Science and Practice*, **2**, 11–3.

Bartram, D., & Brown, A. (2004). Online testing: Mode of administration and the stability of OPQ 32i scores. *International Journal of Selection and Assessment*, **12**, 278–84.

Bauer, T. N., Truxillo, D. M., & Paronto, M. E. (2003). The measurement of applicant reactions to selection. In J. Thomas (Ed.), *Comprehensive Handbook of Psychological Assessment, Vol. 4: Industrial/Organizational Psychology*, (pp. 482–506). New York: Wiley.

Bauer, T. N., Truxillo, D. M., Sanchez, R. J., Craig, J. M., Ferarra, P., & Campion, M. A. (2001). Applicant reactions to selection: Development of the Selection Procedural Justice Scale (SPJS). *Personnel Psychology*, **54**, 387–419.

Bernardin, H. J. (2007). *Human Resource Management: An Experiential Approach* (4th ed). Boston, MA: Mc-Graw Hill.

Bertolino, M., & Steiner, D. D. (2007). Fairness reactions to selection methods: An Italian study. *International Journal of Selection and Assessment*, **15**, 197–205.

Bliesener, T. (1996). Methodological moderators in validating biographical data in personnel selection. *Journal of Occupational and Organizational Psychology*, **69**, 107–20.

Borman W. C., & Motowidlo, S. J. (1997). Task performance and contextual performance: The meaning for personnel selection research. *Human Performance*, **10**, 99–109.

Born, M., & Scholarios, D. (2005). Decision making in selection. In A. Evers, N. Anderson & O. Voskuijl (Eds), *The Blackwell Handbook of Personnel Selection* (pp. 267–90). Oxford, UK: Blackwell.

Bradley, K. M., & Hauenstein, N. M. A. (2006). The moderating effects of sample type as evidence of the effects of faking on personality scale correlations and factor structure. *Psychology Science*, **48**, 313–35.

Breaugh, J. A. (1992). *Recruitment: Science and Practice*. Boston: PWS-Kent.

Breaugh, J. A., & Starke, M. (2000). Research on employee recruitment: So many studies, so many remaining questions. *Journal of Management*, **26**, 405–34.

Buchanan, T., & Smith, J. L. (1999). Using the Internet for psychological research: Personality testing on the World Wide Web. *British Journal of Psychology*, **90**, 125–44.

Burke, M. J., Normand, J., & Raju, N. S. (1987). Examinee attitudes toward computer-administered ability testing. *Computers in Human Behavior*, **3**, 95–107.

Bycio, P., Alvares, K. M., & Hahn, J. (1987). Situational specificity in assessment center ratings: A confirmatory factor analysis. *Journal of Applied Psychology*, **72**, 457–62.

Caligiuri, P. M. (2000). The big five personality characteristics as predictors of expatriate's desire to terminate the assignment and supervisor-rated performance. *Personnel Psychology*, **53**, 67–88.

Callender, J. C., & Osburn, H. G. (1980). Development and test of a new model of validity generalization. *Journal of Applied Psychology*, **65**, 543–58.

Campbell, J. P. (Ed.). (1990). *Personnel Psychology* (Vol. 43).

Campbell, J. P., McCloy, R. A., Oppler, S. H., & Sager, C. E. (1993). A theory of performance. In N. Schmitt & W. C. Borman (Eds), *Personnel Selection in Organizations* (pp. 35–70). San Francisco: Jossey-Bass.

Campbell, J. P., McHenry, J. J., & Wise, L. L. (1990). Modeling job performance in a population of jobs. *Personnel Psychology*, 43, 313–33.

Campbell, S. K., & Catano, V. M. (2004). Using measures of specific abilities to predict training performance in Canadian Forces operator occupations. *Military Psychology*, 16, 183–201.

Campion, M. A., Outtz, J. L., Zedeck, S., Schmidt, F. L., Kehoe, J. F., Murphy, K. R., & Guion, R. M. (2001). The controversy over score banding in personnel selection: Answers to 10 key questions. *Personnel Psychology*, 54, 149–85.

Campion, M. A., Palmer, D. K., & Campion, J. E. (1997). A review of structure in the selection interview. *Personnel Psychology*, 50, 655–702.

Cappelli, P. (2009). The future of the U. S. business model and the rise of competitors. *Academy of Management Perspectives*, 23, 5–10.

Carlson, K. D., Scullen, S. E., Schmidt, F. L., Rothstein, H., & Erwin, F. (1999). Generalizable biographical data validity can be achieved without multi-organizational development and keying. *Personnel Psychology*, 52, 731–55.

Cascio, W. F., Outtz, J., Zedeck, S., & Goldstein, I. L. (1991). Statistical implications of six methods of test score use in personnel selection. *Human Performance*, 4, 233–64.

Casper, S. (2007). *Creating Silicon Valley in Europe: Public Policy Toward New Technology Industries*. Oxford, UK: Oxford University Press.

Chan, D., & Schmitt, N. (1997). Video-based versus paper-and-pencil method of assessment in situational judgment tests: Subgroup differences in test performance and face validity perceptions. *Journal of Applied Psychology*, 82, 143–59.

Chan, D., & Schmitt, N. (2004). An agenda for future research on applicant reactions to selection procedures: A construct-oriented approach. *International Journal of Selection and Assessment*, 12, 9–23.

Chapman, D. S., & Webster, J. (2003). The use of technologies in the recruiting, screening, and selection processes for job candidates. *International Journal of Selection and Assessment*, 11, 113–20.

Christiansen, N. D., Goffin, R. D., Johnston, N. G., & Rothstein, M. G. (1994). Correcting the 16PF for faking: Effects on criterion-related validity and individual hiring decisions. *Personnel Psychology*, 47, 847–60.

Chung-Yan, G. A., Cronshaw, S. F., & Hausdorf, P. A. (2005). A criterion-related validation study of transit operators. *International Journal of Selection and Assessment*, 13, 172–7.

Cleary, T. A. (1969). Test bias: Prediction of grades of Negro and White students in integrated colleges. *Journal of Educational Measurement*, 5, 115–24.

Cober, R. T., Brown, D. J., Levy, P. E., Cober, A. B., & Keeping, L. M. (2003). Organizational websites: Web site content and style as determinants of organizational attraction. *International Journal of Selection and Assessment*, 11, 158–69.

Cohen, J. (1977). *Statistical Power Analysis for the Behavioral Sciences*. New York: Academic Press.

Collins, M. W., & Morris, S. B. (2008). Testing for adverse impact when sample size is small. *Journal of Applied Psychology*, 93, 463–71.

Connelly, B. S., Ones, D. S., Ramesh, A., & Goff, M. (2008). A pragmatic view of dimensions and exercises in assessment center ratings. *Industrial and Organizational Psychology: Perspectives on Science and Practice*, 1, 127–30.

Converse, P. D., Peterson, M. H., & Griffith, R. L. (2009). Faking on personality measures: Implications for selection involving multiple predictors. *International Journal of Selection and Assessment*, 17, 47–60.

Cooper, H., & Hedges, L. V. (Eds.) (1994). *The Handbook of Research Synthesis*. New York: Russell Sage.

Coward, W. M., & Sackett, P. R. (1990). Linearity of ability-performance relationships: A reconfirmation. *Journal of Applied Psychology*, 75, 295–300.

Coyle J. R., & Thorson, E. (2001). The effects of progressive levels of interactivity and vividness in web marketing sites. *Journal of Advertising*, 30, 65–77.

Cronbach, L. J, & Meehl, P. E. (1955). Construct validity in psychological tests. *Psychological Bulletin*, 52, 281–302.

Crowne, D. P., & Marlowe, D. (1960). A new scale of social desirability independent of psychopathology. *Journal of Consulting Psychology*, 24, 349–54.

Davies, M., Stankov, L., & Roberts, R. D. (1998). Emotional intelligence: In search of an elusive construct. *Journal of Personality and Social Psychology*, 75, 989–1015.

Davison, H. K., & Burke, M. J. (2000). Sex discrimination in simulated employment contexts: A meta-analytic investigation. *Journal of Vocational Behavior*, 56, 225–48.

Davison, M. L., & Davenport, E. C. (2002). Identifying criterion-related patterns of predictor scores using multiple regression. *Psychological Methods*, 7, 468–84.

Day, D. V. (2009). Executive selection is a process not a decision. *Industrial and Organizational Psychology: Perspectives on Science and Practice*, 2, 159–62.

De Corte, W., Lievens, F., & Sackett, P. R. (2008). Validity and adverse impact potential of predictor composite formation. *International Journal of Selection and Assessment*, 16, 183–94.

Dilchert, S., & Ones, D. S. (2004, April). *Meta-analysis of practical intelligence: Contender to the throne of g?* Poster session presented at the Annual Conference of the Society for Industrial and Organizational Psychology, Chicago, IL.

Dilchert, S., & Ones, D. S. (2009). Assessment center dimensions: Individual differences correlates and meta-analytic incremental validity. *International Journal of Selection and Assessment*, 17.

Dilchert, S., Ones, D. S., Viswesvaran, C., & Deller, J. (2006). Response distortion in personality measurements: Born to deceive, yet capable of providing valid self-assessments? *Psychology Science*, 48, 209–25.

Dineen, B. R., Ash, S. R., & Noe, R. A. (2002). A web of applicant attraction: Person-organization fit in the context of web-based recruitment. *Journal of Applied Psychology*, 87, 723–34.

Dipboye, R. L., Fontenelle, G. A., & Garner, K. (1984). Effects of previewing the application on interview process and outcomes. *Journal of Applied Psychology*, 69, 118–28.

Donovan, J. J., Dwight, S. A., & Hurtz, G. M. (2003). An assessment of the prevalence, severity, and verifiability of entry-level applicant faking using randomized response technique. *Human Performance*, 16, 81–106.

Dunleavy, E. M., Mueller, L. M., Buonasera, A. K., Kuang, D. C., & Dunleavy, D. G. (2008). On the consequences of frequent applicants in adverse impact analyses: A demonstration study. *International Journal of Selection and Assessment*, 16, 333–44.

Dunn, W. S., Mount, M. K., Barrick, M. R., & Ones, D. S. (1995). Relative importance of personality and general mental ability in managers' judgments of applicant qualifications. *Journal of Applied Psychology*, 80, 500–9.

Dwight, S. A., & Donovan, J. J. (2003). Do warnings not to fake reduce faking? *Human Performance*, 16, 1–23.

Edwards, A. L. (1957). *The Social Desirability Variable in Personality Assessment and Research*. Ft Worth, TX: Dryden.

Ellingson, J. E., Sackett, P. R., & Connelly, B. S. (2007). Personality assessment across selection and development contexts: Insights into response distortion. *Journal of Applied Psychology*, 92, 386–95.

Ellingson, J. E., Sackett, P. R., & Hough, L. M. (1999). Social desirability corrections in personality measurement: Issues of applicant comparison and construct validity. *Journal of Applied Psychology*, 84, 155–66.

Ellingson, J. E., Smith, D. B., & Sackett, P. R. (2001). Investigating the influence of social desirability on personality factor structure. *Journal of Applied Psychology*, 86, 122–33.

Feingold, A. (1994). Gender differences in personality: A meta-analysis. *Psychological Bulletin*, 116, 429–56.

Fernandez-Araoz, C. (2007). *Great People Decisions*. Hoboken, NJ: John Wiley and Sons.

Finger, M. S., & Ones, D. S. (1999). Psychometric equivalence of the computer and booklet forms of the MMPI: A meta-analysis. *Psychological Assessment*, 11, 58–66.

Foldes, H. J., Duehr, E. E., & Ones, D. S. (2008). Group differences in personality: Meta-analyses comparing five U.S. racial groups. *Personnel Psychology*, 61, 579–616.

Foldes, H. J., Ones, D. S., & Sinangil, H. K. (2006). Neither here, nor there: Impression management does not predict expatriate adjustment and job performance. *Psychology Science*, 48, 357–68.

Fox, S., & Spector, P. E. (2000). Relations of emotional intelligence, practical intelligence, general intelligence, and trait affectivity with interview outcomes: It's not all just 'G'. *Journal of Organizational Behavior*, 21, 203–20.

Gandy, J. A., Dye, D. A., & MacLane, C. N. (1994). Federal government selection: The individual achievement record. In G. Stokes, M. Mumford & W. Owens (Eds), *Biodata Handbook: Theory, Research, and Use of Biographical Information in Selection and Performance Prediction* (pp. 275–310). Palo Alto, CA: Consulting Psychologists Press.

Gaugler, B. B., Rosenthal, D. B., Thornton, G. C., & Bentson, C. (1987). Meta-analysis of assessment center validity. *Journal of Applied Psychology*, 72, 243–59.

Geisinger, K. F. (1994). Cross-Cultural Normative Assessment: Translation and Adaptation Issues Influencing the Normative Interpretation of Assessment Instruments. *Psychological Assessment*, 6, 304–12.

Gelade, G. A. (2006). But what does it mean in practice? The Journal of Occupational and Organizational Psychology from a practitioner perspective. *Journal of Occupational and Organizational Psychology*, 79, 153–60.

Gill, C. M., & Hodgkinson, G. P. (2007). Development and validation of the Five Factor Model Questionnaire (FFMQ): An adjectival-based personality inventory for use in occupational settings. *Personnel Psychology*, 60, 731–66.

Gilliland, S. W. (1993). The perceived fairness of selection systems: An organizational justice perspective. *Academy of Management Review*, 18, 694–734.

Goffin, R. D., & Christiansen, N. D. (2003). Correcting personality tests for faking: A review of popular personality tests and an initial survey of researchers. *International Journal of Selection and Assessment*, 11, 340–4.

Goldberg, L. R., Sweeney, D., Merenda, P. F., & Hughes, J. E. (1998). Demographic variables and personality: The effects of gender, age, education, and ethnic/racial status on self-descriptions of personality attributes. *Personality and Individual Differences*, 24, 393–403.

Goldsmith, K., & Walt, C. (2000). New competencies for tomorrow's global leader. *CMA Management*, 73 (11), 20–4.

Goleman, D. (1995). *Emotional Intelligence: Why It Can Matter More than IQ*. New York: Bantam.

Goleman, D. (1998). *Working with Emotional Intelligence*. New York: Bantam Books.

Gottfredson, L. S. (2002). Where and why g matters: Not a mystery. *Human Performance*, 15, 25–46.

Greenberg, J. (2009). Everybody talks about organizational justice, but nobody does anything about it. *Industrial and Organizational Psychology: Perspectives on Science and Practice*, **2**, 181–95.

Griffith, R. L., & McDaniel, M. A. (2006). The nature of deception and applicant faking behavior. In D. Svyantek, R. L. Griffith & M. H. Peterson (Eds), *A Closer Examination of Applicant Faking Behavior* (pp. 1–19). Greenwich, CT: Information Age.

Grigorenko, E. L., & Sternberg, R. J. (2001). Analytical, creative, and practical intelligence as predictors of self-reported adaptive functioning: A case study in Russia. *Intelligence*, **29**, 57–73.

Guion, R. M. (1998). *Assessment, Measurement, and Prediction for Personnel Decisions*. Mahwah, NJ: Erlbaum.

Guttman, A. (2000). *EEO Law and Selection Procedures* (2nd ed). Thousand Oaks, CA: Sage.

Hambleton, R. K., Merenda, P. F., & Spielberger, C. D. (2005). *Adapting educational and psychological tests for cross-cultural assessment*. Lawrence Erlbaum Associates, Hillsdale, NJ.

Harris, M. M. (2000). The internet and industrial/organizational psychology: Practice and research perspectives. *Journal of e-commerce and Psychology*, **1**, 4–23.

Hattrup, K., & Rock, J. (2002). A comparison of predictor-based and criterion-based methods for weighting predictors to reduce adverse impact. *Applied H. R. M. Research*, **7**, 22–38.

Hausknecht, J. P., Day, D. V., & Thomas, S. C. (2004). Applicant reactions to selection procedures: An updated model and meta-analysis. *Personnel Psychology*, **57**, 639–83.

Hedlund, J., & Sternberg, R. J. (2000). Too many intelligences? Integrating social, emotional, and practical intelligence. In R. Bar-On & J. D. A. Parker (Eds), *The Handbook of Emotional Intelligence: Theory, Development, Assessment, and Application at Home, School, and in the Workplace* (pp. 136–67). San Francisco, CA: Jossey-Bass.

Heggestad, E. D., Morrison, M., Reeve, C. L., & McCloy, R. A. (2006). Forced-choice assessments of personality for selection: Evaluating issues of normative assessment and faking resistance. *Journal of Applied Psychology*, **91**, 9–24.

Hermelin, E., Lievens, F., & Robertson, I. T. (2007). The validity of assessment centres for the prediction of supervisory performance ratings: A meta-analysis. *International Journal of Selection and Assessment*, **15**, 405–11.

Herriot, P. (1989). Selection as a social process. In M. Smith & I. T. Robertson (Eds), *Advances in Staff Selection*. Chichester: John Wiley.

Herrnstein, R., & Murray, C. (1994). *The Bell Curve: Intelligence and Class Structure in American Life*. New York: Free Press.

Hodgkinson, G. P. (2006). The role of JOOP (and other scientific journals) in bridging the practitioner-researcher divide in industrial, work and organizational (IWO) psychology. *Journal of Occupational and Organizational Psychology*, **79**, 173–8.

Hodgkinson, G. P., & Healey, M. P. (2008). Cognition in organizations. *Annual Review of Psychology*, **59**, 387–417.

Hodgkinson, G. P., & Payne, R. L. (1998). Graduate selection in three European countries. *Journal of Occupational and Organizational Psychology*, **71**, 359–65.

Hodgkinson, G. P., & Rousseau, D. M. (2009). Bridging the rigour–relevance gap in management research: It's already happening! *Journal of Management Studies*, **46**, 534–46.

Hoffman, E. (2000). *Ace the Corporate Personality Test*. New York: McGraw-Hill.

Hogan, J. C. (1991). Physical abilities. In M. D. Dunnette & L. M. Hough (Eds) *Handbook of Industrial and Organizational Psychology* (Vol. 2, pp. 753–831). Palo Alto, CA: Consulting Psychologists Press.

Hogan, R. (1983). A socio-analytic theory of personality. In M. M. Page (Ed.), *Nebraska Symposium on Motivation 1982. Personality: Current Theory and Research* (pp. 55–89). Lincoln, NE: University of Nebraska Press.

Hogan, R. (2005). In defense of personality measurement: New wine for old whiners. *Human Performance*, 18, 331–41.

Hogan, J., Barrett, P., & Hogan, R. (2007). Personality measurement, faking, and employment selection. *Journal of Applied Psychology*, 92, 1270–85.

Holden, R. R., & Jackson, D. N. (1981). Subtlety, information, and faking effects in personality assessment. *Journal of Clinical Psychology*, 37, 379–86.

Holland, P. W., & Wainer, H. (1993) *Differential item functioning*. Lawrence Erlbaum Associates, Hillsdale, NJ.

Hough, L. M. (1998). Effects of intentional distortion in personality measurement and evaluation of suggested palliatives. *Human Performance*, 11, 209–44.

Hough, L. M., & Dilchert, S. (in press). Personality: Its measurement and validity for employee selection. In J. L. Farr & N. Tippins (Eds), *Handbook of Employee Selection*. New York: Psychology Press.

Hough, L. M., & Ones, D. S. (2001). The structure, measurement, validity, and use of personality variables in Industrial, Work, and Organizational Psychology. In N. Anderson, D. S. Ones, H. K. Sinangil, & C. Viswesvaran (Eds), *Handbook of Industrial, Work and Organizational Psychology* (Vol. 1; pp. 233–77). London: Sage.

Hough, L. M., Ones, D. S., & Viswesvaran, C. (1998, April). Personality correlates of managerial performance constructs. In R. Page (Chair), *Personality determinants of managerial potential, performance, progression and ascendancy*. Symposium conducted at the annual conference of the Society for Industrial and Organizational Psychology, Dallas, TX.

Hough, L. M., & Oswald, F. L. (2000). Personnel selection: Looking towards the future and remembering the past. *Annual Review of Psychology*, 51, 631–64.

Hough, L. M., Oswald, F. L., & Ployhart, R. E. (2001). Determinants, detection, and amelioration of adverse impact in personnel selection procedures: Issues, evidence, and lessons learned. *International Journal of Selection and Assessment*, 9, 152–94.

Howard, A. (1996). *The Changing Nature of Work*. San Francisco: Jossey-Bass.

Huffcutt, A. I., & Roth, P. L. (1998). Racial group differences in employment interview evaluations. *Journal of Applied Psychology*, 83, 179–89.

Hunter, J. E., & Hunter, R. F. (1984). Validity and utility of alternate predictors of job performance. *Psychological Bulletin*, 96, 72–98.

Hunter, J. E., & Schmidt, F. L. (2004). *Methods of Meta-Analysis*. Thousand Oaks, CA: Sage.

Hunter, J. E., Schmidt, F. L., & Hunter, R. (1979). Differential validity of employment tests by race: A comprehensive review and analysis. *Psychological Bulletin*, 86, 721–35.

Hyde, J. S. (2005). The gender similarities hypothesis. *American Psychologist*, 60, 581–92.

Jeannet, P. (2000). Managing with a global mindset. London: Financial Times/Prentice-Hall.

Jensen, A. R. (1980). *Bias in Mental Testing*. New York: Free Press.

Jensen, J. B. (1998). *The g Factor: The Science of Mental Ability*. Westport, CT: Praeger Publishers.

Jone, J. W. (2001). Defining the best job search websites. *Journal of e-commerce and Psychology*, 2, 4–8.

Judge, T. A., & Cable, D. M. (1997). Applicant personality, organizational culture, and organization attraction. *Personnel Psychology*, 50, 359–94.

Kehoe, J. F. (2002). General mental ability and selection in private sector organizations: A commentary. *Human Performance*, 15, 97–106.

Kehoe, J. F. (2008). Commentary on Pareto-optimality as a rationale for adverse impact reduction: What would organizations do? *International Journal of Selection and Assessment*, 16, 195–200.

Kluger, A. N., & Rothstein, H. R. (1993). The influence of selection test type on applicant reactions to employment testing. *Journal of Business and Psychology*, 8, 3–25.

Kuncel, N. R., & Borneman, M. J. (2007). Toward a new method of detecting deliberately faked personality tests: The use of idiosyncratic item responses. *International Journal of Selection and Assessment*, 15, 220–31.

Lance, C. E. (2008). Why assessment centers do not work the way they are supposed to. *Industrial and Organizational Psychology: Perspectives on Science and Practice*, 1, 84–97.

Landy, F. J. (2008). Stereotypes, bias, and personnel decisions: Strange and stranger. *Industrial and Organizational Psychology: Perspectives on Science and Practice*, 1, 379–92.

Li, A., & Bagger, J. (2006). Using the BIDR to distinguish the effects of impression management and self-deception on the criterion validity of personality measures: A meta-analysis. *International Journal of Selection and Assessment*, 14, 141.

Lievens, F. (2008). Research on selection in an international context: Current status and future directions. In M. M. Harris (Ed.), *Handbook of Research in International Human Resource Management* (pp. 107–23). New York: Lawrence Erlbaum.

Lievens, F., Dilchert, S., & Ones, D. S. (in press). The importance of exercise and dimension factors in assessment centers: Simultaneous examinations of construct-related and criterion-related validity. *Human Performance*.

Lievens, F., & Harris, M. M. (2003). Research on internet recruitment and testing: Current status and future directions. In C. L. Cooper & I. T. Robertson (Eds), *International Review of Industrial and Organizational Psychology* (Vol. 18, pp. 131–65). Chichester, UK: John Wiley & Sons.

Lievens, F., & Highhouse, S. (2003). The relation of instrumental and symbolic attributes to a company's attractiveness as an employer. *Personnel Psychology*, 56, 75–102.

Lynn, R., & Vanhanen, T. (2006). *Race Differences in Intelligence: An Evolutionary Analysis*. Augusta, GA: Washington Summit Books.

Maher, K., & Silverman, R. E. (2002, January). Online job sites yield few jobs, users complain. *The Wall Street Journal*, January 2, A1, A13.

Marcus, B. (2006). Relationships between faking, validity, and decision criteria in personnel selection. *Psychology Science*, 48, 226–46.

Marquardt, M. J., & Berger, N. O. (2000). *Global Leaders for the 21st Century*. New York: State University of New York.

Matthews, G., Zeidner, M., & Roberts, R. D. (2002). *Emotional Intelligence: Science and Myth*. Cambridge, MA: MIT Press.

Maxwell, S. E., & Arvey, R. D. (1993). The search for predictors with high validity and low adverse impact: Compatible or incompatible goals? *Journal of Applied Psychology*, 78, 433–7.

Mayer, J. D., Caruso, D. R., & Salovey, P. (1999). Emotional intelligence meets traditional standards for emotional intelligence. *Intelligence*, 27, 267–98.

McDaniel, M. A., Whetzel, D. L., Schmidt, F. L., & Maurer, S. D. (1994). The validity of the employment interview: A comprehensive review and meta-analysis. *Journal of Applied Psychology*, 79, 599–616.

McFarland, L. A. (2003). Warning against faking on a personality test: Effects on applicant reactions and personality test scores. *International Journal of Selection and Assessment*, 11, 265–76.

McFarland, L. A., & Ryan, A. M. (2000). Variance in faking across noncognitive measures. *Journal of Applied Psychology*, 85, 812–21.

McFarland, L. A., Ryan, A. M., & Ellis, A. (2002). Item placement on a personality measure: Effects on faking behavior and test measurement properties. *Journal of Personality Assessment*, **78**, 348–69.

McManus, M. A., & Ferguson, M. W. (2003). Biodata, personality, and demographic differences of recruits from three sources. *International Journal of Selection and Assessment*, **11**, 175–83.

Mead, A. D., & Drasgow, F. (1993). Equivalence of computerized and paper-and-pencil cognitive ability tests: A meta-analysis. *Psychological Bulletin*, **114**, 449–58.

Mesmer-Magnus, J. R., & Viswesvaran, C. (2006). Assessing response distortion in personality tests: A review of research designs and analytic strategies. In R. Griffith & M. Peterson (Eds), *A Closer Examination of Applicant Faking Behavior* (pp. 83–111). Greenwich, CT: Information Age.

Mook, D. G. (1983). In defense of external invalidity. *American Psychologist*, **38**, 379–87.

Morgeson, F. P., Campion, M. A., Dipboye, R. L., Hollenbeck, J. R., Murphy, K., & Schmitt, N. (2007). Reconsidering the use of personality tests in personnel selection contexts. *Personnel Psychology*, **60**, 683–729.

Morris, S. B., & Lobsenz, R. E. (2000). Significance tests and confidence intervals for the adverse impact ratio. *Personnel Psychology*, **53**, 89–112.

Moscoso, S., & Salgado, J. E. (2004). Fairness reactions to personnel selection techniques in Spain and Portugal. *International Journal of Selection and Assessment*, **12**, 187–96.

Moses, J. L., & Boehm, V. R. (1975). Relationship of assessment center performance to management progress of women. *Journal of Applied Psychology.* **60**, 527–29.

Mount, M. K., Oh, I.-S., & Burns, M. (2008). Incremental validity of perceptual speed and accuracy over general mental ability. *Personnel Psychology*, **61**, 113–39.

Murphy, K. A. (1986). When your top choice turns you down: Effect of rejected job offers on the utility of selection tests. *Psychological Bulletin*, **99**, 128–33.

Murphy, K. R., & Dzieweczynski, J. L. (2005). Why don't measures of broad dimensions of personality perform better as predictors of job performance? *Human Performance*, **18**, 343–57.

Neisser, U. (Ed.). (1998). *The Rising Curve: Long-term Gains in IQ and Related Measures.* Washington, DC: American Psychological Association.

Nikolaou, I., & Judge, T. A. (2007). Fairness reactions to personnel selection techniques in Greece. *International Journal of Selection and Assessment*, **15**, 206–19.

Nye, C. D., Do, B., Drasgow, F., & Fine, S. (2008). Two-step testing in employee selection: Is score inflation a problem? *International Journal of Selection and Assessment*, **16**, 112–20.

Odenwald, S. (1996). Global work teams. *Training and Development*, **50**, 54–8.

Ones, D. S. (2009, August). Employee Green Behaviors A Taxonomy for the Green Economy. In S. Dilchert and D. S. Ones (Chairs), *Environmentally friendly worker behaviors, senior leader wrongdoing, and national level outcomes.* Symposium conducted at the annual meeting of the Academy of Management, Chicago, Illinois.

Ones, D. S., & Dilchert, S. (2009a, August). Green behaviors of workers: A taxonomy for the green economy. In S. Dilchert & D. S. Ones (Chairs), *Environmentally Friendly Worker Behaviors, Senior Leader Wrongdoing, and National Level Outcomes.* Symposium conducted at the annual meeting of the Academy of Management, Chicago, IL.

Ones, D. S., & Dilchert, S. (2009b). How special are executives? How special should executive selection be? Observations and recommendations. *Industrial and Organizational Psychology: Perspectives on Science and Practice*, **2**, 163–70.

Ones, D. S., Dilchert, S., Viswesvaran, C., & Judge, T. (2007). In support of personality assessments in organizational settings. *Personnel Psychology*, **60**, 995–1027.

Ones, D. S., Dilchert, S., Viswesvaran, C., & Salgado, J. F. (in press). Cognitive abilities. In J. L. Farr & N. Tippins (Eds), *Handbook of Employee Selection*. Mahwah, NJ: Erlbaum.

Ones, D. S., Rubenzer, S. J., & Faschingbauer, T. R. (2004). Predicting presidential success. In S. J. Rubenzer & T. R. Faschingbauer (Eds), *Personality, Character and Leadership in the White House* (pp. 38–59). Washington, DC: Brassey's.

Ones, D. S., & Viswesvaran, C. (1997). Personality determinants in the prediction of aspects of expatriate job success. In Z. Aycan (Ed.), *Expatriate Management: Theory and Research* (pp. 63–92). London, UK: JAI.

Ones, D. S., & Viswesvaran, C. (1998). Gender, age, and race differences on overt integrity tests: Results across four large scale job applicant datasets. *Journal of Applied Psychology*, **83**, 35–42.

Ones, D. S., & Viswesvaran, C. (1999). Relative importance of personality dimensions for expatriate selection: A policy capturing study. *Human Performance*, **12**, 275–94.

Ones, D. S., & Viswesvaran, C. (2001). Integrity tests and other criterion-focused occupational personality scales (COPS) used in personnel selection. *International Journal of Selection and Assessment*, **9**, 31–9.

Ones, D. S., & Viswesvaran, C. (2007a). A research note on the incremental validity of job knowledge and integrity tests for predicting maximal performance. *Human Performance*, **20**, 293–303.

Ones, D. S., & Viswesvaran, C. (2007b). Labor market influences on personality scale scores among job applicants: Four field studies in personnel selection settings. *Zeitschrift für Personalpsychologie*, **6**, 71–84.

Ones, D. S., Viswesvaran, C., & Dilchert, S. (2005a). Cognitive ability in personnel selection decisions. In A. Evers, N. Anderson & O. Voskuijl (Eds), *Handbook of Personnel Selection* (pp. 143–73). Oxford, UK: Blackwell.

Ones, D. S., Viswesvaran, C., & Dilchert, S. (2005b). Personality at work: Raising awareness and correcting misconceptions. *Human Performance*, **18**, 389–404.

Ones, D. S., Viswesvaran, C., & Reiss, A. D. (1996). The role of social desirability in personality testing in personnel selection: The red herring. *Journal of Applied Psychology*, **81**, 660–79.

Ones, D. S., Viswesvaran, C., & Schmidt, F. L. (1993). Comprehensive meta-analysis of integrity test validities: Findings and implications for personnel selection and theories of job performance. *Journal of Applied Psychology*, **78**, 679–703.

Oppler, E. S., Lyons, B. D., Ricks, D. A., & Oppler, S. H. (2008). The relationship between financial history and counterproductive work behavior. *International Journal of Selection and Assessment*, **16**, 416–20.

Ortner, T. M. (2008). Effects of changed item order: A cautionary note to practitioners on jumping to computerized adaptive testing for personality assessment. *International Journal of Selection and Assessment*, **16**, 249–57.

Outtz, J. L., (2002). The role of cognitive ability tests in employment selection. *Human Performance*, **15**, 161–71.

Pace, V. L., & Borman, W. C. (2006). The use of warnings to discourage faking on non-cognitive inventories. In R. Griffith & M. Peterson (Eds), *A Closer Examination of Applicant Faking Behavior* (pp. 283–304). Greenwich, CT: Information Age.

Pace, V. L., Xu, X., Penney, L. M., Borman, W. C., & Bearden, R. M. (2005), April. Using warnings to discourage personality test faking: An empirical study. In J. P. Bott & C. C. Rosen (Chairs), *Moving from Laboratory to Field: Investigating Situation in Faking Research*. Symposium conducted at the annual conference of the Society for Industrial and Organizational Psychology, Los Angeles, CA.

Perry, E. L., Simpson, P. A., NicDomhnaill, O. M., & Siegel, D. M. (2003). Is there a technology age gap? Associations among age, skills, and employment outcomes. *International Journal of Selection and Assessment*, 11, 141–9.

Petrides, K. V., & Furnham, A. (2001). Trait emotional intelligence: Psychometric investigation with reference to established trait taxonomies. *European Journal of Personality*, 15, 425–48.

Pfeffer, J. (1994). *Competitive Advantage through People*. Boston: Harvard Business School Press.

Phillips, J. M., & Gully, S. M. (2002). Fairness reactions to personnel selection techniques in Singapore and the United States. *International Journal of Selection and Assessment*, 13, 1186–205.

Ployhart, R. E., & Ryan, A. M. (1997). Toward and explanation of applicant reactions: An examination of organizational justice and attribution frameworks. *Organizational Behavior and Human Decision Processes*, 72, 308–35.

Ployhart, R. E., & Schneider, B. (2005). Multilevel selection and prediction: Theories, methods, and models. In A. Evers, O. Voskuijl & N. Anderson (Eds), *Handbook of Selection* (pp. 495–516). Oxford, UK: Blackwell.

Potosky, D., & Bobko, P. (1997). Computer versus paper and pencil administration mode and response distortion in noncognitive selection tests. *Journal of Applied Psychology*, 82, 293–9.

Potosky, D., Bobko, P., & Roth, P. L. (2005). Forming composites of cognitive ability and alternative measures to predict job performance and reduce adverse impact: Corrected estimates and realistic expectations. *International Journal of Selection and Assessment*, 13, 304–15.

Potosky, D., Bobko, P., & Roth, P. L. (2008). Some comments on Pareto thinking, test validity, and adverse impact: When 'and' is optimal and 'or' is a trade-off. *International Journal of Selection and Assessment*, 16, 201–5.

Pulakos, E. D., & Schmitt, N. (1996). An evaluation of two strategies for reducing adverse impact and their effects on criterion-related validity. *Human Performance*, 9, 241–58.

Quinones, M. A., Ford, K. J., & Teachout, M. S. (1995). The relationship between work experience and job performance: A conceptual and meta-analytic review. *Personnel Psychology*, 48, 887–910.

Rees, C. J., & Metcalfe, B. (2003). The faking of personality test questionnaire results: Who's kidding whom? *Journal of Managerial Psychology*, 18, 156–65.

Reeve, C. L., & Bonaccio, S. (2009). Measurement reliability, the Spearman–Jensen effect and the revised Thorndike model of test bias. *International Journal of Selection and Assessment*, 17, 61–8.

Reich, R. (1991). *The work of nations*. New York: Knopf.

Reynolds, D. H, Sinar E. F., & McClough A. C. (2000, April). *Evaluation of a web-based selection procedure*. Paper presented at the annual conference of the Society for Industrial and Organizational Psychology, New Orleans, LA.

Richman, W. L., Kiesler, S., Weisband, S., & Drasgow, F. (1999). A meta-analytic study of social desirability distortion in computer-administered questionnaires, traditional questionnaires, and interviews. *Journal of Applied Psychology*, 84, 754–75.

Roberts, R. D., Zeidner, M., & Matthews, G. (2001). Does emotional intelligence meet traditional standards for an intelligence? New data and conclusions. *Emotion*, 1, 196–231.

Robertson, I. T., Gratton, L., & Sharpley, D. (1987). The psychometric properties and design of managerial assessment centres: dimensions into exercises won't go. *Journal of Occupational Psychology*, 60, 187–95.

Roth, P. L., Bevier, C. A., Bobko, P. L., Switzer, F. S., & Tyler, P. (2001). Ethnic group differences in cognitive ability in employment and educational settings: A meta-analysis. *Personnel Psychology*, 54, 297–330.

Roth, P. L., Bobko, P., & Switzer, S. S. (2006). Modeling the behavior of the 4/5ths rule for determining adverse impact: Reasons for caution. *Journal of Applied Psychology*, 91, 507–22.

Rothstein, H. R., Schmidt, F. L., Erwin, F. W., Owens, W. A., & Sparks, C. P. (1990). Biographical data in employment selection: Can validities be made generalizable? *Journal of Applied Psychology*, 75, 175–84.

Rousseau, D. M. (1990). New hire perceptions of their own and their employer's obligations: A study of psychological contracts. *Journal of Organizational Behavior*, 11, 389–400.

Russell, C. J., Matson, S. E., Devlin, S. E., & Atwater, D. (1990). Predictive validity of biodata items generated from retrospective life experience essays. *Journal of Applied Psychology*, 75, 569–80.

Ryan, A. M., & Ployhart, P. E. (2000). Applicants' perceptions of selection procedures and decisions: A critical review and agenda for the future. *Journal of Management*, 26, 565–606.

Ryan, A. M., Ployhart, R. E., & Friedel, L. A. (1998). Using personality testing to reduce adverse impact: A cautionary note. *Journal of Applied Psychology*, 83, 298–307.

Ryan, A. M., & Tippins, N. T. (2004). Attracting and selecting: What psychological research tells us. *Human Resource Management*, 43, 305–18.

Rynes, S. L., Brown, K. G., & Colbert, A. E. (2002). Seven common misconceptions about human resource practices: Research findings versus practitioner beliefs. *Academy of Management Executive*, 16, 92–102.

Saad, S., & Sackett, P. R. (2002). Investigating differential prediction by gender in employment-oriented personality measures. *Journal of Applied Psychology*, 87, 667–74.

Sackett, P. R., & Dreher, G. F. (1984). Situation specificity of behavior and assessment center validation strategies: A rejoinder to Neidig and Neidig. *Journal of Applied Psychology*, 69, 187–90.

Sackett, P. R., & Ellingson, J. E. (1997). The effects of forming multi-predictor composites on group differences and adverse impact. *Personnel Psychology*, 50, 707–21.

Sackett, P. R., & Wilk, S. L. (1994). Within-group norming and other forms of score adjustment in pre-employment testing. *American Psychologist*, 49, 929–54.

Saks, A. M. (2005). The impracticality of recruitment research. In A. Evers, N. Anderson & O. Voskuijl (Eds), *The Blackwell Handbook of Personnel Selection* (pp. 47–72). Oxford, UK: Blackwell.

Salgado, J. F. (1997). The Five Factor Model of personality and job performance in the European Community. *Journal of Applied Psychology*, 82, 30–43.

Salgado, J. F., Anderson, N., Moscoso, S., Bertua, C., De Fruyt, F., & Rolland, J. P. (2003). International validity generalization of GMA and cognitive abilities: A European community meta-analysis. *Personnel Psychology*, 56, 573–605.

Salgado, J. F., & De Fruyt, F. (2005). Personality in personnel selection. In A. Evers, N. Anderson, & O. Voskuijl (Eds), *The Blackwell Handbook of Personnel Selection* (pp. 174–98). Oxford, UK: Blackwell.

Salgado, J. F., & Moscoso, S. (2002). Comprehensive meta-analysis of the construct validity of the employment interview. *European Journal of Work and Organizational Psychology*, 11, 299–324.

Salgado, J., Viswesvaran, C., & Ones, D. S. (2001). Predictors used for personnel selection: An overview of constructs, methods, and techniques. In N. Anderson, D. S. Ones, H. K. Sinangil & C. Viswesvaran (Eds), *Handbook of Industrial, Work, and*

Organizational Psychology: Personnel Psychology (pp. 165–99). Thousand Oaks, CA: Sage.

Salovey, P., & Mayer, J. D. (1990). Emotional intelligence. *Imagination, Cognition, and Intelligence*, **9**, 185–211.

Schippmann, J. S. (1999). *Strategic Job Modeling: Working at the Core of Integrated Human Resources*. Mahwah, NJ: Lawrence Erlbaum.

Schmidt, F. L. (1991). Why all banding procedures in personnel selection are logically flawed. *Human Performance*, **4**, 265–78.

Schmidt, F. L. (1992). What do data really mean? Research findings, meta-analysis, and cumulative knowledge in psychology. *American Psychologist*, **47**, 1173–81.

Schmidt, F. L. (2002). The role of general cognitive ability and job performance: Why there cannot be a debate. *Human Performance*, **15**, 187–210.

Schmidt, F. L., & Hunter, J. E. (1977). Development of a general solution to the problem of validity generalization. *Journal of Applied Psychology*, **62**, 529–40.

Schmidt, F. L., & Hunter, J. E. (1996). Measurement error in psychological research: Lessons from 26 research scenarios. *Psychological Methods*, **1**, 199–223.

Schmidt, F. L., & Hunter, J. E. (1998). The validity and utility of selection methods in personnel psychology: Practical and theoretical implications of 85 years of research findings. *Psychological Bulletin*, **124**, 262–74.

Schmidt, F. L., & Hunter, J. E. (1999). Theory testing and measurement error. *Intelligence*, **27**, 183–98.

Schmidt, F. L., Hunter, J. E., & Outerbridge, A. N. (1986). Impact of job experience and ability on job knowledge, work sample performance, and supervisory ratings of job performance. *Journal of Applied Psychology*, **71**, 432–9.

Schmidt, F. L., & Kaplan, L. B. (1971). Composite versus multiple criteria: A review and resolution of the controversy. *Personnel Psychology*, **24**, 419–34.

Schmidt, F. L., & Rader, M. (1999). Exploring the boundary conditions for interview validity: Meta-analytic validity findings for a new interview type. *Personnel Psychology*, **52**, 445–64.

Schmidt, F. L., Viswesvaran, C., & Ones, D. S. (2000). Reliability is not validity and validity is not reliability. *Personnel Psychology*, **53**, 901–12.

Schmidt, F. L., & Zimmerman, R. D. (2004). A counterintuitive hypothesis about employment interview validity and some supporting evidence. *Journal of Applied Psychology*, **89**, 553–61.

Schmitt, N. (1993). Group composition, gender and race effects on assessment center ratings. In H. Schuler, J. Farr, & M. Smith (Eds), *Personnel Selection in Industrial Research and Development* (pp. 315–32). Hillsdale, NJ: Erlbaum.

Schmitt, N., & Chan, D. (1998). *Personnel Selection: A Theoretical Approach*. Thousand Oaks, CA: Sage.

Schmitt, N., Clause, C., & Pulakos, E. (1996). Subgroup differences associates with different measures of some common job relevant constructs. In C. L. Cooper & I. T. Robertson (Eds), *International Review of Industrial and Organizational Psychology* (pp. 115–39). New York: Wiley.

Schmitt, N., Oswald, F. L., Kim, B. H., Gillespie, M. A., & Ramsay, L. J. (2004). The impact of justice and self-serving bias explanations of the perceived fairness of different types of selection tests. *International Journal of Selection and Assessment*, **12**, 160–71.

Schmitt, N., Oswald, F. L., Kim, B. H., Gillespie, M. A., Ramsay, L. J., & Yoo, T.-Y. (2003). Impact of elaboration on socially desirable responding and the validity of biodata measures. *Journal of Applied Psychology*, **88**, 979–88.

Schmitt, N., Rogers, W., Chan, D., Sheppard, L., & Jennings, D. (1997). Adverse impact and predictive efficiency of various predictor combinations. *Journal of Applied Psychology*, **82**, 719–30.

Schneider, B. (1987). The people make the place. *Personnel Psychology*, **40**, 437–53.

Schreurs, B., Derous, E., Proost, K., Notelaers, G., & De Witte, K. (2008). Applicant selection expectations: Validating a multidimensional measure in the military. *International Journal of Selection and Assessment*, **16**, 170–6.

Schuler, H. (1993). Social validity of selection situations: Fairness in selection. In H. Schuler, J. L. Farr & M. Smith (Eds), *Personnel Selection and Assessment: Individual and Organizational Perspectives* (pp. 11–26). Hillsdale, NJ: Erlbaum.

Schulte, Ree, & Carretta (2004). Emotional intelligence: Not much more than g and personality. *Personality and Individual Differences*, **37**, 1059–68.

Schutte, N. S., Malouff, J. M., Hall, L. E., Haggerty, D. J., Cooper, J. T., Golden, C. J., & Dornheim, L. (1998). Development and validation of a measure of emotional intelligence. *Personality and Individual Differences*, **25**, 167–77.

Seiler, S. N., & Kuncel, N. R. (2005, April). *Modeling the individual differences determinants of faking: Integration and extension*. Paper presented at the annual conference of the Society for Industrial and Organizational Psychology, Los Angeles, CA.

Shackleton, V., & Newell, S. (1991). Management selection: A comparative survey of methods used in top British and French companies. *Journal of Occupational Psychology*, **64**, 23–36.

Shackleton, V., & Newell, S. (1994). European management selection methods: A comparison of five countries. *International Journal of Selection and Assessment*, **2**, 91–102.

Shackleton, V., & Newell, S. (1997). International assessment and selection. In N. Anderson & P. Herriot (Eds), *International Handbook of Selection and Assessment*. Chichester, UK: Wiley.

Short, J., Williams, E., & Christie, B. (1976). *The Social Psychology of Telecommunications*. New York: Wiley.

Siegfried, J. (1994). *The Status of Common Sense in Psychology*. Westport, CT: Ablex.

Silvester, J., Anderson, N., Haddleton, E., Cunningham-Snell, N., & Gibb, A. (2000). A cross-modal comparison of telephone and face-to-face selection interviews in graduate recruitment. *International Journal of Selection and Assessment*, **8**, 16–21.

Sinangil, H. K., & Ones, D. S. (2001). Expatriate management. In N. Anderson, D. S. Ones, H. K. Sinangil & C. Viswesvaran (Eds), *Handbook of Industrial, Work and Organizational Psychology* (Vol. 1, pp. 424–43). London: Sage.

Slaughter, J. E., & Greguras, G. J. (2009). Initial attraction to organizations: The influences of trait inferences. *International Journal of Selection and Assessment*, **17**, 1–18.

Slaughter, J. E., Zickar, M. J., Highhouse, S., & Mohr, D. C. (2004). Personality trait inferences about organizations: Development of a measure and assessment of construct validity. *Journal of Applied Psychology*, **89**, 85–103.

Smithikrai, C. (2007). Personality traits and job success: An investigation in a Thai sample. *International Journal of Selection and Assessment*, **15**, 134–8.

Song, K. M. (2005, June 22). Faking your type to 'pass' a personality test. *Seattle Times*, p. F1.

Sparrow, P. R. (2006). International management: Some key challenges for industrial and organizational psychology. In G. P. Hodgkinson & J. K. Ford (Eds), *International Review of Industrial and Organizational Psychology* (Vol. 21, pp. 189–265). Chichester, UK: Wiley.

Spreitzer, G. M., McCall, M. W., Jr., & Mahoney, J. D. (1997). Early identification of international executive potential. *Journal of Applied Psychology*, **82**, 6–29.

Stahl, G. K. (2001). Using assessment centers as tools for global leadership development. In Mendenhall, M. E., Kühlmann, T. M. & Stahl, G. K. (Eds), *Developing Global Business Leaders: Policies, Processes, and Innovations* (pp. 197–210). Westport, CT: Greenwood.

Stark, S., Chernyshenko, O. S., Chan, K.-Y., Lee, W. C., & Drasgow, F. (2001). Effects of the testing situation on item responding: Cause for concern. *Journal of Applied Psychology*, **86**, 943–53.

Steiner, D. D., & Gilliland, S. W. (1996). Fairness reactions to personnel selection techniques in France and the U. S. *Journal of Applied Psychology*, **81**, 134–41.

Sternberg, R. J., & Hedlund, J. (2002). Practical intelligence, g, and work psychology. *Human Performance*, **15**, 143–60.

Sternberg, R. J., Forsythe, G. B., Hedlund, J., Horvath, J. A., Wagner, R. K., Williams, W. M., *et al.* (2000). *Practical Intelligence in Everyday Life*. New York: Cambridge University Press.

Straus, S., Miles, J., & Levesque, L. (2001). The effects of videoconference, telephone, and face-to-face media on interviewer and applicant judgments in employment interviews, *Journal of Management*, **27**, 363–379.

Thorndike, E. L. (1920). Intelligence and its uses. *Harper's Magazine*, **140**, 227–35.

Thorndike, R. L. (1949). *Personnel Selection: Test and Measurement Techniques*. New York: Wiley.

Tippins, N. T. (2009). Internet alternatives to traditional proctored testing: Where are we now? *Industrial and Organizational Psychology: Perspectives on Science and Practice*, **2**, 2–10.

Tippins, N. T., Beatty, J., Drasgow, F., Gibson, W. M., Pearlman, K., Segall, D. O., & Shepherd, W. (2006). Unproctored internet testing in employment settings. *Personnel Psychology*, **59**, 189–225.

Tourangeau, R. (1987). Attitude measurement: A cognitive perspective. In H. Hippler, N. Schwarz, & S. Sudman (Eds), *Social Information Processing and Survey Methodology* (pp. 149–62). New York: Springer.

Tourangeau, R., & Smith, T. W. (1996). Asking sensitive questions: The impact of data collection mode, question format, and question context. *Public Opinion Quarterly*, **60**, 275–304.

Truxillo, D. M., Bauer, T. N., & Campion, M. A. (2009). Organizational justice interventions: Practicalities, concerns, and potential. *Industrial and Organizational Psychology: Perspectives on Science and Practice*, **2**, 211–4.

U. S. Bureau of Census (1975). *Historical Statistics of the United States: Colonial Times to 1970s*. Washington, DC: US Department of Commerce.

van de Ven, A. (2007). *Engaged Scholarship*. Oxford, UK: Oxford University Press.

Van Rooy, D. L., Alonso, A., & Fairchild, Z. (2003). In with the new, out with the old: Has the technological revolution eliminated traditional job search process? *International Journal of Selection and Assessment*, **11**, 170–74.

Van Rooy, D. L., & Viswesvaran, C. (2004). Emotional intelligence: A Meta-analytic investigation of predictive validity and nomological net. *Journal of Vocational Behavior*, **65**, 71–95.

Van Rooy, D. L., Alonso, A., & Viswesvaran, C. (2005). Group differences in emotional intelligence test scores: Theoretical and practical implications. *Personality and Individual Differences*, **38**, 689–700.

Van Rooy, D. L., Dilchert, S., Viswesvaran, C., & Ones, D. S. (2006). Multiplying intelligences: Are general, emotional, and practical intelligences equal? In K. R. Murphy (Ed.), *The Case Against Emotional Intelligence: What are the Problems and How Can They be Fixed?* Mahwah, NJ: Erlbaum.

Van Rooy, D. L., Viswesvaran, C., & Pluta, P. (2005). An examination of construct validity: What is this thing called emotional intelligence? *Human Performance*, **18**, 445–62.

Vanderpool, M., & Catano, V. M. (2008). Comparing the performance of Native Americans and predominantly White military recruits on verbal and non-verbal measures of cognitive ability. *International Journal of Selection and Assessment*, **16**, 239–48.

Vasilopoulos, N. L., Cucina, J. M., & McElreath, J. M. (2005). Do warnings of response verification moderate the relationship between personality and cognitive ability? *Journal of Applied Psychology*, **90**, 306–22.

Vinchur, A. J., Schippmann, J. S., Switzer, F. S., & Roth, P. L. (1998). A meta-analytic review of predictors of job performance for salespeople. *Journal of Applied Psychology*, **83**, 586–97.

Vinson, G. A., Connelly, B. S., & Ones, D. S. (2007). Relationships between personality and organization switching: Implications for utility estimates. *International Journal of Selection and Assessment*, **15**, 118–33.

Vispoel, W. P. (1999). Creating computerized adaptive tests of music aptitude: Problems, solutions and future directions. In F. Drasgow & J. B. Olson-Buchanan (Eds), *Innovations in Computerized Assessments* (pp. 151–176). Mahwah, NJ: Erlbaum.

Viswesvaran, C. (2003). Introduction to special issue: Role of technology in shaping the future of staffing and assessment. *International Journal of Selection and Assessment*, **11**, 107–12.

Viswesvaran, C., Deller, J., & Ones, D. S. (2007). Personality measures in personnel selection: Some new contributions. *International Journal of Selection and Assessment*, **15**, 354–8.

Viswesvaran, C., & Ones, D. S. (1999). Meta-analysis of fakability estimates: Implications for personality measurement. *Educational and Psychological Measurement*, **54**, 197–210.

Viswesvaran, C., & Ones, D. S. (2002). Agreements and disagreements on the role of General Mental Ability (GMA) in Industrial, Work and Organizational Psychology. *Human Performance*, **15**, 211–31.

Viswesvaran, C., Sinangil, H. K., Ones, D. S., & Anderson, N. (2001). Where we have been, where we are, (and where we could be). In N. Anderson, D. S. Ones, H. K. Sinangil & C. Viswesvaran (Eds), *Handbook of Industrial, Work, and Organizational Psychology* (Vol. 1: Personnel psychology, pp. 1–9). Thousand Oaks, CA: Sage.

Voskuijl, O. (2005). Job analysis: Current and future perspectives. In A. Evers, O. Voskuijl & N. Anderson (Eds), *Handbook of Selection* (pp. 27–46). Oxford, UK: Blackwell.

Voskuijl, O., Evers, A., & Geerlings, S. (2005). Is the obvious obvious? Considerations about ethical issued in personnel selection. In A. Evers, O. Voskuijl & N. Anderson (Eds), *Handbook of Selection* (pp. 98–117). Oxford, UK: Blackwell.

Wagner, R. (1949). The employment interview: A critical summary. *Personnel Psychology*, **2**, 279–94.

Wall, T. (2006). Is JOOP of only academic interest? *Journal of Occupational and Organizational Psychology*, **79**, 161–5.

Waters, L. K. (1965). A note on the "fakability" of forced-choice scales. *Personnel Psychology*, **18**, 187–91.

Weekley, J. A., & Ployhart, R. E. (Eds). (2006). *Situational Judgment Tests: Theory, Measurement, and Application*. Mahwah, NJ: Lawrence Erlbaum Associates.

Whitley, R. (2006). Project-based firms: New organizational forms or variations on a theme? *Industrial and Corporate Change*, **15**, 77–99.

Whitman, D. S., Van Rooy, D. L., Viswesvaran, C., & Alonso, A. (2008). The susceptibility of a mixed model measure of emotional intelligence to faking: A Solomon four-group design. *Psychology Science*, **50**, 44–63.

Whitman, D. S., Van Rooy, D. L., Viswesvaran, C., & Kraus, E. (2009). Testing the second-order factor structure and measurement equivalence of the Wong and Law

Emotional Intelligence Scale across gender and ethnicity. *Education and Psychological Measurement*, **69**, 1059–74.

Zickar, M. J., & Drasgow, F. (1996). Detecting faking on a personality instrument using appropriateness measurement. *Applied Psychological Measurement*, **20**, 71–87.

Zickar, M. J., & Robie, C. (1999). Modeling faking good on personality items: An item level analysis. *Journal of Applied Psychology*, **84**, 551–63.

Zusman, R. R., & Landis, R. S. (2002). Applicant preferences for web-based versus traditional job postings. *Computers in Human Behavior*, **18**, 285–96.

Chapter 6

DOING DIVERSITY RIGHT: AN EMPIRICALLY BASED APPROACH TO EFFECTIVE DIVERSITY MANAGEMENT

Derek R. Avery

Department of Psychology, University of Houston, Houston, TX, USA

Patrick F. McKay

School of Management and Labor Relations, Rutgers, The State University of New Jersey, Piscataway, NJ, USA

Three recent workplace trends combine to illustrate the existence of a significant organizational problem: managing diversity. First, demographic diversity in the workplace is increasing. For instance, the proportions of (a) older workers, (b) women, and (c) those belonging to traditionally underrepresented racial and ethnic minority groups in the labor market are rising around the globe (Toossi, 2007; Wrench, 2007). Second, many forms of employment discrimination remain prevalent (e.g., Avery, McKay, and Wilson, 2008; Deitch *et al.*, 2003; Murray and Syed, 2005; Ozgener, 2008; Tung, 2008; Wrench, 2007) and claims seem to be rising as well (McDonald and Dear, 2008). In fact, the financial settlements associated with claims in the United States alone climbed nearly 600% between 1992 and 2005 (cf. Goldman, Gutek, Stein, and Lewis, 2006). Third, companies appear more proficient at retaining employees belonging to dominant groups than those who do not (Hom, Roberson, and Ellis, 2008; Windzio, 2008; Zatzick, Elvira, and Cohen, 2003). Collectively, these occurrences suggest that as demographic diversity grows, many organizations are experiencing, and may continue to experience, considerable difficulty managing it and capitalizing on its highly touted prospective benefits.

The purpose of this chapter is to aid in this regard by integrating and synthesizing recent empirical research demonstrating what works and what does

International Review of Industrial and Organizational Psychology, 2010, Volume 25.
Edited by G. P. Hodgkinson and J. K. Ford. Copyright © 2010 John Wiley & Sons, Ltd

not with respect to diversity management. By consolidating this literature, we seek to accomplish three goals. First, we hope to help identify best practices to assist practitioners in their efforts to advocate and support organizational diversity efforts. Second, we look to clarify common misconceptions about what we have learned and what we have yet to learn about the effective management of demographic differences in organizational settings. Finally, we propose a research agenda for future study of workplace diversity.

Before commencing our review, it is important that we acknowledge recent related contributions by Kulik and Roberson (2008) and Avery (in press). In their chapter, Kulik and Roberson reviewed diversity recruitment, diversity training, and mentoring from the perspective of helping organizations realize how to maximize the efficacy of these initiatives in a diverse workforce. Avery reviewed the literature relating to impediments to equitable promotions in organizations and how organizations might seek to rectify them. It is our intent to extend what they have done. In the sections that follow, we briefly identify why effective diversity management is vital in today's world, describe what the research tells us about how to do it, and conclude with our suggestions for research to come.

WHY DIVERSITY MANAGEMENT IS NECESSARY

Diversity, in and of itself, is not a new construct, as there have always been men and women of various skin colors, religions, ages, abilities, and sexual orientations. Given that people have never been homogenous, many readers may wonder why diversity management should be any more critical now than in the past. In other words, if we have always been diverse, and, thus, always managed diversity – what's different now? The answer to this question is a complex one, rooted in at least three events: globalization, changing population demographics, and increased integration on the heels of civil rights movements.

More than at any time in the past, the business dealings of nations around the world are tied to one another, creating a global economy. Companies routinely export and import their goods and services across national borders. Many organizations operate in multiple locales, requiring them to employ and manage a diverse group of people (Jackson, Schuler, and Werner, 2009). Even companies that operate exclusively within a single country are not immune to the impact of globalization. The global economy is a part of their external environment and, therefore, influences factors like supply, demand, and legislation. Moreover, immigrants may comprise a considerable portion of their workforce or clientele.

In addition to the impact of globalization, many local labor forces are experiencing changes resulting in heightened demographic diversity. Despite past arguments to the contrary (e.g., Friedman and DiTomaso, 1996), projections continue to indicate that higher birth rates and immigration will result in sizable shifts in the racial and ethnic composition of the US population as a whole and workplaces therein (e.g., Toossi, 2007). Furthermore, populations in Western nations around the globe are aging, with the proportion of older workers growing at faster rates than other age categories (Dixon, 2003; Lende, 2005; US General Accounting Office, 2001). As the employee mean age increases, young workforce entrants will encounter an older employee base than in previous generations.

Finally, workforces of many companies are becoming more demographically heterogeneous because of civil rights movements and the legislation these activities have helped to spur. In the United States, for example, traditionally underrepresented groups like women, Black people, Hispanics, and Asian Americans are far more prevalent now than they were before the Civil Rights Act of 1964, which has yielded more integrated work settings (Tomaskovic-Devey *et al.*, 2006). Similar pressures toward equality and integration also exist outside the United States. In fact, "diversity issues in Europe have gained much publicity over the last two years, with increased pressure from governments and the European Commission for discrimination to be tackled" (Singh and Point, 2006, p. 364).

The result of these three occurrences is that there is more diversity in a wider range of workplaces. Traditional approaches to diversity management were designed to account for the previously smaller presence and fewer forms of diversity. Because these practices were not tailored to fit the current status quo, it is not surprising that they are largely ineffective in helping today's organizations manage diversity effectively. Whether or not one believes in the prospective benefits of workplace diversity, research clearly indicates that ineffective diversity management can prove quite costly to the bottom line. In addition to the millions of dollars that can be lost via discrimination lawsuits, companies also face the prospect of reputational damage further compounding losses when diversity is managed poorly (James and Wooten, 2006). For instance, whereas diversity awards for sound practice tend to facilitate positive corporate stock performance, lawsuits have the opposite effect (Roberson and Park, 2007; Wright, Ferris, Hiller, and Kroll, 1995).

McKay, Avery, and Morris (2009) found that aggregated employee and managerial perceptions that their business unit was supportive of equal opportunity and inclusion (i.e., diversity climate) positively influenced unit performance. Furthermore, performance was greatest when both parties agreed that the climate was hospitable for diversity. Evidence also suggests that diversity climate helps to facilitate the positive effects of racioethnic and sex diversity on unit performance (Gonzalez and DeNisi, 2009). In short, diversity management has grown significantly in importance over a fairly brief period of time. Consequently, the next section focuses on research illustrating how organizations might manage diversity more effectively.

RESEARCH IMPLICATIONS FOR EFFECTIVE
DIVERSITY MANAGEMENT

One of the most studied aspects of diversity is its relationship with performance at both the group and organizational levels (see Horwitz and Horwitz, 2007; Shoobridge, 2006; or van Knippenberg and Shippers, 2007 for recent reviews of this literature). The bottom line from this body of research is that there is no consistent simple relationship (i.e., main effect) between diversity and performance (Kochan *et al.*, 2003). The common failure to detect a consistent relationship is likely a result of the effect of diversity being contingent on how it is managed. Specifically, when diversity is well managed, it can become a potential asset for the employing organization by introducing a variety of skills and perspectives. Conversely, when it is not, it probably detracts from performance by promoting competition and conflict among dissimilar individuals (Cox, 1994).

We believe the key to effective diversity management lies in creating an atmosphere within the organization wherein employees of all types are (a) allowed and encouraged to participate in organizational processes and (b) recognized and rewarded equitably for their contributions. Such an atmosphere is captured within the concept of diversity climate, which was introduced to the literature in the early 1990s by Kossek and Zonia (1993) and Cox (1994). The former claimed that, "diversity climate includes an abstract component, which is a general perception toward the importance of employer efforts to promote diversity, and a specific component which refers to attitudes toward the probable beneficiaries of these efforts (i.e. white women and racioethnic minority men and women) in one's unit" (p. 63). Cox offered a relatively similar definition of the construct, but expanded it in proposing that diversity climate operates at the individual, group, and organizational levels.

Individual-level factors are those regarding people that influence their openness to diversity. Specifically, Cox identified identity structures, prejudice, stereotyping, and personality. Group-level factors are those properties of groups that are likely to promote or inhibit tensions with other groups such as cultural differences, ethnocentrism, or a history of intergroup conflict. Organizational factors are more macro characteristics that pertain to an organization's likelihood of treating employees of all backgrounds fairly. These include integration of both formal and informal structures and bias in human resource systems.

Much of the subsequent research on diversity management has focused on a single level of Cox's (1994) multilevel conceptualization. In doing so, some studies have focused explicitly on diversity climate (e.g., McKay *et al.*, 2007), whereas others have been more implicit and may not have referred to it by name despite its relevance (e.g., Brief *et al.*, 1995). We aim to cover both here to provide a comprehensive assessment of how diversity climate influences the efficacy of diversity management. We begin by reviewing research on the antecedents or causes of diversity climate. If organizations are to manage their diversity climates, it is imperative to understand how they develop and evolve. Subsequently, we examine the outcomes of diversity climate to illustrate how they influence organizational effectiveness.

Antecedents of Diversity Climate

Leadership

Nearly all organizational phenomena can be traced to leadership. This explains, in part, why researchers have placed so much emphasis on understanding this topic. Regarding diversity, we begin our review of the antecedents of diversity climate with leadership because few things are more important to the success or failure of diversity initiatives as top management support. In fact, a qualitative study involving structured interviews with diversity managers of eight multinational corporations identified support from top management as the key determinant of diversity initiative success (Wentling, 2004). This coincides with universal consensus in an earlier survey of 12 diversity experts on the importance of top management support (Wentling and Palma-Rivas, 1998). Perhaps Gilbert and Ivancevich (2001, p. 1344) put it best when they concluded that "unless it is championed by the CEO, organization wide cultural change to value diversity is likely to be ineffective."

The seminal study was conducted by Brief *et al.* (1995). Building on Milgram's (1964) classic research on compliance, they proposed that people would discriminate in selecting among job applicants if given instructions to do so. In a laboratory experiment manipulating whether race was to be used as a criterion in a selection exercise, they found that participants were significantly more likely to discriminate against Black applicants when they received instructions to use race as a factor. In a follow-up study, Brief *et al.* (2000) found that business justifications (e.g., business-related reasons for discrimination) predicted discrimination against minorities in a hiring scenario and that this effect was moderated by the legitimacy of the individual giving the justification and the level of modern racism of the participant. Specifically, the justification only enhanced the propensity to discriminate when the individual giving the order was a legitimate authority figure. Moreover, those higher in modern racism were no more likely to discriminate than those lower in modern racism unless a justification was provided.[1] Brief and his colleagues referred to this phenomenon, whereby individuals are permitted to act on their biases, as releasing the beast.

---

[1] Modern racism differs from blatant, old-fashioned racism in that it is more covert as a result of social norms against explicitly racist behavior. Thus, modern racism is more likely to emerge when seemingly nondiscriminatory justifications for such behavior exist.

In attempting to replicate the results of Brief *et al.* (2000), Ziegert and Hanges (2005) were unable to find an interaction between modern racism and their manipulation of what they termed "climate for bias" in a hiring scenario. They did find that climate moderated the effects of implicit racial bias (i.e., negative racial attitudes that lie outside of conscious awareness), such that implicit racism affected actual discrimination only when a business justification was provided. Petersen and Dietz (2000) reported a similar interaction involving right-wing authoritarianism. While those low in right-wing authoritarianism did not comply with orders to discriminate against out-group members, those high in right-wing authoritarianism were complicit. More recently, the same authors examined employees' organizational commitment as a moderator of the influence of leader's demographic preferences. Their results indicated that the propensity to engage in discriminatory compliance was greater among employees who were highly committed to the organization (Petersen and Dietz, 2008). Thus, it seems evident that many employees may act in a discriminatory manner if they believe such actions are consistent with the perspective held by those at higher organizational levels.

The studies discussed thus far have looked at how managers can lead their subordinates to discriminate. It is encouraging to note, however, that managers can use their powers of influence for good as well. For instance, a recent two-study experiment involving undergraduates (Umphress *et al.*, 2008) found that those high in social dominance orientation (SDO; i.e., beliefs that hierarchical identity group structures are legitimate and desirable) were more likely than those lower in SDO to discriminate against members of lower status groups (i.e., women and Black applicants) when making selection decisions. However, when given orders to focus on relevant information such as job performance, SDO had significantly less impact. Clearly, leaders and managers have a considerable influence on what does and does not occur in their workplaces. Their preferences, in conjunction with the policies and procedures they enact, help to shape the organization's diversity climate.

Community

Although leaders have considerable influence on diversity climate via what takes place within the organization, employees and organizations are nested within communities. What happens in the community influences the people who live there. When these individuals come to work, they bring to work any attitudinal predispositions or biases they may have accumulated in their community (Brief, Butz, and Dietch, 2004). Consequently, we can expect the composition and climates of the communities in which employees reside to influence the diversity climate of their employers.

Research has detected relationships between communities and climate at the individual and unit levels of analyses. At the individual level, White employees who lived closer to Black people or experienced more interethnic conflict in their neighborhoods responded less favorably to organizational diversity (Brief et al., 2005). The authors interpreted these findings using social conflict theory (Levine and Campbell, 1972) to suggest that ethnic conflict or threat at home translates into less favorable attitudes toward dissimilarity, which manifest themselves in both home and work settings. More recently, Avery et al. (2008) discovered that the impact of racioethnic dissimilarity with one's supervisor on perceived discrimination depended on the level of racioethnic dissimilarity the employee experienced at home. Together, these studies illustrate the potential impact of community characteristics on individual-level indicators of diversity climate.

At the organizational level, McKay and Avery (2006) developed theory describing how community characteristics help to shape the diversity climates within organizations. Though their treatment principally concerned cues that applicants interpret during job site visits, the general premise should extend in other ways as well. Organizations based in communities embroiled in conflict or rife with racioethnic tension are likely to experience similar happenings within their walls as well. In an empirical study, Pugh et al. (2008) detected a relationship between community composition and an organization's diversity climate. Although there was no main effect, they found that the proportion of minorities in the firm's surrounding community moderated the impact of employee diversity on diversity climate in a way that the relationship was weaker when the community contained more minorities.

Human Resource Management Consequences of Diversity Climate

We now shift gears to examine how diversity climate affects various areas of human resource management (HRM). The section begins by assessing the impact of diversity climate on how organizations select and place new employees. Subsequently, the effects of diversity climate on performance appraisals, compensation, and employee retention are examined.

Personnel Selection

Many of the articles reviewed in the leadership section help to illustrate how that aspect of an organization's diversity climate can influence personnel selection. Notably, those studies showed how (a) prejudice or vigilance against it can be contagious within organizations and (b) organizational-level factors can influence individual-level behaviors, ultimately resulting in biased or equitable personnel selection decisions. Other key indicators of diversity climate, however, are the demographic composition of the employing firm and the employee selection techniques a firm uses to screen applicants. These conditions should have bearing on who is more or less likely to be selected.

According to Cox (1994), a company's demographic profile is an indicator of its diversity climate. Specifically, he argued that the more integrated a company's personnel are across hierarchical levels, the more hospitable its diversity climate. Organizational research on the effects of demographic composition has shown some key linkages to selection. Most often, these results conform to a pattern known as homosocial reproduction (Kanter, 1977) wherein organizations tend to hire individuals whose demographics match that of incumbent employees (Reskin, McBrier, and Kmec, 1999). For instance, the odds of hiring a minority or female employee are significantly higher if the incumbent being replaced was a minority or woman (Konrad and Pfeffer, 1991), or if the job involves low wages, or has few skill requirements (Kmec, 2006). In addition, an organization is more likely to hire a woman if it already has a higher proportion of women at or above the level for which she is being considered (Cohen, Broschak, and Haveman, 1998).

Decades of research has demonstrated that various selection techniques differ on the extent of adverse impact against minority groups (Roth et al., 2001; Schmidt and Hunter, 1998). Recently, scholars (e.g., Kravitz, 2008; McKay and Davis, 2007; Ployhart and Holtz, 2008) have suggested that an organization's choice of selection devices to use in screening has implications for the success (or failure) of their diversity efforts by impacting the hiring rates of minority job applicants. Traditional selection systems, such as those that include cognitive ability tests and unstructured interviews, could hamper diversity efforts. Studies indicate that Black people and Hispanics earn significantly lower scores on cognitive ability tests than their White counterparts (Roth et al., 2001). In addition, Black–White disparities in interview scores (disfavoring Blacks people) are markedly larger for unstructured versus structured interviews (the latter contains questions based on job analyses, standardized questions, and structured scoring schemes; Huffcutt et al., 2001; Huffcutt and Roth, 1998). Furthermore, personality tests and biographical data have been identified as valid, low-adverse impact selection devices (Bobko et al., 1999). Moreover, personality testing has the potential to identify job candidates who may be more supportive of a company's diversity programs (Arthur and Doverspike, 2005; McKay and Davis, 2007).

Employee Placement

After a job candidate has been hired, he or she must be placed in a position within the company. Although many candidates are hired to fill a specific vacancy within the organizational chart, companies often have some degree of discretion in deciding the placement of a new hire. Considerably less research has examined the potential relationship between diversity climate and placement, but there is reason to suspect that such a linkage exists.

Lefkowitz (1994) discovered a two-pronged organizational sorting phenomenon that he labeled "ethnic drift." First, newly hired employees were disproportionately more likely to be assigned to work for a supervisor belonging to their ethnic group. Second, if reassigned within the first five months of their tenure, those who did not draw initial assignments matching them with an ethnically similar supervisor were likely to be matched in this manner during reassignment. While somewhat less prevalent, Lefkowitz observed a similar trend concerning employee sex, suggesting that personnel often may be clustered within organizations on a demographic basis. Though we could find no subsequent inquiry replicating or extending this finding, research showing that organizational segregation (particularly by race and ethnicity) continues to exist (Tomaskovic-Devey et al., 2006) suggests this phenomenon is likely to have continued. We believe this tendency to segregate organizations demographically is less likely to occur in organizations with more hospitable diversity climates. Individuals in such organizations and the workgroups that they comprise should be less averse to diversity and dissimilarity, which should help curtail tendencies to want to group similar employees together (Fujimoto, Härtel, and Härtel, 2004; Hobman, Bordia, and Gallois, 2004).

Performance Appraisals

Clearly, an organization's diversity climate should have an impact on its performance appraisals. At the individual level, biased employees could create obstacles for dissimilar coworkers and subordinates, making it more difficult for them to perform up to their potential. At the group level, competition fueled by ethnocentrism may lead to rivalry and conflict that detracts from individual, group, and organizational performance, which would be reflected in appraisals. At the organizational level, biases in HR systems make it impossible for all employees to enjoy equal employment opportunity. For example, if an organization has an implicit tendency to provide more favorable ratings than deserved to members of a particular identity group, employees who do not belong to this group will be in a position of relative disadvantage.

Research at all three levels has provided support for the preceding conclusions. Three of the aforementioned studies (Brief et al., 2000; Umphress et al., 2008; Ziegert and Hanges, 2005) illustrated that individual-level biases, in the form of modern racism, social dominance orientation, and implicit racism, can interact with leader's expectations to influence how employees view and rate others (average ΔR^2 for interactions was 0.04). Other evidence indicates that performance judgments are affected by individual openness to dissimilarity with those more open being less likely to exhibit bias (Härtel et al., 1999). At the group level, research indicates that the composition of one's workgroup peers influences appraisal ratings (e.g., Pazy and Oron, 2001; Sackett, DuBois, and Noe, 1991) so evaluations tend to be less disparate when there is less severe underrepresentation of women and minorities. The effects tend to be moderate in size as context can change the magnitude of group differences considerably (e.g., male–female $d = -0.55$ when the group is between 1% and 10% female and 0.26 when the percentage ranges from 51 to 60; Sackett *et al.*) At the organizational or unit level, a recent study (McKay, Avery, and Morris, 2008) showed that diversity climate, conceptualized as "as employees' shared perceptions that an employer utilizes fair personnel practices and socially integrates underrepresented employees into the work environment" (p. 350), influenced the size of racioethnic differences in objective performance ratings (i.e., yearly sales/hour ratios) among retail sales employees. In fact, though there were significant differences between minority (i.e., Black people and Hispanic) and majority (i.e., White people) salespeople favoring the latter in stores with inhospitable diversity climates (Black–White difference $= -\$8.90$/hr; Hispanic–White difference $= -\$23.40$/hr.), this was not the case in hospitable diversity climates (Black–White difference $= \$7.41$/hr.; Hispanic–White difference $= -\$1.21$/hr.). This difference, which is likely attributable to greater equity of opportunity present in stores with favorable diversity climates, also should be reflected in performance appraisals.

Compensation

Much has been made in the practical and scholarly literatures of pay gaps between the sexes and racioethnic groups. Despite a good deal of argument concerning the degree to which these gaps reflect differences in human capital, there are many studies indicating that discrimination is at least partially responsible. Of importance here is the research within this literature linking diversity climate to pay disparities.

Joshi, Liao, and Jackson (2006) recently conducted a study examining the influence of similarity to those in one's surroundings on sex and racioethnic differences in compensation. Their findings revealed similar, yet distinct differences for the two identity markers. On the one hand, sex differences in pay disfavoring women were smaller when there were more minority or female managers in the unit. On the other hand, racioethnic differences disfavoring minorities were smaller when there was a greater presence of minority co-workers. Although Joshi*et al.* did not detect an effect of minority manager presence on minority salaries, a more recent study found that having an ethnically similar supervisor corresponded in the receipt of 4.5% more money annual pay (Avey, West, and Crossley, 2008). This represented a nice extension to the literature demonstrating effects of workplace composition on wages (Reskin *et al.*, 1999).

Employee Retention

Without question, the most extensively researched outcomes of diversity climate pertain to employee retention. Several studies have shown positive linkages between individual-level perceptions of diversity climate and key outcomes related to turnover. For instance, Avery et al. (2007) showed that perceived organizational value of diversity relates negatively to the number of days an employee is absent from work per year and can help to reduce commonly observed racioethnic differences in absenteeism. Several other researchers have reported significant positive relationships with precursors to turnover such as job satisfaction, organizational commitment, and turnover intentions (Gonzalez and DeNisi, 2009; Hicks-Clarke and Iles, 2000; Hopkins, Hopkins, and Mallette, 2001). In fact, favorable diversity climate perceptions appear to facilitate commitment and well-being, thereby decreasing employees' propensity to consider leaving the organization (McKay et al., 2007; Miner-Rubino and Cortina, 2007).

Qualitative research also provides some measure of support for the assertion that diversity climate aids in retaining employees. Gilbert and Ivancevich (2001) compared and contrasted two organizations with differing approaches to diversity management. Whereas one was actively involved in managing its diversity, the other was not. The authors used three indicators of employee attachment to test their hypotheses: commitment, attitudinal attachment, and absenteeism. Their results indicated that men and women of all racioethnic backgrounds were more attached to the organization that valued diversity than the one that did not. The same pattern was detected across all groups for commitment, although the difference across the two organizations did not reach conventional levels of statistical significance for minorities (which could have been a power issue, $n = 63$). Looking at absenteeism, only minorities exhibited the expected pattern and were absent less often at the company that placed greater value on diversity. Taken together, the research reviewed in this section indicates diversity climates should aid in retaining employees by keeping them satisfied, healthy (psychologically and physically), and committed.

THE RESEARCH-BASED APPROACH

Because diversity climate helps determine whether diversity's effects are positive, negative, or null (Gonzalez and DeNisi, 2009), the preceding sections contained a review of literature on its antecedents and consequences. This research is clearly important because it has enhanced our understanding of how diversity climates are formed and the outcomes that they influence. Unfortunately, however, these findings are scattered about the literature and have not been integrated. Additionally, many of the scholars responsible for producing this literature have focused more on the theoretical implications of their findings while ignoring their practical implications. Many practitioners who stand to benefit the most from this work are either unable to locate it or unsure what to make of it if they do. In this section, we integrate the findings to derive an empirically based approach to diversity management.

In planning to implement or alter an organization's diversity climate, it is imperative to begin at the top. Leaders can have a considerable impact on the type of climate their organizations develop with respect to diversity. To ensure that their impact is positive, leaders need to do the following three things: (1) assess their own beliefs and biases, (2) examine HR policies, and (3) become active advocates of equal employment opportunity and inclusion.

Assessing Own Beliefs

Because we are motivated to feel positively about ourselves (Tajfel and Turner, 1985), people often tend to be reluctant to engage in honest self-appraisal, lest they discover something unfavorable. One such unfavorable reality is that we harbor prejudices, albeit to different degrees. Because of growing consensus regarding the unacceptability of prejudice and bias, many individuals are motivated internally and externally to appear unbiased (Plant and Devine, 1998). Such motivation may lead people to try to convince themselves, as a first step toward convincing others, that they are unprejudiced.

Unfortunately, attempts to deceive ourselves often fail to persuade others about who we are and what we believe (Norton et al., 2006). Accordingly, leaders may take on an air of hypocrisy as they profess their support for diversity when they lack sincerity. This can have the unintended consequence of undermining the very diversity efforts leaders are trying, at least consciously, to reinforce. If employees suspect that their leaders do not really value diversity, why would they? Thus, their failure to support diversity or actions to oppose it may stem from their perceptions that leadership, and by extension the organization, doesn't support diversity.

If leaders are to be honest in assessing their valuation of diversity, many are apt to come to the conclusion that they are ambivalent about diversity. In fact, a recent national study (National Urban League, 2004) showed that fewer than half of American employees believe their employer is seriously committed to diversity. Should leaders recognize such an internal ambivalence, they may find that education about diversity can aid in altering their diversity mindset. According to van Knippenberg and Schippers (2007, p. 531), a diversity mindset, "refers to people's understanding of how diversity may affect their work group or organization, their understanding of the appropriate way to deal with diversity, and their associated evaluations of diversity." Discovering the realities and disconfirming the myths about dissimilar others may inspire in leaders a commitment to learning about difference.

Translating this commitment from the leader to the organization can hold immense organizational potential. For example, Ely and Thomas (2001) identified three perspectives organizations may adopt with respect to diversity. The first, discrimination-and-fairness, endorses managing diversity because it is the fair thing to do and helps to avoid costly discrimination suits. The second perspective, known as access-and-legitimacy, views diversity management as a means to gain entry into diverse customer markets. Finally, the integration-and-learning paradigm sees diversity as an opportunity for individuals to learn from those who are different, thereby contributing to greater organizational performance. Ely and Thomas found that only the integration-and-learning perspective produces consistent positive results. Subsequent research (Homan, van Knippenberg, and van Kleef, 2007; van Dick *et al.*, 2008) has echoed this notion by showing diversity beliefs to moderate the effect of group diversity in a way that diversity facilitates team members' desire to stay and their performance by enhancing their identification with the group and the quality of information exchange when diversity beliefs are favorable. Thus, when leaders truly believe in diversity and convey this belief to their employees, diversity becomes an organizational asset.

Examining HR Policies

Human resource management policies that intend to discriminate are probably a rarity in today's organizations. Given the presence of laws actively prohibiting demographic discrimination along several bases, it is in a company's best interests not to discriminate. Unfortunately, it takes more than merely good intentions to provide an atmosphere promoting equal opportunity and inclusion. Sound HR policies are needed to ensure the creation and maintenance of a healthy and productive diversity climate.

Perhaps the biggest reason for the failure of many organizational HR policies is that they are not designed with diversity in mind. Many organizations have taken the approach of opening their doors to diversity, but not changing a thing (Cox, 1994). R. R. Thomas (1999b) makes a clever analogy between this tendency and a popular fable involving a giraffe inviting an elephant into his home without making any adjustments to accommodate their differences. Companies cannot continue to use the policies and procedures of the past to manage the workforce of the present. Instead, they must develop new means of managing that are tailored to deal with differences. In fact, a recent study showed that recognition of the importance of people's valued identities corresponds in higher levels of employee creativity and satisfaction and lower absenteeism (Thatcher and Greer, 2008). This coincides with earlier research demonstrating that identity-conscious HR policies (i.e., those that specifically acknowledge employee identities) correspond in greater female and minority representation in management than identity-blind policies (Konrad and Linnehan, 1995).

Accordingly, various aspects of HRM probably will need to change. Research suggests companies utilize new and different ways to recruit employees (see Kulik and Roberson, 2008 for a comprehensive review). For instance, Kravitz (2008) proposed using targeted recruitment to help reduce adverse impact in selection, an idea later supported mathematically and empirically by Newman and Lyon (2009). Criteria for employee selection and performance appraisal should be updated to reflect the new types of knowledge, skills, and abilities the organization hopes to employ by diversifying its personnel (Stone, Stone-Romero, and Lukaszewski, 2007). This may include decreasing reliance on traditional measures that may adversely impact minorities' selection and promotion ratios (McKay and Davis, 2007). It likely entails revamping compensation systems to ensure that (a) organizational rewards are valued by the employees they are intended to motivate and (b) pay inequity patterns of the past (e.g., Barnum, Liden, and DiTomaso, 1995) are discontinued. To embrace diversity companies also might consider adopting nontraditional and, perhaps, even unconventional approaches to work scheduling and job design (Friday and Friday, 2003; Hall and Parker, 1993). In short, if diversity is made to fit into the organizational practices of the past, it is unlikely to contribute positively to organizational functioning.

Companies should pay particular attention to the ways they go about developing talent (Kulik and Roberson, 2008). It is not a coincidence that organizations that emphasize employee development strategies also employ and promote more women than those that don't (Goodman, Fields, and Blum, 2003). Additionally, when paired with a strategic diversity management plan that establishes responsibility for diversity management, employee development and diversity training efforts are more effective in increasing the proportion of female and Black managers (Kalev, Dobbins, and Kelly, 2006). For a list of particular strategies, though they are not necessarily empirically based, we refer readers to a recent chapter by Kossek, Lobel, and Brown (2006).

Diversity Advocacy

Many readers are likely to view this third suggestion as intuitive. Who would think that they can develop a hospitable diversity climate without diversity advocacy? The key to this suggestion, however, lies in the meaning of advocacy. Whereas many might interpret this to mean that the organization and its representatives does not condone or engage in unfair practices. We take it one step further in proposing that advocacy involves actively campaigning against injustice.

Being a diversity advocate does not entail simply not being racist or sexist. It means taking a proactive stance against bigotry and intolerance. In fact, research on people who are relatively unbiased shows that they are characterized by a desire to disconfirm stereotypes (Wyer, 2004). Note that this differs from merely not holding stereotypes in that it necessitates having the commitment to move from a passive state (i.e., I don't endorse stereotypes) to an active one (i.e., I actively seek to disprove them). This helps explain why many instances of leadership passivity regarding diversity send powerful signals to organizational personnel that serve to undermine the efficacy of diversity initiatives (Avery and Johnson, 2007).

Many companies continue to reward employees holding more traditional views on diversity. In fact, a recent study showed that those higher in modern sexism (i.e., views that sexism and discrimination against women are things of the past and that women are too demanding in seeking change) received significantly more promotions than those lower in modern sexism (Watkins-Baskerville et al., 2006). If firms go against this trend by encouraging a higher standard regarding diversity beliefs among their employees, they can expect greater commitment to learning from diversity. Leaders must model this behavior by being visible in their diversity advocacy. HRM systems should recognize, support, and reward advocacy efforts designed to enhance the organization's diversity climate. We should point out that these advocacy efforts are not limited to inside the organization. To the extent that companies play an active role in shaping positive intergroup relations within the communities they are embedded in, they can expect to reap long-term benefits in the form of more favorable diversity climates (Brief et al., 2004).

AN AGENDA FOR FUTURE RESEARCH

Although a myriad of suggestions have potential relevance to managing diversity, critical research needs include (a) specifying the links between human resource practices, diversity climate, and work outcomes; (b) determining the processes through which diversity climate relates to work outcomes; (c) examining diversity climate effects on work outcomes from a multi-level perspective; (d) assessing the between-firm implications of diversity climate for organizational performance; and (e) clarifying the relationship between composition and climate.

Specifying the Links between HR Practices, Diversity Climate, and Work Outcomes

Much of the work on diversity climate has focused on its links with work outcomes. Ambiguity exists, however, regarding the HR practices that are associated with supportive diversity climates. This uncertainty renders scholars largely unable to inform managers as to how they could develop HR systems that fully leverage diversity to their firm's competitive advantage. To rectify this situation, scholars should engage in greater conceptual development to clearly articulate how HR practices might relate to diversity climate in business units and firms. Two theoretical perspectives, in combination, that would be useful in this instance are strategic human resource management (SHRM) and organizational climate.

SHRM theory states that firms will maximize the accomplishment of their objectives to the extent that their HR practices are aligned with firm strategy (Becker and Gerhart, 1996; Lepak et al., 2006). HR practices are hypothesized to be antecedents of organizational climate (i.e., the way things are done around here; Reichers and Schneider, 1990) because they serve a prescriptive function by informing employees as to what work behaviors should be valued and rewarded by the organization, thereby resulting in a discernible climate for *something* (e.g., innovation, safety, service, or diversity; Bowen and Ostroff, 2004). Furthermore, climate has been theorized to link to firm performance through its influence on workers' cognitive states (e.g., work attitudes) and behaviors (e.g., work effort; Kopelman, Brief, and Guzzo, 1990). Lepak et al. (2006) further noted that organizational climate has implications for employees' motivation, ability, and opportunity to perform. Thus, HR practices that foster supportive climates should enhance workers' likelihood of contributing to the achievement of organizational strategic objectives. Accordingly, recent work indicates that climate mediates the HR practices–firm performance relationship (Collins and Smith, 2006; Gelade and Ivery, 2003).

Extending the above theory and research to diversity climate, diversity scholars should conduct studies to uncover the HR practices associated with pro-diversity work climates. Some likely practices in this regard include valid selection systems, extensive training programs, employee participation, cooperation, formal performance appraisal systems, and merit-based promotions. Practices of this nature are likely to mitigate demographic group disparities in work experiences (e.g., Foley, Kidder, and Powell, 2002; Gutek, Cohen, and Tsui, 1996; McKay and McDaniel, 2006), thereby allowing employees to contribute fully to organizational effectiveness. Moreover, additional work is needed to determine the particular practices or configurations of practices that are most pivotal for precipitating supportive diversity climates (e.g., Delery and Doty, 1996; Lepak et al., 2006).

Determining the Processes through which Diversity Climate Relates to Work Outcomes

A notable limitation of diversity climate research is that it has examined its moderating effects on outcomes while largely excluding relevant mediation processes. Although McKay et al. (2007) demonstrated that organizational climate mediated the relationship between diversity climate and turnover intentions, their study was conducted at the individual level of analysis. In contrast, we are unaware of any work that has delved into the "black box" (Lawrence, 1997) to explicate *how* diversity climate, measured at the aggregate level, relates to group and organizational level work outcomes. This limitation is especially relevant to studies that have focused on various forms of numerical demographic diversity (e.g., Gonzalez and DeNisi, 2009; Joshi *et al.*, 2006; Kochan *et al.*, 2003), yet this concern also applies to recent aggregate-level diversity climate investigations (e.g., Gonzalez and DeNisi, 2009; McKay *et al.*, 2008).

To pursue this line of research, future investigators must incorporate theoretically grounded constructs that are likely to link diversity climate and work outcomes. Especially relevant to this issue is Cox's (1994) Interactional Model of Cultural Diversity (IMCD). According to the model, diversity climate relates to first-level (e.g., attendance, turnover, and work quality) and second-level organizational effectiveness outcomes (e.g., market share, and profitability) through employees' affective outcomes (e.g., job/career satisfaction and organizational identification) and achievement outcomes (e.g., job performance ratings and promotions).

Using the IMCD as a starting point, scholars could hypothesize individual employee attitudinal and/or performance indicators that are apt to influence subsequent firm- or unit-level performance indicators. For instance, McKay *et al.* (2008) proposed that diversity climate should moderate Black–White and Hispanic–White mean differences in employee sales performance through a social exchange process. Because of group status differences and related probability of experience racial–ethnic discrimination, Black and Hispanic personnel, relative to their White peers, were expected to place greater value on firm efforts to instill a supportive diversity climate in retail store units. To reciprocate this organizational goodwill, these employees were posited to work harder to sell the firms products, thus increasing their sales per hour. Though unmeasured, a likely mediator of the effects McKay *et al.* (2008) reported is perceived organizational support (POS; Rhoades and Eisenberger, 2002). A supportive diversity climate, especially among Black and Hispanic sales associates, should invoke strong perceptions of POS, thereby resulting in improved sales performance and reduced racial–ethnic disparities in performance. Another potential mediator in this regard is organizational identification. Because a pro-diversity work climate ensures that all employees enjoy equality of opportunity and integrated in the firm's social fabric, workers are more likely to identify with the firm because it serves their interests. Viewing the firm's interests as their own, these employees should work more diligently toward the firm's strategic objectives, resulting in improved firm performance (Ashforth and Mael, 1989; Hogg and Terry, 2000). While these examples are speculative, we hope they inform thinking as to potential mediators of diversity climate effects on work outcomes.

Examining the Multilevel Effects of Diversity Climate on Work Outcomes

With exceptions (e.g., Gonzalez and DeNisi, 2009; McKay *et al.*, 2008), the majority of diversity climate research has been conducted at a single-level of analysis. Because of this, the current diversity climate literature offers an incomplete picture of how the construct relates to relevant organizational outcomes. At the extreme, one could infer that this research presents a somewhat artificial view of diversity climate's relations with criteria, considering that by their very nature, organizations are multilevel (Kozlowski and Klein, 2000). To fully understand diversity climate's influence on organizational outcomes (at various levels of aggregation), multilevel studies are necessary. For instance, individual-level studies indicate that diversity climate relates to absenteeism (Avery et al., 2007) and turnover intentions (McKay et al., 2007); however, it is uncertain as to whether aggregate-level diversity climate has any bearing on these outcomes, in spite of theory suggesting that it might (e.g., the IMCD; Cox, 1994). Moreover, the studies above failed to control for potentially relevant organizational-level contextual features such as racial–ethnic and sex demography of coworkers and supervisors, both of which have been shown to influence employee outcomes (Elvira and Cohen, 2001; Joshi et al., 2006; Zatzick, Elvira, and Cohen, 2003).

Investigators should utilize data-analytic techniques (e.g., hierarchical linear modeling) that allow control for aggregate-level organizational features while examining diversity climate's relations with individual-level criteria. Inquiries in this regard could be extended to determine diversity climate's implications for various outcomes such as discrimination claiming, grievances, and sexual harassment (Goldman et al., 2006), perceived advancement opportunities (Foley et al., 2002), and access to developmental assignments (Lyness and Terrazas, 2006; Lyness and Thompson, 2000).

Assessing the Between-Firm Implications of Diversity Climate for Organizational Performance

An important question that remains in the diversity climate literature is "Does diversity climate serve as a source of competitive advantage between firms?" Research that speaks to this question has been primarily qualitative in nature, focusing only on a small number of firms (Ely and Thomas, 2001; Gilbert and Ivancevich, 2001; Robinson and Dechant, 1997). The strong claim of the "business case for diversity" is that diversity should improve business performance by facilitating personnel recruitment, bringing a greater variety of ideas to bear on organizational problems, fostering greater creativity, and increasing access to diversity customer markets. While intuitively appealing, the business case has yet to be subjected to rigorous empirical examination, so it remains equivocal as to whether diversity climate differentiates financial performance between firms. We strongly advocate future diversity work that indulges this issue and offer some suggests for how it might proceed.

First, between-firm studies should sample from an industry for which diversity climate has particular relevance to firm performance (Lepak et al., 2006).

A strong initial candidate for such a study would be the service industry because it has strong customer interface requirements and customer service is a strong differentiator between firms. This latter concern is pivotal given customer service research that has illuminated the strong attitudinal component of customer service (Borucki and Burke, 1999; Schneider and Bowen, 1985), suggesting a potential diversity climate→ work attitude → customer service performance → firm performance pathway. Second, between-firm studies should focus on employees in core jobs that are most pivotal to the achievement of a firm's objectives (Lepak et al., 2006). For example, if the retail industry serves as the source of data, then sales associates, as opposed to HR employees, should serve as the focal referent group. Third, assuming a between-study designed to extend SHRM and organizational climate theory predictions to diversity climate, researchers should be careful to choose valid, reliable informants as sources of HR practices data (e.g., HR directors or line managers; Lepak et al., 2006). Failure to do so could result in misidentification of the HR practices utilized in the organization, thus compromising internal validity. Finally, as applicable to most research on diversity, between-firm studies should be longitudinal in nature to determine the line of causality between diversity climate and organizational performance.

Clarifying the Composition–Climate Relationship

Several authors (e.g., Cox, 1994) have argued that composition influences climate, so more integrated units should have climates more supportive of diversity. A recent longitudinal study, however, failed to show that composition predicts climate (Kossek, Markel, and McHugh, 2003). Moreover, correlations between sex and racioethnic composition and diversity climate in other research have proven relatively small (i.e., <0.20) and inconsistent, with some being negative and others positive (Gonzalez and DeNisi, 2009; McKay et al., in press; Pugh et al., 2008). This likely reflects the fact that it is not merely the level of overall employee diversity that influences climate, but how the diversity is distributed. Many organizations are relatively diverse at lower hierarchical levels, but homogenous at the top. This is evidenced by the fact that while women and minorities represent 46.4% and 29.7% of the US workforce, respectively, they hold only 25.6% and 12.8%, respectively, of all executive management positions (Bureau of Labor Statistics, 2007, Table 11). In instances of such representational imbalance, it is unlikely that a higher level of overall diversity present would facilitate a hospitable climate. Conversely, having diversity at higher levels promotes employee commitment to diversity (D. A. Thomas, 1999a) and greater equity in human resource management outcomes (e.g., Joshi et al., 2006).

Another body of work that is relevant here is that of examining demographic fault lines, which involve the alignment of multiple demographic categories within a particular context (Lau and Murnighan, 1998). For instance, a group with 20 Black and White men and women could have 5 Black men, Black women, White men, and White women (weak fault line) or 10 Black men and 10 White women (strong fault line). Research on this topic has linked fault lines to cohesion and conflict, with stronger fault lines resulting in less of the former and more of the latter (Li and Hambrick, 2005). Thus, while research using simple demographic statistics is likely to yield little relation to diversity climate, more sophisticated measures (e.g., hierarchical distributions, and fault lines) appear to show more promise in this regard. We urge future researchers to (a) conduct longitudinal investigations and (b) examine potential moderators of the composition–climate relationship.

REFERENCES

Ashforth, B. E., & Mael, F. (1989). Social identity and the organization. *Academy of Management Review*, 14, 20–39.

Arthur, W., Jr., & Doverspike, D. (2005). Achieving diversity and reducing discrimination in the workplace through human resource management practices: Implications of research and theory for staffing, training, and rewarding performance. In R. L. Dipboye & A. Colella (Eds), *Discrimination at Work: The Psychological and Organizational Bases* (pp. 305–27). San Francisco, CA: Jossey-Bass.

Avery, D. R. (in press). Why the playing field remains uneven: Impediments to promotions in organizations. To appear In S. Zedeck (Ed.), *Handbook of Industrial & Organizational Psychology*. Washington, DC: American Psychological Association.

Avery, D. R., & Johnson, C. D. (2007). Now you see it, now you don't: Mixed messages regarding workplace diversity. In K. M. Thomas (Ed.), *Diversity Resistance in Organizations: Manifestations and Solutions* (pp. 221–47). Mahwah, NJ: Lawrence Erlbaum Associates.

Avery, D. R., McKay, P. F., & Wilson, D. C. (2008). What are the odds? How demographic similarity affects the prevalence of perceived employment discrimination. *Journal of Applied Psychology*, 93, 235–49.

Avery, D. R., McKay, P. F., Wilson, D. C., & Tonidandel, S. (2007). Unequal attendance: The relationships between race, organizational diversity cues, and absenteeism. *Personnel Psychology*, 60, 875–902.

Avey, J. B., West, B. J., & Crossley, C. D. (2008). The association between ethnic congruence in the supervisor-subordinate dyad and subordinate organizational position and salary. *Journal of Occupational & Organizational Psychology*, 81, 551–66.

Barnum, P., Liden, R. C., & Ditomaso, N. (1995). Double jeopardy for women and minorities: Pay differences with age. *Academy of Management Journal*, 38, 863–80.

Becker, B., & Gerhart, B. (1996). The impact of human resource management on organizational performance: Progress and prospects. *Academy of Management Journal*, 39, 779–801.

Bobko, P., Roth, P. L., & Potosky, D. (1999). Derivation and implications of a meta-analytic matrix incorporating cognitive ability, alternative predictors, and job performance. *Personnel Psychology*, 52, 561–89.

Borucki, C. C., & Burke, M. J. (1999). An examination of service-related antecedents to retail store performance. *Journal of Organizational Behavior*, 20, 943–62.

Bowen, D. E., & Ostroff, C. (2004). Understanding HRM-firm performance linkages: The role of the "strength" of the HRM system. *Academy of Management Review*, **29**, 203–21.

Brief, A. P., Buttram, R. T., Elliott, J. D., Reizenstein, R. M., & McCline, R. L. (1995). Releasing the beast: A study of compliance with orders to use race as a selection criterion. *Journal of Social Issues*, **51**, 177–93.

Brief, A. P., Butz, R. M., & Deitch, E. A. (2004). Organizations as reflections of their environments: The case of race composition. In R. Dipboye & A. Colella (Eds), *The Psychological and Organizational Bases of Discrimination at Work* (pp. 199–248). San Francisco: Jossey-Bass.

Brief, A. P., Dietz, J., Cohen, R. R., Pugh, S. D., & Vaslow, J. B. (2000). Just doing business: Modern racism and obedience to authority as explanations for employment discrimination. *Organizational Behavior and Human Decision Processes*, **81**, 72–96.

Brief, A. P., Umphress, E. E., Dietz, J., Burrows, J. W., Butz, R. M., & Scholten, L. (2005). Community matters: Realistic group conflict theory and the impact of diversity. *Academy of Management Journal*, **48**, 830–44.

Bureau of Labor Statistics. (2007). Characteristics of the employed, Table 11 – Employed persons by detailed occupation, sex, race, and Hispanic or Latino ethnicity. *Current Population Survey*. Retrieved on February 9, 2009 from http://www.bls.gov/cps/cpsaat11.pdf

Civil Rights Act of 1964, (Pub. L. 88B352), U.S.C. § 2000d et seq.; 28 C.F.R. § 42.101 et seq., 34 C.F.R. § 100.1 et seq., and 45 C.F.R. §80.1 et seq.

Cohen, L. E., Broschak, J. P., & Haveman, H. A. (1998). And then there were more? The effect of organizational sex composition on the hiring and promotion of managers. *American Sociological Review*, **63**, 711–27.

Collins, C. J., & Smith, K. G. (2006). Knowledge exchange and combination: The role of human resource practices in the performance of high-technology firms. *Academy of Management Journal*, **49**, 544–60.

Cox, T., Jr. (1994). *Cultural Diversity in Organizations: Theory, Research, & Practice*. San Francisco: Berrett-Koehler.

Deitch, E. A., Barsky, A., Butz, R. M., Chan, S., Brief, A. P., & Bradley, J. C. (2003). Subtle yet significant: The existence and impact of everyday racial discrimination in the workplace. *Human Relations*, **56**, 1299–324.

Delery, J. E., & Doty, D. H. (1996). Modes of theorizing in strategic human resource management: Tests of universalistic, contingency, and configurational performance predictions. *Academy of Management Journal*, **39**, 802–35.

Dixon, S. (2003). Implications of population ageing for the labour market. *Labour Market Trends*, **111**(2), 67–76.

Elvira, M. M., & Cohen, L. E. (2001). Location matters: A cross-level analysis of the effects of organizational sex composition on turnover. *Academy of Management Journal*, **44**, 591–605.

Ely, R. J., & Thomas, D. A. (2001). Cultural diversity at work: The effects of diversity perspectives on work group processes and outcomes. *Administrative Science Quarterly*, **46**, 229–73.

Foley, S., Kidder, D. L., & Powell, G. N. (2002). The perceived glass ceiling and justice perceptions: An investigation of Hispanic law associates. *Journal of Management*, **28**, 471–96.

Friday, S. S., & Friday, E. (2003). Racioethnic perceptions of job characteristics and job satisfaction. *Journal of Management Development*, **22**, 426–42.

Friedman, J. J., & DiTomaso, N. (1996). Myths about diversity: What managers need to know about changes in the U.S. labor force. *California Management Review*, **38**(4), 54–77.

Fujimoto, Y., Härtel, C. E. J., & Härtel, G. F. (2004). A field test of the diversity-openness moderator model in newly formed groups: Openness to diversity affects group decision effectiveness and interaction patterns. *Cross Cultural Management,* **11**(4), 4–16.

Gelade, G. A., & Ivery, M. (2003). The impact of human resource management and work climate on organizational performance. *Personnel Psychology,* **56**, 383–404.

Gilbert, J. A., & Ivancevich, J. M. (2001). Effects of diversity management on attachment. *Journal of Applied Social Psychology,* **31**, 1331–49.

Goldman, B. M., Gutek, B. A., Stein, J. H., & Lewis, K. (2006). Employment discrimination in organizations: Antecedents and consequences. *Journal of Management,* **32**, 786–830.

Gonzalez, J. A., & DeNisi, A. S. (2009). Cross-level effects of demography and diversity climate on organizational attachment and firm effectiveness. *Journal of Organizational Behavior,* **30**, 21–40.

Goodman, J. S., Fields, D. L., & Blum, T. C. (2003). Cracks in the glass ceiling: In what kinds of organizations do women make it to the top? *Group & Organization Management,* **28**, 475–501.

Gutek, B. A., Cohen, A. G., & Tsui, A. (1996). Reactions to perceived sex discrimination. *Human Relations,* **49**, 791–813.

Hall, D. T., & Parker, V. A. (1993). The role of workplace flexibility in managing diversity. *Organizational Dynamics,* **22**, 5–18.

Härtel, C. E. J., Douthitt, S. S., Härtel, G., & Douthitt, S. Y. (1999). Equally qualified but unequally perceived: Openness to perceived dissimilarity as a predictor of race and sex discrimination in performance judgments. *Human Resource Development Quarterly,* **10**(1), 79–89.

Hicks-Clarke, D., & Iles, P. (2000). Climate for diversity and its effects on career and organisational attitudes and perceptions. *Personnel Review,* **29**, 324–45.

Hobman, E. V., Bordia, P., & Gallois, C. (2004). Perceived dissimilarity and work group involvement: The moderating effects of group openness to diversity. *Group & Organization Management,* **29**, 560–87.

Hogg, M. A., & Terry, D. J. (2000). Social identity and self-categorization processes in organizational contexts. *Academy of Management Review,* **25**, 121–40.

Hom, P. W., Roberson, L., & Ellis, A. D. (2008). Challenging conventional wisdom about who quits: Revelations from corporate America. *Journal of Applied Psychology,* **93**, 1–34.

Homan, A. C., van Knippenberg, D., & Van Kleef, G. A. (2007). Bridging faultlines by valuing diversity: Diversity beliefs, information elaboration, and performance in diverse work groups. *Journal of Applied Psychology,* **92**, 1189–99.

Hopkins, W. E., Hopkins, S. A., & Mallette, P. (2001). Diversity and managerial value commitment: A test of some proposed relationships. *Journal of Managerial Issues,* **13**, 288–306.

Horwitz, S. K., & Horwitz, I. B. (2007). The effects of team diversity on team outcomes: a meta-analytic review of team demography. *Journal of Management,* **33**, 987–1015.

Huffcutt, A. I., Conway, J. M., Roth, P. L., & Stone, N. J. (2001). Identification and meta-analytic assessment of psychological constructs measured in employment interviews. *Journal of Applied Psychology,* **86**, 897–913.

Huffcutt, A. I., & Roth, P. L. (1998). Racial group differences in employment interview evaluations. *Journal of Applied Psychology,* **83**, 179–89.

Jackson, S. E., Schuler, R. S., & Werner, S. (2009). *Managing Human Resources* (10th edition). Mason, OH: South-Western Cengage Learning.

James, E. H., & Wooten, L. P. (2006). Diversity crises: How firms manage discrimination lawsuits. *Academy of Management Journal,* **49**, 1103–18.

Joshi, A., Liao, H., & Jackson, S. E. (2006). Cross-level effects of workplace diversity on sales performance and pay. *Academy of Management Journal*, **49**, 459–81.

Kalev, A., Dobbin, F., & Kelly, E. (2006). Best practices or best guesses? Assessing the efficacy of corporate affirmative action and diversity policies. *American Sociological Review*, **71**, 589–617.

Kanter, R. M. (1977). *Men and Women of the Corporation*. New York: Basic Books.

Kmec, J. A. (2006). White hiring agents' organizational practices and out-group hiring. *Social Science Research*, **35**, 668–701.

Kochan, T., Bezrukova, K., Ely, R., et al. (2003). The effects of diversity on business performance: Report of the Diversity Research Network. *Human Resource Management*, **42**, 3–21.

Konrad, A., & Linnehan, F. (1995). Formalized human resource management structures: Coordinating equal opportunity or concealing organizational practices. *Academy of Management Journal*, **38**, 787–820.

Konrad, A. M., & Pfeffer, J. (1991). Understanding the hiring of women and minorities in educational institutions. *Sociology of Education*, **64**, 141–57.

Kopelman, R. E., Brief, A. P., & Guzzo, R. A. (1990). The role of climate and culture in productivity. In B. Schneider (Ed.), *Organizational Climate and Culture* (pp. 282–318). San Francisco, CA: Jossey-Bass.

Kossek, E. E., Lobel, S. A., & Brown, J. (2006). Human resource strategies to manage workforce diversity: Examining 'the business case'. In A. M. Konrad, P. Prasad & J. K. Pringle (Eds), *Handbook of Workplace Diversity* (pp. 53–74). Thousand Oaks, CA: Sage.

Kossek, E. E., Markel, K. S., & McHugh, P. P. (2003). Increasing diversity as an HRM change strategy. *Journal of Organizational Change Management*, **16**, 328–52.

Kossek, E. E., & Zonia, S. C. (1993). Assessing diversity climate: A field study of reactions to employer efforts to promote diversity. *Journal of Organizational Behavior*, **14**, 61–81.

Kozlowski, S. W. J., & Klein, K. J. (2000). A multilevel approach to theory and research in organizations: Contextual, temporal, and emergent processes. In K. J. Klein & S. W. J. Kozlowski (Eds), *Multilevel Theory, Research, and Methods in Organizations* (pp. 3–90). San Francisco, CA: Jossey-Bass.

Kravitz, D. A. (2008). The diversity-validity dilemma: Beyond selection—the role of affirmative action. *Personnel Psychology*, **61**, 173–93.

Kulik, C., & Roberson, L. (2008). Diversity initiative effectiveness: What organizations can (and cannot) expect from diversity recruitment, diversity training, and formal mentoring programs. In A. P. Brief (Ed.), *Diversity at Work* (pp. 265–317). New York, NY: Cambridge University Press.

Lau, D. C., & Murnighan, J. K. (1998). Demographic diversity and faultlines: the compositional dynamics of organizational groups. *Academy of Management Review*, **23**, 325–40.

Lawrence, B. S. (1997). The black box of organizational demography. *Organization Science*, **8**, 1–22.

Lefkowitz, J. (1994). Race as a factor in job placement: Serendipitous findings of 'ethnic drift.' *Personnel Psychology*, **47**, 497–513.

Lende, T. (2005). Older workers: Opportunity or challenge? *Canadian Manager*, **30**(1), 20–30.

Lepak, D. P., Liao, H., Chung, Y., & Harden, E. E. (2006). A conceptual review of human resource management systems in strategic human resource management. *Research in Personnel and Human Resource Management*, **25**, 217–71.

Levine, R. A., & Campbell, D. T. (1972). *Ethnocentrism: Theories of Conflict, Ethnic Attitudes, and Group Behavior*. New York: Wiley.

Li, J., & Hambrick, D. C. (2005). Factional groups: A new vantage on demographic faultlines, conflict, and disintegration in work teams. *Academy of Management Journal*, 48, 794–813.

Lyness, K. S., & Terrazas, J. M. (2006). Women in management: An update on their progress and persistent challenges. In G. Hodgkinson & J. K. Ford (Eds), *International Review of Industrial and Organizational Psychology* (pp. 267–94), Volume 22, West Sussex, England: Wiley.

Lyness, K. S., & Thompson, D. E. (2000). Climbing the corporate latter: Do female and male executives follow the same route? *Journal of Applied Psychology*, 85, 86–101.

McDonald, P., & Dear, K. (2008). The incidence and patterns of discrimination and harassment affecting working women in Australia. *Women's Studies Journal*, 22, 37–48.

McKay, P. F., & Avery, D. R. (2006). What has race got to do with it? Unraveling the role of racioethnicity in job seekers' reactions to site visits. *Personnel Psychology*, 59, 395–429.

McKay, P. F., Avery, D. R., & Morris, M. A. (2008). Mean racial-ethnic differences in employee sales performance: The moderating role of diversity climate. *Personnel Psychology*, 61, 349–374.

McKay, P. F., Avery, D. R., & Morris, M. A. (2009). A tale of two climates: Diversity climate from subordinates' and managers' perspectives and their role in store unit sales performance. *Personnel Psychology*.

McKay, P. F., Avery, D. R., Tonidandel, S., Morris, M. A., Hernandez, M., & Hebl, M. R. (2007). Racial differences in employee retention: Are diversity climate perceptions the key? *Personnel Psychology*, 60, 35–62.

McKay, P. F., & Davis, J. L. (2007). Traditional selection methods as resistance to diversity in organizations. In K. M. Thomas (Ed.), *Diversity Resistance in Organizations: Manifestations and Solutions* (pp. 151–74). Boca Raton, FL: Taylor & Francis.

McKay, P. F., & McDaniel, M. A. (2006). A reexamination of Black-White mean differences in work performance: More data, more moderators. *Journal of Applied Psychology*, 91, 538–54.

Milgram, S. (1964). Group pressure and action against a person. *Journal of Abnormal and Social Psychology*, 69, 137–43.

Miner-Rubino, K., & Cortina, L. M. (2007). Beyond targets: Consequences of vicarious exposure to misogyny at work. *Journal of Applied Psychology*, 92, 1254–69.

Murray, P., & Syed, J. (2005). Critical issues in managing age diversity in Australia. *Asia Pacific Journal of Human Resources*, 43, 210–24.

National Urban League. (2004). *Diversity practices that work: The American worker speaks*. Retrieved on January 1, 2009 from http://www.nul.org/Publications/PDF/ERAC-NUL.pdf.

Newman, D. A., & Lyon, J. S. (2009). Recruitment efforts to reduce adverse impact: Targeted recruiting for personality, cognitive ability, and diversity. *Journal of Applied Psychology*, 94, 298–317.

Norton, M. I., Sommers, S. R., Apfelbaum, E. P., Pura, N., & Ariely, D. (2006). Color blindness and interracial interaction: Playing the political correctness game. *Psychological Science*, 17, 949–53.

Ozgener, S. (2008). Diversity management and demographic differences-based discrimination: The case of Turkish manufacturing industry. *Journal of Business Ethics*, 82, 621–31.

Pazy, A., & Oron, I. (2001). Sex proportion and performance evaluation among high-ranking military officers. *Journal of Organizational Behavior*, 22, 689–702.

Petersen, L., & Dietz, J. (2000). Social discrimination in a personnel selection context: The effects of an authority's instruction to discriminate and followers' authoritarianism. *Journal of Applied Social Psychology*, 30, 206–20.

Petersen, L., & Dietz, J. (2008). Employment discrimination: Authority figures' demographic preferences and followers' affective organizational commitment. *Journal of Applied Psychology*, **93**, 1287–1300.

Plant, E. A., & Devine, P. G. (1998). Internal and external motivation to respond without prejudice. *Journal of Personality and Social Psychology*, **75**, 811–32.

Ployhart R. E., & Holtz, B. C. (2008). The diversity-validity dilemma: Strategies for reducing racioethnic and sex subgroup differences and adverse impact in selection. *Personnel Psychology*, **61**, 153–72.

Pugh, S. D., Dietz, J., Brief, A. P., & Wiley, J. W. (2008). Looking inside and out: The impact of employee and community demographic composition on organizational diversity climate. *Journal of Applied Psychology*, **93**, 1422–8.

Reichers, A. E., & Schneider, B. (1990). Climate and culture: An evolution of constructs. In B. Schneider (Ed.), *Organizational Climate and Culture* (pp. 5–39). San Francisco, CA: Jossey-Bass.

Reskin, B. F., McBrier, D. B., & Kmec, J. A. (1999). The determinants and consequences of workplace sex and race composition. *Annual Review of Sociology*, **25**, 335–61.

Rhoades, L., & Eisenberger, R. (2002). Perceived organizational support: A review of the literature. *Journal of Applied Psychology*, **87**, 698–714.

Roberson, Q. M., & Park, H. J. (2007). Examining the link between diversity and firm performance: The effects of diversity reputation and leader racial diversity. *Group & Organization Management*, **32**, 548–68.

Robinson, G., & Dechant, K. (1997). Building a business case for diversity. *Academy of Management Executive*, **11**, 21–31.

Roth, P. L., BeVier, C. A., Bobko, P., Switzer, F. S. III, & Tyler, P. (2001). Ethnic group differences in cognitive ability in employment and educational settings: A meta-analysis. *Personnel Psychology*, **54**, 297–330.

Sackett, P. R., DuBois, C. L. Z., & Noe, A. W. (1991). Tokenism in performance evaluation: The effects of work group representation on male-female and white-black differences in performance ratings. *Journal of Applied Psychology*, **76**, 263–7.

Schmidt, F. L., & Hunter, J. E. (1998). The validity and utility of selection methods in personnel psychology: Practical and theoretical implications of 85 years of research findings. *Psychological Bulletin*, **124**, 262–74.

Schneider, B., & Bowen, D. E. (1985). Employee and customer perceptions of service in banks: Replication and extension. *Journal of Applied Psychology*, **70**, 423–33.

Shoobridge, G. E. (2006). Multi-ethnic workforce and business performance: Review and synthesis of the empirical literature. *Human Resource Development Review*, **5**, 92–137.

Singh, V., & Point, S. (2006). (Re)presentations of gender and ethnicity in diversity statements on European company websites. *Journal of Business Ethics*, **68**, 363–79.

Stone, D. L., Stone-Romero, E. F., & Lukaszewski, K. M. (2007). The impact of cultural values on the acceptance and effectiveness of human resource management policies and practices. *Human Resource Management Review*, **17**, 152–65.

Tajfel H., & Turner, J. C. (1985). The social identity theory of intergroup behavior. In S. Worchel & W. G. Austin (Eds), *Psychology of Intergroup Relations* (2nd ed., pp. 7–24). Chicago: Nelson-Hall.

Thatcher, S. M. B., & Greer, L. L. (2008). Does it really matter if you recognize who I am? The implications of identity comprehension for individuals in work teams. *Journal of Management*, **34**, 5–24.

Thomas, D. A. (1999a). Beyond the simple demography-power hypothesis: How Blacks in power influence white-mentor-black-protégé developmental relationships. In

A. J. Murrell, F. J. Crosby & R. J. Ely (Eds), *Mentoring Dilemmas: Developmental Relationships Within Multicultural Organizations* (pp. 157–72). Mahwah, NJ: Lawrence Erlbaum.

Thomas, R. R., Jr. (1999b). *Building a House for Diversity: A Fable About a Giraffe & an Elephant Offers New Strategies for Today's Workforce*. New York: AMACOM.

Tomaskovic-Devey, D., Zimmer, C., Stainback, K., Robinson, C., Taylor, T., & Mc-Tague, T. (2006). Documenting desegregation: segregation in American workplaces by race, ethnicity, and sex, 1966–2003. *American Sociological Review*, 71, 565–88.

Toossi, M. (2007). Labor force projections to 2016: more workers in their golden years. *Monthly Labor Review*, 130(11), 33–52.

Tung, R. L. (2008). Do race and gender matter in international assignments to/from Asia Pacific? An exploratory study of attitudes among Chinese and Korean executives. *Human Resource Management*, 47, 91–110.

Umphress, E. E., Simmons, A. L., Boswell, W. R., & Triana, M. (2008). Managing discrimination in selection: The influence of directives from an authority and social dominance orientation. *Journal of Applied Psychology*, 93, 982–93.

U.S. General Accounting Office. (2001). *Older Workers: Demographic Trends Pose Challenges for Employers and Workers*. Washington, DC: Author.

van Dick, R., van Knippenberg, D., Hägele, S., Guillaume, Y. R. F., & Brodbeck, F. C. (2008). Group diversity and group identification: The moderating role of diversity beliefs. *Human Relations*, 61, 1463–92.

van Knippenberg, D., & Schippers, M. C. (2007). Work group diversity. *Annual Review of Psychology*, 58, 515–41.

Watkins-Baskerville, M. B., Kaplan, S., Brief, A. P., Shull, A., Dietz, J., Mansfield, M., & Cohen, R. (2006). Does it pay to be a sexist? The relationship between modern sexism and career outcomes. *Journal of Vocational Behavior*, 69, 524–37.

Wentling, R. M. (2004). Factors that assist and barriers that hinder the success of diversity initiatives in multinational corporations. *Human Resource Development International*, 7, 165–80.

Wentling, R. M., & Palma-Rivas, N. (1998). Current status and future trends of diversity initiatives in the workplace: diversity experts' perspective. *Human Resource Development Quarterly*, 9, 235–53.

Windzio, M. (2008). Organizational ecology of immigrant employment and organizational buffer zones: Who leaves first when the organization gets into trouble? *Social Science Research*, 37, 1171–87.

Wrench, J. (2007). *Diversity Management and Discrimination: Immigrants and Ethnic Minorities in the EU*. London: Ashgate.

Wright, P., Ferris, S. P., Hiller, J. S., & Kroll, M. (1995). Competitiveness through management of diversity: Effects on stock price valuation. *Academy of Management Journal*, 38, 272–87.

Wyer, N. A. (2004). Not all stereotypic biases are created equal: Evidence for a stereotype-disconfirming bias. *Personality and Social Psychology Bulletin*, 30, 706–20.

Zatzick, C. D., Elvira, M. M., & Cohen, L. E. (2003). When more is better? The effects of racial composition on voluntary turnover. *Organization Science*, 14, 483–96.

Ziegert, J. C., & Hanges, P. J. (2005). Employment discrimination: The role of implicit attitudes, motivation, and a climate for racial bias. *Journal of Applied Psychology*, 90, 553–62.

Chapter 7

POSITIVE ORGANIZATIONAL BEHAVIOR AT WORK

James Campbell Quick
College of Business, University of Texas at Arlington, Arlington, TX, USA

Cary L. Cooper
Lancaster University Management School, Lancaster University, Lancaster, UK

Philip C. Gibbs
Centre for Organisational Health & Well-Being, School of Health & Medicine, Lancaster University, Lancaster, UK

Laura M. Little
Terry College of Business, University of Georgia, Athens, GA, USA

Debra L. Nelson
Department of Management, Spears School of Business, Oklahoma State University, Stillwater, OK, USA

INTRODUCTION

Organizational behavior (OB) is the study of understanding, predicting, and controlling group and individual human behavior in organizational settings. Interdisciplinary in nature, with its origins in psychology, anthropology, medicine, sociology, and management, OB has evolved as researchers advance theory and offer implications for leaders (Nelson and Quick, 2009). Our knowledge of conflict management, political behavior, emotions at work, performance management, motivation, and teamwork has grown as research in OB has accumulated.

International Review of Industrial and Organizational Psychology, 2010, Volume 25.
Edited by G. P. Hodgkinson and J. K. Ford. Copyright © 2010 John Wiley & Sons, Ltd

OB researchers have been influenced by psychology and management, as these fields have moved toward the positive. Positive organizational behavior (POB) is an extension of the positive psychology initiative developed by Martin E.P. Seligman (cf. Seligman and Csikszentmihalyi, 2000) and earlier foundational psychologists, including Hersey et al. (see Wright and Quick, 2009). Positive organizational scholarship (POS), spearheaded by Kim Cameron and his colleagues, focuses on identifying human strengths and exceptional organizational performance (cf. Cameron, Dutton, and Quinn, 2003). Both positive psychology and POS are points of departure for POB, which we define as a focus on positive states, traits, and processes within organizations (Nelson and Cooper, 2007). Our view is inclusive, and we welcome the variance that it facilitates. By encompassing a range of variables within POB, we can reflect the diversity that exists in positive organizational research.

OB has always involved positive research, but because of its roots in medicine and psychology it suffers from an emphasis on disease and dysfunction. The leader's role is to diagnose problems and provide solutions. A vital part of OB is to resolve negative situations, and we do not advocate abandoning the study of dysfunction in organizations. Instead, we propose a balanced approach in which the positive side receives its share of research attention. We need more knowledge of what goes right in organizations and how to encourage it, and the processes that enable individuals and teams to thrive.

The first section of this chapter reviews POB's roots in positive psychology as well as the emergence of POS. It explores the foundational work of Luthans and his colleagues (cf. Luthans et al., 2007), with attention to the concept of positive psychological capital (PsyCap). As a higher-order construct, PsyCap comprises hope, optimism, self-efficacy, and resilience and has garnered attention among POB researchers.

The second section of the chapter considers positive states, traits, and processes and reflects the breadth and complexity of POB. Positive states are considered for their malleability and relationships with job performance. Of the host of traits that favorably impact an organization, we highlight three: character, hardiness, and resilience. Too, there are processes that facilitate the positive at work, and we focus on communication, forgiveness, and thriving.

It is important to distinguish between health as the absence of disease and health as the presence of positive attributes. In the third section of the chapter, we consider eustress, the healthy side of stress, as a new area for research and propose that the process of generating eustress should complement the process of preventing and resolving distress. Next we explore the notion of healthy workplaces, with attention to the American Psychological Association's (APA) lauding organizations that exemplify healthy work.

The fourth section gives voice to both the skeptic and the critic. It's easy to slip into an advocacy role in POB because of its positive nature and fit with our time, but we must strike a balance between advocacy and science.

By examining POB from the viewpoint of skepticism and scholarly criticism, we can ensure that POB researchers advance the positive paradigm with full awareness of the challenges that scholarly rigor poses. The chapter concludes with a focus on the future of POB. We take the latitude to imagine what POB can do to grow. We also discuss workplace relevance and application. How do we develop positive states and processes in the workplace? How do we sustain them? Given global economic challenges, how viable is the POB movement, and should it change course to accommodate the evolving context within which we work? We summarize in this chapter the fresh ideas being explored in the relatively new field of POB. We hope that the chapter can serve as a catalyst for research that elevates the positive aspects of organizational life so that a balance of the positive and the negative is attained within the larger field of OB.

ROOTS OF POB: POSITIVE PSYCHOLOGY

In 1998 the president of the APA, Martin Seligman, delivered an address detailing the activities in which psychologists should be engaged in the twenty-first century (see Seligman, 1999). He called for a reorientation in science that emphasizes the most positive human qualities, and he called this "positive psychology." Seligman *et al.* (2005) state how positive psychology has now become "an umbrella term for the study of positive emotions, characteristics, processes and institutions that assist both individuals and organizations to thrive" (p. 410). Not only is it a unified approach to the study of topics like strengths and happiness, it is also a systematized attempt to promote the optimal human condition.

Seligman and colleagues, Mihalyi Csikszentmihalyi, Christopher Peterson, Raymond Fowler, George Vaillant, Ed Diener, Donald Clifton, Kathleen Hall Jamieson, and Bob Nozick, attempted to craft a new scientific framework for positive psychology. Seligman and Csikszentmihalyi (2000) urged a shift away from healing and repairing human functioning to building on the positive qualities that help individuals and societies flourish. To facilitate research and practice and to highlight what they considered gaps in understanding, positive psychology was divided into three levels of inquiry (Peterson and Park, 2003), which constitute the three pillars to positive psychology (Seligman, 2002a; Seligman, 2003).

The first level of inquiry studies hope, confidence, and trust (Seligman and Csikszentmihalyi, 2000). This approach values subjective experiences characterized as being either retrospective (satisfaction and well-being), present (happiness and flow), or forward-looking (optimism and hope). The second-level studies strengths and virtues (Peterson and Seligman, 2004), including the capacity for love, courage, forgiveness, and perseverance

(Seligman and Csikszentmihalyi, 2000). The third-level studies positive institutions and communities such as democracy, strong families, and free inquiry. Peterson and Park (2003) explain how institutions and civic virtues can promote positive emotions that in turn enable individuals to be better citizens (more responsible, engaged, altruistic, and tolerant).

How Did Positive Psychology Emerge?

The idea of positive psychology came to Seligman (2002a) while gardening with his daughter one summer. After he finished shouting at her, she replied that if she could stop whining, he could stop being such a grouch. He realized that rather than focus on his daughter's weaknesses, he should nurture her strengths. This inspired Seligman to think about psychology and other social and behavioral sciences, and he became critical of them for ignoring positive qualities. He concluded that psychology had become focused on pathology and how to treat mental health and fix human functioning (Seligman, 2003).

Seligman and Csikszentmihalyi (2000) noted the significant increases in Western governmental funding for psychologists to address mental health issues following World War II. The empirical focus became negatively oriented, despite a minority of humanists who focused on curing mental illness and individual suffering (Seligman, 2002b). Thus a high demand developed for research to investigate psychologic disorders and the negative consequences and effects of environmental stressors (Seligman and Csikszentmihalyi, 2000), which could then be used to help prevent such outcomes (Seligman, 2002b). Seligman recognized how psychologists of the time helped identify effective treatments for a range of maladies. However, he argued that psychology as a discipline has a much broader remit and should also be concerned with improving quality of life and promoting well-being (Seligman, 2004). The positive psychology movement was born in an attempt to remedy this imbalance (Seligman, Parks, and Steen, 2004).

How Does Positive Psychology Differ from Humanistic Psychology?

Some argue that many of positive psychology's concepts appear to echo themes expressed by humanistic psychologists (e.g. Fineman, 2006). Noted humanists Abraham Maslow and Carl Rogers shared a vision in attempting to influence the positive human qualities of self-actualization, hope, creativity, and love (Gable and Haidt, 2005). At first glance, both movements seem to occupy the same territory. Both attempt to understand positive characteristics rather than the negative pathological factors detrimental to human functioning. Martin (2007) stated that humanistic psychologists such as Maslow could have written the proposed positive psychology agenda if it weren't for the latter movement being more experimental. Maslow's (1954) book, *Motivation and Personality*, even contained a chapter titled "Toward a Positive Psychology." This poses an intriguing question: Were theorists such as Maslow and Rogers positive psychologists before positive psychology? (Fineman, 2006).

Although Seligman and others built on the foundations of humanistic psychologists, they distanced themselves from the humanistic psychology movement (Seligman, Parks, and Steen, 2004; Seligman *et al.*, 2005). They considered it narrow and lacking a cumulative empirical base (Seligman and Csikszentmihalyi, 2000). Positive psychology endeavored to adopt the traditional psychologist's scientific methods and treatment practices while creating a new, scientifically vital approach for what is right and best (Linley and Joseph, 2004). Consequently, Seligman and Csikszentmihalyi (2000) state that positive psychology will "reorient psychology back to its two neglected missions–making normal people stronger and more productive, and making high human potential actual" (p. 8).

Strengths and Talents

Positive psychology is empirically oriented, meaning it encourages the validation of psychometrically robust diagnostic tools. An early priority for positive psychologists was to identify human strengths and virtues. Seligman (2004) explains that no progress could be made without agreement on a classification system. Consequently, with his colleague Peterson, he went on to develop the character, strengths, and virtues (CSV: Peterson and Seligman, 2004). CSV was an attempt to counter the negatively oriented *Diagnostic and Statistical Manual of Mental Disorders* published by the American Psychiatric Association (2000). Rather than classify psychological disorders that hinder people, CSV attempts to describe strengths and virtues that help people thrive (Peterson, Park, and Seligman, 2005a). Seligman (2002a) argues that although they possess similarities, strengths are not the same as talents: Strengths are moral traits more susceptible to development, whereas talents are more innate and mechanical (either individuals have a particular talent or they do not have).

CSV features six virtues that Seligman and colleagues argue are universal. Peterson and Seligman (2004) categorize them thus: *wisdom and knowledge* (creativity, curiosity, judgment, love of learning, and perspective); *courage* (bravery, honesty, perseverance, and zest); *humanity* (kindness, love, and social intelligence); *justice* (fairness, leadership and teamwork); *temperance* (forgiveness, modesty, prudence and self-regulation); and *transcendence* (appreciation of beauty, gratitude, hope, humor, and religion). Seligman labels a person's unique qualities their signature strengths (Seligman, 2002a,b) and argues that rather than focus on correcting perceived character flaws, attention should focus on heightening signature strengths (Park, Peterson, and Seligman, 2004), which leads to greater emotional satisfaction (Peterson, Park, and Seligman, 2005b).

Recent Developments

Seligman *et al.* (2005) reviewed the progress of the positive psychology movement, highlighting developments in journals, books, undergraduate and postgraduate courses, conferences, and networking groups. Similarly, topics such as well-being and happiness, once regarded as unscientific, are now the subject of studies by serious academics and scientists (Linley and Joseph, 2004; Linley *et al.*, 2006). Positive psychology has helped reclaim virtue and character as topics of investigation, as well as further the understanding of positive phenomena (Seligman, 2005). Peterson *et al.* (2008) investigated why certain character strengths were associated more highly with greater life satisfaction among Swiss and American adults. Previous research had highlighted the links between the long-term effects of strengths and satisfaction among adults (see Isaacowitz, Vaillant, and Seligman, 2003). Hope, love, zest, and curiosity seemed to link highest with life satisfaction across both samples. The most robust predictor was gratitude in the American sample and perseverance in the Swiss sample. It was concluded that these findings may be congruent with national stereotypes.

Seligman *et al.* (2005) also highlighted how positive psychology has helped validate interventions for increasing happiness and decreasing depressive symptoms for up to six months. One example required individuals to apply their signature strengths in a novel way every day for a week. Positive interventions such as these might one day supplement the more traditional focus on repairing human functioning.

In the years since Seligman first called for a new science of human strengths, positive psychology has advanced considerably. Roberts (2006) notes how the rapid increase in empirical efforts to study well-being at work have influenced the formation of associated movements such as POS and POB. Gable and Haidt (2005) found rapid growth in positive psychology and evaluated the need for such a movement. They concluded in favor of positive psychology, finding a greater potential for understanding what is good and right with people. They believed that the time was right for an organized positive psychology movement, "In the past five years, many investigators have been getting on the train and discovering that it is taking them to interesting places and new frontiers" (Gable and Haidt, 2005, p. 107).

POSITIVE ORGANIZATIONAL SCHOLARSHIP

POS is a relatively new movement within the management and organizational sciences, often used as an umbrella term incorporating a range of perspectives around the theme of positivity (Dutton and Glynn, 2008). Cameron, Dutton, and Quinn (2003) introduced the term as a way to recognize those elements in organizations that optimize performance. Cameron and Caza (2004) define POS as, "a new movement in organizational science that focuses on the dynamics leading to exceptional individual and organizational performance such as developing human strength, producing resilience and restoration and fostering vitality" (p. 731).

The term "positive organizational scholarship" describes the orientation of the movement (Bernstein, 2003; George, 2004). Positive refers to the examination of generative dynamics and states that accentuate an affirmative bias of positive phenomena (Cameron, 2003). It does not disregard the absence or presence of negative phenomena so much as it examines the contrary aspects to positive phenomena (Cameron and Caza, 2004; Sonenshein, 2005). Organizational refers to understanding organizational generative dynamics and states at the micro and macro levels, as well as how these operate within and across organizations (Cameron, 2003). POS is inclusive as well as expansive, incorporating traditional studies of organizational phenomena such as organizational design, leadership, and organizational change while attempting to develop new positive insights (Cameron, Dutton, and Quinn, 2003). Finally, scholarship refers to the scientific rigor underpinning the methodological procedures chosen to investigate positive phenomena (Cameron, 2003). It attempts to rectify criticisms of previous research that was deemed unscientific because it drew largely from religious, spiritual, and philosophical perspectives (Bernstein, 2003).

Dutton and Glynn (2008) describe how POS stems from three features. The first focuses on the notion of flourishing and investigates how certain states, processes, and conditions unfold (Cameron, Dutton, and Quinn, 2003). The second feature focuses on strengths and capabilities (Cameron, 2003), while the third highlights the generative dynamics that explain flourishing and help facilitate capabilities (Dutton and Sonenshein, 2007).

All three components are investigated at an individual, group, and organizational level (Cameron, 2007b). At the individual level Keyes (2002) likens flourishing to optimal human functioning. A POS perspective investigates particular states and processes, such as optimism, health and well-being, happiness, resilience, self-efficacy, and satisfaction (Dutton and Sonenshein, 2007; Losada and Heaphy, 2004). At the group level, POS is concerned with communal flourishing – understanding the dynamics of team creativity, flow, and synergy (Cameron and Caza, 2004). At the organizational level POS investigates how organizations thrive (Dutton et al., 2006) by focusing on dynamics such as resilience, optimism, courage, and integrity (Dutton and Sonenshein, 2007). The POS perspective lends itself to investigating interactions across these levels of organizations. Dutton and Sonenshein (2007) call this the dyadic level, which is concerned with understanding how flourishing relationships are facilitated (e.g., among peers, or between employees and their immediate manager).

Dutton and Sonenshein (2007) highlight how a number of intellectual disciplines influenced POS development, but none more so than positive psychology. POS and positive psychology share a similar orientation, emphasizing promotion of individual and collective strengths, vitality, optimal functioning, and flourishing (Cameron, Dutton, and Quinn, 2003).

How Does POS Differ from Positive Psychology?

In many ways POS moves parallel to positive psychology by drawing attention away from non-positive phenomena to investigating positive conditions in which organizations and employees thrive (Caza and Cameron, 2008). POS has been called the organizational equivalent of positive psychology because it attempts to understand what organizations are doing right, as opposed to focusing on what they're doing wrong (Dutton and Sonenshein, 2007).

POS is not dominated purely by positivity, though, as it recognizes the importance of negativity and bottom-line organizational issues (Cameron, 2003). Research has shown that understanding negative states is important in explaining how to nurture the resilience to overcome them, which in turn can enable individuals, groups, and organizations to flourish (Fredrickson and Dutton, 2008; Sutcliffe and Vogus, 2003). POS also addresses the limited amount of research that investigates positive institutions and communities, positive psychology's third pillar of inquiry (Gable and Haidt, 2005; Roberts, 2006).

POS adopts perspectives from sociology, anthropology, social work, and organization theory (Dutton, Glynn, and Spreitzer, 2006), while taking into account various processes such as leadership, culture, and climate that encourage positive dynamics (Cameron and Caza, 2004). Roberts (2006) suggests that "organizational scholarship has a particular opportunity to enrich and complicate the positive psychology agenda by more deeply contextualizing psychologists' accounts of positive subjective experiences and states" (p. 294). As a result, POS can be seen as a complementary movement to positive psychology that adopts a multidimensional, multilevel approach focusing on positive phenomena in organizational contexts; thus, it draws on a number of perspectives in an attempt to contextualize its relevance for organizational studies (Cameron, Dutton, and Quinn, 2003).

Key Assumptions

Four assumptions encompass the POS perspective (Dutton and Glynn, 2008). First, POS assumes that factors leading to extraordinary states (thriving) are not necessarily the same as those leading to problematic states (stress). To create a thriving environment it's not enough to simply remove environmental stressors (Dutton, Glynn, and Spreitzer, 2006). Second, POS assumes that organizational resources, both collective and human, are dynamic and can take place from within systems (Dutton and Glynn, 2008). Glynn and Wrobel (2007) call this "endogenous resourcefulness," that is, resources and capabilities, including strength-based skills, which can reveal the hidden potential within systems. Third, POS assumes that flourishing is embedded in a context. Therefore, context plays a crucial role in developing collective and individual strengths in organizations (Dutton and Glynn, 2008). Finally, POS assumes a normative basis by focusing on dynamics within OB that are believed to be "positive" topics worthy of scientific investigation (Dutton and Glynn, 2008).

Recent Developments

Although still a relatively new movement, POS has flourished. Roberts (2006) highlighted how it has contributed to organizational studies, and a number of journals, papers, and books plus various institutions have helped promote the domains of positive inquiry (Dutton and Sonenshein, 2007). In a review of empirical articles that align with the POS perspective, Caza and Cameron (2008) categorized 20 of these domains into six themes: individual virtue and concern, leadership, organizational virtue and performance, positive relationships and performance, absence of negativity, and PsyCap.

In line with these themes, several POS antecedents provide macrolevel perspectives on positive psychology, community psychology, pro-social behavior, organization development, corporate social performance, and POB (Caza and Cameron, 2008). All can be seen as further evidence of how POS is contributing to the study of the mechanisms and outcomes associated with positive organizing (Fredrickson and Dutton, 2008).

EMERGENCE OF POSITIVE ORGANIZATIONAL BEHAVIOR

POB has roots in positive psychology, but it considers both the positive and the negative, building strengths while improving weaknesses (Luthans and Youssef, 2007). In the workplace, where success necessitates higher and higher performance (Sutcliffe and Vogus, 2007), POB answers the call for the study of what goes right in organizations: identifying human strengths, producing resilience and restoration, fostering vitality, and cultivating extraordinary individuals (Cameron, Dutton, and Quinn, 2003; Luthans and Youssef, 2003) by focusing on positive states, traits, and processes (Nelson and Cooper, 2007).

By states we refer to the continuum from fleeting emotions to vigor, optimism, and self-efficacy. The malleable nature of states makes them a critical aspect of POB as a result of their potential for training and development (Luthans and Church, 2002; Luthans and Youssef, 2007). Positive states represent positive psychological resources that can give an advantage in the workplace; indeed, many positive states have been linked to positive outcomes at work (Kluemper, Little, and DeGroot, 2009; Simmons, Nelson, and Quick, 2003). Traits, on the other hand, are relatively enduring, stable, and develop over one's life span. Traits include various aspects of personality, including core self-evaluation (Judge *et al.*, 1998), character, virtue, and resilience. Given their more stable nature, traits can be important in the development of states (Luthans and Youssef, 2007) as well as in determining individual fit within organizations (Kristof-Brown, Zimmerman, and Johnson, 2005). The processes of communication, forgiveness, compassion, and thriving involve courses of action that facilitate positive outcomes (Macik-Frey, Quick, and Quick, 2005; Peterson and Seligman, 2004).

Although most definitions of POB include traits and processes, some would suggest a focus on states, particularly states that are measurable (Luthans and Youssef, 2007). As the founding fathers of POB research, Luthans (2002) defined POB as, "the study and application of positively oriented human resource strengths and psychological capacities that can be measured, developed, and effectively managed for performance improvement in today's workplace" (p. 59). They argue that extensive theory and practical application, including the ability to develop and validate measures, are essential if the study of positive constructs is to bear fruit. Further, Luthans, Luthans, and Luthans (2004) propose four psychological resource capacities that meet these characteristics: hope, self-efficacy, optimism, and resiliency.

With its scholarly roots in clinical psychology, hope has been defined as a positive motivational state derived from the combination of successful agency (willpower) and pathways (waypower) (Snyder *et al.*, 1991). Those with hope believe in their ability to set goals and accomplish them. The derivation of hope comes from goal-setting theory (Locke and Latham, 1984), specifically from the idea that goals can provide crucial anchors in cognition (Lee, Locke, and Latham, 1989). Hope can be developed through goal-setting training (Snyder, 2000) and has been found to positively relate to health (Simmons *et al.*, 2003) and performance (Luthans, 2002; Luthans, Youssef, and Avolio, 2007).

Self-efficacy is grounded in Bandura's social cognitive theory and features confidence in the ability to mobilize the resources needed to execute a task (Bandura, 1986; Stajkovic and Luthans, 1998). Self-efficacy can be developed through mastery, vicarious learning, persuasion, and psychological and physical arousal (Bandura, 1997). It is related to leadership effectiveness (Luthans *et al.*, 2001), creativity (Tierney and Farmer, 2002), several types of decision making (May *et al.*, 2003; Nilsson, Schmidt, and Meek, 2002) and work-related performance (Bandura and Locke, 2003).

Optimism is an attributional style in which positive events are portrayed through personal, permanent, and pervasive causes and negative events through external, temporary, and situation-specific causes (Seligman, 2006).

Carver and Scheier (1981) argue that optimism influences outcomes through its self-regulatory nature. They theorize that all human behavior can be cast in goal terms and argue that becoming aware of a discrepancy between a goal and the present situation initiates an assessment process. If an individual perceives that this discrepancy can be reduced to achieve desirable outcomes, they will continue to exert efforts to this end, whereas if they perceive that desirable outcomes are unattainable, they will reduce effort. From this perspective, it is expected that optimists continue to strive, work hard, and cope with the problems they encounter, while pessimists give up (Lee, Ashford, and Jamieson, 1993; Scheier and Carver, 1987; Scheier et al., 1989). Like hope, optimism can be developed through goal-setting training and has been related to a variety of positive outcomes such as contextual performance, job satisfaction, and commitment (Kluemper, Little, and DeGroot, 2009).

Resiliency is the capacity to rebound from adversity and embrace positive events such as progress and increased responsibility (Luthans, 2002). Luthans describes resiliency as being of interest to the POB movement because of its learned component. Resiliency allows individuals to learn from setbacks. It can be developed in the workplace through using one's assets (knowledge, skills, abilities, personality traits, or social relationships) to reduce and handle risks (stress, conflict, or job insecurity) (Luthans and Youssef, 2007). Through resiliency, individuals view adversity as a learning experience. Resiliency has been shown to relate to self-fulfillment and supervisor-rated performance (Luthans et al., 2005).

Luthans and Church (2002) argue that hope, self-efficacy, optimism, and resiliency contribute more to our learning when combined. As noted earlier, PsyCap comprises a higher-order construct that reflects the combination of these four lower-order constructs. It has been shown to relate to performance and satisfaction in the workplace (Luthans et al., 2007). Beyond these four state-like positive constructs, a variety of other states, traits, and processes have been studied to better understand the positive in the workplace, and it is to this broader body of work that we turn next.

What Is Positive?

The three sets of positive constructs in OB discussed in here are positive states, positive traits, and positive interpersonal processes. These are three separate, distinct sets of constructs. First, positive states include a spectrum from discrete emotions to more stable and yet malleable states. We focus on the positive emotions of happiness, interest, contentment, and the state of vigor. Second, positive traits represent more enduring attributes that are less prone to fluctuation, including character, self-reliance, personality hardiness, and resilience. Third, positive interpersonal processes focus on the human exchanges that occur in organizational settings; the discussion focuses on healthy communication, forgiveness, and thriving.

Positive States, Positive Emotions

Emotions are a feature of our affective systems and are characterized as being intense, short-lived, and having a definite cause (Watson and Clark, 1992). Therefore, emotions, unlike our general mood, are said to be composed of components including appraisal, physiological, and expressive changes and attribution (Russell, 2003). Emotions are referred to as positive and negative but also areassessed as discrete entities (Cropanzano *et al.*, 2003). Positive emotions are said to build an individual's thought-action capacities (Fredrickson, 1998), while negative emotions focus the individual to be more critical and discerning (George and Zhou, 2002). Positive emotions impact on behavior because they broaden the scope of attention, cognition, and action and build physical, intellectual, and social resources, whereas negative emotions narrow one's focus (Fredrickson, 1998). Thus, negative emotions can result in effortful processing and analysis, again in contrast to the heuristic processing that results from positive emotions (cf. Elsbach and Barr, 1999).

Positive emotions also can undo negative consequences associated with negative emotions. Studies have shown that experiencing a positive emotion can reverse cardiovascular arousal associated with negative emotions (Fredrickson and Levenson, 1998). When one is experiencing the negative consequences of negative emotion (say, fear of public speaking), these negative effects may be undone by inducing a positive emotion (relaxing the individual so that he can get through it) (Fredrickson *et al.*, 2000). Other states, not least the POB constructs of hope, self-efficacy, optimism, and resiliency, are more stable, develop over a longer period, and often have no known proximal salient cause.

To illustrate the impact of emotions and states in the workplace, we discuss the emotions of happiness, interest, and contentment, as well as the positive state of vigor. These were chosen because their impact on work life has been studied extensively.

Happiness (Lazarus, 1991) has been called joy, exhilaration, or mirth (Ruch, 1993). Izard (1977) says joy arises when the situation is safe and familiar. Other research found that joy was a result of events seen as accomplishments or progress toward goals (Izard, 1977; Lazarus, 1991). Joy is characterized by approach-related behavior that creates the urge to play and engage physically, socially, intellectually, and artistically (Fredrickson, 1998; Lyubomirsky, King, and Diener, 2005). Play has been related to both manipulative-cognitive and social-affective skill acquisition (Boulton and Smith, 1992). Happiness has also been related to constructs such as unselfishness (Feingold, 1983), income (Graham, Eggers, and Sukhtankar, 2004), and judgment accuracy (Ambady and Gray, 2002).

Interest has been defined as synonymous with curiosity and intrigue and is thought to be related to intrinsic motivation (Deci and Ryan, 1985). Interest is the most experienced emotion, and it arises in contexts that are considered safe and that offer possibility (Izard, 1977). Interest is associated with approach-related thoughts but may not be characterized by physical action. Instead, interest may reside in feelings of engagement and animation. Interest increases one's knowledge base and has been characterized as the primary instigator of personal growth and the development of intelligence.

Contentment is a low-arousal emotion associated with tranquility and satisfaction (Ellsworth and Smith, 1988). It is not usually associated with action but with thought and has been characterized as creating an urge to savor experiences (Fredrickson, 1998). Contentment has been shown to relate to broadening attention and thought-action (Fredrickson and Branigan, 2005).

Vigor is an affect experienced at work that combines elements of an emotion and a mood state (Shirom, 2007; Shirom *et al.*, 2008). Vigor at work involves feelings of physical strength, emotional energy, and cognitive liveliness resulting from an appraisal of one's energy resources (Shirom, 2004). Vigor at work is an internal, energetic resource or the affective representation of the individual's energy reservoirs related to the job. It is related to motivational processes that initiate and sustain behavior at work. Vigor encompasses arousal as well as positive feelings and has been proposed to stem from cognitive appraisal of job demands and resources (Lazarus, 1991; Shirom, 2004). Individuals who believe they can manage their job demands will experience vigor in relation to their jobs.

Vigor relates to various behaviors because of its nature as a state and because of the cognitive, physical, and emotional resources associated with specific approach-action tendencies (Fredrickson, 2002; Frijda, Kuipers, and Schure, 1989). Positive affect and emotions prompt individuals to engage with their environment and partake in activities that produce pleasurable outcomes. Individuals who feel vigorous at work can broaden their range of options and creatively solve problems as well as build social connectivity. While research has not linked vigor to work-related outcomes, vigor has been related to athletic and scholastic performance (Beedie, Terry, and Lane, 2000; Lane *et al.*, 2005). Research on zest, a relatively new construct somewhat near vigor on the spectrum of positive states, has linked zest to work-related outcomes to include work as a calling, work satisfaction, and life satisfaction (Peterson *et al.*, 2009).

Positive Traits

Of the four positive traits addressed in this chapter – strong character, self-reliance, personality hardiness, and resilience – character is important as the core of exceptional leadership in a crisis (Cooper *et al.*, 2006). Character (ethos) refers to the habitual qualities within individuals (Wright and Goodstein, 2007); it is the positive trait that enables the individual to behave in ways that are good, moral, and healthy. Character can be challenging to define, however, as Wright and Goodstein (2007) note in their major review of the literature on individual character and organizational-level virtue. Gavin *et al.* (2003) explore the role of character in executive health with a focus on personal integrity. They define character as a three-dimensional construct of emotional intelligence, moral approbation, and self-transcendent values.

Wright and Goodstein (2007) bring attention to the multidimensionality of character in two ways. First they trace the concept of character through history and across cultures. Then they include a classification of character strengths and virtues (see Peterson and Seligman (2004) for an expanded discussion). Wright and Goodstein's (2007) classification lists six categories of character strengths, each category including several specific strengths: wisdom and knowledge (creativity, curiosity, and open-mindedness), courage (bravery, integrity, and vitality), humanity (love, kindness, and emotional intelligence), justice (citizenship, fairness, and leadership), temperance (forgiveness, humility, and self-control), and transcendence (hope, humor, and spirituality). Although this classification scheme has been well articulated, several key tasks remain, not least the reliable and valid operationalization of the relevant constructs and an analysis of their impact on actions, behaviors, and performance.

A distinguishing characteristic of moral and healthy individuals is the reflection of these strengths of character in their actions. Strengths of character are a basis for individual actions in specific organizational contexts aimed at contributing to the greater good. Therefore, character strengths can contribute to organizational-level virtue.

Paradoxically, the individual acting based on strength of character may be labeled negative by those in the specific organizational context. An example might be the individual who reacted "negatively" to the social pressures at Enron (Cooper *et al.*, 2006). Using Wright and Goodstein's (2007) framework, companies that lack organizational-level virtue are immoral and unhealthy organizations in which a "negative" response becomes a display of positive and individual strength of character. Organizations that respond to such negative feedback by correcting what is bad move toward organizational-level virtue. When the bad is corrected, it then becomes positive.

A second positive trait is that of self-reliance (Quick, Nelson, and Quick, 1987). Self-reliance is a behavioral trait identified by British pediatrician John Bowlby and American psychologist Mary Ainsworth in their extended research on children (Ainsworth and Bowlby, 1991). We consider self-reliance an enduring trait of healthy individuals that extends into adulthood and spans social contexts, from work to home and from home to work. This pattern has been labeled interpersonal attachment because of the flexibility in self-reliance. Paradoxically, the individual seems strong and autonomous, but this appearance is anchored in secure interpersonal attachments. The dependency is for information, evaluative feedback on performance, emotional sustenance, and protection from either psychological or physical threats. Hence, as appropriate to task and circumstance, the self-reliant individual acts with autonomy, yet when faced with threat or limitation asks for help.

Self-reliance is anchored in attachment, which is one of two instinctual behaviors in humans. The second is exploratory behavior, which refers to the mastery of one's environment. Exploratory behavior was the basis for Christopher Columbus' crossing the Atlantic to reach the New World and for the space flight that placed an American on the moon. Exploratory behavior leads to potentially dangerous actions that display conquest when executed well. Hazan and Shaver (1990) suggest that exploratory behavior is the basis for work in adulthood.

Hazan and Shaver (1990) suggest that attachment behavior leads to the experience of safety and security, making it the basis for romantic love. In addition, Quick, Nelson, and Quick (1987) found attachment behavior to be a basis for secure interpersonal working relationships among executives. Thus attachment behavior complements exploratory behavior. Both are essential to full human development.

As Ainsworth and Bowlby (1991) demonstrate, self-reliance is rooted in childhood and becomes an enduring trait over time. They found, as did Joplin, Nelson, and Quick (1999) in their research with adults in organizations, that there are two negative alternatives to self-reliance, also labeled as interdependent attachment. Ainsworth and Bowlby (1991) labeled these negative alternatives as dismissive and preoccupied attachment styles. Joplin, Nelson, and Quick (1999) called them, respectively, counterdependent and overdependent attachment styles. Both are negative traits with adverse consequences, including social dysfunctions, performance problems, and psychological woes such as burnout (cf. Atkinson and Zucker, 1997).

In a study of 161 employees and their supervisors at an assisted living center, Simmons et al. (2009) concluded that self-reliance, which they label secure attachment, is a positive psychological strength with important implications for working adults. Specifically, they found secure attachment to have a positive relationship with hope and trust and a negative relationship with burnout. They discovered that trust has a significant and positive relationship with supervisory-rated performance. These findings are consistent with both the foundational research on self-reliance (Ainsworth and Bowlby, 1991) and the extended research among adults in work (Joplin, Nelson, and Quick, 1999) and non-work (Hazan and Shaver, 1990) settings.

A third positive trait, personality hardiness, was identified by Salvadore Maddi and his colleagues in their study of Illinois Bell Telephone executives (Maddi, 2006). This trait is actually a three-dimensional construct, similar to the notion of character, the dimensions being commitment, control, and challenge. While personality hardiness is not new, it is a positive trait that is legitimately a strength factor within the emerging positive agenda. We see, too, its consistency with character strengths and virtues such as curiosity, temperance, and self-control (cf. Peterson and Seligman, 2004).

Commitment stands in contrast to isolation and is defined as curiosity and engagement with the environment. Commitment leads to the experience of activities as interesting and enjoyable. Control stands in contrast to powerlessness and is the ability to influence events. Control leads to personal choice at work and at home. Challenge contrasts with threat and is the use of change as a stimulus for personal development. These three hardiness dimensions lead to a process of transformational coping through which life events are transformed into experiences that are subjectively less stressful. This transformation may enable individuals to view events from a broader life perspective and possibly even alter outcomes.

Think of personality hardiness as a protective shield against life's difficulties. Philanthropist William T. Grant funded a study beginning in 1937 that aimed to counterbalance medical research too weighted toward disease (Vaillant, 1977). Over the next four decades this study of healthy, successful men was transformed into a longitudinal study of their adult development and adaptation to life. Psychoanalyst George E. Vaillant joined the research team in 1967 and over the next 10 years identified five mature adaptive mechanisms: sublimation, altruism, suppression, anticipation, and humor. They proved to be the distinguishing characteristics of those who had the best outcomes within the cohort. In addition, Vaillant found that all members of the cohort had experienced trauma, tragedy, or significant loss at some point but that these experiences were not what defined the life. Rather, the mature mechanisms formed a shield that enabled those in the study to transform their lives in positive ways.

A fourth positive trait, resilience, merits revisiting here for its overlap with personality hardiness and self-reliance. This trait focuses on one's capacity to rebound from tragedy. Coutu (2002) suggests that resilience under stress is more important than either experience or training in determining success or failure in life. This is a powerful trait for organizational members, especially in challenging positions. Maddi and Khoshaba (2008) extend the personality hardiness trait and build on the earlier notions of transformational coping with the intention of enabling individuals to face their problems. Teaching people transformational coping skills enables them to enhance their personality hardiness under stress. The three key transformational coping skills are to understand the stressful event, to interpret the event in a broader life perspective, and to take action to alter the course and outcome of event. Vaillant (1977) classifies denial, distortion, and delusional projection as psychotic mechanisms that fall even below the immature adaptive mechanisms. Hence denial and avoidance become regressive coping mechanisms that fail.

By building on personality hardiness through transformational coping, Maddi and Khoshaba (2008) chart a path to increasing positive attitudes and emotions. Further, aligned with the positive trait of self-reliance, their concept of resilience leads to developing patterns of support that are based on giving and getting assistance when necessary.

Positive Interpersonal Processes

Positive interpersonal processes focus on the human exchanges that occur in organizational settings. Positive interpersonal processes are a third positive set of constructs distinct from either positive states or positive traits. Our discussion targets healthy communication, forgiveness, and thriving as three positive processes in organizations.

Healthy communication is one important aspect of working together when "working together" is taken for its intrapersonal as well as interpersonal meaning (Nelson and Quick, 2009). Broadly framed, interpersonal communication occurs between two or more people and results in a shared meaning. Healthy communication may be considered heartfelt communication, the absence of which has significant adverse consequences. In his classic work, Lynch (1977) documents the medical consequences of loneliness, where loneliness is the absence of deep human connection and heartfelt communication. The consequences take the form of morbidity, as in cardiovascular disease, and mortality, as in premature death. Lynch's (2000) follow-up volume offers insights into the medical consequences of loneliness and explores what he now labels communicative disease. Communicative disease is characterized by loneliness and social isolation.

Healthy communication is the key to unlocking social support (Macik-Frey, Quick, and Quick, 2005). Macik-Frey and her colleagues explored the development of communication competence as the basis for developing social support. They found that emotional intelligence, cognitive complexity, and gender and personality (locus of control, self-reliance, and hardiness) were all variables that influenced communication competence and moderated the linkage between interpersonal communication and social support.

At the social and interpersonal level, communication becomes unhealthy when it becomes defensive, extreme (violence) or breaks down completely (silence). The caveat here is that silence can be an appropriate listening device that enables the communicator to unravel momentary confusion or the listener to sort out emotional reactions to a message that, if expressed, might turn the communication negative. Nelson and Quick (2009) include a detailed discussion of key aspects of healthy interpersonal communication, including reflective listening, nondefensive communication behavior, proxemics, and gestures and facial expressions. Quick and Macik-Frey (2004) discuss deep-level interpersonal communication in the workplace.

One aspect of the communication process that is neither well studied nor particularly well understood is the intrapersonal dimension, wherein we tell ourselves stories that may not be true. Pennebaker's (1997) approach to expressive writing is one pathway through which one can become more familiar with this inner dialogue. Awareness of one's inner communication affords an opportunity to change the self-talk if needed. Cognitive-behavioral therapy is predicated on the idea that negative self-talk is a major source of psychological dysfunction (Dobson, 2001). Transformation is the art of replacing negative thoughts and self-talk with positive thoughts and self-talk (Dobson and Dobson, 2009). Research and clinical practice in this domain can provide the scholarly foundations for advancing our understanding of this intrapersonal dimension in the context of workplace behavior.

In summary, healthy communication builds social support and positive bonds in the workplace. Healthy communication and interpersonal exchange can take the form of helping. Schein (2009) presents guidelines for offering, giving, and receiving help in one-on-one, group, and organizational relationships. Healthy communication with oneself (self-talk) enables the individual to "get it together" in an integrated way characterized by personal integrity (Quick *et al.*, 2004). We suggest that when this happens, it triggers a greater likelihood that individuals will work in supportive collaboration.

The second positive interpersonal process is forgiveness. Forgiveness in organizations is irrelevant unless negative events have occurred and harm has been produced (Cameron, 2007a). The concern with forgiveness grows out of the broader program of POS, which advocates emphasizing what goes right in organizations rather than what goes wrong, what is life-giving rather than life-depleting, what is experienced as good rather than bad, what inspires rather than distresses, and what brings joy rather than stress and anxiety (Cameron, Dutton, and Quinn, 2003). The central fact here is that the positive and the negative are often intertwined, making it impossible to study the positive in a one-sided way (Cameron, 2007a). Wrongdoing, sometimes intentional, in organizations does occur, and it results in pain, whether physical from an injury on the job or emotional from harsh words or loss caused, for example by the wrongful death of a colleague.

Forgiveness, which is considered a specialized form of mercy, can be healing and transformative (Peterson and Seligman, 2004). However, it takes risk, effort, and learning. Forgiveness is rarely one-directional. Furthermore, it does not necessarily bypass legal or personal responsibility. Peterson and Seligman (2004) distinguish between forgiveness and forgivingness, the latter being the tendency to forgive. Forgiveness can lead to emotional freedom from the suffering associated with the harmful act. Harbored emotion from a harmful event damages the one who carries it more than it does the person to whom it's directed.

Forgiveness involves asking for forgiveness when you have wronged another and forgiving yourself for any wrongdoing. Forgiveness can be cathartic, although the healing consequences may not be apparent immediately. Peterson and Seligman (2004) note the theoretical traditions from theology that underpin mercy and forgiveness. From a theologic perspective, Buechner (1993: 28) finds power in forgiveness:

When somebody you've wronged forgives you, you're spared the dull and self-diminishing throb of guilty conscience. When you forgive somebody who wronged you, you're spared the dismal corrosion of bitterness and wounded pride. For both parties, forgiveness means the freedom again to be at peace inside their own skins and to be glad in each other's presence.

While this is true, it does not mean that the event is forgotten. Learning and development can occur at the same time as emotional release and freedom. Human excellence often springs from challenging, even harmful, circumstances (Cameron, 2007a). As a result, forgiveness is a powerful process in organizations. For Peterson and Seligman (2004), forgiveness falls under the virtue strength of temperance.

The third positive interpersonal process, thriving, stands squarely on the positive side of the organizational ledger and is the psychological state in which individuals experience both vitality and a sense of learning at work (Spreitzer and Sutcliffe, 2007). Thriving in organizations contributes to self-development, health, performance, and positive contagion. Self-development and growth are foundational for the individuals' ability to explore their worlds, fulfill their resident potential, and find satisfaction with work and life. Both physical health and psychological health are positive outcomes of the thriving process.

Thriving is an interpersonal process in organizations, just as performance is primarily a collective characteristic. Taking a concept from the study of disease epidemics and converting it to the positive lets us see how thriving can have a contagious impact at work. Positive effect, positive emotion, and positive energy can spread from person to person (Spreitzer and Sutcliffe, 2007). In this way vitality and well-being can become "epidemic" within the organization, to the benefit of all.

In a parallel process, thriving can have spillover effects in individuals' home and family lives. Just as there may be negative spillover where employees carry home unresolved conflicts (Quick *et al.*, 1997), there also is the potential for positive spillover from the positive energy and vitality of thriving at work. Cameron (2007a) suggests that positive and negative dynamics are frequently correlated, thus offering positive potential where negative circumstances may exist.

HEALTHY WORK

The translation of POB concepts into the workplace can be explored by examining what constitutes healthy individuals and, in turn, healthy work. The roots of health, as more than the absence of disease, go back to Aristotle's writings on eudeamonism, the realization of the individual's true potential (Rothman, 1993). Antonovsky (1987) described a sense of coherence in terms of its association with salutogenesis (health and well-being) as opposed to pathogenesis (disorder and disease). Among the proponents of a positive view of health are

Ryff and Singer (1998), who proposed that the "goods" necessary for positive health include having a purpose in life, supportive connections with others, positive self-regard, and mastery. In addition, they proposed a broader view of health that encompasses wellness and mind-body concepts.

As noted earlier, Seligman and Csikszentmihalyi's (2000) call for positive psychology noted that psychology's preoccupation with pathology was a product of traumatic events such as World War II. Even in such times, they argued, individuals can be identified whose attributes (strengths) buffer them from illness. From this followed studies of individual characteristics associated with health.

In attempting to study health as the presence of the positive, we know that personal factors and environmental or organizational factors play a role, and we recognize the interdependence of healthy individuals and healthy organizations. In this section we consider eustress as an individual influence on health and then explore what constitutes the organizational influence of healthy work and healthy workplaces.

Eustress

Eustress is the motivational side of stress, and it complements the more widely studied (and experienced) negative side, or distress. A discussion of eustress is in keeping with our emphasis on positive states, because eustress is indicated by the presence of positive states within individuals. Eustress also exemplifies health defined as the presence of the positive, rather than simply the absence of the negative.

The positive motivational side of stress, which Selye (1976a, 1976b) termed "eustress," has been conspicuously neglected in the literature. Quick et al. (1997) described eustress in their model of preventive stress management as being associated with healthy outcomes. Simmons (2000) called for a more holistic model incorporating both eustress and distress. He illustrated the holistic approach with a bathtub analogy. Two elements make for a good bath – water level and temperature – and two things determine the water level – the flow of water into and out of the tub. Likewise, the *simultaneous* flow of *both* hot and cold water into the bathtub determines the temperature. Our current approach is like studying a bathtub with a single faucet – cold water, representing distress. We know a lot about the sources of cold water, and we can tell individuals how to decrease or increase the flow. We also know quite a bit about the physiological, behavioral and psychological consequences of sitting in cold water for a long time. Our knowledge of cold water (distress) is important, but it does not present a complete understanding of the water (stress) in the tub. Simmons (2000) argued that a more complete model of stress would acknowledge that the bathtub does indeed have two faucets and that both are necessary to get the water level and temperature just right.

Much of the psychological support for eustress as a construct comes from Lazarus and Folkman's (1984) work concerning cognitive appraisals of stressors. Appraisals can be positive (challenge) or negative (threat), and these are not the bipolar opposites of a single continuum. Instead, challenge and threat responses may occur simultaneously, even as a result of the same stressor. The immediate psychological effects of positive appraisals are positive emotions (Folkman and Lazarus, 1985).

The physiological support for eustress demonstrates that the stress response is more complex than simply a negative reaction; in fact, there are both positive and negative physiological manifestations (Nelson and Simmons, 2004). Frankenhauser (1979, 1983, 1986) provided support for the idea that different psychological processes affect the physiological response in different ways. Through a series of experiments, she and her colleagues consistently found that two components of psychological arousal determined cortisol and catecholamine responses. The psychological state characterized by positive emotions was labeled "effort," while the state characterized by negative emotions was labeled "distress."

Rose's (1987) longitudinal study of air traffic controllers provides further evidence of the ways in which cognitive appraisals affect the stress response. Over three years, the cortisol values of 201 men were measured every 20 minutes for five hours on three or more days and compared with both objective and subjective assessments of workload. Those air traffic controllers who showed the highest increases in cortisol in response to increased workload reported greater job satisfaction and were rated by peers as more competent. The high-cortisol responders also showed lower illness rates than those with lower cortisol levels. Rose described the controllers who experienced cortisol increases associated with challenging work as engaged rather than stressed. In their review of Rose's study, Ganster and Schaubroeck (1991) described the healthy state of physiological arousal experienced by the controllers as eustress.

Nelson and Simmons (2004) defined eustress as a positive psychological response to a stressor, as indicated by the presence of positive psychological states. Eustress captures the extent to which the cognitive appraisal of a stressor is perceived to enhance well-being. The holistic stress model (Simmons and Nelson, 2007) incorporates both distress and eustress to present a more complete picture of stress at work. The model incorporates both eustress and distress as separate responses and contains seven central tenets:

- Demands or stressors are inherently neutral.
- The cognitive appraisal of any given demand or stressor produces a simultaneous positive and negative response. It is the response to demands that has positive and/or negative valence based on the degree of attraction and/or aversion the individual experiences toward the event.
- Individual differences/traits affect the way in which demands are appraised; therefore, they moderate the relationship between demands and responses. Positive and negative responses are complex and mixed; therefore, they manifest themselves in a variety of physiological, psychological, and behavioral indicators. Degrees of both positive and negative indicators of response

will be present for any given demand. (This model does not focus on physiological indicators because they are less observable by managers interacting with employees and therefore less subject to managerial intervention.)

- Individuals select strategies to either eliminate or alleviate their negative responses to demands, or to accentuate their positive responses. These strategies can be focused either on the perceived demand or the perceived response.
- Positive and negative responses differentially affect valued outcomes at work.
- The relationship between responses and outcomes is moderated by both explicit and implicit contracts that govern what is expected of and accepted from employees at work.

The holistic stress model has been examined in studies of hospital nurses, university professors, clergy, and assisted living center workers (Little, Simmons, and Nelson, 2007; Nelson and Simmons, 2003; Simmons and Nelson, 2001). Results regarding its eustress component indicated that hope, positive affect, meaningfulness, manageability, and engagement hold promise as indicators of eustress.

Emotions also may indicate eustress. As observed earlier, because emotions are associated with an object, they require cognitive appraisals and are associated with action readiness (Fredrickson, 2002). Whether emotions are positive or negative depends on whether they motivate approach or avoidance actions. The positive emotions that may be good indicators of eustress include joy, contentment, love, excitement, and happiness (Simmons and Nelson, 2007). In summary, both positive psychological states such as hope and engagement and positive emotions such as joy and excitement are indicators of the eustress response.

Individuals who try to manage the distress response are engaged in coping. The complement to coping with distress is savoring eustress (Nelson and Simmons, 2004). To savor the positive response means enjoying it with anticipation, dwelling on it with satisfaction, and/or attempting to prolong it. Just as there are individuals who engage in effective coping, there are individuals who are more likely to engage in savoring. Future research should focus on identifying individual differences related to savoring eustress at work.

Returning to the distress focus in stress research, Quick et al. (1997) developed a comprehensive model with a three-tiered approach to distress prevention, focusing on the elimination of stressors (primary prevention), boosting resilience (secondary prevention), and obtaining professional help to manage symptoms of distress (tertiary prevention). As a complement to distress resolution and prevention, leaders who recognize that healthy workers are productive workers must also engage in eustress generation (Nelson and Simmons, 2004).

Efforts to generate hope may constitute one form of eustress generation. Hope may be viewed as having the will to accomplish valued goals (Snyder et al., 1996). Leaders can generate hope by helping workers set meaningful goals, by allocating resources for high performance and by creating meaningful dialogues with employees. Research should focus on identifying those aspects of work settings that employees respond to with eustress, determine why employees find their work pleasurable, and determine how to promote this type of work experience.

Healthy Workplaces

Perhaps what characterizes healthy workplaces best is the notion of balance. Healthy work promotes the positive in individuals and organizations while preventing or resolving the negative. Ryff and Singer (1998) presented three principles in framing a positive view of what constitutes health:
    Health is a philosophical position in relation to the meaning of a good life; it is more than simply a medical condition.

1. Health encompasses the mind (mental) and the body (physical) and how they interact. The dualism between mind and body is not a functional perspective when considering health.
2. Health is a multidimensional, dynamic process rather than a discrete end state.

On the basis of these three principles, Quick and Macik-Frey (2007) proposed that healthy organizations work to ensure three major health-related outcomes for their members. Health in this case mirrors the attributes of healthy individuals but is applied in a broader sense to the organization as a whole.

- Leading a life of purpose
  - Clear mission and goals
  - Give back to the community
  - Integrity
  - Quality focus
  - Principled
  - Opportunities for growth
  - Recognize achievement
- Quality connections to others
  - Open, honest communication norms
  - Fairness in practices
  - Opportunity
  - Trust and safety norms
  - Mutual purpose and sense of belonging to the bigger whole
  - Diversity of people, skills, and ideas
  - Cohesiveness and positive affiliation
  - Pride in group accomplishments
  - Interdependent workers (high autonomy with strong social supports)
- Positive self-regard and mastery

- Balance
- Growth opportunities
- Support systems for problems
- Fitness support systems
- Positive physical work environment
- High safety focus

Quick and Macik-Frey (2007) further proposed that organizational health can be promoted through the development of positive strength factors within individuals. Two such factors, communication competence and interpersonal interdependence, were suggested as keys to healthy organizational functioning. This positive, competence-based approach extended the view of healthy organizations by applying principles of positive psychology and POB. Organizations that work to encourage the three major aspects of health enumerated earlier are encouraging healthy work.

Since 1999, the APA's Psychologically Healthy Workplace Program has honored organizations that foster employee health and well-being while enhancing organizational performance and productivity. Several practices distinguish psychologically healthy workplaces, including

- employee involvement,
- work–life balance,
- employee growth and development,
- health and safety, and
- employee recognition.

The 2008 national winners included Porter Keadle Moore, LLP, an Atlanta-based accounting firm; Westminster Savings Credit Union (British Columbia), Nike Tennessee, Cooperativa de Seguros Multiples de Puerto Rico, a nonprofit insurance company; and the Arkansas Educational Television Network. Each of these organizations uses a comprehensive set of practices to promote healthy work (www.phwa.org), and the outcomes are significant. The five awardees boast average staff turnover of 11%, compared to the US national average of 40%. Twenty-one percent of employees in the winning organizations reported chronic work stress versus the US national average of 34%, and whereas the national rate of job satisfaction was 66%, in the winning organizations it was 80% (American Psychological Association, 2007).

Winners of the 2008 APA Best Practices award incorporated various programs for enhancing healthy work. Ascend One, a Maryland financial services company, offers telecommuting, and half of its contact center employees do telecommute. The employees report greater job satisfaction and work–life balance, and the company enjoys greater productivity, improved retention, and lower facility costs. The Dayton, Ohio, Marriott started an on-site adult learning center that features two hours of tutoring a week per employee. Mathematics, adult literacy, and basic computing are among the courses offered, along with GED preparation. This has been accompanied by a 75% drop in voluntary turnover and an all-time company high in engagement scores.

Opportunities abound to expand our view of healthy organizations. The triple-bottom-line concept – people, planet, and profit – expands the traditional financial view of effectiveness to include ecological and social performance (Elkington, 1994). The goal is sustainability, meaning that organizations succeed without undermining the environment or exploiting people – meeting the needs of the present without compromising the ability of future generations to meet their own needs.

Corporate sustainability takes many forms, including recycling, alternative energy generation, water and waste management, sustainable land use, conscious consumption, and dematerialization. Alcoa, the world leader in aluminum production, has specific goals regarding reductions in materials usage, landfill waste, energy intensity, and mercury greenhouse gas emissions (Alcoa, 2007). All of these goals serve to reduce Alcoa's environmental footprint.

In the most macro sense, corporate sustainable performance contributes to the health of the organization, its people, the planet and future generations. Individuals who work in organizations with sustainability initiatives may themselves be sustained by the first of Ryff and Singer's (1998) "goods in life," which is *leading a life of purpose*. Yet the evidence that sustainable practices can improve employees' health is scarce (Bichard, 2009). Employees who believe that their behaviors and their work contribute to a more sustainable world should be more productive, satisfied, and committed, but these remain empirical questions. For some organizations, like Alcoa, employee health and safety are important elements in the company's sustainability strategy.

A GROUNDED COUNTERBALANCE

Cameron (2007a) points out that in this new POB domain, the positive and the negative are often intertwined so that it is difficult to study the positive in a one-sided way. Conceptually and theoretically, however, there is a risk of one-sidedness in our thinking. Freud differentiated among three "systems of thought" (Schwartz, 1990) – the animistic (mythological), the religious, and the scientific. According to Freud, the scientific system of thought holds that there is no longer any room for human omnipotence. Thus, our knowledge of ourselves and our world must be grounded in incremental, uncertain, scientific knowledge. The extremes of dogmatism and skepticism must be rejected as grounds for knowledge (Payne, 1978). As new domains of knowledge advance, it is essential to be reminded of the epistemological foundations of knowledge. We suggest that advancing knowledge requires the dialectic process of argument, debate, and alternative views of the evidence. This process grounds our knowledge and counterbalances any one-sided view of what we know and how we know it.

We agree with Bowlby (1988) that authority has no place in science. This is part of the grounds for the failure of dogmatism as a basis of knowing anything. There are no infallible authorities, there are no self-evident principles, and there are no indubitable facts (Payne, 1978). The risk in the positive domain is being carried away by a flight of fantasy that is not grounded in human struggle. Skepticism embraces uncertainty in a way that suggests that nothing is knowable and therefore everything is to be always questioned. That is the extreme of the unfettered skeptic. We reject the ultimate claims of dogmatism and skepticism as the basis for our knowledge.

What we embrace is a scientific grounding of new knowledge on the basis of dialogue, debate, argument and competing ideas, theories, and evidence. Because there is no certain evidence or knowledge, we see a role for both the skeptic and the critic in the scientific enterprise. For an in-depth reading of critical realist philosophy that aims to understand behavior by identifying generative mechanisms, believing that causal mechanisms cannot be truly isolated, turn to Van de Ven (2007), Rousseau, Manning, and Denyer (2008) and Hodgkinson and Rousseau (2009). This is nowhere more important than in the domain of the positive, whose flip side is the negative. Wright and Quick (2009) include a point–counterpoint set of four debate commentaries in their special issue on the emerging positive agenda in the *Journal of Organizational Behavior*. Luthans and Avolio (2009a) advance the point perspective while Hackman (2009a) offers the counterpoint. Hackman (2009a) is adamant that his role is that of skeptic, not critic, in the emerging POB discussion. The fundamental distinction between the two roles is essential to the health of the debate.

The Role of the Skeptic

While we reject skepticism as the ultimate basis for knowledge, we accept the importance of the skeptic in the advancement of new knowledge. The advocate puts forth new evidence as a basis for claiming an advance in science and theory. The skeptic responds with doubts. Unquestioned theory should be a concern for any scientist because the scientist is best characterized as inquisitive.

Hartshorne (1963) sets forth an excellent model for how to raise doubts, in his case concerning the Bible. He suggests that unquestioned faith can become dogma in the absence of questions. Hence he explores the doubts about biblical faith from several perspectives, including the epistemological, the psychological, and the sociological. He reasons that one should see the validity in these points of view rather than deny it. Hartshorne's (1963) approach to biblical faith reflects the religious level of thinking as identified by Freud, a level in which humankind does not surrender its role as the real center of the universe. At the religious level of thought, humanity acknowledges the existence of God but holds to the idea that God is controllable though prayer, through religious practices, and by adherence to specific conventions. The individual bound by religious thought never truly surrenders control nor acknowledges humanity's limitations in the known universe.

By transcending this level of thinking in his skeptical approach to biblical faith, Hartshorne (1963) arrives at Freud's scientific level of thinking, which demands rigorous inquiry, the serious exploration of doubts, and a quest for the truth. Hartshorne concludes that one of biblical faith has the capacity to stand firm in the face of questions. This leaves the faithful as neither dogmatic nor lost to skepticism but secure because of a transcendent level of attachment (Quick et al., 1996). For a contemporary discussion grounded in the same foundation as Hartshorne's, read Berger and Zijderveld's (2009) examination of faithful convictions that are distinguished from dogmatic fanaticism.

As we shift focus to POB, Hackman (2009a, 2009b) plays the role of skeptic to ensure that the emergent science does not become dogmatic. He is impressed with the passion and productivity that have characterized POB research, but he fears that the research is accumulating so rapidly that it may outstrip the field's conceptual, methodological, and ideological foundations. He articulates his doubts in the form of six concerns. His posing questions keep POB from becoming the new true religious set of beliefs within the broader OB domain. Were that to happen, it would be dogmatic, and ultimately dogmatism is illegitimate as a basis for knowing anything. This is illustrated in the Christian church's view of Earth as the center of the universe, which Galileo and Copernicus debunked. Note that Hackman (2009a, 2009b) does not play the critic in the POB drama because the critic analyzes and judges. No, he is ensuring that we reflect and question, so that whatever we think we know, we really do know.

The initial point perspective on POB by Luthans and Avolio (2009a, 2009b) buoys Hackman's (2009a) counterpoint. Both show how the point–counterpoint dynamic leads to more in-depth inquiry. Just as Hartshorne (1963) does not want the individual of deep faith to deny legitimate uncertainties, so Luthans and Avolio (2009b) do not deny the legitimacy of Hackman's concerns about POB. Each view in the point–counterpoint debate answers the other in the dialectic. That is as it should be as new theory and science are advanced on firm grounds, not all of which are agreed upon.

Luthans and Avolio (2009a, 2009b) conclude the point perspective by exploring more deeply the role of the negative in the study of POB. The acknowledgement in this case is the hallmark of the best in intellectual and scientific inquiry. They finish by demonstrating how POB relates to their work in authentic leadership development. In tandem, the point–counterpoint dialectic ensures that a firm foundation underpins the advancement of POB as it pushes the boundaries of knowledge.

The Role of the Critic

One may argue that much of what we know is simply common sense. Payne (1978) suggests that we should always doubt uncriticized common sense. Criticism is different from simply being skeptical. While the critic may be connotatively seen in a negative way, this is not grounded denotatively. To be critical requires observation and thoughtful reflection. The critic, therefore, is one who engages in observation that leads to analysis, evaluation, and judgment. Criticism is anchored in careful evaluation of the evidence.

The critic often is cast as the devil's advocate, taking the opposite view on the basis of this evidence. This line of reasoning ties in to Cameron's (2007a) concern that the positive should not become one sided. As observed earlier, this concern is particularly important in the domain of the positive. Synthesis is not the same as analysis, thus presenting the risk that what is created will fail. And, imagination and fantasy are not grounded in concrete reality, thus presenting the risk of the positive being unrealistic.

Cameron, Dutton, and Quinn (2003), Luthans and Avolio (2009a, 2009b), Nelson and Cooper (2007) and Peterson and Seligman (2004) are among those on the leading edge of creating the new positive agenda to include POB, POS, and positive psychology. While elements of this strength-based approach in human endeavor have long roots, the breadth and magnitude of the new positive agenda have grown dramatically in just one decade, as Hackman (2009a, 2009b) points out. The scientists and practitioners working in the positive domain are creating constructs that they believe work. However, akin to new aircraft designs that must be wind tunnel and otherwise tested, the research from these scholars must be examined, hopefully by a thoughtful analyst or impartial judge. The builders and the testers are best when different people.

The critic is equally essential to overcoming the risk of positive proposals being unrealistic. Linus Pauling was one of only two scientists to win Nobel Prizes in different fields (the Nobel Prize in chemistry and the Nobel Peace Prize). Asked how he got so many ideas, he replied that he had lots of ideas, but he only kept the good ones. Imagination is the source of creative ideas, not all of which will work in the real world. The critic exists to ensure that only the good ideas survive. Therefore, as POB continues to advance, critics play a key role in ensuring that it adds value to the wider domain of OB.

How Do We Know What We Know?

We know what we know not because it is obvious – that would be dogmatic – but through rigorous and systematic advancement of scientific knowledge that is grounded in public evidence and open to debate. The debate comes between the advocates and the critics, the creators and the testers, those working to advance new material, and those doubting it. While we cannot achieve certain knowledge in any domain of scientific inquiry, we know that we are not lost in skepticism so that everything is uncertain. It is in this middle ground, on the basis of a balance between dogmatism and skepticism, that we find the best hope for the advancement of our science.

CONCLUSION: THE FUTURE OF POB

Hackman (2009a) suggested that the POB paradigm is a reaction to the pathology orientation in individual and organizational psychology, whether in workplace stress or individual differences. But he emphasized that even though it is called positive *organizational* behavior, it is still rooted at the individual level of analysis. Indeed, POS at its inception was transforming individual constructs to the generic or organizational level rather than devising new organizational-specific positive constructs. This was followed by researching positive constructs, to validate them and build conceptual frameworks around them. Now we seem stuck at the definitional level of debating whether POB constructs are just the opposite end of the continuum from negative constructs or an extension of individual states at a macro organizational level. This is exemplified by the notion that individual resilience translates to the organizational level constructs of organizational well-being and organizational-level happiness. Luthans and Avolio (2009a) highlight the six questions we have been obsessed with over the last six years:

1. What is, and what is not, POB?
2. What role did positive psychology play in establishing POB?
3. What is the distinction between POB and OB?
4. What is the difference between POB and current positive approaches such as strength-based management and POS?
5. What role does the negative play in POB?
6. How does POB continue to advance the science in related fields, such as leadership?

We have attempted here to summarize many of the historical debates that have arisen in connection with these questions, but what is arguably the most important question, "Where do we go from here?" remains. In any new sub-areas of a field, academicians have a need to define the parameters and determine what contribution each subfield makes. This is usually the first step in deciding if we have discovered a new "academic gold seam." However, spending too much time mapping the boundaries may obscure insights and very different but novel perspectives. Albert Einstein wrote that "your imagination is the preview of life's coming attractions." Perhaps the second academic step, after groping for definitions of POB, is to do more positively oriented organizational research. Then we can let the findings help to define the field and what contributions POB can make.

For example, hundreds of studies have been conducted on organizational stress, the majority concentrating on the negative job characteristics associated with negative individual (physical and mental ill health) and organizational (sickness absence and job dissatisfaction) outcomes (for the details of a number of these studies, see Cartwright and Cooper, 2009). On the one hand we know that lack of control at work, overload, role conflict or ambiguity, and abusive management are all associated with negative individual and organizational health outcomes. On the other hand we know very little about what job and organizational factors are associated with successful organizations (for some evidence and a discussion of the issues, see Cartwright and Cooper, 2008). Defining "successful" is never easy, but it is possible that some of these factors may not be the opposite of those found in the workplace stress literature. Consequently, the best-fit model for predicting organizational health or ill health is likely to incorporate the independent variables derived from both the negatively and positively oriented studies. Perhaps at this stage of POB development we need a more inductively oriented approach that reveals the most propitious conceptual models for understanding effective OB.

Numerous issues call out for more research. Given the global economic crisis, will accentuating the positive resonate with business leaders to prevent or resolve suffering? Will the positive agenda go on the back burner as organizations struggle to survive? From the POB perspective, exploring "the positives" may help us resolve subterranean problems. For example, in this recession people in many organizations will experience job insecurity and as a consequence may be reluctant to take sick leave; so sickness absence may decline, only to be replaced by presenteeism – people going to work earlier and staying later and coming to work even if they are ill. Exploring the underpinnings of what appears to be a positive – high commitment and lower absenteeism – may help us identify effective and ineffective aspects of the phenomenon. How ironic that at a time of despondency about the economy and our banking or business practices we should be concerned about accentuating the positives for fear that attention will be on correcting the negatives. Ultimately, the organizational sciences need to encompass both extremes of behavior if we are to overcome our current and future dilemmas.

Protective Armor

It is interesting how POB characteristics can become "protective armor" for individuals, groups, and even work organizations. POB characteristics need to become mechanisms of psychological protection in the workplace, deflecting turmoil. How do we translate POB into practice (while understanding that not all positive behaviors lead automatically to positive outcomes)? Charismatic leadership, for example, can be perceived positively in certain contexts, but not all. The models we begin to create must factor in the dynamics of context, time and culture. As Fineman (2006) observed, acceptable positive behavior in one cultural context is anathema in another. He illustrates this by contrasting American and British culture. The American cultural script includes positive self-promotion, expressive optimism, and "being noticed," which contrasts with British individualism that has traditionally been more guarded, forged from the manners of rural gentry and yeomen as well as from Victorian stoicism, and the value placed on understatement and self-control. So understanding context is important to understanding what attributes are perceived as positive, as well as the impact of those attributes.

New Pathways ... and Questions

Hackman (2009b) highlights one of the challenges ahead when he says POS clearly can help guide adaptation as individuals address the inevitable stresses of life. But this is only half the story. The other half is his hope that research within the POB paradigm will give as much attention to identifying those organizational conditions that promote growth as it does to strategies for adapting to work circumstances. Hackman suggests that this is the real challenge. Let's ask ourselves the unconventional questions rather than go down the traditional, safe academic path. What can the emotional contagion literature bring to POB? Are hope and optimism contagious? How do we create positive emotional contagion? What does it mean at an organizational level to have fun at work? To what extent is managing people by reward, instead of fault finding, more or less effective? What positive organizational cultural values work? Unless we focus on replicating POB insights and converting what we find into organizational reality, we are left with an interesting but otherwise useless academic exercise. In Ralph Waldo Emerson's words, "what we call results are beginnings."

POB enables us to include in our academic armory a different view of the world of OB. As Luthans and Avolio (2009a) suggest, the goal of OB, to include POB, is to better the human condition in order for individuals, groups, and organizations to grow while being more effective.

Caza and Cameron (2008) highlighted some interesting opportunities for POS and positivity. First, more clarity is needed with regard to what is positive. This is crucial for the continued development of the field. Second, positive–negative interactions need to be explored holistically rather than focusing on one end of the continuum. A growing body of evidence and case examples holds that positive behaviors require negative conditions and vice versa. Caza and Cameron (2008) state that "there is no need for forgiveness without offense, and resilience is meaningless without hardship" (p. 22). However, research also shows that a concept such as pride can produce both negative and positive outcomes (Losada and Heaphy, 2004). Hence the interactions of both positive and negative phenomena need to be addressed to provide a deeper understanding of how POB characteristics can become "protective armour."

Finally, consider the current economic climate and the challenges it will create for the POB field. Because many organizations are struggling to survive, how seriously will they address POB characteristics aimed at protecting individuals in the workplace? How can POB and positivity help the practitioners of this vision defend their existence in times of trouble? We hope that the work reviewed in this chapter has laid the foundations for the science and practice of POB to flourish.

ACKNOWLEDGMENT

The authors wish to thank Sheri Schember Quick, Thomas A. Wright, Alankrita Pendey and John Dycus for their assistance.

REFERENCES

Ainsworth, M.D.S., & Bowlby, J. (1991). An ethological approach to personality development. *American Psychologist,* **46,** 331–41.

Alcoa (2007). Sustainability Highlights. Retrieved from: http://www.alcoa.com/global/en/about_alcoa/sustainability/pdfs/sustain_highlights07.pdf

Ambady, N., & Gray, H. (2002). On being sad and mistaken: mood effects on the accuracy of thin-slice judgments. *Journal of Personality and Social Psychology,* **83**(4), 947–61.

American Psychiatric Association (2000). *Diagnostic and Statistical Manual of Mental Disorders,* 4th (Ed.). Washington DC: Author.

American Psychological Association (2007). *Stress in America Survey.* Washington DC: Author.

Antonovsky, A. (1987). *Unraveling the Mystery of Health: How People Manage Stress and Stay Well.* San Francisco, CA: Jossey-Bass.

Atkinson, L., & Zucker, K.J. (1997). *Attachment and Psychopathology.* New York: The Guilford Press.

Bandura, A. (1986). *Social Foundations of Thought and Action: A Social Cognitive Theory.* Englewood Cliffs, NJ: Prentice-Hall, Inc.

Bandura, A. (1997). *Self-Efficacy: The Exercise of Control.* New York: Freeman.

Bandura, A., & Locke, E.A. (2003). Negative self-efficacy and goal effects revisited. *Journal of Applied Psychology,* **88**(1), 87–99.

Beedie, C., Terry, P., & Lane, A. (2000). The profile of mood states and athletic performance: Two meta-analyses. *Journal of Applied Sport Psychology,* **12**(1), 49–68.

Berger, P., & Zijderveld, A. (2009). *In Praise of Doubt: How to have Convictions without Becoming a Fanatic.* New York: HarperOne.

Bernstein, S.D. (2003). Positive organizational scholarship: Meet the movement: An interview with Kim Cameron, Jane Dutton and Robert Quinn. *Journal of Management Inquiry,* **12**(3), 266–71.

Bichard, E. (2009). Creating a healthy work environment through sustainable practices: Future challenges. In S. Cartwright & C.L. Cooper (Eds), *The Oxford Handbook of Organizational Well-Being* (pp. 542–62). Oxford, UK: Oxford University Press.

Boulton, M., & Smith, P. (1992). The social nature of play fighting and play chasing: Mechanisms and strategies underlying cooperation and compromise. In J.H. Barkow,

L. Cosmides, & J. Tooby (Eds), *The Adapted Mind: Evolutionary Psychology and the Generation of Culture* (pp. 429–44). New York: Oxford University Press.

Bowlby, J. (1988). *A Secure Base*. New York: Basic Books.

Buechner, F. (1993). *Wishful Thinking: A Theological ABC*. New York: HarperCollins.

Cameron, K.S., Dutton J.E., & Quinn, R.E. (Eds) (2003). *Positive Organizational Scholarship: Foundations of a New Discipline*. San Francisco: Berrett-Koehler.

Cameron, K.S. (2003). Organizational virtuousness and performance. In K.S. Cameron, J.E. Dutton, & R.E. Quinn (Eds), *Positive Organizational Scholarship: Foundations of a New Discipline* (pp. 48–65). San Francisco: Berrett-Koehler.

Cameron, K.S. (2007a). Forgiveness in organizations. In D.L. Nelson & C.L. Cooper (Eds), *Positive Organizational Behavior* (pp. 129–42). London: SAGE Publications.

Cameron, K.S. (2007b). Positive organizational scholarship. In S. Clegg & J. Bailey (Eds), *International Encyclopedia of Organizational Studies* (129–42). Beverly Hills: Sage.

Cameron, K.S., & Caza, A. (2004). Contributions to the discipline of positive organizational scholarship. *American Behavioral Scientist*, **47**, 731–9.

Cartwright, S., & Cooper, C.L. (Eds) (2008). *Oxford Handbook of Personnel Psychology*. Oxford: Oxford University Press.

Cartwright, S., & Cooper, C.L. (Eds) (2009). *Oxford Handbook of Organizational Wellbeing*. Oxford: Oxford University Press.

Carver, C.S., & Scheier, M.F. (1981). The self-attention-induced feedback loop and social facilitation. *Journal of Experimental Social Psychology*, **17**(6), 545–68.

Caza, A., & Cameron, K.S. (2008). Positive organizational scholarship. In C.L. Cooper & S. Clegg (Eds), *Handbook of Macro-Organizational Behavior* (pp. 99–116). New York: Sage.

Cooper, C.L., Quick, J.C., Quick, J.D., & Gavin, J.H. (2006). Strength of character: exceptional leadership in a crisis. In R. Burke & C.L. Cooper (Eds), *Inspiring Leaders* (pp. 272–95). London: Rutledge, Taylor and Francis.

Coutu, D.L. (2002). How resilience works. *Harvard Business Review*, **80**, 46–50, 52, 55.

Cropanzano, R., Weiss, H.M., Hale, J.M.S., & Reb, J. (2003). The structure of affect: Reconsidering the relationship between negative and positive affectivity. *Journal of Management*, **29**(6), 831–57.

Deci, E.L., & Ryan, R.M. (1985). *Intrinsic Motivation and Self-Determination in Human Behavior*. New York: Plenum.

Dobson, D., & Dobson, K.S. (2009). *Evidence-Based Practice of Cognitive-Behavioral Therapy*. New York: The Guilford Press.

Dobson, K.S. (2001). *Handbook of Cognitive-Behavioral Therapies*, 2nd (Ed.). New York: The Guilford Press.

Dutton, J.E., & Glynn, M. (2008). Positive organizational scholarship. In C. Cooper & J. Barling (Eds), *Handbook of Organizational Behavior*. Thousand Oaks, CA: Sage.

Dutton, J., Glynn, M., & Spreitzer, G. (2006). Positive Organizational Scholarship. In J. Greenhaus & G. Callanan (Eds), *Encyclopedia of Career Development* (pp. 641–4). Thousand Oaks, CA: Sage Publishers.

Dutton, J.E., & Sonenshein, S. (2007). Positive organizational scholarship. In S. Lopez & A. Beauchamps (Eds), *Encyclopedia of Positive Psychology*. Malden, MA: Blackwell Publishing.

Dutton, J.E., Worline, M.C., Frost, P.J., & Lilius, J. (2006). Explaining compassion organizing. *Administrative Science Quarterly*, **51**(1), 59–96.

Elkington, J. (1994). Toward the sustainable corporation: Win-win-win business strategies for sustainable development. *California Management Review*, **36**, 90–100.

Ellsworth, P.C., & Smith, C.A. (1988). Shades of joy: Patterns of appraisal differentiating positive emotions. *Cognition and Emotion*, 2, 301–31.

Elsbach, K., & Barr, P.S. (1999). The effects of mood on individual use of structured decision protocols. *Organizational Science*, 10, 181–98.

Feingold, A. (1983). Happiness, unselfishness and popularity. *The Journal of Psychology*, 115(1), 3–5.

Fineman, S. (2006). On being positive: concepts and counterpoints. *Academy of Management Review*, 31(2), 270–91.

Folkman, S., & Lazarus, R.S. (1985). If it changes it must be a process: Study of emotion and coping during three stages of a college examination. *Journal of Personality and Social Psychology*, 48, 150–70.

Frankenhauser, M. (1979). Psychobiological aspects of life stress. In S. Levine & H. Ursin (Eds), *Coping and Health* (pp. 203–23). New York: Plenum Press.

Frankenhauser, M. (1983). The sympathetic-adrenal and pituitary-adrenal response to challenge: Comparison between the sexes. In T.M. Dembroski, T.H. Schmidt, & G. Blumchen (Eds), *Biobehavioral Bases of Coronary Heart Disease* (pp. 91–105). New York: Karger.

Frankenhauser, M. (1986). A psychobiological framework for research on human stress and coping. In M.H. Appley & R. Trumbull (Eds), *Dynamics of Stress: Physiological, Psychological and Social Perspectives* (pp. 101–16). New York: Plenum Press.

Fredrickson, B.L. (2002). Positive emotions. In C.R. Snyder & S.J. Lopez (Eds), *Handbook of Positive Psychology* (pp. 120–34). Oxford: Oxford University Press.

Fredrickson, B.L. (1998). What good are positive emotions? *Review of General Psychology*, 2, 300–19.

Fredrickson, B.L., & Branigan, C. (2005). Positive emotions broaden the scope of attention and thought-action repertoires. *Cognition and Emotion*, 19, 313–32.

Fredrickson, B.L., & Levenson, R. (1998). Positive emotions speed recovery from the cardiovascular sequelae of negative emotions. *Cognition and Emotion*, 12(2), 191–220.

Fredrickson, B.L., Mancuso, R.A., Branigan, C., & Tugade, M.M. (2000). The undoing effect of positive emotions. *Motivation and Emotion*, 24, 237–58.

Fredrickson, B.L., & Dutton, J.E. (2008). Unpacking positive organizing: Organizations as sites of individual and group flourishing. *The Journal of Positive Psychology*, 3(1), 1–3.

Frijda, N.H., Kuipers, P., & Schure, E. (1989). Relations among emotion, appraisal and emotional action readiness. *Journal of Personality and Social Psychology*, 57(2), 212–28.

Gable, S., & Haidt, J. (2005). What (and why) is positive psychology. *Review of General Psychology*, 9(2), 103–10.

Ganster, D.C., & Schaubroeck, J. (1991). Work stress and employee health. *Journal of Management*, 17, 235–71.

Gavin, J.H., Quick, J.C., Cooper, C.L., & Quick, J.D. (2003). A spirit of personal integrity: The role of character in executive health. *Organizational Dynamics*, 32(2), 165–79.

George, J.M. (2004). Positive organizational scholarship: Foundations of a new discipline. *Administrative Science Quarterly*, 49, 325–30.

George, J.M., & Zhou, J. (2002). Understanding when bad moods foster creativity and good ones don't: the role of context and clarity of feelings. *Journal of Applied Psychology*, 87(4), 687–97.

Glynn, M.A., & Wrobel, K. (2007). My family, my firm: how family relationships function as endogenous organizational resources. In J.E. Dutton & B.R. Ragins (Eds), *Exploring Positive Relationships at Work: Building a Theoretical and Research Foundation* (pp. 307–23). Mahwah, NJ: Erlbaum.

Graham, C., Eggers, A., & Sukhtankar, S. (2004). Does happiness pay? An exploration based on panel data from Russia. *Journal of Economic Behavior and Organization*, 55(3), 319–42.

Hackman, J.R. (2009a). The perils of positivity. *Journal of Organizational Behavior*, 30(2), 309–19.

Hackman, J.R. (2009b). The point of POB: Rejoinder. *Journal of Organizational Behavior*, 30(2), 321–2.

Hartshorne, M.H. (1963). *The Faith to Doubt*. Englewood Cliffs, NJ: Prentice-Hall.

Hazan, C., & Shaver, P.R. (1990). Love and work: An attachment-theoretical perspective. *Journal of Personality and Social Psychology*, 59, 270–80.

Hodgkinson, G.P., & Rousseau, D.M. (2009). Bridging the rigour-relevance gap in management research: It's already happening! *Journal of Management Studies* 46(3), 534–46.

Isaacowitz, D.M., Vaillant, G.E., & Seligman, M.E.P. (2003). Strengths and satisfaction across the adult lifespan. *The International Journal of Aging and Human Development*, 57(2), 181–201.

Izard, C.E. (1977). *Human Emotion*. New York: Plenum Press.

Joplin, J.R.W., Nelson, D.L., & Quick, J.C. (1999). Attachment behavior and health: Relationships at work and home. *Journal of Organizational Behavior*, 20(6), 783–96.

Judge, T.A., Locke, E.A., Durham, C.C., & Kluger, A.N. (1998). Dispositional effects on job and life satisfaction: The role of core evaluations. *Journal of Applied Psychology*, 83(1), 17–34.

Keyes, C. (2002). The mental health continuum: From languishing to flourishing in life. *Journal of Health and Social Behavior*, 43(2), 207–22.

Kluemper, D., Little, L.M., & DeGroot, T. (2009). State or trait: Effects of state optimism on job-related outcomes. *Journal of Organizational Behavior*, 30(2), 209–31.

Kristof-Brown, A.L., Zimmerman, R.D., & Johnson, E.C. (2005). Consequences of individual's fit at work: A meta-analysis of person-job, person-organization, person-group and person-supervisor fit. *Personnel Psychology*, 58(2), 281–342.

Lane, A., Whyte, G., Terry, P., & Nevill, A. (2005). Mood, self-set goals and examination performance: the moderating effect of depressed mood. *Personality and Individual Differences*, 39(1), 143–53.

Lazarus, R.S. (1991). *Emotion and Adaption*. New York: Oxford University Press.

Lazarus, R.S., & Folkman, S. (1984). *Stress, appraisal and coping*. New York: Springer Publishing Company.

Lee, C., Ashford, S., & Jamieson, L. (1993). The effects of type A behavior dimensions and optimism on coping strategy, health and performance. *Journal of Organizational Behavior* 14(2), 143–57.

Lee, T., Locke, E., & Latham, G. (1989). *Goal Setting Theory and Job Performance*. Hillsdale, NJ: Erlbaum.

Linley, P.A., & Joseph, S. (2004). Applied positive psychology: A new perspective for professional practice. In P.A. Linley & S. Joseph (Eds), *Positive Psychology in Practice* (pp. 3–12). Hoboken, NJ: Wiley.

Linley, P.A., Joseph, S., Harrington, S., & Wood, A.M. (2006). Positive psychology: past, present and (possible) future. *The Journal of Positive Psychology*, 1(1), 3–16.

Little, L.M., Simmons, B.L., & Nelson, D.L. (2007). Health among leaders: Positive and negative affect, engagement and burnout, forgiveness and revenge. *Journal of Management Studies*, 44, 243–60.

Locke, E., & Latham, G. (1984). *Goal Setting*. Englewood Cliffs, NJ: Prentice-Hall.

Losada, M., & Heaphy, E. (2004). The role of positivity and connectivity in the performance of business teams: A nonlinear dynamics model. *American Behavioral Scientist*, 47(6), 740–65.

Luthans, F. (2002). The need for and meaning of positive organizational behavior. *Journal of Organizational Behavior*, **23**(6), 695–706.

Luthans, F., & Avolio, B.J. (2009a). The "point" of positive organizational behavior. *Journal of Organizational Behavior*, **30**(2), 291–307.

Luthans, F., & Avolio, B.J. (2009b). Inquiry unplugged: Building on Hackman's potential perils. *Journal of Organizational Behavior*, **30**(2), 323–28.

Luthans, F., Avolio, B.J., Avey, J., & Norman, S. (2007). Positive psychological capital: Measurement and relationship with performance and satisfaction. *Personnel Psychology*, **60**(3), 541–72.

Luthans, F., Avolio, B.J., Walumbwa, F.O., & Weixing, L. (2005). The psychological capital of Chinese workers: Exploring the relationship with performance. *Management and Organization Review*, 1, 249–71.

Luthans, F., & Church, A. (2002). Positive organizational behavior: developing and managing psychological strengths. *Executive-ADA Then Briercliff*, **16**(1), 57–75.

Luthans, F., Luthans, K., Hodgetts, R., & Luthans, B. (2001). Positive approach to leadership (PAL) implications for today's organizations. *Journal of Leadership and Organizational Studies*, **8**(2), 3.

Luthans, F., Luthans, K., & Luthans, B. (2004). Positive psychological capital: Beyond human and social capital. *Business Horizons*, **47**(1), 45–50.

Luthans, F., & Youssef, C. (2007). Emerging positive organizational behavior. *Journal of Management*, **33**(3), 321.

Luthans, F., Youssef, C., & Avolio, B. (2007). *Psychological Capital: Developing the Human*. Competitive Edge: Oxford University Press.

Lynch, J.J. (1977). *The Broken Heart: The Medical Consequences of Loneliness*. New York: Basic Books.

Lynch, J.J. (2000). *The Cry Unheard: New Insights into the Medical Consequences of Loneliness*. Baltimore, MD: Bancroft Press.

Lyubomirsky, S., King, L., & Diener, E. (2005). The benefits of frequent positive affect: Does happiness lead to success? *Psychological Bulletin*, **131**(6), 803–55.

Macik-Frey, M., Quick, J.C., & Quick, J.D. (2005). Interpersonal communication: The key to social support for preventive stress management. In C.L. Cooper (Ed.), *Handbook of Stress, Medicine and Health, Second Edition* (pp. 265–92). Boca Raton, FL: CRC Press.

Maddi, S.R. (2006). Hardiness: the courage to grow from stresses. *The Journal of Positive Psychology*, **1**(3), 160–8.

Maddi, S.R., & Khoshaba, D.M. (2008). *Resilience at Work: How to Succeed no Matter what Life Throws at You*. New York: MJF Books.

Martin, M.W. (2007). Happiness and virtue in positive psychology. *Journal for the Theory of Social Behaviour*, **37**(1), 89–103.

Maslow, A.H. (1954). *Motivation and Personality*. New York: Harper.

May, D., Chan, A., Hodges, T., & Avolio, B. (2003). Developing the moral component of authentic leadership. *Organizational Dynamics*, **32**(3), 247–60.

Nelson, D.L., & Cooper, C.L.E. (2007). *Positive Organizational Behavior*. London: SAGE Publications.

Nelson, D.L., & Quick, J.C. (2009). *Organizational Behavior: Science, the Real World and You*, 6th (Ed.). Mason, OH: Southwestern/Cengage.

Nelson, D.L., & Simmons, B.L. (2003). Health psychology and work stress: a more positive approach. In J.C. Quick and L.E. Tetrick (Eds), *Handbook of Occupational Health Psychology* (pp. 97–119). Washington, DC: American Psychological Association.

Nelson, D.L., & Simmons, B.L. (2004). Eustress: An elusive construct, an engaging pursuit. In P.L. Perrewé & D.C. Ganster (Eds), *Research in Occupational Stress and Well*

Being (Vol. 3): Emotional and Physiological Processes and Positive Intervention Strategies (pp. 265–322). Oxford, UK: Elsevier.

Nilsson, J., Schmidt, C., & Meek, W. (2002). Reliability generalization: An examination of the career decision-making self-efficacy scale. *Educational and Psychological Measurement*, **62**(4), 647.

Park, N., Peterson, C., & Seligman, M.E.P. (2004). Strengths of character and well-being. *Journal of Social and Clinical Psychology*, **23**, 603–19.

Payne, R. (1978). Epistemology and the study of stress at work. In C.L. Cooper & R. Payne (Eds), *Stress at Work* (pp. 259–83). Chichester, England: John Wiley and Sons.

Pennebaker, J.W. (1997). *Opening Up: The Healing Power of Expressing Emotions*. New York: Guilford Publications, Inc.

Peterson, C., & Park, N. (2003). Positive psychology as the evenhanded positive psychologist views it. *Psychological Inquiry*, **14**, 141–6.

Peterson, C., Park, N., Hall, N., & Seligman, M.E.P. (2009). Zest and work. *Journal of Organizational Behavior*, **30**(2), 161–72.

Peterson, C., Park, N., & Seligman, M.E.P. (2005a). Assessment of character strengths. In G.P. Koocher, J.C. Norcross, & S.S. Hill III (Eds), *Psychologists' Desk Reference*, 2nd (Ed.) (pp. 93–8). New York: Oxford University Press.

Peterson, C., Park, N., & Seligman, M.E.P. (2005b). Orientations to happiness and life satisfaction: the full life versus the empty life. *Journal of Happiness Studies*, **6**, 25–41.

Peterson, C., Ruch, W., Beermann, U., Park, N., & Seligman, M.E.P. (2008). Strengths of character, orientation to happiness and life satisfaction. *The Journal of Positive Psychology*, **2**(3), 149–56.

Peterson, C., & Seligman, M.E.P. (2004). *Character Strengths and Virtues*. Oxford and NewYork: American Psychological Association and Oxford University Press.

Quick, J.C., Gavin, J.H., Cooper, C.L., & Quick, J.D. (2004). Working together: Balancing head and heart. In R.H. Rozensky, N.G. Johnson, C.D. Goodheart, & W.R. Hammond (Eds), *Psychology Builds a Healthy World* (pp. 219–32). Washington, DC: American Psychological Association.

Quick, J.C., & Macik-Frey, M. (2004). Behind the mask: Coaching through deep interpersonal communication. *Consulting Psychology Journal: Practice and Research*, **56**(2), 67–74.

Quick, J.C., & Macik-Frey, M. (2007). Healthy, productive work: positive strength through communication competence and interpersonal interdependence. In D.L. Nelson & C.L. Cooper (Eds), *Positive Organizational Behavior* (pp.25–39). London: Sage Publications.

Quick, J.C., Nelson, D.L., & Quick, J.D. (1987). Successful executives: How independent? *Academy of Management Executive*, **1**(2), 139–45.

Quick, J.C., Quick, J.D., Nelson, D.L., & Hurrell, J.J. (1997). *Preventive Stress Management in Organizations*. Washington, D.C.: American Psychological Association.

Quick, J.D., Nelson, D.L., Matuszek, P.A.C., Whittington, J.L., & Quick, J.C. (1996). Social support, secure attachments and health. In C.L. Cooper (Ed.), *Handbook of Stress, Medicine and Health* (pp. 269–87). Boca Raton, FL: CRC Press, Inc.

Roberts, L.M. (2006). Shifting the lens on organizational life: The added value of positive scholarship. *Academy of Management Review*, **31**, 292–305.

Rose, R.M. (1987). Neuroendocrine effects of work stress. In J.C. Quick, R.S. Bhagat, J.E. Dalton, & J.D. Quick (Eds), *Work Stress: Health Care Systems in the Workplace* (pp. 130–47). New York: Praeger.

Rothman, J.C. (1993). *Aristotle's Eudaemonia, Terminal Illness and the Question of Life Support*. New York: P. Lang.

Rousseau, D.M., Manning, J., & Denyer, D. (2008). Evidence in management and organizational science: assembling the field's full weight of scientific knowledge through syntheses. *The Academy of Management Annals*, **2**, 475–515.

Ruch, W. (1993). Exhilaration and humor. In M. Lewis & J.M. Haviland (Eds), *The Handbook of Emotions* (pp. 605–16). New York: Guilford Publications.

Russell, J. (2003). Core affect and the psychological construction of emotion. *Psychological Review*, **110**(1), 145–72.

Ryff, C.D., & Singer, B. (1998). The contours of positive human health. *Psychological Inquiry*, **9**(1), 1–28.

Scheier, M., & Carver, C. (1987). Dispositional optimism and physical well-being: The influence of generalized outcome expectancies on health. *Journal of Personality*, **55**(2), 169–210.

Scheier, M., Magovern, G., Abbott, R., *et al.* (1989). Dispositional optimism and recovery from coronary artery bypass surgery: The beneficial effects on physical and psychological well-being. *Journal of Personality and Social Psychology*, **57**(6), 1024–40.

Schein, E.H. (2009). *Helping*. San Francisco: Barrett-Koehler Publishers.

Schwartz, H.S. (1990). *Narcissistic Process and Corporate Decay. The Theory of the Organization Ideal*. New York and London: New York University Press.

Seligman, M.E.P. (1999). The president's address (Annual Report). *American Psychologist*, **54**, 559–62.

Seligman, M.E.P. (2002a). *Authentic Happiness: Using the New Positive Psychology to Realize your Potential for Lasting Fulfillment*. New York: Free Press.

Seligman, M.E.P. (2002b). Positive psychology, positive prevention and positive therapy. In C.R. Snyder & S.J. Lopez (Eds), *Handbook of Positive Psychology* (pp. 3–9). New York: Oxford.

Seligman, M.E.P. (2003). Positive psychology: fundamental assumptions. *The Psychologist*, **16**, 126–27.

Seligman, M.E.P. (2004). Foreword. In P.A. Linley & S. Joseph (Eds), *Positive Psychology in Practice* (pp. xi–xiii). Hoboken, NJ: John Wiley.

Seligman, M.E.P. (2005). Positive psychology, positive prevention and positive therapy. In C.R. Snyder & S.J. Lopez (Eds), *Handbook of Positive Psychology* (275–83). Oxford: Oxford University Press.

Seligman, M.E.P. (2006). *Learned Optimism: How to Change Your Mind and Your Life*. New York: Vintage Books.

Seligman, M.E.P., & Csikszentmihalyi, M. (2000). Positive psychology: an introduction. *American Psychologist*, **55**(1), 5–14.

Seligman, M.E.P., Parks, A.C., & Steen, T. (2004), A balanced psychology and a full life. *The Royal Society*, **359**, 1379–81.

Seligman, M.E.P., Steen, T.A., Park, N., & Peterson, C. (2005). Positive psychology progress: Empirical validation of interventions. *American Psychologist*, **60**(5), 410–21.

Selye, H. (1976a). *Stress in Health and Disease*. Boston: Butterworths.

Selye, H. (1976b). *The Stress of Life: Revised Edition*. New York: McGraw-Hill.

Shirom, A. (2004). Feeling vigorous at work? The construct of vigor and the study of positive affect in organizations. *Research in Organizational Stress and Well-being*, **3**, 135–65.

Shirom, A. (2007). Explaining vigor: On the antecedents and consequences of vigor as a positive affect at work. In D.L. Nelson & C.L. Cooper (Eds), *Positive Organizational Behavior* (pp. 86–100). London: Sage.

Shirom, A., Toker, S., Berliner, S., Shapira, I., & Melamed, S. (2008). The effects of physical fitness and feeling vigorous on self-rated health. *Health Psychology*, **27**(5), 567–75.

Simmons, B., Nelson, D., & Quick, J. (2003). Health for the hopeful: A study of attachment behavior in home health care nurses. *International Journal of Stress Management*, 10(4), 361–75.

Simmons, B.L. (2000). *Eustress at work: Accentuating the positive*. Unpublished *doctoral dissertation*, Oklahoma State University, Stillwater, OK.

Simmons, B.L., Gooty, J., Nelson, D.L., & Little, L.M. (2009). Secure attachment: Implication for hope, trust, burnout and performance. *Journal of Organizational Behavior*, 30(2), 233–47.

Simmons, B.L., & Nelson, D.L. (2001). Eustress at work: The relationship between hope and health in hospital nurses. *Health Care Management Review*, 26, 7–18.

Simmons, B.L., & Nelson, D.L. (2007). Eustress at work. In D.L. Nelson & C.L. Cooper (Eds), *Positive Organizational Behavior* (pp. 40–53). London: Sage Publications.

Snyder, C. (2000). *Handbook of Hope: Theory, Measures, and Applications*. New York: Academic Press.

Snyder, C., Harris, C., Anderson, J., *et al.* (1991). The will and the ways: development and validation of an individual-differences measure of hope. *Journal of Personality and Social Psychology*, 60(4), 570–85.

Snyder, C.R., Sympson, S.C., Ybasco, F.C., Borders, T.F., Babyak, M.A., & Higgins, R.L. (1996). Development and validation of the state hope scale. *Journal of Personality and Social Psychology*, 70, 321–35.

Sonenshein, S. (2005). Positive organizational scholarship. In P.H. Werhane & R.E. Freeman (Eds), *The Blackwell Encyclopedia of Management, Vol. II, Business Ethics* (pp. 410–14). Oxford: Blackwell Publishing.

Spreitzer, G.M., & Sutcliffe, K.M. (2007). Thriving in organizations. In D.L. Nelson & C.L. Cooper (Eds), *Positive Organizational Behavior* (pp. 74–85). London: Sage Publications.

Stajkovic, A.D., & Luthans, F. (1998). Self-efficacy and work-related performance: A meta-analysis. *Psychological Bulletin*, 124(2), 240–61.

Sutcliffe, K.M., & Vogus, T.J. (2003). Organizing for resilience. In K. Cameron, J.E. Dutton, & R.E. Quinn (Eds), *Positive Organizational Scholarship*. San Francisco: Berrett-Koehler.

Tierney, P., & Farmer, S. (2002). Creative self-efficacy: its potential antecedents and relationship to creative performance. *Academy of Management Journal*, 45(6), 1137–48.

Vaillant, G.E. (1977). *Adaptation to Life*. Boston: Little, Brown and Company.

Van de Ven, A.H. (2007). *Engaged Scholarship*. New York: Oxford University Press.

Watson, D., & Clark, L.A. (1992). Affects separable and inseparable: On the hierarchical arrangement of the negative affects. *Journal of Personality and Social Psychology*, 62(3), 489–505.

Wright, T.A., & Goodstein, J. (2007). Character is not "dead" in management research: A review of individual character and organizational-level virtue. *Journal of Management*, 33(6), 928–58.

Wright, T.A., & Quick, J.C. (2009). The emerging positive agenda in organizations: Greater than a trickle, but not yet a deluge. *Journal of Organizational Behavior*, 30(2), 147–59.

Chapter 8

TEAM COGNITION AND ADAPTABILITY IN DYNAMIC SETTINGS: A REVIEW OF PERTINENT WORK

Sjir Uitdewilligen
Department of Organization and Strategy, Maastricht University, Maastricht, The Netherlands

Mary J. Waller
Schulich School of Business, York University, Toronto, ON, Canada

Fred R.H. Zijlstra
Department of Work and Social Psychology, Maastricht University, Maastricht, The Netherlands

INTRODUCTION

Given the increased unpredictability, complexity, and turbulence of organizational and economic environments, organizations are relying on teams of individuals to analyze situations, solve problems, make decisions, negotiate agreements, and generally keep things running. Teams provide an efficient means of arranging work in many organizational structures (Zaccaro and Bader, 2003), and researchers, for some time, have trained their focus on understanding how teams successfully and unsuccessfully manage the aforelisted tasks. One particular team characteristic has emerged as critical, given the dynamic situations within which many teams now find themselves embedded: *adaptability*.

It is no longer adequate, in countless organizational situations, for teams to follow the "rational" prescription of scanning the environment, collecting and analyzing data, developing alternatives, and solving problems or making decisions. Teams may be peppered with nonroutine events as they struggle to

International Review of Industrial and Organizational Psychology, 2010, *Volume 25*.
Edited by G. P. Hodgkinson and J. K. Ford. Copyright © 2010 John Wiley & Sons, Ltd

follow accepted guidelines and operating procedures (Stachowski, Kaplan, and Waller, 2009). Team decision rules meant for relatively stable conditions may become obsolete as competitors run and change at Internet speed. Instead, these and similar situations that call for proactive anticipation and agile adaptation require teams with members who are connected in very particular ways.

In this chapter, we present a review of recent research published within the last 15 years about those "particular ways" – specifically the shared mental models, transactive memory, and team situation awareness (TSA) – that are suggested to enable teams to sense and manage unexpected events in their dynamic task environments. Briefly, *shared mental models* are mental representations of knowledge, relationships, or systems that are similar across team members. *Transactive memory* has been defined as the division of cognitive labor in a team with respect to encoding, storing, and retrieving knowledge from different domains (Lewis *et al.*, 2007) – or more colloquially, the system of knowing who on the team knows what. Finally, *team situation awareness* differs from shared mental models and transactive memory in that it is shared *contextual* knowledge about the current situation, team members' knowledge of each other's goals, and their current and future activities and intentions (Roth, Multer, and Raslear, 2006).

Overall, much of the research reviewed in this chapter suggests that each of these team cognitive structures facilitate the coordination and communication necessary in teams attempting to successfully anticipate and react to turbulent, dynamic task settings. In our conclusion to the chapter, however, we question the building assumption that these types of shared cognition *always* facilitate the adaptability needed by teams facing unexpected and turbulent situations and explain how the level and type of dynamism in teams' environments may significantly influence the positive effects of shared mental models, transactive memory, and shared situation awareness in teams. Additionally, given our focus on these aspects of shared cognition, we pay particular attention in this review to work pertaining to "action" teams; that is, teams that face unpredictable, dynamic, and complex task environments, and both react to and influence those environments (Chen, Thomas, and Wallace, 2005; Marks, Zaccaro, and Mathieu, 2000). Where appropriate in our review, we highlight how each of the three types of shared cognition is thought to facilitate adaptability in teams, and we include suggestions for future research.

ADAPTABILITY

Several models of team adaptation have appeared in the team literature (it refers to the literature about teams) in recent years. Referring to their advanced conceptual model of team adaptation, Burke and colleagues define team adaptation as "a change in team performance, in response to a salient cue or cue stream that leads to a functional outcome for the entire team" (Burke et al., 2006, p. 1190). These scholars suggest that teams adapt in a recursive, cyclical nature over time to their changing contexts, and specifically suggest that teams with accurate and flexible mental models and heightened levels of TSA will be better able than other teams to notice and correctly identify important changes in their task situations. LePine (p. 1154) refers to team adaptation as a "nonscripted" response that calls for action other than learned routines, or as a "response to an unforeseen change that creates problems for which the team has had limited experience or training," and suggests that individuals' cognition levels provide an important antecedent to team-level adaptation. Marks, Zaccaro, and Mathieu (2000, p. 972) refer to team adaptation as occurring when "teams are able to derive and use new strategies and techniques for confronting novel elements in their environments." Marks and colleagues also suggest that the similarity and accuracy of teams' mental models will facilitate team adaptation efforts. Chen, Thomas, and Wallace (2005) suggest that the transfer of training in teams involves adaptive expertise, or "the capacity to modify knowledge, skill, and other characteristics acquired during training to meet novel, difficult, and complex situations" (p. 828).

Thus, the recent work on adaptation in teams is fairly consistent in characterizing team adaptation as change undertaken by a team in terms of (1) specific task performance behavior, (2) strategies for planned behavior, or (3) collective knowledge, in response to or anticipation of some unexpected, novel, nonroutine, complex event. This work is also consistent in suggesting that elements of shared cognition in teams, most often shared mental models, facilitate teams' efforts to make these necessary and often time-pressured changes. Consequently, we turn now to review the literature on shared mental models to better understand the role of this form of shared cognition as a shaper of team outcomes.

SHARED MENTAL MODELS

Probably the most widely researched concept pertaining to shared cognition is the shared mental model notion (Cannon-Bowers, Salas, and Converse, 1993; Klimoski and Mohammed, 1994; Mathieu et al. , 2000) and the related concept of shared schema (Rentsch and Hall, 1994). Mental models are organized knowledge structures consisting of the content as well as the structure of the concepts in the mind of individuals that represent a specific task or knowledge domain (Johnson-Laird, 1983; Kieras and Bovair, 1984; Orasanu and Salas, 1993). Reasoning based on mental models is a form of top–down information processing in the sense that cumulated knowledge from past experiences is used to make sense of information environments and to guide action (Abelson and Black, 1986; Hodgkinson and Healey, 2008; Johnson-Laird, 1983; Walsh,

1995). Hence, mental models are functional structures that enable people to describe, explain, and predict a system with which they interact (Gentner and Stevens, 1983; Hodgkinson and Healey, 2008: Rouse and Morris, 1986). For example, machine operators may possess a mental model that depicts the cause and effect relations of the internal functioning of a machine. To the extent that their mental models properly mirror the actual functioning of the machine, operators will be able to deduce what the parameters on the machine display signify about the system's state and be able to infer the consequences of alternative actions.

Since the introduction of the concept of mental models to team research in a number of seminal theory papers (e.g., Cannon-Bowers *et al.*, 1993; Klimoski and Mohammed, 1994; Kraiger and Wenzel, 1997; Rentsch and Hall, 1994), team researchers have embraced this concept and provided an ongoing stream of articles and studies covering team-level properties of mental models, which we refer to here as *shared mental model theory*. The basic tenet of shared mental model theory is that congruence in team members' mental models facilitates efficient teamwork and consequently leads to high performance (Cannon-Bowers, Salas, and Converse, 1993). On the basis of this principle, researchers have suggested that shared mental models may facilitate team performance and decision making in a wide variety of situations (e.g., Langfield-Smith, 1992; Smith and Dowell, 2000; Stout *et al.*, 1999; Walsh and Fahey, 1986) and facilitate team adaptation in challenging and novel situations (Burke *et al.*, 2006; Marks *et al.*, 2000; McIntyere and Salas, 1995; Waller, 1999; Waller, Gupta, and Giambatista, 2004).

The field has now reached a point where a substantial number of empirical studies have been published in the area, allowing us to draw more informed conclusions regarding the consequences, antecedents, mediators, and contingencies of shared mental models. Here we seek to provide an update of the state of the field and focus in particular on the empirical evidence that has been found, identifying some outstanding issues for which empirical tests are still wanting. In the following section, we first describe some conceptual issues related to shared mental models. After this we discuss team outcomes and processes that are associated with shared mental models and the measurement techniques that have been used to elicit mental models from team members. Then we review antecedents of shared mental models and contingency factors that influence the impact of shared mental models. We end with some outstanding issues in research on shared mental models and present directions for further research.

Types of Shared Mental Models

Researchers in the area have generally agreed that different types of mental models may be active simultaneously in teams. Klimoski and Mohammed

(1994) suggested that at any given point in time, multiple mental models may be shared among the members of a team. Regarding mental model types, Cooke *et al.* (2000) distinguished between three types of knowledge that individuals' mental models may contain: (1) declarative knowledge, containing the facts, figures, rules, relations, and concepts of a task domain; (2) procedural knowledge, consisting of the steps, procedures, sequences, and actions required for task performance; and (3) strategic knowledge, consisting of the superseding task strategies and knowledge of when they apply. It has also been suggested variously that mental models may consist of collections of these different knowledge types (Klimoski and Mohammed, 1994) and that each type of knowledge may be considered as a separate mental model (Banks and Millward, 2007).

Whereas the aforementioned division applies to the type or form of mental models, team members may also hold mental models for different aspects of their task. Cannon-Bowers *et al.* (1993) identified mental models for four aspects of a task that may be required for successful team performance: (1) a model of the *equipment* used in the execution of the task, (2) a model representing aspects of the *task* itself, such as task processes, strategies, and likely scenarios, (3) a *team interaction mental* model, representing team members interaction and communication patterns, roles, and responsibilities, (4) a *team member* model, containing knowledge about other teammates' knowledge, skills, abilities, attitudes, beliefs, and tendencies. An examination of empirical studies on shared mental models indicates that most researchers have used a somewhat simpler division, and have, on the basis of a classical distinction of Morgan *et al.* (1986) between a taskwork track and a teamwork track of team development, collapsed the first two and the second two mental model types into task and team mental models (e.g., Cooke *et al.*, 2003; Fleming *et al.*, 2003; Lim and Klein, 2006; Mathieu *et al.*, 2005; Mathieu *et al.*, 2000). However, many other scholars have focused on a single mental model (e.g., Ellis, 2006; Marks *et al.*, 2002; Marks, Zaccaro, and Mathieu, 2000; Rentsch and Klimoski, 2001).

In sum, shared mental models are a configural type of team construct indicating the degree of similarity among the mental models of members of a team (Kozlowski and Klein, 2000; Mathieu *et al.*, 2005).

Outcomes of Shared Mental Models

Direct Effects of Shared Mental Models

Previous reviews of shared mental models have indicated that despite several articles and chapters describing shared mental models, the empirical record of evidence supporting the beneficial effects of shared mental models on team performance is still wanting (Klimoski and Mohammed, 1994; Kraiger and Wenzel, 1997; Mohammed, Klimoski, and Rentsch, 2000). An investigation of studies appearing in the trail of these publications indicates that researchers have clearly taken these comments to heart and have gone beyond applying mental models merely *a posteriori* to explain relationships between team behavior and performance; instead, researchers have moved towards directly eliciting the mental models held by team members and relating them to a variety of team outcomes. Over the past two decades, an accumulating body of research has supplied evidence for a direct effect between the similarity of team members' mental models and team task performance in a large variety of domains, including simulation studies (e.g., Cooke, Kiekel, and Helm, 2001; Cooke *et al.*, 2003; Ellis, 2006; Fleming *et al.*, 2003; Gurtner *et al.*, 2007; Marks *et al.*, 2002; Marks, Zaccaro, and Mathieu, 2000; Mathieu *et al.*, 2005; Mathieu *et al.*, 2000) and also field studies on air traffic control teams (Smith-Jentsch, Mathieu, and Kraiger, 2005), work teams (Rentsch and Klimoski, 2001), combat teams (Lim and Klein, 2006), and basketball teams (Webber *et al.*, 2000).

Similarity and Accuracy

Several scholars have indicated that it is not only similarity or overlap in team mental models but also the accuracy of those mental models that is required to benefit team effectiveness (Cooke *et al.*, 2000; Rentsch and Hall, 1994). Team mental model accuracy refers to the extent to which the mental models of the team members adequately represent the structure of the system it models (Stout, Salas, and Kraiger, 1997). Mental model accuracy is most often assessed by comparing participants' mental models with a referent mental model developed by one or a few task experts (e.g., Cook *et al.*, 2001; Lim and Klein, 2006) or by having experts rate the quality of participants' mental models (e.g., Ellis, 2006; Marks *et al.*, 2000). Team mental model accuracy is subsequently calculated as the average accuracy of the team members' mental models (Cooke *et al.*, 2003; Lim and Klein, 2006; Webber *et al.*, 2000).

Results of a number of studies indicate that team mental model accuracy is sometimes (Cooke *et al.*, 2001; Cooke *et al.*, 2003; Edwards *et al.*, 2006; Lim and Klein, 2006; Marks *et al.*, 2000) but not always (e.g., Webber *et al.*, 2000) directly related to team performance. Interestingly Marks *et al.* (2000) found an interaction between the effects of mental model similarity and accuracy on performance, such that teams with less accurate mental models seemed to benefit more from mental model similarity than teams with more accurate mental models. Additionally, in a study directly comparing the predictive accuracy of team mental model similarity and accuracy, Edwards *et al.* (2006) found that mental model accuracy was a stronger predictor of team performance than mental model similarity.

Scholars have posited that shared mental models influence team performance through their effect on team interaction processes (Cannon-Bowers *et al.*, 1993; Klimoski and Mohammed, 1994), and this seems to have been supported by empirical studies indicating mediating effects of coordination, communication, and collaboration processes on the relationship between shared mental models and team performance (Marks *et al.*, 2000; Mathieu *et al.*, 2005; Mathieu *et al.*, 2000). Below, we review in greater detail work that has examined each of these three mediating processes.

Coordination

Congruence in team members' mental models is considered to affect team functioning through its effect on team coordination processes. Coordination processes refer to those behaviors that are aimed at attuning the resources and activities of individual team members towards the concerted goal directed behavior of the team as a unit (Cannon-Bowers *et al.*, 1995). A crucial aspect of coordination is the harmonization of interdependent activities performed by the different members of the team. Shared mental models are expected to affect team coordination by providing mutual expectations from which accurate, timely predictions can be drawn about the behavior of other team members (Cannon-Bowers *et al.*, 1993). In particular, shared expectations are considered to facilitate tacit coordination – coordination based on unspoken assumptions about what actions other members are likely to pursue and what information they require (Wittenbaum, Vaughan, and Stasser, 1998).

Especially in high-workload situations, implicit coordination may be the optimal way to manage intrateam interdependencies because it requires only a limited amount of communication overhead, time, and cognitive energy (Entin and Serfaty, 1999; Macmillan, Entin, and Serfaty, 2004). It is, therefore, not surprising that a number of studies have indicated that coordination mediates the relationship between mental model similarity and performance (e.g., Marks *et al.*, 2002; Mathieu *et al.*, 2000, 2005).

Apart from facilitating coordination through attuning actions, overlapping knowledge also comprises a source of robustness for a social cognitive system in the face of error and interruption (Hutchins, 1995). In case a team member is unable to perform his or her appointed responsibilities, cognitive redundancy makes it possible for the team as a whole to perform its team task because another team member may be able to take over execution of the task. Salas and colleagues (2005) emphasized the importance of shared mental models in two processes related to the robustness of the system: mutual performance monitoring and backup behavior. The ability to keep track of other team members' task performance while executing one's own task and to correct errors and assist others if necessary is important to guarantee consistent team performance, in particular under nonroutine, stressful circumstances (Marks and Panzer, 2004). Empirical evidence indicating backup behavior as a significant mediator between mental model similarity and team performance seems to support this reasoning (Marks *et al.*, 2002). Thus, a shared understanding about team tasks enables members to assess if other team members are falling short of task performance and to give assistance if required.

Communication

Research also suggests that shared mental models are positively related to the quality of communication in teams (Marks *et al.*, 2000; Mathieu *et al.*, 2000, 2005). Marks *et al.* (2000) found that mental model similarity was positively related to quality of team communication as well as to team performance; additionally, mental model accuracy was positively related to team performance, but a linear relation between mental model accuracy and quality of team communication was not supported in these researchers' results. Team members with similar mental models are also more likely to communicate information that is required by others at the time it is required, and in a way that is understood by the recipient (Fussel and Krauss, 1989; Krauss and Fussell, 1991). Especially during periods with strong time constraints and high stress levels, the ability to communicate can be highly reduced (Kleinman and Serfaty, 1989); therefore, in order to function effectively as a team with minimum amounts of communication, it is essential for team performance that members share a similar understanding of the task situation. This allows team members to coordinate implicitly without the need for overt communication (Kleinman and Serfaty, 1989; Salas, Cannon-Bowers, and Johnston, 1997). Ironically, however, maintaining a shared understanding may be especially problematic under stressful circumstances (Driskell, Salas, and Johnston, 1999). Ellis (2006) found that acute stress negatively affected team interaction model similarity and accuracy, which consequently had a negative impact on performance. This suggests that, for those situations in which a shared understanding is most essential for task performance, maintaining this shared understanding may be most difficult.

Collaboration

With respect to collaboration, the existence of shared mental models can reduce a team's investment in time and resources for reaching consensus, and can decrease the occurrence of friction due to cognitive divergence and misunderstanding. Research on group[1] negotiations has indicated that a common understanding of each party's problems and possible solutions constitutes an essential ingredient for reaching the maximum joint outcome (Swaab *et al.*, 2007). In newly formed teams, members often require a considerable

---

[1] We will use the terms "group" and "team" interchangeably in the present review, reverting as much as possible to the terms used by the original authors of the articles we describe.

proportion of their time getting to know each other and establishing a shared understanding of the task structure and the actions that are appropriate for performance (Bettenhausen and Murnighan, 1985). Constructing a shared understanding about the nature of the task and the norms for team interaction may involve political processes and negotiation (Walsh and Fahey, 1986). Therefore, teams in which shared mental models are present before task performance may need less time for clarifying and agreeing upon strategies. Consequently, such teams may have more time and resources for task execution and performance monitoring than other teams. Klimoski and Mohammed (1994) have suggested that if team members even perceive that their mental models are similar, this perception may lead to positive affective reactions and facilitate the development of trust within the team.

Measurement of Mental Models

The measurement of mental models is a topic that has garnered increasing interest and concern among team researchers. On the basis of a review of the various techniques available to measure mental models, Mohammed, Klimoski, and Rentsch, 2000 concluded that researchers must base their choice of measurement technique on a careful consideration of the research question and research context. They also called for the inclusion of multiple measurement techniques in single studies in order to assess their relative benefits and increase their predictive validity.

In a number of methodological articles and reviews, researchers have noted a wide variety of elicitation, representation, and analysis techniques available for assessing mental models that could be applied to a team context (see, e.g., Cooke et al., 2000; Hodgkinson and Healey, 2008; Langan-Fox, Code, and Langfield-Smith, 2000; Mohammed, Klimoski, and Rentsch, 2000). Elicitation techniques have included cognitive interviewing, questionnaires, process tracing and verbal protocol analysis, text-based content analysis, and a variety of conceptual methods including visual card sorting, repertory grid, causal mapping, ordered tree technique, and matrix based, and pairwise ratings. Analysis and representation methods included pathfinder networks, multidimensional scaling, and UCINET techniques based on proximity ratings, cause-mapping based on interviews and questionnaire data, and text-based cause mapping involving the systematic coding of documents and transcripts.

Whereas Mohammed, Klimoski, and Rentsch (2000) indicated that the most common elicitation methodologies in the study of team mental models were similarity ratings and Likert scale questionnaires, it seems that the popularity of Likert scale questions has decreased while the use of similarity ratings and concept mapping seems to have increased in recent empirical studies. With similarity ratings, researchers typically derive, by means of a task analysis, a number of concepts that are relevant for team task execution. Respondents are asked to rate the similarity in terms of causality, relatedness, proximity, or association they perceive between these concepts. Outcomes of this ratings process are subsequently subjected to systems such as Pathfinder or UCINET to derive and analyze the mental models (see Edwards *et al.*, 2006; Mathieu *et al.*, 2000 for examples). With concept mapping methods, team members are asked to place concepts in a prespecified hierarchical structure (Mohammed *et al.*, 2000). For example, Marks and colleagues (2000) asked team members to indicate on a timeline the sequence of actions they themselves would take, as well as the actions the other team members would be taking at the same time during team task performance. Similarity is typically subsequently calculated by assigning points for each instance in which team members located similar concepts or actions within the predefined structure. Using a different method, Carley (1997) employed a textual analysis technique that helped automate the approach for deriving mental models from written text. In her study, participants answered an open-ended essay question regarding their team task. Concepts were derived from the words team members used in their texts, and the relationships among those concepts were obtained from the proximity of the location of these concepts within the text.

Webber *et al.* (2000) distinguished between consistency measures of similarity and consensus measures in their work. According to this conceptualization, consistency only requires similarity in rank ordering between raters, whereas consensus requires essentially the same ratings. Webber and colleagues' results indicated that although team mental model consistency was not significantly related with team performance, team mental model consensus was. On the other hand, Smith-Jentsch, Mathieu, and Kraiger (2005) only found significant relationships between mental model similarity and team performance with a consistency-based measure of similarity and not with a consensus measure of this construct.

Some researchers have suggested that in particular situations, there may not be one single most accurate mental model; instead, multiple mental models of equally high quality may exist at the same time (Marks *et al.*, 2000; Smith-Jentsch *et al.*, 2001). Mathieu *et al.* (2005) noted that measures of mental model accuracy that depend on a single referent or "ideal" model cannot distinguish mental model similarity from mental model quality at the high end of the continuum; that is, if team members' mental models highly resemble the referent model, they will, as an artifact of the measurement method, also highly resemble each other. To remedy this limitation, they developed a measure of *quality* as an alternative to *accuracy* of mental models that does not depend on reference to "ideal" models; as a result, the new measure leaves open the possibility of several structurally different, high-quality mental models. These researchers derived referent task mental models by identifying clusters among the mental models of a group of experienced flight simulation players and referent team mental models by clustering mental models of a sample of team researchers.

To summarize, it appears that the techniques often used by researchers to measure various aspects of mental models provide relatively straightforward measures of accuracy and similarity. However, these techniques may be restricted in that participants' mental models are constructed with a limited amount of concepts that are often predefined by the researchers. This may render these measurement techniques less than optimal means to investigate richer and more idiosyncratic aspects of mental models, such as mental model complexity (Curseu, Schruijer, and Boros, 2007) or flexibility in the cognitive processes and structures that may facilitate adaptation (Chen *et al.*, 2005; Eisenhardt and Tabrizi, 1995). However, a number of recent advances in the measurement of individual-level mental models reported in *Organizational Research Methods* seem to provide a promising avenue for more complex operationalizations of the structural aspects of shared mental models (e.g., Clarkson and Hodgkinson, 2005; Hodgkinson, Maule, and Bown, 2004; Nadkarni and Narayanan, 2005; Wright, 2008).

Antecedents of Shared Mental Models

A number of researchers have investigated the conditions under which accurate and shared mental models are most likely to arise in teams. Kraiger and Wenzel (1997) suggested four categories of antecedents of team mental models: environmental, organizational, team, and individual. Klimoski and Mohammed (1994) emphasize group formation, development, and training as important factors that may affect the course and speed of team mental model development. There is supportive evidence for each of these aspects.

Team researchers have indicated the necessity of considering the broader system context in which a team operates for understanding the functioning of individual teams (Arrow, McGrath, and Berdahl, 2000; Hackman, 2003; Kozlowski, Gully, Nason, and Smith, 1999). One way in which the environmental context influences team functioning is by shaping the mental models the team members bring with them to their team task. Although some researchers have set out to identify aspects of mental models that are generic and transfer over different contexts (Druskat and Pescosolido, 2002; Johnson *et al.*, 2007), most mental models are learned and developed within, and are idiosyncratic to, a specific context – for example, a department, organization, or industry. As individuals spend time within an organization, they learn and become socialized as to the "dominant logic" prevailing within that organization (Prahalad and Bettis, 1986). Also, selection criteria used in member recruitment and self-selection processes may contribute to ensure that organization members hold similar orientations to their work and tasks (Klimoski and Mohammed, 1994).

Two field studies provide support for this kind of contextual influence on shared mental model formation. In a study addressing the antecedents of team member mental model similarity, Rentsch and Klimoski (2001) found that similarity in education and organizational level, average team experience, and whether a team member was actively recruited to the team were positively related to mental model similarity. In a study among navy personnel, Smith-Jentsch et al. (2001) found that higher ranking personnel had more accurate team mental models—as measured by similarity to a referent model – than lower-ranking personnel. Additionally, they found that higher-ranking individuals and individuals who had spent more time in the navy held more similar mental models of teamwork than lower-ranking officers and individuals who had spend less time in the navy.

Whereas such organizational assimilation effects can lead to congruence of mental models within teams from a single organization, for teams consisting of members originating from different organizations (e.g., temporary teams such as interagency crisis management teams), it may be particularly difficult to attain such a shared understanding (e.g. Smith and Dowell, 2000). Cronin and Weingart (2007) noticed that when members hold different functional backgrounds in which different mental models prevail, teams may suffer from "perceptual gaps" – misunderstanding between team members about what is needed for the team to be successful.

There also is some evidence of task contextual influences on team members' mental models. In an experimental simulation, Driskell and colleagues (1999) found that, relative to teams performing in a low-stress condition, team members performing the task in a high-stress environment became more individualistic and self-focused, which manifested in more individual and less collective representations of the task. Building on these findings, Ellis (2006) conducted an experimental study in which he directly investigated the effects of acute stress on team cognition. The results of his study indicated that acute stress negatively affected the similarity and the accuracy of team members' team interaction mental models as well as their transactive memory systems (TMSs).

Another oft-investigated antecedent of shared mental models is the effect of team training. Several studies have measured mental models repeatedly over time during team training or task execution; results, however, are inconclusive and inconsistent. Cooke et al. (2003) found that their teamwork mental model showed improvement in team knowledge accuracy over time, but their task knowledge measure showed no change between two sessions. Xinwen et al. (2006) found a significant increase in task mental model similarity but not in team interaction mental model similarity when teams increased the time spent on task implementation. Mathieu et al. (2000, 2005), as well as Edwards and colleagues (2006), did not find a significant increase in similarity and accuracy of team members' mental models over time. Levesque, Wilson, and Wholey

(2001) actually found that the mental models of software development team members became less similar over time as team member interaction decreased due to increased specialization. This seems to imply that simply having team members train and work together on a task may not be sufficient to increase the accuracy and similarity of team members' mental models, and deliberate actions may have to be taken in order to ensure that mental models remain congruent. One way to do this is by administering training programs that are specifically aimed at improving the similarity and accuracy of team members' mental models. A distinction should be made here between individual-level training programs in which team members are individually trained in facilitating adequate team mental models, and team-level training programs in which the team is trained as a whole to collectively execute the task. Individual-level training programs can improve the accuracy of the team members' mental models; however, they can only indirectly enhance the similarity in team members' mental models by increasing the similarity of each team member's mental model with an ideal mental model (and hence with each others' mental models). Team-level training programs, on the other hand, can directly increase mental model similarity; through team interactions, team members are encouraged to explore, harmonize, integrate, and conjointly construct their mental models (Van den Bossche et al., 2006).

At the individual level, Day, Arthur, and Gettman (2001) found that the improvements in accuracy of individuals' knowledge structures of a task developed together with the acquisition of skill in executing the task. Stout, Salas, and Kraiger (1997) found that after receiving training aimed to improve their knowledge structures, navy helicopter pilots' mental models became more consistent and displayed more resemblance to an expert mental model, which translated to improved performance on a subsequent team task. Smith-Jentsch and colleagues (2001) found that after exposure to a computer based training program, trainees' teamwork mental models became more similar to an expert mental model; moreover, they became more consistent and more similar to the mental models of other trainees. Finally, the work of Marks et al. (2000) indicated that teams with members who received video-based team interaction training developed more accurate and more similar mental models than teams in a control condition.

Some researchers have suggested that because team members often have different roles within a team, team training should not simply be aimed at increasing similarity in mental models, but instead at increasing the understanding team members have of the roles and accompanying requirements and contributions of the other members (Blickensderfer, Cannon-Bowers, and Salas, 1998; Marks et al., 2002; Volpe et al., 1996). Cross training has been defined by Volpe and colleagues (1996) as "an instructional strategy in which each team member is trained in the duties of his or her teammates" (p. 87). Marks and colleagues (2002) conducted two studies on the effect of three types of cross training differing in depth and method: (1) positional clarification, consisting of a verbal presentation of information about the roles of the other team members; (2) positional modeling, consisting of verbal discussions and observation of other members' roles; and (3) positional rotation in which team members gain active experience in carrying out the duties of their team members. In the first experiment, they included only positional clarification and positional modeling training, and found that both were positively related to team interaction mental model similarity. In the second experiment, they also included positional rotation, and they found that all training conditions positively influenced mental model similarity and that positional modeling was more effective than positional clarification. Cooke *et al.* (2003) designed a cross-training program in which team members were trained either actively in executing the role of all the other members or passively in only learning the role knowledge of the other team members. The results of their study indicated that only the active cross training condition was effective in facilitating the development of shared mental models and accurate knowledge structures regarding the other team members' roles. In sum, cross-training seems to provide an effective method for facilitating the development of shared mental models; however, results are inconsistent regarding the type and depth of cross training that is required to gain these positive effects.

The effectiveness of team training on mental model accuracy and similarity may also be moderated by individual difference variables. Day *et al.* (2001) found that general cognitive ability was positively related to mental model accuracy at the end of a training period, and Edwards *et al.* (2006) found that general cognitive ability was a significant predictor for the development of accurate and similar mental models.

Marks *et al.* (2001) suggested that teams alternate between *action periods* in which they engage in acts that contribute directly to the goals of the team and *transition periods* in which teams focus on evaluation and planning activities that play a more supportive role towards team goal accomplishment. Given an ongoing sequence of team performance episodes, these transition episodes may have both a forward looking function during which team members actively prepare for the task ahead and a backward-looking evaluative function, during which team members collectively make sense of their functioning in preceding task episodes. These transition periods may provide a particularly good time for team leaders to play a role shaping and developing shared mental models (Hackman and Wageman, 2005; Kozlowski *et al.*, 1996).

Previous research indicates that both forward- and backward-oriented transition processes may function to facilitate the construction of shared mental models for ensuing task periods. Stout *et al.* (1999) found that the quality of the planning process prior to a team mission was positively related to the similarity in team members' mental models. Similarly, Marks *et al.* (2000) found that teams receiving leader briefings before the actual performance episode developed more accurate and more similar mental models than teams in a control condition. Other studies indicate that team feedback and debriefs, taking place after task performance episodes, can positively affect the development of rich and accurate mental models (Ellis and Davidi, 2005; Xinwen *et al.*, 2006). In particular, guided team self-corrections during which the team is guided in critically reflecting on and discussing its own functioning, fosters the construction of more accurate (Smith-Jentsch *et al.*, 2008) and more similar (Blickensderfer *et al.*, 1997) mental models. A study by Rasker, Post, and Schraagen (2000) suggested that the extent to which a team has the ability to engage in performance monitoring and self-corrections, positively relates to the ability of the team to construct high-quality mental models. More generally, it can be stated that the extent to which a team explicates and overtly reflects on its objectives, processes, and strategies positively relates to the quality and similarity of team members' mental models (Gurtner *et al.*, 2007; Massey and Wallace, 1996; Müller, Herbig, and Petrovic, 2009).

Contingency Factors Influencing the Impact of Shared Mental Models

Cannon-Bowers and Salas (2001) have called for research specifying the conditions under which shared mental models may affect various team-level outcomes. Various authors have suggested contingency variables that could influence when shared mental models are more or less important for team functioning. Stout, Cannon-Bowers, and Salas (1996) theorized that the importance of mental model similarity is contingent on the demands a task poses on the team. If task demands are low and team members have ample time, shared mental models may be less important than when task demands are high and the team has inadequate time to communicate and strategize. Supporting this line of reasoning, Minionis, Zaccaro, and Perez (1995) found that shared mental models enhanced performance on tasks requiring interdependence among team members, but had no significant impact on tasks that could be completed without coordinated team actions.

Espinosa, Lerch, and Kraut (2004) noted that teams may make use of two types of mechanisms to manage interdependencies: implicit team cognition–based mechanisms and explicit mechanisms based on schedules, plans, and procedures. They argue that there may be complementarities, trade-offs, and interactions between these mechanisms and that various team and contextual variables may influence which mechanism may be most suitable for teams to complete a specific task. For example, if team coordination can be efficiently managed by configuration management systems such as project schedules or electronic planning systems, shared mental models may be less important for team performance.

Finally, the work of Kellermanns *et al.* (2008) demonstrated that mental model similarity improves decision-making quality. However, when a team has strong norms for constructive confrontation – that is, when team members value open expression, disagreement, and the avoidance of negative affect – these findings suggest that less, instead of more, mental model similarity improves decision making quality. The authors reasoned that mental model dissimilarity indicates a diversity of perspectives from which teams can reap benefits as long as they have norms that help them avoid the negative consequences of conflict.

Additive and Compatible Mental Models

Klimoski and Mohammed (1994) noted the ambiguous nature of the term "shared" in that it may refer to overlapping or similar knowledge as well as to divided or different knowledge; similarly, Cannon-Bowers and Salas (2001) added that "shared" may also refer to similar or identical knowledge and to compatible and complimentary knowledge. Although the majority of studies on shared mental model theory seem to concern the beneficial effects of congruence in team member's mental models, there seems to be general recognition that not all knowledge should be held by all team members (Cannon-Bowers and Salas, 2001; Klimoski and Mohammed, 1994; Rentsch and Hall, 1994). Cannon-Bowers, Salas, and Converse (1993) suggest the possibility that different mental models may be accurate. They argue that it is not so much the overlap in team members' mental models that is related to team performance, but the common expectations that team members derive from these models. Accordingly, they suggested that teams may not need similar so much as compatible and supplementary knowledge structures, for example, differences in expertise.

When team members have distinct team roles, they are likely to develop knowledge structures considering their own specific subtasks, which do not necessarily have to be shared among the team members. In effect, it would often be cognitively impossible or at least inefficient if all knowledge were held by all team members (Banks and Millward, 2000; Mohammed and Dumville, 2001). The theory of distributed cognition (Banks and Millward, 2000; Hutchins, 1995) indicates that it is not merely overlap in knowledge that is required, but instead that the team as a whole needs to be able to understand the complexity of the system. Some empirical evidence suggests that similarity in team mental models may not always be beneficial for team performance. Cooke *et al.* (2003) found that teams with members who had a thorough understanding of their own roles but lower similarity in taskwork knowledge tended to be the best performing teams. Similarly, Banks and Millward (2007) found in a simulation study that even though similarity in members' declarative knowledge was positively related to team performance, similarity in members' procedural knowledge was negatively related to performance.

The shared mental model perspective emphasizes the effects of mental models on team interaction behavior (Cannon-Bowers *et al.*, 1993; Mathieu *et al.*, 2000, 2005), while the distributed cognition perspective of team mental models focuses on the extent to which the team members' mental models cover the relevant task environment – that is, provide the requisite expertise to perform a variety of actions and perceive and interpret a variety of stimuli (Conant and Ashby, 1970; Weick, 1979). This implies that two opposing mechanisms may intervene between mental model similarity and team performance. On the one hand, mental model similarity facilitates team interaction processes; on the other hand, mental model diversity may be required to ensure the requisite variety of expertise and skills in complex task environments. The effect of similarity in mental models on team performance may depend on the relative importance of each of these mechanisms in accomplishing the particular team task at hand.

Other researchers have associated diversity in underlying knowledge structures with the ability to generate a wide range of perspectives and alternative solutions (Milliken and Martins, 1996; Simons, Pelled, and Smith, 1999). The integration of these various viewpoints is considered to lead to deep information processing, the emergence of new insights (Jehn, Northcraft, and Neale, 1999; Levine and Resnick, 1993), and team ability to reconsider assumptions and come to more creative and high quality solutions (De Dreu and West, 2001; Nemeth, 1986; van Knippenberg, De Dreu, and Homan, 2004). However, because mental models are essentially interpretations and simplifications of an external system (Fiske and Taylor, 1991), they may compromise the ability to make decisions in complex environments (Walsh, 1995; Weick, 1979). Moreover, Starbuck and Milliken (1988) posited that knowledge structures function as lenses that filter the information that is received from the environment and determine how this information is interpreted. Thus, it may be that diversity in team members' mental models facilitate the probability that important information is noticed by at least one team member.

Beyond Input–Process–Output Conceptions

Most team researchers have explicitly or implicitly embedded the construct of shared mental model in an input–process–output (I–P–O) framework of team performance, in which team inputs are considered to impact team processes that in turn shape team outcomes (Hackman, 1987; McGrath, 1964). Recently, however, authors have warned against adopting overly simplistic interpretations of the I–P–O framework by pointing to interaction effects that may occur between inputs and processes, and by emphasizing the temporal and ongoing nature of team functioning (Ilgen *et al.*, 2005; Marks, Mathieu, and Zaccaro, 2001). In consonance with this dynamic view, Marks *et al.* (2001) categorized team cognition constructs as *emergent states*, which they define as "constructs that are typically dynamic in nature and vary as a function of team context, inputs, processes, and outcomes" (p. 357). They argued that team emergent states describe dynamic properties of the team and should be distinguished from team processes, which describe the nature of team member interaction. Since team cognitive structures can both serve as inputs and outputs of team processes, a cyclical framework – one that takes into account the observation that outcomes and emergent states from previous cycles may be inputs in subsequent performance cycles – may be more appropriate than a purely linear view of the relationship between team inputs, processes, and outputs. Despite the increasing recognition among researchers for this more dynamic temporal perspective on team cognition, longitudinal studies that address antecedents and consequences of changes in shared mental models over time are still scarce. An alternative way by which researchers can provide for a more dynamic view of team cognition is by distinguishing between the relatively stable notion of the mental models and the more dynamic concept of situation awareness (SA) described later in this chapter.

Future Directions

A recent review on diversity literature (Harrison and Klein, 2007) warned against the problems of adopting overtly simplified conceptualizations of diversity and suggested that researchers go beyond simply looking at similarity and diversity. Similarly, team researchers may look at more complex compositions of knowledge within teams. Research by Walsh and colleagues seems to indicate that for some tasks only the mental models of the most influential member may be important for team functioning (Walsh and Fahey, 1986; Walsh, Henderson, and Deighton, 1988). But what happens if a team is divided into two equally powerful subteams that possess equally appropriate but different mental models of the team task (cf. Cronin and Weingart, 2007)? And, what are the effects on team functioning if one member holds a more accurate mental model than the other members? Under what circumstances are such minority members able to influence the other members to accept their understanding of the task?

Future research may also go beyond similarity and accuracy to take into account characteristics such as the flexibility or complexity of the mental models, or the extent to which the team's mental model covers the relevant task environment. Previous research on individual-level mental models indicates that experts hold more detailed mental models than novice task performers (Murphy and Wright, 1984; Tanaka and Taylor, 1991). Complexity of mental models is considered to increase the amount of information that can be garnered from the environment (Bartunek, Gordon, and Weathersby, 1983; Starbuck and Milliken, 1988).

Another promising future direction, proposed by Huber and Lewis (2010), is cross understanding, or each member's understanding of the mental models of the other team members. The cross-understanding notion bears similarity to the transactive memory concept in that it comprises team members' understanding of the knowledge of other members. However, unlike a TMS, cross understanding does not necessarily imply a distribution of expertise. Huber and Lewis (2010) indicate that team members may also benefit from an understanding of other members' mental models when knowledge within the team is not differentiated. For instance, Rentsch and Woehr (2004) indicated that team effectiveness may be a function not only of the similarity in team members' cognitions but also of the extent to which "a team member's schema of a target matches the target's actual schema" (2004: 22).

Of the three types of shared cognition reviewed in this chapter, the literature on shared mental models is the most mature and wide ranging. However, many teams scholars have focused their attention away from the "sharedness" of mental representations and instead on the understanding of the distribution of *different* knowledge and expertise across team members. The literature on and understanding of these *transactive memory systems* in teams has grown in recent years, and we turn now to a review of this work.

TRANSACTIVE MEMORY SYSTEMS

The theory of transactive memory was developed by Wegner and colleagues (1985, 1987) to explain how individuals can expand their own limited memory capacity with external aids, including other people. Wegner uses the analog of a computer to describe how transactive memory functions. Computers with separate hard disks can share each other's memory if they have a directory containing an abbreviated record of the contents and location of the other memory systems (Wegner, 1995). Correspondingly, a group's transactive memory consists of the knowledge of the individual members of the group combined with members' knowledge of the content of information held by other members of the group.

Initially, Wegner and colleagues (1985) developed the notion of transactive memory as a theory describing the interpersonal division of memory tasks in intimate couples. For instance, in an experiment testing this theory, Wegner, Erber, and Raymond (1991) compared performance on a memory task between natural pairs – couples that had been in close dating relationships for at least three months – with impromptu pairs of strangers they had put together specifically for the experiment. They found that if pairs could decide how they would divide the memory tasks between them, the natural pairs were clearly superior, whereas when the researchers assigned a structure for how the memory task should be divided between the members, the impromptu pairs outperformed their natural counterparts. These results indicate that the memory advantage that natural pairs develop through prolonged interaction is based on an efficient, implicit structure for dividing memory tasks. When pairs are forced to adopt an alternative structure, however, this benefit breaks down, and the persistence of their previously established structure may even negatively influence the adoption of a new structure.

Although transactive memory theory was originally developed to explain how intimate couples formed a division of labor for remembering and accessing information, soon researchers noticed the merit of the concept for explaining group and team-level phenomena. Moreland and colleagues applied the notion of transactive memory to the group level in order to explain the performance advantage of groups that had been trained together relative to groups whose members had been trained apart (Liang, Moreland, and Argote, 1995; Moreland, Argote, and Krishnan, 1996; 1998). Their reasoning was that during the collective training process, group members not only achieve individual task experience but also develop an understanding of the knowledge and fields of expertise of their group members. This knowledge of "who knows what" enables group members to arrange their tasks in such a way as to optimally benefit from the variety of experience available within the group as a whole. In this way, the group can make optimal use of their cognitive resources; specifically, remembering and accessing a specific information element will cost the group member with the most experience with that type of information fewer cognitive resources than it would cost the other, less experienced and less knowledgeable group members. In sum, a TMS functions in groups as a cognitive structure that bridges the gap between individual and group-level information processing by efficiently tying together contributions of individual members into collective group performance (Hinsz, Tindale, and Vollrath, 1997; Larson and Christensen, 1993).

Early in the development of the concept, scholars referred to the content of transactive memory as pertaining mainly to facts and information; later, scholars broadened the concept to also include knowledge of team members' skills or expertise (Moreland and Myaskovsky, 2000) and external relationships (Austin, 2003). Scholars have emphasized the importance of a TMS for groups functioning in a wide variety of domains, including work teams (Austin 2003; Lewis, 2004; Littlepage et al., 2008; Zhang et al., 2007), action teams (Ellis, 2006; Pearsall and Ellis, 2006), disaster response groups (Majchrzak, Jarvenpaa, and Hollingshead, 2007), management teams (Rau, 2005; Rulke, Zaheer, and Anderson, 2000), and virtual teams (Cramton, 2001; Griffith and Neale, 2001; Kanawattanachai and Yoo, 2007).

Conceptual Aspects of TMSs

With the notion of a TMS, scholars refer to two separate but interrelated components of cognitive structures and group interaction processes that enable groups to efficiently divide their cognitive labor with respect to the encoding, storage, retrieval, and communication of information among their members (Hollingshead, 2001; Lewis *et al.*, 2007; Moreland, 1999). The *knowledge component*, often referred to simply as transactive memory, refers to the memory content, skill base, or external relationships of the individual members in combination with the metaknowledge of who knows what within the team. Whereas this transactive memory component emerges as a team-level compositional construct from the knowledge components of the individual group members, the *process component* consists of the dynamic interaction processes involved in the acquisition, storage and retrieval of information among the group members, and therefore comprises a pure group-level construct (Hollingshead, 2001; Kozlowski and Klein, 2000; Lewis, 2003).

This dual component structure manifests itself in the various frameworks and dimensions of TMSs that have been proposed by scholars. Some scholars have focused specifically on the structural aspects of TMSs. For instance, Moreland (1999) distinguishes between three structural aspects of TMSs: (1) the accuracy in team members' understanding of each other's knowledge, (2) the extent to which group members agree about who holds what knowledge, and (3) the complexity in terms of the extent of specialization of expertise within the group and the level of detail of this understanding. Austin (2003) identifies four structural aspects of TMSs: knowledge stock, consensus, specialization, and accuracy. *Knowledge stock* refers to the total knowledge of the group that is composed of the knowledge of the individual members. *Specialization* refers to degree of differentiation in knowledge and expertise of the different team members. *Accuracy* considers the extent to which team members are correct in identifying knowledge of other group members.

Regarding the process component of TMSs, scholars have relied heavily on Wegner and colleagues' (1985) model, which includes directory updating, information allocation, and information retrieval. *Directory updating* refers to the establishment or refinement of team members' representations of each others' knowledge base. *Information allocation* refers to the process of forwarding information to the group member considered to hold expertise within the area relevant for that information. *Retrieval coordination* refers to the process of accessing information from team members based on an understanding of their relative expertise.

Others have proposed alternative TMS frameworks that include both structure and process components. For instance, Liang *et al.* (1995) identified three components reflecting the operation of a TMS among group members: memory differentiation (i.e., the tendency of group members to remember different aspects of the task processes; task coordination (i.e., the ability of the group members to work together efficiently) and task credibility, (i.e., the level of trust in the knowledge of the other group members). This tripartite framework also served as input for a collection of studies by Lewis (2003), who developed and validated a measure for assessing TMSs in the field, thereby providing additional support for the dimensionality and validity of Liang and colleagues' framework. Similarly, Brandon and Hollingshead (2004) identified three dimensions of a TMS: accuracy, the extent to which group members perceptions about other group members' knowledge are accurate; sharedness, the degree to which team members have a shared understanding of the division of expertise within the group; and validation, the extent to which the team members contribute their expertise knowledge during actual task performance. In addition, they introduced the concept of TMS convergence, reflecting the extent to which groups are characterized by high levels on each of these dimensions. In a somewhat similar vein, Faraj and Sproull (2000) identified (1) knowing where knowledge is distributed among the team members, (2) recognizing when knowledge is needed, and (3) bringing to bear expertise in a timely manner. Unlike the other dimensions reviewed earlier, which are explicitly identified by their originators as TMS dimensions, Faraj and Sproul locate their constructs under the umbrella of "expertise coordination."

Overall, it appears that a variety of comparable but slightly deviating frameworks of the dimensions of TMSs have been developed by scholars in this area. Some frameworks cover only structural aspects of the TMS notion, others only process aspects, while still others cover both aspects of TMSs.

TMS Outcomes

Outcomes of TMSs have been studied extensively both at the dyadic level and in larger groups and teams (Peltokorpi, 2008). Our focus here is on the group- and team-level studies; however, given the theoretical foundation provided by the dyad-level research, in our discussion of the development of the TMS construct, we mention and elaborate on findings from this research stream whenever relevant and appropriate. Regarding the outcomes of TMSs, we rely on the general finding that people in intimate relationships develop efficient implicit systems for remembering and retrieving information, providing them with an advantage over impromptu couples on collective memory tasks (Hollingshead, 1998a, 1998b; Johansson, Andersson, and Rönnberg, 2000; Wegner et al., 1991).

A number of studies compared the performance of work groups in which the individual members were trained apart, with groups in which the members were trained together (e.g., Liang, Moreland and Argote, 1995; Moreland et al., 1996, 1998). The latter groups outperformed groups consisting of individually trained members, suggesting that in addition to task related skills, groups that are trained together also develop a TMS with beneficial effects for group performance. Liang *et al.* (1995) scored videotapes of group tasks on typical TMS behaviors and found that the difference in performance between the two conditions could be attributed to the higher amount of transactive memory behaviors displayed by the collectively trained groups. Additional experiments confirmed that this effect was due to the development of a TMS, as opposed to general group building benefits (Moreland, 1999), or improved communication (Moreland and Myaskovsky, 2000).

In addition to studies demonstrating the beneficial effects of TMSs in experimental group settings, a number of studies have demonstrated positive performance outcomes in field settings. In a study of continuing work teams in a sporting goods company, Austin (2003) found positive relationships between the task and external relationship aspects of TMSs and internal and external team performance measures. Lewis (2004) similarly found positive relationships among MBA consultancy teams between TMS development – measured by means of her field scale covering the components of specialization, coordination, and credibility – and team-rated performance, client-rated performance, and the ability of the team to continue working well in the future. Using the same scale in a cross-sectional study among 193 nurse and physician anesthetists, Michinov, *et al.* (2008) found that TMSs predicted members' perceptions of team effectiveness, job satisfaction, and team identification. Also using Lewis' TMS questionnaire, in a multiorganizational study Zhang and colleagues (2007) found that TMSs resulted in effective performance across diverse organizational settings. Similarly, Rau (2005) found a positive relationship between awareness of the location of expertise within management teams and an objective measure of performance. Finally, in a study of software development teams, Faraj and Sproull (2000) found a strong relation between expertise coordination and team performance.

TMS Development

Scholars have asserted that TMSs develop naturally as group members form awareness about each others' knowledge and expertise base and develop processes and routines for dividing and accessing information among them (Hollingshead, 1998a; Wegner, 1987). Brandon and Hollingshead (2004) identified three interdependent processes of TMS development: (1) team members must perceive that they are cognitively dependent on each other to perform their task; (2) they must develop knowledge structures linking specific tasks to expertise to group members – so called task-expertise-person units; and (3) they must reconcile these perceptions among the group members. When group members perceive dependence on each other for reaching goals, the development of a TMS begins with directory updating; group members start acquiring information about the knowledge and skills of the other members through self-disclosure or shared experiences and form knowledge structures representing the associations among task, expertise, and people (Brandon and Hollingshead, 2004; Wegner, 1995). The concept of directory updating can also be found in research on expertise recognition; studies in this area suggest that group members are able to indicate the individual with most expertise after a brief discussion period (Henry, 1995), and that this recognition and utilization of expertise is positively related to performance on a wide variety of tasks (Austin, 2003; Henry, 1995; Littlepage, Robinson, and Reddington, 1993; Stasser, Stewart, and Wittenbaum, 1995).

Studies indicate that active sharing of information about expertise early on in group development processes, facilitates the development of an effective TMS. In a study examining the encoding process of a TMS, Rulke and Rau (2000) found that in groups that had developed high quality TMSs, members declared expertise early during group interaction and increased the frequency of expertise evaluations over time. Similarly, in a study on the development of TMS in virtual teams, Kanawattanachai and Yoo (2007) found that the frequency and volume of task-oriented communications, particularly in the early stages of team development, were important for the development of expertise location and cognition-based trust.

It is not only actual expertise but also team members' perceptions about each other's expertise that influences the amount of specialization and diversification that occurs. If people perceive others to have expertise that is different from their own, they are more likely to focus on processing information from their own areas of expertise while trusting the others to take care of information from their areas of expertise (Hollingshead, 2000, 2001). Borgatti and Cross (2003) proposed and tested a model specifying four factors that influence the likelihood that an individual will seek information from another person: (1) awareness that the other has the knowledge; (2) the extent to which the knowledge is perceived as valuable; (3) the ability to timely access the knowledge from that person; and (4) the perceived costs involved in accessing the knowledge. These researchers found that the perceived knowledge and accessibility factors mediated the relationship between physical proximity and information seeking, while the cost factor did not.

Scholars have identified a variety of ways in which group members form an understanding of each others' expertise. Group members can self-disclose their expertise by communicating their qualifications and relevant experiences or by indicating their ignorance regarding a topic. Alternatively, team members can infer the expertise of their coworkers by monitoring their actions and judging their contributions. Finally, they can actively question and evaluate each others' expertise (Hollingshead, 1998a; Rulke and Rau, 2000). However, initial group interaction is not a necessary prerequisite for the development of a TMS. Moreland and Myaskovsky (2000) found that groups with members who were trained apart but who received information about one another's skills performed nearly as well as groups that had been trained together. Even in the case of no direct information regarding expertise, team members may use available stereotypes, such as gender roles, to infer expertise of others (Hollingshead and Fraidin, 2003). However, although stereotypes may in some instances provide basic information about a person's expertise, the benefits of using such highly inferential information may easily become overshadowed by its drawbacks. In particular, research from the social identity tradition indicates that relying merely on stereotypes may result in the development of subgroup biases and suboptimal team performance arising from inaccurate perceptions (van Knippenberg, De Dreu, and Homan, 2004).

The existence of an initially varied distribution of expertise in teams facilitates the development of a TMS (Lewis, 2004). Hollingshead (2001) argued that when team members perceive their own expertise to differ from those of others, they are encouraged to specialize even more by gathering additional knowledge and skills in their own field of expertise while leaving information outside of their specialization area to be processed by other team members. The reasoning behind this is that information can be most efficiently processed and stored by the team member who is most knowledgeable regarding that specific type of information. Therefore, responsibility for information elements is implicitly or explicitly allocated to the member who is perceived to have most expertise with regard to that specific information (Hollingshead, 2001; Wittenbaum, Stasser, and Merry, 1996). In this way, over time the initial transactive memory structure deepens as team members increasingly differentiate their knowledge and each member specializes in his or her area of expertise (Hollingshead, 2001; Wegner, 1995). In a longitudinal study of knowledge–worker teams, Lewis (2004) examined how TMSs emerge and develop over time. She found that initially distributed expertise, member familiarity, and frequent face-to-face communication supported the development of TMSs. In another study, Lewis (2005) investigated if groups may also develop TMSs that facilitates group learning beyond the basic transfer of concrete knowledge from one task to a similar other task (i.e., single loop learning). She found that after experience with several tasks, groups TMSs include abstract principles that facilitate the generalization of team knowledge from one task domain to another across distinct but related tasks (i.e., double loop learning).

Parallel to the development of knowledge directories specifying where knowledge is located within the group, the TMS is further extended by the formation of effective transactive *processes* (Lewis et al., 2007, Lewis et al., 2005). In enacting a TMS, group members develop standardized interaction routines in an attempt to facilitate the efficient allocation and accessing of knowledge from each other during ongoing task performance (Gersick and Hackman, 1990; Kanki, Folk, and Irwin, 1991). Research on the retrieval processes of TMSs suggests that apart from verbal communications, nonverbal and paralinguistic communications, referring to the manner in which something is communicated rather than the actual meaning of the words, also play an important role in the effectiveness of transactive retrieval processes (Hollingshead, 1998b).

Antecedents of TMSs

Variables that can affect TMS development include communication, group size, social network, time, group members' tenure, group training, and turnover within the group (Moreland, 1999). Antecedents of TMSs were tested in a number of studies, all using Lewis' field scale. Akgün et al. (2005) found that team stability, team member familiarity, and interpersonal trust were positively related to the development of TMSs in new product development teams. Lewis (2004) also found that initially distributed expertise was positively related to the emergence of a TMS and that this effect was even stronger if members were familiar with each other. In a study of daycare workgroups, Peltokorpi and Manka (2008) found that interpersonal communication, group potency, supportive supervision, and self-reported group performance were positively related to the group's TMS, and that variability in TMS development mediated the relationships between those antecedent factors and group performance.

The personality composition of the team may also affect TMS development, especially regarding the extent to which team members actively share expertise-specific information, critically evaluate other members' expertise, and share and request information (Pearsall and Ellis, 2006; Rulke and Rau, 2000). For example, Pearsall and Ellis (2006) found that team members' dispositional assertiveness was positively related to the formation of TMSs. Using a team-level operationalization of personality constructs, De Vries, Van den Hooff, and De Ridder (2006) found that agreeableness in teams' communication styles was positively related to team members' willingness to share information, and teams' extraversion in communication style was positively related to individuals' eagerness and willingness to share information. As can be seen from the studies reported earlier, researchers have operationalized these predictor variables at different levels, leaving open the question of how individual-level traits translate to team-level factors that impact team-level TMS outcomes.

Another antecedent to the development of a TMS is the extent to which team members depend on each other for reaching their goals (Brandon and Hollingshead, 2004). Zhang and colleagues (2007) found that task interdependence, cooperative goal interdependence, and support for innovation were positively related to the quality of teams' TMSs in terms of differentiation, coordination, and credibility. In a study of dyads, Hollingshead (2001) employed an experimental design that enabled the comparison of four incentive systems that represented a continuum of outcome interdependence, ranging from a condition in which the members only received points if both members recalled the information correctly (integration condition) to a condition in which the members received points only if one member recalled the information correctly (differentiation condition). Under the integration condition, participants were more likely to specialize in remembering different information than their partners, whereas under the integration condition participants were more likely to remember the same information.

Some scholars have applied computational modelling to logically validate propositions regarding the antecedents of TMSs. For instance, Choi and Robertson (2008) found that communication quantity and the existence of a social network in the form of a referral network were positively related to TMS consensus, while group size was negatively related to this particular outcome. Palazzolo and colleagues (2006) tested a model in which communication density mediated the relationship between initial and final transactive memory states. These researchers found that the starting knowledge level of individual members was negatively related to TMS development because of decreased communication density, whereas accuracy of expertise recognition was positively related to TMS development because of its facilitating effect on future communicative interactions. Overall team size was negatively related to TMS development. Palazzolo and colleagues (2006) argued that this may be due to people's cognitive limitations; that is, it may be more difficult to become familiar and cognitively acquainted with all members of a large group versus a smaller group. Relatedly, Ren, Carley, and Argote (2006) found that larger groups and groups functioning in more dynamic task and knowledge environments benefited more from "knowing what others know" than smaller groups and groups functioning in more stable environments.

Apart from the benefits of training team members collectively rather than apart, which are evident in many TMS studies (Lewis et al., 2005; Liang et al., 1995; Moreland et al., 1996; Moreland and Myaskovsky, 2000), specific team skills training may also facilitate the formation of a TMS. An experimental study by Pritchard and Ashleigh (2007) indicated that teams receiving team training aimed at the development of a range of skills including problem-solving, interpersonal relationships, goal setting, and role allocation developed higher-quality TMSs than teams that did not receive the skills training.

Finally, given that TMSs develop idiosyncratically in groups and TMS development is contingent on the expertise of group members, changes in group composition are generally found to be devastating to group performance (Lewis, 2003; Moreland et al., 1996, 1998). Moreover, when the composition of a team is changed, the old TMS structure may interfere with the development of a new TMS structure. Lewis et al. (2007, Study 1) found that groups that experienced partial membership changes retained the TMS communication structure observed at the outset, which resulted in ineffective TMS processes. In a follow up study they found that these detrimental effects could be overcome by actively encouraging the retained group members to reflect on their knowledge structures (Lewis et al., 2007, Study 2).

Measurement of TMSs

In studies of dyads, pertinent TMS constructs are often operationalized indirectly, inferred from the collective output of the dyad on memory tasks (Hollingshead, 1998a, 1998b, 2001; Wegner, 1987). The reasoning behind this approach is that the more information a pair of individuals is able to accurately recall, the higher the quality of their TMS. A comparison of recall performance of individual members with the collective recall performance of dyads allows researchers to disentangle the individual members' memory contributions from the collective memory component.

A wider variety of measurement techniques have been used to study TMSs in group settings than have been used in the study of dyadic TMSs. Lewis (2003) has distinguished among three methods for measuring group-level TMSs: recall measures, measures that capture observed behaviors, and self-report measures of group members' expertise.

Observation measures are based on the scoring by raters of behavior indicative of TMS functioning. Following the work of Moreland et al. (Liang et al., 1995; Moreland, 1999; Moreland and Myaskovsky, 2000) one method commonly applied entails the use of independent judges to provide overall ratings of the quality of each team's TMS, based on their observations of the quality and/or extent of memory differentiation, task coordination, and task credibility within the teams (e.g., Pritchard and Ashleigh, 2007; Rulke and Rau, 2000). Other researchers have coded the actual behaviors involved in the transactive memory processes. For instance, Ellis (2006) used additive indexes of the occurrence of directory updating, information allocation, and retrieval coordination behavior among the team members, while Rulke and Rau (2000) conducted a more fine-grained analysis of the encoding process of the TMS.

Researchers have also used self-report measures of TMSs. These measures have been in the form of Likert scale questionnaire measures that reflect the various dimensions of TMSs enumerated. Faraj and Sproull (2000), for example, developed a Likert scale item-based questionnaire measure for expertise coordination in which they asked participants to indicate if they knew how knowledge was distributed among the team members, how team members recognized when their expertise was needed, and the extent to which they brought their expertise to bear in a timely manner. Lewis (2003) developed and validated a questionnaire measure of TMS for use in field settings, consisting of 15 items covering her "knowledge specialization," "credibility," and "coordination" dimensions. Given its ease of administration, this instrument has been adopted in a growing number of field (e.g., Michinov et al., 2008;

Peltokorpi and Manka, 2008; Zhang *et al.*, 2007) and experimental (Pearsall and Ellis, 2006; Pearsall, Ellis, and Stein, 2009) studies.

Another form of self-report measures, known as expertise identification measures, have been used mainly in field studies of teams. Adopting this method, researchers start with an analysis of the field and interviews with field experts to formulate a list of possible areas of expertise, knowledge, or skills. Then team members are asked to indicate from this list their own and their team members' areas of expertise. Measures of the group's knowledge stock are calculated by aggregating the fields of expertise of all individual team members, and team TMS consensus is calculated by assessing the level of agreement concerning the location of expertise within the team (e.g., Austin, 2003; Rau, 2005; Rulke *et al.*, 2000; Yuan, Fulk, and Monge, 2007).

Contingency Variables

Finally, some researchers have started to analyze the factors that influence under what circumstances a TMS is more or less important for team performance. Akgün *et al.* (2005) found that task complexity moderated the relationship between TMS and product success, such that when tasks were more complex, the positive effect of a TMS on product success was higher than when tasks were less complex. Rau (2005) found that the level of relationship conflict in teams moderated the effect of awareness of the location of expertise within a team on team performance. Awareness of expertise location had a positive effect on performance under low levels of relationship conflict, but had an insignificant effect under high levels of relationship conflict.

In an experimental study, Ellis (2006) found that acute stress negatively affected the functioning of teams' TMSs. However, a subsequent experimental study by Pearsall, Ellis, and Stein (2009) indicated that not all types of stress are detrimental to team performance. Hindrance stressors – demands or circumstances that interfere with work achievement and are associated by team members with negative outcomes – negatively affect a team's TMS, whereas challenge stressors – demands or circumstances that are associated by team members with potential gains – exert a positive effect on the team's TMS.

Future Directions

As becomes clear from the above review, several authors have indicated that a TMS consists of transactive memory knowledge structures as well as transactive processes (Hollingshead, 2001; Lewis, 2003; Wegner *et al.*, 1985). However, much remains unclear regarding the relationship between these two components. In empirical studies, researchers generally have not made a distinction between process and knowledge components, but instead have included both together under the rubric of TMS. However, although interrelated, they clearly constitute separate factors; as Lewis and coauthors indicated, "TMS structure and processes operate synergistically within a group's TMS, but in distinctly different ways, with TMS structure providing the initial guidance for transactive processing" (p. 162). Future studies could usefully further assess the relative importance of these components and their interactive effects in the effective functioning of TMSs. Furthermore, apart from the developmental aspects, most scholars have considered the TMS notion as a relatively stable construct. Contextual variables that may vary over time are generally not explicitly taken into account, although studies by Ellis (2006) and Pearsall and colleagues (2009) indicate that TMSs may be affected in the short term by contextual factors such as team stress. This implies a need for further work to explore the interplay between the enduring properties of TMSs and situational variables that might moderate their effects on team processes and outcomes.

Finally, several scholars have alluded to the distinctions and overlap between the shared mental models concept and the TMS concept. In their review of research and theory on teams in organizations, Ilgen et al. (2005) observed that these two constructs, which dominate the recent literature on team cognition, ironically point to opposing conclusions regarding integration and differentiation of knowledge within the team. Whereas work on shared mental models emphasizes the benefits that can be gained from having overlapping knowledge among team members, the literature on TMSs emphasizes the advantages of diversification of the team's knowledge base. Other scholars, however, have pointed to the similarities between the two concepts. Mohammed and Dumville (2001) argued that the notion of shared mental model is the broader concept that encompasses aspects of the transactive memory construct. Moreover, several scholars have noted the similarity between what Cannon-Bowers and colleagues (2003) referred to as team member mental models and the "knowing who knows what" component of a TMS (Austin, 2003; Kerr and Tindale, 2004). We agree that shared mental models and TMSs are partly overlapping; however, the relationship between the two constructs may be more complex in the sense that they could also have interactive effects on performance and that they could be causally related concepts (Brandon and Hollingshead, 2004; Ellis, 2006; Lewis, 2003). A TMS and shared mental models could reinforce each other such that a TMS will be more effective when team members also hold similar mental models. On the other hand, under some circumstances they could be supplementary in that it may suffice for a team to have either a TMS or shared mental models to facilitate team information processing. Finally, longitudinal studies may clarify if the existence of shared mental models may facilitate the development of a TMS in a team and vice versa. Empirical studies on the relationship between these two central team cognition constructs could further the formation of a more complete understanding of the cognitive structures and processes that are important for effective team functioning.

While teams researchers have focused intently on understanding more about the shared cognitive constructs of mental models and transactive memory, a third, less-prevalent team-level construct has been defined and described in extant literature: TSA. We next turn to a review of the work on TSA for three central reasons. First, existing work suggests that the concept of TSA is similar to and yet distinctive from shared mental models and TMSs, particularly concerning its role in team adaptability in dynamic environments. Second, most theorizing about TSA has been published in extant literatures not routinely accessed by many team researchers; by including a review of the concept here, we hope to increase the accessibility of this literature to those researchers. Finally, and of related concern, knowledge about SA has been pioneered by researchers focusing outside the team context; our understanding of TSA could be greatly broadened with more team-level empirical research and specification. We hope here to foster more interest in the concept among researchers of groups and teams.

TEAM SITUATION AWARENESS

Even though various scholars have alluded to the crucial role of TSA in adaptive team performance (Burke *et al.*, 2006; Cooke *et al.*, 2000; Orasanu, 1990), unlike shared mental models and TMSs, there is only a scant empirical record of this concept.

Whereas mental models are cognitive representations of the general functioning of a system, SA refers to the knowledge and understanding of a dynamic system at a specific point in time (Durso and Gronlund, 1999; Endsley, 1995). As such, it refers to a more ephemeral and transitive type of knowledge that is developed while engaging in task performance – and one that is constantly being updated and recreated subject to changes in the task situation and performance requirements (Adams, Tenney, and Pew, 1995; Fracker and Vidulich, 1991). Correspondingly, scholars have referred to TSA as a team's awareness and understanding of a complex and dynamic situation at any point in time (e.g., Endsley, 1995; Salas, *et al.*, 1995). The concept of TSA is closely related to the notion of team situation models, which are defined by Rico and colleagues as "dynamic, context-driven mental models concerning key areas of the team's work" (2008: 164), and that have been characterized by Cooke and colleagues (2000, p. 157) as team knowledge that is "in a constant state of flux."

Because a team's ability to form an appropriate understanding of the task environment plays an important role in its adjustment to unanticipated events, the concept of TSA is crucial for understanding the sustained performance and viability of teams (Ancona, 1990; Ancona and Caldwell, 1992; Burke *et al.*, 2006) and the organizations in which they function (Bourgeois, 1985; Daft and Weick, 1984; Eisenhardt, 1989). Particularly for teams functioning in high-reliability organizations, the timely recognition of cues signaling non-routine situations, and the incorporation of those cues in the collective team-level representations, is pivotal to safe and efficient operations (Waller, 1999; Weick, Sutcliffe, and Obstfeld, 2005). Accordingly, scholars have emphasized the importance of achieving and maintaining an adequate understanding of the situation in a variety of fields including medicine (Gaba, Howard, and Small, 1995); Helmreich and Schaefer, 1994), aviation (Endsley, 1995; Mosier and Chidester, 1991; Orasanu, 1990), nuclear power plant operations (Hogg et al., 1995; Sebok, 2000; Waller et al., 2004), military command-and-control (Kaempf et al., 1996), and railroad operations (Roth, Multer, and Raslear, 2006). In order to clarify the concept of TSA, we first briefly introduce the general concept of SA as it has been developed at the individual level. Then we explain the different ways scholars have conceptualized TSA at the team level. We describe its relation to shared mental models and briefly describe measurement methods scholars have applied to this more ephemeral form of team cognition. Finally, we provide a short overview of the few empirical studies that have been conducted on TSA.

Conceptualization

The concept of SA developed in the field of aviation, where it was used to explain the superior performance of some fighter pilots during World War I (Endsley, 1995). Because several studies indicate that a breakdown in SA constituted an important factor in many aviation accidents (Endsley, 1988; Jentsch et al., 1999; Salas et al., 1995), it is not surprising that SA has continued to receive much attention among aviation psychologists and in the related field of Human Factors.

The most widely cited definition of SA is given by Endsley as "the perception of the elements in the environment within a volume of time and space, the comprehension of their meaning, and the projection of their status in the near future" (Endsley, 1988, p. 97). Endsley thus considered SA to be composed of three hierarchical levels. The first level pertains to the perception of the individual elements in the environment, the second to the integration of the elements into a comprehension of the current situation, and the third to the projection and anticipation of future states. She posed SA as a central aspect of individual information processing, linking attention and perception of incoming information to decision making and action execution (Endsley, 1995).

Scholars have made a distinction between situation assessment, referring to the processes involved in acquiring and maintaining an understanding of the situation (i.e., perception, comprehension, and projection), and the situation awareness that encompasses the resulting knowledge or awareness of the situation (Sarter and Woods, 1991). Situation assessment is considered a goal-directed process (e.g., Durso and Gronlund, 1999; Endsley, 1995; Sarter and Woods, 1991). It involves more than merely being conscious of, and attending to, the environment; instead, it implies an active assessment of the environment with respect to specific goals (Smith and Hancock, 1995). Accordingly, SA, which constitutes the outcome of the situation assessment processes, has been referred to as a metagoal – an overriding goal that must be achieved before task goal completion is possible (Selcon and Taylor, 1991).

Situation assessment as a process bears close resemblance to the activities of scanning, interpretation, understanding, and action involved in sensemaking (Weick, 1995). Moreover, the result of situation assessment – SA – comes close to what Weick described as the substance of sensemaking, or the linkages between cues, frames, and connections. However, the situation assessment approach stands in contrast with Weick's sensemaking perspective in that he emphasizes the idiosyncratic and subjective nature of the processes of giving meaning to and constructing an understanding of the situation, while scholars studying SA have often implicitly assumed the existence of an optimal or "true" referent to which a person's or team's situational understanding can be compared (see, e.g., Endsley, 1995; Mosier and Chidester, 1991).

Emergent Aspects of TSA

Although TSA is generally considered as an emergent phenomenon originating from the SA of the individual members, different specifications exist concerning how this higher level phenomena is shaped and constrained by its lower-level constituents (Chan, 1998; Kozlowski and Klein, 2000). Wellens (1993) and Endsley (1995) conceptualized TSA as the distribution and overlap of the SA of the individual team members. They argued that optimal TSA could be obtained by the separation of the responsibilities for SA of the team members in such a way that it maximizes the coverage of the relevant environment while at the same time leverages sufficient overlap to ensure efficient group coordination. Hence, according to this view, optimal TSA strikes a balance between the differentiation and integration of team members' personal awareness of the situation.

Others, however, have argued that TSA can not be fully captured by the aggregation or overlap of the individual team members' knowledge, but instead must also involve team interaction processes such as communication, coordination, task allocation, and planning (Salas et al., 1995; Schwartz, 1990). Cooke et al. (2000, 2001) proposed the concept of holistic TSA, which arises when team processes transform the knowledge of the individual team members into effective collective knowledge. They asserted that this holistic team-level understanding does not reside with the individual team members, nor can it be conceptualized as a collection of individual knowledge; rather, they maintained, it constitutes the knowledge on which the team's actions are based.

Some authors have adopted a more top–down, systems approach that considers how collectives form and maintain overall SA of dynamic systems (Artman and Garbis, 2004; Artman and Waern, 1999; Heath and Luff, 1992). These scholars build on Hutchins' (1991, 1995) notion of distributed cognition which takes the joint cognitive system as the focal point of analysis. In line with the sociotechnical system approach (Trist and Bamforth, 1951), cognition is considered to be an embedded property of the cognitive system – the collection of individuals plus the available technology – and not merely a compilation of the cognition of individual team members. Therefore, studies from a distributed cognition perspective often consist of case studies that describe how TSA is maintained in specific naturalistic settings, such as cockpits, control rooms, or medical dispatch centres (Artman and Waern, 1999; Blandford and Wong, 2004; Heath and Luff, 1992; Hutchins, 1995). Particular emphasis is placed on the role of structural aspects, supportive technology, and artifacts in understanding how SA is represented and propagated through the system (Artman and Garbis, 1998). For example, Roth et al. (2006) described how in railroad operations, employees developed a variety of informal cooperative strategies that enhanced overall system safety by improving shared SA. The strategies used included alerting others of unusual or unexpected conditions and overhearing or overseeing activities of others. The use of open communication channels that could be sampled by all members of the system played an important role in enabling informational redundancy.

Distributed TSA

Other scholars have emphasized the distributed aspects of TSA, acknowledging that by distributing SA responsibilities among their members, teams can reach broader coverage of the task environment and potentially locate and process more task relevant information (Endsley, 1995; Stanton et al., 2006; Wellens, 1993). In order to maximize the extent to which they are able to gain awareness coverage of their relevant task environment, teams may distribute their situation assessment function among the different members by spatially or functionally splitting up their task environment and assigning responsibility for each subsection to a different member (Artman, 1999, 2000). For example, teams may spatially split up their task environment, as is the case in air traffic control (i.e., individuals monitor different geographic sectors), or team members may be assigned responsibility for different functional aspects, as may be the case in fire fighting teams (i.e., some members may attend to the fire while others keep track of victims involved in the incident). On the other hand, by maintaining overlapping areas of responsibility, teams can attain redundancy, which may increase the probability that important information will become noticed by at least one member (Hollenbeck et al., 1995). Particularly in environments requiring high levels of vigilance, the cost of missing pieces of information may be higher than the costs of functional redundancy.

Apart from a horizontal, geographical, or functional distribution, teams may also decide to adopt a vertical distribution of TSA tasks. Stanton and colleagues (2006) theorized that distributed SA may entail different individuals being involved in different levels of SA; some individuals may be engaged in task perception, some in comprehension and others in projection. For example in military organizations, although a large number of people may span the boundary with the external environment, only a small group of people at the top of the organizational hierarchy may be involved in the actual interpretation of the organizational environment (see Kaempf et al., 1996 for an example). This, however, summons the classical dilemma between central command and distributed responsibility; is it better for teams to hold one central person responsible or to make all team members responsible for maintaining overall awareness of the situation? On the one hand, in complex situations, individual members may quickly become overloaded with information, making it difficult to maintain SA. On the other hand, assigning overall SA tasks to some members may free up cognitive resources from other members, thereby allowing them to fully concentrate on executing other tasks.

Particularly in high-workload situations, it may be beneficial for teams if one individual with a cognitively central position within the group is responsible for compiling and keeping active the higher-order situational knowledge. Studies on the role of working memory in the formation of SA suggest that the availability of sufficient attentional resources is crucial for forming and maintaining SA (Carretta, Perry, and Ree, 1996; Endsley, 1995; Gugerty and Tirre, 2000). For instance, in a study investigating 311 civilian aircraft accidents, Jentsch et al. (1999) found that captains were significantly more likely to lose SA when flying themselves then when the first officer was flying. This indicates that the additional workload involved in flying the aircraft negatively affected the ability to maintain SA. Similarly, Bigley and Roberts (2001) observed that for members of temporary response organizations, "the cognitive or perceptual requirements of particular tasks can be so demanding that individuals performing them are not able to maintain an awareness of the surrounding system" (p. 1291). These authors found that in such cases, responsibilities for SA were shifted to someone in a better position and with sufficient cognitive resources to build and maintain an overall understanding.

Awareness of Other Members

TSA does not exclusively relate to the external task environment; it may also include awareness of the team's internal situation or, in other words, understanding of the current status and needs of the other team members (Endsley, 1995; Marks and Panzer, 2004). Scholars have addressed this internal aspect of

TSA using labels such as shared workspace awareness (Gutwin and Greenberg, 2004), mutual awareness (Artman and Waern, 1999), and mutual organizational awareness (Macmillan, Entin, and Serfaty, 2004). However, because a proliferation of different terms for similar constructs may lead to confusion, we propose the basic distinction between *external TSA* – the awareness and understanding of the task environment and *internal TSA* – the awareness of the current status and needs of the team and the team members. Note that this division runs parallel to distinction between *teamwork mental models* – knowledge about the team's structure and about characteristics of the other team members – and *taskwork mental models* – knowledge about task processes, strategies, and likely scenarios of the task system that the team faces.

Whereas most studies and theories have focused on external TSA, some processes have been related to internal TSA. For example, Heath and colleagues noted the importance of rendering activities visible in order to facilitate the development of internal TSA (Heath and Luff, 1992; Heath *et al.*, 2002). By rendering visible selective aspects of their activities, team members encourage others to pay attention to features of their task that become potentially relevant to others. Although this ascribes a relatively passive role to the observer, others have pointed to the more active process of team monitoring, or "observing the activities and performance of other team members" (Dickinson and McIntyre, 1997, p. 25), in maintaining internal TSA. In a study with teams performing in a simulated flight simulation, Marks and Panzer (2004) found that team monitoring was positively correlated with both coordination and feedback processes, which in turn improved team performance. There is thus some indirect evidence for the relationship between internal team SA and team performance; however, apart from a few studies, a coherent framework of the activities, processes, and technological devices team members may apply to maintain and understand the internal status of the team is still lacking.

The Relationship between Shared Mental Models and TSA

Although no study has yet been undertaken to directly address the relationship between shared mental models and TSA, research at the individual level indicates that team members' mental models play an important role in the development of TSA for two main reasons (Stout, Cannon-Bowers, and Salas, 1994). First, mental models influence the content of TSA. Because mental models focus attention onto specific aspects of the situation and determine how this information becomes interpreted (Endsley, 1995; Mogford, 1997; Sarter and Woods, 1991), team members' mental models determine to a considerable extent how team members understand the task situation at any point in time. Second, mental models facilitate the development of TSA. Because the maintenance, integration, and projection of information take place in working memory, the ability to concurrently store and operate using different pieces of information is considered to be the main bottleneck for acquiring and maintaining SA (Fracker and Vidulich, 1991; Wickens, 1984). Therefore, scholars have argued that mental models facilitate the attainment of SA by diminishing the load on working memory capacity (for a review see Durso and Gronlund, 1999). For example, Sohn and Doane (2004) conducted an experiment investigating the relative effects of working memory and memory retrieval structures – essentially a basic type of mental model – on flight SA. They demonstrated that individuals who had acquired retrieval structures through experience in a particular domain could use these structures to take the load necessary for acquiring SA off working memory capacity. The quality of the retrieval structures of experienced pilots emerged as a better predictor for SA than their working memory capacity.

The relationship between mental models and SA however is not unidirectional; rather, as argued by Waller and Uitdewilligen (2009), team members' momentary understandings of the situation can evoke and shape particular cognitive structures. For example, when a situation is perceived as a crisis, team members access different mental models from those accessed when they perceive a situation as serious but routine. Adams and colleagues (1995) nicely depicted this iterative process using Neisser's (1976) model of the perceptual cycle. This model shows how cognitive structures – mental models – influence what aspects of the environment people explore, which determines the type of information that becomes available from the environment – SA – which in turn modifies the original cognitive structures, and so on.

The aforementioned close relationship between individual-level mental models and SA leads us to speculate how shared mental models and TSA relate to each other at the team level. First, it is likely that if team members share an understanding regarding how aspects of the environment, task, and team function in general, they are also more likely to construe a common understanding of the task and team situation at a specific point in time. Second, as argued above, to the extent that mental models direct team members' focus of attention and interpretation processes, similarity in mental models may lead members to focus on similar information sources and draw similar interpretations from them. This in turn may aid rapidity of response, but also increase the danger of collective myopia. Conversely, highly divergent mental models may lead to a wider sampling of environmental information and a wide variety of interpretations, which may lead to more complete and more elaborate TSA. On the other hand, this may pose a greater burden of information processing on the team as a whole, leading to conflicting and ambiguous understanding. However, as research integrating these team cognitive structure concepts is still lacking, statements about how they relate to each other remain speculative. For example, does similarity in mental models always lead to similarity in TSA? And, can similar TSA also trigger different mental models in different team members? More research is needed on how characteristics of a teams' shared mental models – accuracy, similarity, complexity – relate to characteristics of their TSA.

Measures of TSA

One reason for the scarcity of studies on TSA is probably the difficulty involved in developing assessment methods that take into account the dynamic nature of the concept (Cooke et al., 2000). Another explanation can be found in the challenge of deriving meaningful team-level variables from individual-level SA indicators. At the individual level, a variety of methods has been developed for assessing SA, including questionnaires, query measures, implicit performance measures, and behavioral checklists (Cooke et al., 2001; Durso and Gronlund, 1999; Endsley, 1995b). Dynamic aspects of SA can be assessed by repeatedly administering measures over time. Team-level SA measures may be constructed from these individual measures by creating collective indexes – for instance, on the basis of aggregated accuracy, similarity, or distribution. Alternatively, some authors have argued that TSA should be directly assessed as a holistic team-level situation understanding; by targeting measures to the team as a whole instead of to each member separately (Cooke et al., 2000; Hogg et al., 1995). However, when team tasks have conjunctive or disjunctive properties (Steiner, 1972), it may very well be the SA of the best or worst performing team member that drives team performance (Endsley, 1995b; Sebok, 2000).

Questionnaires measures often consist of Likert scale questions with which participants or observers are directly questioned about situation assessment quality (e.g., Taylor, 1990). They can be administered during and/or after task performance. A disadvantage of administering SA questionnaires after a task has been completed is that respondents may confuse SA with task performance outcomes. Moreover, SA questionnaires have often been developed for specific domains – mainly pilot performance and air traffic control – and hence may not directly be generalizable to other settings.

Query measures assess the extent to which participants are aware of task relevant information at a specific point in time. Questions about the present or anticipated future state of the situation are administered, while the simulation is frozen at random moments. For instance, in the case of the Situation Awareness Global Assessment Technique (SAGAT) technique developed by Endsley (1995), a simulator task is stopped at random points and information about the task is collected from operators while they answer the SA questions. SA accuracy is subsequently measured by comparing the answers of the operators with objective data registered by the simulator (computer), and SA similarity can be assessed by comparing the answers of the different team members (Bolstad et al., 2005; Cooke et al., 2001). An advantage of this method is that by repeatedly administering queries, researchers can develop a dynamic picture of TSA as it develops over time. The main disadvantage, however, is the intrusiveness of the method. Because the task has to be stopped every time queries are administered, the measurement often interferes with the natural execution of the task. This makes administration of the method problematic particularly in field settings, as it is rarely possible to interrupt a task in order to administer a measurement. Moreover, after the first round of queries, participants may anticipate the queries that follow, and the questions may focus participants on aspects of the task to which they would otherwise not attend. Finally, assessment of the accuracy of team members' SA is only possible if objectively correct answers to the queries can be determined. For lower levels of SA that refer to simple facts about the situation, this will not be problematic; however, for higher levels of SA that refer to interpretations about the situation, it may not always be possible to determine the "true situation."

Implicit measures assess SA indirectly by scoring behavior or performance on tasks or subtasks which are selected or constructed specifically to require SA in order to be successfully accomplished (Cooke and Gorman, 2006; Dwyer *et al.*, 1997; Patrick *et al.*, 2006). However, although this method allows researchers to induce the quality of TSA, it does not provide any information about the content of team member's SA nor does it provide a dynamic picture of TSA over time.

Another method that may be particularly suited to assess TSA is content analysis applied to the content of team communications obtained by video, audio, and/or written text recordings (Langan-Fox, Anglim, and Wilson, 2004; Waller *et al.*, 2004; Waller and Uitdewilligen, 2009). This approach provides the type of data amenable to continuous measurement, and can capture the dynamic and continuous nature of the TSA construct. Although communication is only an indirect measure of team members' knowledge and is therefore not likely to cover the complete content of awareness of the individual team members, it does nevertheless include those aspects deemed appropriate to share in an open forum. Hence, coding and analyzing the content of team communications should enable researchers to gain insights into the process of collective sensemaking.

Empirical Studies

As we mentioned before, the number of studies directly assessing TSA is low. Studies that do assess TSA generally are exploratory in nature and have small sample sizes. Here, we simply give a summation of the results that have been found in these studies. In a study investigating two person pilot crews, Prince *et al.* (2007) found that an observer-based measure of TSA accuracy administered during a high-fidelity simulation as well as a TSA measure collected in a preceding low-fidelity scenario were significantly correlated with performance scores of the teams on the high-fidelity simulation. In a study using a synthetic team training task in which three person teams learned to operate an uninhabited air vehicle, Cooke *et al.* (2001) found that TSA accuracy and similarity, measured by queries regarding mission progress that were randomly administered during the mission, were positively correlated with team performance. In a simulation study using a query measure of TSA, Bolstad *et al.* (2005) found that frequency of communication among team members and a social network measure of physical distance predicted TSA similarity. Hogg *et al.* (1995) developed a query measure of TSA specifically for nuclear power plant control rooms, which they administered holistically – to the team as a whole instead of separately to each member. They found that scores on this TSA measure accurately reflected the difficulty of different types of disturbances that were introduced into the simulation scenario; the more difficult the disturbances, the stronger the teams experienced a decrease in the accuracy of their TSA. In an experimental study using this same measure, Sebok (2000) compared TSA – operationalized as the average accuracy of the SA of the team members – in normal (four-person) with small (two-person) teams before and during system disturbances, under two interface conditions. The first interface condition was a "Conventional nuclear power plant interface condition", characterized by noncomputerized displays where operators' stations were located several meters apart. The second condition was an "advanced interface condition" characterized by computerized displays, large-screen overview display, and co-located seating arrangement. Although she did not find main effects for plant interface and team size, Sebok found an interaction effect indicating that normal sized teams had better TSA in the conventional plant interface condition while smaller teams had better TSA in the advanced interface condition.

Other studies have not directly assessed TSA but have focused on the processes in which teams engaged while forming an understanding of the situation. For instance, in a study of air traffic controllers, Hauland (2008) assessed team situation assessment behaviours using eye-movement data and found that during the handling of nonroutine events, team performance improved when the two operators simultaneously accessed information regarding future traffic. In a study of nuclear power plant control teams, Waller and colleagues (2004) found that the time team members spent engaging in team situation assessment behaviors was positively related to their ability to adapt to nonroutine events.

Future Directions

Although it is neither as mature nor as coherent as the literatures concerning shared mental models or TMSs, the existing work on team situational awareness may be more applicable to the dynamic, transitive nature of the turbulent environments facing many action teams. More work in the area needs to be done, both theoretically and empirically, to further understanding of how individuals' situational awareness translates to the team-level version of the construct. Through the integration of the various conceptualizations of team situational awareness and the critique of extant methods of assessment for operationalizing this potentially important concept, we hope our review here will help motivate such work.

ADAPTATION AND SHARED COGNITION

In our review of the recent literature on shared mental models, TMSs, and TSA, we have emphasized issues of adaptability in action teams facing dynamic environments. In this, the final section of our chapter, we suggest why these shared cognitive structures may not always facilitate adaptability in such teams, and we suggest two important moderators of the relationship between shared cognition and team adaptability. Specifically, we seek to address the question as to whether the shared cognitive structures so efficient under relatively stable or even moderately dynamic circumstances actually hinder teams' abilities to adapt to radically changing environments.

Shared Mental Models and Team Adaptation

In their cyclical model of team adaptation, Burke *et al.* (2006) emphasized the importance of shared mental models for the formulation and execution of new plans and strategies in novel environments. They stated that "[in] the absence of shared mental models adaptive team performance is not possible, because members do not have compatible views of equipment, tasks, and team member roles and responsibilities, which allow members to adapt proactively" (p. 1194). Similarly, Marks *et al.* (2001) posed that under high environmental dynamism, the positive relationship between mental model similarity and accuracy and team performance will be even more pronounced than under low degrees of environmental dynamism. In particular, they argued that when faced with novel nonroutine situations, similar and accurate mental models enable teams to engage in real-time interpretations of information and effective coordination. The results of their study support the reasoning that mental model similarity becomes more important for performance when teams operate in novel environments. Moreover, they found that a priori accuracy of team members' mental models was not very important in novel environments, leading them to suggest that teams with similar mental models would eventually form accurate ones as well.

However, scholars from other fields have pointed out that cognitive structures may function as barriers to radical change and lead to rigidity (Hodgkinson, 1997, 2005; Porac and Thomas, 1990; Reger and Palmer, 1996; Tushman, Newman, and Romanelli, 1986; Tushman and Romanelli, 1985).

Studies of mental model accuracy indicate that it is important for team functioning that the team's mental models appropriately represent the underlying structure of the environment (Cooke et al., 2001; Edwards et al., 2006; Lim and Klein, 2006). This implies that in a changing environment, alterations in the underlying structure of the environment should be matched with corresponding modifications in team members' mental models. Under low or moderate environmental dynamism, teams may adapt by making incremental changes to their mental models. Under extreme environmental dynamism, however, teams may need to completely redevelop their knowledge structures (Gersick, 1991). Because structures that may have been effective under previous circumstances may become dysfunctional in the new situation, failure to update team knowledge structures in a timely manner may lead to severe performance decrements (e.g., Weick, 1990, 1993). As March noted, "mutual learning has a dramatic long-run degenerate property under conditions of exogenous turbulence" (1991, p. 80).

More specifically, and as Cannon-Bowers et al. (1993) noted, if a threshold of similarity in mental models is surpassed, team's cognitive functioning may become overtly rigid; similarly, Klimoski and Mohammed noted that although often seen as functional, shared mental models may have a "dark side" as well (1994, p. 419). Mental models tend to be obstinate and enduring, and changes in mental models often lag behind changes in the environment (Fiske and Taylor, 1991; Hodgkinson, 1997, 2005; Reger and Palmer, 1996). Particularly when teams have successfully functioned in environments that have been stable for a relatively long period of time, their knowledge structures may become engrained and taken for granted, making them less amenable to change in the short term (Audia, Locke, and Smith, 2000; Lant, Milliken, and Batra, 1992; March, 1991).

The first phase of team adaptation is the recognition and interpretation of cues signalling a need for change, while the second phase is the formulation of plans and strategies to deal with the challenges of the changing environment (Burke et al., 2006; Waller, 1999). The effect of shared mental models on both phases of the adaptation processes is dubious. Concerning the first phase, because mental models guide perception and interpretation processes (Neisser, 1976; Starbuck and Milliken, 1988), similarity in mental models may cause team members to attend to similar situational cues and diagnose these cues in similar ways. As Walsh (1995: 281) noted in his review of work on strategic decision making, "[while] these knowledge structures may transform complex information environments into tractable ones, they may also blind strategy makers, for example, to important changes in their business environments, compromising their ability to make sound strategic decisions" (see also Zajac and Bazerman, 1991). Therefore, Cohen and Levinthal (1990) suggested that in order to evaluate and utilize outside knowledge under conditions of rapid and uncertain change, it is best to expose a fairly broad range of prospective "receptors" to the environment. Hence, teams with very similar mental models may fail to – or lack the absorptive capacity to – perceive and diagnose cues that fall out of the scope of their knowledge structures, and thereby miss early indications of upcoming environmental upheaval.

Concerning the second phase of team adaptation, the formulation of new and groundbreaking plans and strategy requires the kind of improvisation and creativity processes that are often associated more with cognitive diversity than with cognitive similarity (Bantel, 1994; Bantel and Jackson, 1989; Hoffman and Maier, 1961; Jehn et al., 1999). Diversity in underlying knowledge structures has been associated, if adequately managed, with the ability to generate a wide range of perspectives and alternative solutions and the tendency to engage in deep information processing to integrate these various viewpoints (Milliken and Martins, 1996; van Knippenberg et al., 2004). A thorough elaboration of perspectives and information is related to successful problem solving, the emergence of new insights (Jehn et al., 1999; Levine and Resnick, 1993), and a team's ability to reconsider assumptions and produce more creative and high-quality solutions (de Dreu and West, 2001; Nemeth, 1986). So, although similarity in mental models may lead to highly efficient team coordination processes, it may not be the optimal configuration for the adaptive planning processes teams require under extreme environmental change.

TMSs and Team Adaptation

Lewis states that "knowing whether the effects of a TMS persist in dynamic task environments is critical to understanding the real impact of TMSs in organizations" (2005, p. 581). Ren and colleagues (2006) found in a study using computational modeling that knowing "who knows what" is particularly important for groups' functioning in volatile task and knowledge environments. However, the functionality of a TMS seems to depend on the stability of the membership and expertise specialization within the team (Lewis, 2005).

Particularly under circumstances requiring team adaptation, team composition may be far from stable. For example, research on top management teams indicates increases in turnover under turbulent circumstances (Keck and Tushman, 1993; Wiersema and Bantel 1994) and teams in fast-response organizations may often have to engage in plug-and-play teaming, composing teams with those members who happen to be available at the time (Bigley and Roberts, 2001; Faraj and Xiao, 2006). Moreover, modest levels of turnover can be an optimal strategy for increasing exploration in the face of environmental turbulence (March, 1991). Finally, teams may bring in outsiders to challenge the status quo and increase the variety of perspectives the team can draw on when facing novel situations (Bogner and Barr, 2000; Choi and Levine, 2004).

Various studies of TMS show the detrimental effects of breaking up and re-arranging group membership (Lewis, 2003; Moreland, Argote, and Krishnan,

1996, 1998; Wegner *et al.*, 1991). More specifically, Lewis *et al.* (2007) found that when teams had partial membership loss, remaining members rigidly adhered to their previous TMS structures, which resulted in decreased performance.

Team Situation Awareness and Adaptive Performance

Numerous scholars have pointed to the pivotal role of an integrated representation and awareness of the important elements of the task environments for adaptive team performance (Bourgeois, 1985; Hogg, *et al.*, 1995; Waller *et al.*, 2004). Scholars have represented situation representations as knowledge structures that are subject to continuous transformations (Cooke *et al.*, 2000; Rico *et al.*, 2008; Salas *et al.*, 1995), as they are considered to "change with changes in the situation" (Cooke *et al.*, 2000, p. 154). However, studies about if and when teams actually update their situation representations given changes in the external environment are scarce (for an exception, see Waller and Uitdewilligen, 2009). Because of the important role the accuracy of team situation representations play in team functioning, it is of pivotal importance for teams to readjust their situation representations after significant changes in the environment (Burke *et al.*, 2006; Rico *et al.*, 2008). Studies on cognitive fixation suggest that people tend to stick to their original interpretations of situations even when faced with evidence disconfirming these interpretations (Einhorn and Hogarth, 1978; Lord, Ross, and Lepper, 1979). When a situation is defined in a particular way, people have a natural tendency to favour confirmatory information and discount or ignore discordant evidence (Einhorn and Hogarth, 1978).

Studies on attentional narrowing and cognitive tunnelling indicate that team members may become so preoccupied with a single aspect of the environment that they may fail to attend to other aspects and fail to update their SA (Huey and Wickens, 1993). For instance, in an incident described by Wiener *et al.* (1993), during a routine flight on the night of December 29, 1972, the pilot, first, and second officer of a Lockheed 1011 noted that the nose-landing gear light did not indicate "down and locked". In the ensuing moments, while the crew became so involved discussing the underlying causes and attempting to solve this problem, their attention was distracted from their instruments and they failed to notice a warning signal indicating a sudden drop in altitude. It was this failure to notice an unexpected change in a timely manner that eventually led to the crash of the aircraft. This is a telling example of how a team that formed an initially correct understanding of the situation became so preoccupied with their original understanding that they failed to notice significant changes that had taken place, necessitating an update of their SA. The example illustrates again the importance of taking into account the temporal aspects of team cognition; it is not the correct TSA at a single point in time but the frequent updating of TSA that is the key to adaptive team performance.

Flexibility

From our previous analysis, it appears that shared cognitive structures may facilitate as well as impede team adjustment to novel environments. However, work is lacking that would enable us to predict the help or hindrance of shared cognition in teams facing dynamic environments. *What would enable teams with shared cognitive structures to be flexible in radically changing environments – that is, to be able to quickly and accurately update not only their shared mental models, transactive memory, and team situation awareness, but update the assumptions on which these structures were created?* We propose that two sources of flexibility may help teams in these situations: flexibility embedded in the cognitive structures themselves, and flexibility in the team processes.

Burke *et al.* (2006) suggested that in the face of radical change, team members may require flexible mental models; however, not much is known about what may make knowledge structures particularly flexible or rigid. Some scholars have suggested that flexibility may depend on the structural aspects of the cognitive structures. For example, Weick's observation (1979) that loose coupling in structural configurations allows for adaptation and adaptability may hold not only for organizational but also for cognitive structures. Lyles and Schwenk (1992) proposed that loose coupling between core and peripheral features in cognitive structures facilitates organizational adaptation. Work by Yayavaram and Ahuja (2008) indicates that the structure by which different knowledge elements are coupled together or the way they are subdivided into different clusters may affect the ability to recombine knowledge elements for innovation.

Additionally, the level of abstraction of knowledge structures may be related to their adaptability to different task situations. At the highest level of abstraction, team members may develop a form of metacognitive knowledge, referring to an understanding of their cognitive structures and conditional knowledge that facilitates deciding on when and why to apply various cognitive actions (Doyle and Ford, 1998; Hinsz, 2004; Lorch, Lorch, and Klusewitz, 1993). For example, Lewis (2005) showed that when teams were trained in more than one task in the same domain, they developed a more abstract understanding of the task domain, enabling them to recognize common elements between tasks, which in turn facilitated the application of prior knowledge and expertise distribution structures to novel contexts.

Other scholars have looked at team processes that foster flexibility required for adaptive behavior. Whereas most studies on guided team self-corrections and reflexivity indicate that these processes are related to quality and similarity in team knowledge structures under relatively stable circumstances

(Blickensderfer *et al.*, 1997; Smith-Jentsch *et al.*, 2008), the extent to which a team explicates and overtly reflects on its objectives, processes, and strategies is also likely to positively influence the team's ability to adapt to more extreme environmental jolts (Gurtner *et al.*, 2007). For example, Lewis *et al.* (2007) found that when teams faced changes in membership, invoking reflexivity in team members helped prevent the rigid adherence to obsolete TMSs by the team members who were left behind. Finally, a study by Kray and Galinsky (2003) suggested that the activation of a counterfactual mindset – that is, focusing team members on what might have been and fostering the formation of alternative representations – may minimize cognitive rigidity resulting from the failure of groups to seek disconfirming information in respect of their initial hypothesis when engaged in problem solving tasks.

CONCLUSION

In this chapter, we have reviewed recent empirical and theoretical work on three types of shared cognition in teams: shared mental models, transactive memory systems and team situation awareness. We have focused this review in particular on aspects of shared cognition that affect the adaptability of teams facing dynamic, unpredictable task environments. Additionally, we have suggested that both the inherent structural characteristics of shared cognition and the reflexivity of teams moderate the influence these types of shared cognition have on team performance in such environments.

Our suggestions for future research are included in the body of the review at the end of each section, and we do not reiterate them here. However, our overall reading of the literature reviewed above reminded us of two important aspects concerning research collaboration in the groups and teams literature. First, and following an elegant call for such collaboration (Poole *et al.*, 2005), over the past several years researchers across several disparate academic fields have added much to our knowledge regarding shared cognition in teams, and many signs of cross-field collaboration have begun to appear. For example, the formation of INGRoup – the Interdisciplinary Network for Group Research – in 2006 has provided an annual means for groups' researchers across disciplines such as industrial/organizational psychology, social psychology, organizational behavior, and communication, to meet and explore new agendas and methods for studying team shared cognition and other issues in small group research. A quick perusal of the reference list included here will illustrate the need for such cross-disciplinary dialogue to continue in the area of shared cognition in teams. Such dialogue is particularly important regarding the consistent use of terminology concerning shared cognition in teams, which in turn will increase the ability of researchers to perform cross-study analyses and better summarize our knowledge in this area (Hodgkinson and Healey, 2008).

Additionally, as organizational environments become more complex and fast-paced, and as organizations turn to teams to successfully anticipate and react to these environments, researchers will be challenged to find increasingly accurate means to measure shared cognition and related behaviors in dynamic environments – either simulated or real. Developing better and more accurate measures will likely necessitate "an earnest dialogue with computer scientists and mathematicians who may have the tools necessary to aid us in automating the coding of behavioral data and detecting patterns of behavior in groups" (Ballard et al., 2008, p. 345). Ultimately, more precise measures may also lead to better cross-study comparison as well as information for the training of teams working in these environments. What an exciting time to be studying team cognition, when new developments in techniques and methods open up new opportunities to deepen our understanding of temporal and dynamic aspects of team cognition that hitherto have remained beyond the grasp of our knowledge.

REFERENCES

Abelson, R.P., & Black, J.B. (1986). Introduction. In J.A. Galambos, R.P. Abelson & J.B. Black (Eds), *Knowledge Structures* (pp. 1–18). Hillsdale, NJ: Lawrence Erlbaum Associates Publishers.

Adams, M.J., Tenney, Y.J., & Pew, R.W. (1995). Situation awareness and the cognitive management of complex systems. *Human Factors*, 37, 85–104.

Akgün, A.E., Byrne, J., Keskin, H., Lynn, G.S., & Imamoglu, S.Z. (2005). Knowledge networks in new product development projects: A transactive memory perspective. *Information and Management*, 42, 1105–20.

Ancona, D.G. (1990). Outward bound: Strategies for team survival in an organization. *Academy of Management Journal*, 33, 334.

Ancona, D.G., & Caldwell, D.F. (1992). Bridging the boundary: External activity and performance in organizational teams. *Administrative Science Quarterly*, 37, 634–61.

Arrow, H., McGrath, J.E., & Berdahl, J.L. (2000). *Small Groups as Complex Systems: Formation, Coordination, Development, and Adaptation*. Thousand Oaks, CA: Sage.

Artman, H. (1999). Situation awareness and co-operation within and between hierarchical units in dynamic decision. *Ergonomics*, 42, 1404–18.

Artman, H. (2000). Team situation assessment and information distribution. *Ergonomics*, 43, 1111–28.

Artman, H., & Garbis, C. (1998). *Situation awareness as distributed cognition*. Paper presented at the European Conference on Cognitive Ergonomics, Cognition and Cooperation, Limerick, Ireland.

Artman, H., & Waern, Y. (1999). Distributed cognition in an emergency co-ordination center. *Cognition, Technology and Work*, 1, 237–46.

Audia, P.G., Locke, E.A., & Smith, K.G. (2000). The paradox of success: An archival and a laboratory study of strategic persistence. *Academy of Management Journal*, 43, 837–53.

Austin, J.R. (2003). Transactive memory in organizational groups: the effects of content, consensus, specialization, and accuracy on group performance. *Journal of Applied Psychology*, 88, 866–78.

Ballard, D.I., Tschan, R., & Waller, M.J. (2008). All in the timing: Considering time at multiple stages of group research. *Small Group Research*, **39**, 328–51.

Banks, A.P., & Millward, L.J. (2000). Running shared mental models as a distributed cognitive process. *British Journal of Psychology*, **91**, 513–31.

Banks, A.P., & Millward, L.J. (2007). Differentiating knowledge in teams: The effect of shared declarative and procedural knowledge on team performance. *Group Dynamics: Theory, Research, and Practice*, **11**, 95–106.

Bantel, K.A. (1994). Strategic planning openness. *Group and Organization Management*, **19**, 406–24.

Bantel, K.A., & Jackson, S.E. (1989). Top management and innovations in banking: Does the composition of the top team make a difference? *Strategic Management Journal*, **10**, 107–24.

Bartunek, J.M., Gordon, J.R., & Weathersby, R.P. (1983). Developing "complicated" understanding in administrators. *Academy of Management Review*, **8**, 273–84.

Bettenhausen, K., & Murnighan, J.K. (1985). The emergence of norms in competitive decision-making groups. *Administrative Science Quarterly*, **30**, 350–72.

Bigley, G.A., & Roberts, K.H. (2001). The incident command system: High-reliability organizing for complex and volatile task environments. *Academy of Management Journal*, **44**, 1281–99.

Blandford, A., & William Wong, B.L. (2004). Situation awareness in emergency medical dispatch. *International Journal of Human-Computer Studies*, **61**, 421–52.

Blickensderfer, E., Cannon-Bowers, J.A., & Salas, E. (1997). Theoretical bases for team self correction: Fostering shared mental models. In M.M. Beyerlein, D.A. Jackson & S.T. Beyerlein (Eds), *Advances in Interdisciplinary Studies of Work Teams* (pp. 249–79). Greenwich, CT: JAI.

Blickensderfer, E., Cannon-Bowers, J.A., & Salas, E. (1998). Crosstraining and team performance. In J.A. Cannon-Bowers & E. Salas (Eds.)*Making Decisions under Stress: Implications for Individual and Team Training* (pp. 299–311). Washington, DC: American Psychological Association.

Bogner, W.C., & Barr, P.S. (2000). Making Sense in Hypercompetitive Environments: A Cognitive Explanation for the Persistence of High Velocity Competition. *Organization Science*, **11**, 212–26.

Bolstad, C.A., Cuevas, H.M., Gonsalez, C., & Schneider, M. (2005). *Modeling shared situation awareness*. Paper presented at the 14th Conference on Behavior Representation in Modeling and Simulation (BRIMS), Los Angeles, CA.

Borgatti, S.P., & Cross, R. (2003). A relational view of information seeking and learning in social networks. *Management Science*, **49**, 432–45.

Bourgeois, L.J. (1985). Strategic goals, perceived uncertainty, and economic performance in volatile environments. *Academy of Management Journal*, **28**, 548–73.

Brandon, D.P., & Hollingshead, A.B. (2004). Transactive memory systems in organizations: Matching tasks, expertise, and people. *Organization Science*, **15**, 633–44.

Burke, C.S., Stagl, K.C., Salas, E., Pierce, L., & Kendall, D. (2006). Understanding team adaptation: A conceptual analysis and model. *Journal of Applied Psychology*, **91**, 1189–207.

Cannon-Bowers, J.A., Salas, E., & Converse, S. (1993). Shared mental models in expert team decision making. In N.J. Castellan, Jr. (Ed.), *Individual and Group Decision Making* (pp. 221–46). Hillsdale, NJ: Lawrence Erlbaum Associates.

Cannon-Bowers, J.A., Tannenbaum, S.I., Salas, E., & Volpe, C.E. (1995). Defining competencies and establishing team training requirements. In R. Guzzo & E. Salas (Eds), *Team Effectiveness and Decision Making in Organizations* (pp. 333–80). San Fransisco: Jossey-Bass.

Cannon-Bowers, J.A., & Salas, E. (2001). Reflections on shared cognition. *Journal of Organizational Behavior*, 22, 195–202.

Carley, K.M. (1997). Extracting team mental models through textual analysis. *Journal of Organizational Behavior*, 18, 533–58.

Carretta, T.R., Perry, D.C., & Ree, M.J. (1996). Prediction of situational awareness in F-15 pilots. *International Journal of Aviation Psychology*, 6, 21–41.

Chan, D. (1998). Functional relations among constructs in the same content domain at different levels of analysis: A typology of composition models. *Journal of Applied Psychology*, 83, 234–46.

Chen, G., Thomas, B.A., & Wallace, J.C. (2005). A multilevel examination of the relationships among training outcomes, mediating regulatory processes, and adaptive performance. *Journal of Applied Psychology*, 90, 827–41.

Choi, H.S., & Levine, J.M. (2004). Minority influence in work teams: the impact of newcomers. *Journal of Experimental Social Psychology*, 40, 273–80.

Choi, T., & Robertson, P.J. (2008). Transactive memory systems and group performance: A simulation study of the role of shared cognition. *Academy of Management Proceedings*, (**0896-7911**), 1–6.

Clarkson, G.P., & Hodgkinson, G.P. (2005). Introducing Cognizer™: A comprehensive computer package for the elicitation and analysis of cause maps. *Organizational Research Methods*, 8, 317–41.

Cohen, W.M., & Levinthal, D.A. (1990). Absorptive capacity: A new perspective on learning and innovation. *Administrative Science Quarterly*, 35, 128–52.

Conant, R.C., & Ashby, R.W. (1970). Every good regulator of a system must be a model of that system. *International Journal of Systems Science*, 1, 89–97.

Cooke, N.J., & Gorman, J.C. (2006). Assessment of team cognition. In W. Karwowski (Ed.), *International Encyclopedia of Ergonomics and Human Factors*, 2nd (Ed.). Boca Raton, FL: CRC Press.

Cooke, N.J., Kiekel, P.A., & Helm, E.E. (2001). Measuring team knowledge during skill acquisition of a complex task. *International Journal of Cognitive Ergonomics*, 5, 297–315.

Cooke, N.J., Kiekel, P.A., Salas, E., Stout, R., Bowers, C., & Cannon-Bowers, J. (2003). Measuring team knowledge: A window to the cognitive underpinnings of team performance. *Group Dynamics: Theory, Research, and Practice*, 7, 179–99.

Cooke, N.J., Salas, E., Cannon Bowers, J.A., & Stout, R.J. (2000). Measuring team knowledge. *Human Factors*, 42, 151–73.

Cramton, C.D. (2001). The mutual knowledge problem and its consequences for dispersed collaboration. *Organization Science*, 12, 346–71.

Cronin, M.A., & Weingart, L.R. (2007). Representational gaps, information processing, and conflict in functionally diverse teams. *Academy of Management Review*, 32, 761–73.

Curseu, P.L., Schruijer, S., & Boros, S. (2007). The effects of groups' variety and disparity on groups' cognitive complexity. *Group Dynamics: Theory, Research, and Practice*, 11, 187–206.

Daft, R.L., & Weick, K.E. (1984). Toward a model of organizations as interpretation systems. *Academy of Management Review*, 9, 284–95.

Day, E.A., Arthur, W., Jr., & Gettman, D. (2001). Knowledge structures and the acquisition of a complex skill. *Journal of Applied Psychology*, 86, 1022–33.

De Dreu, C.K.W., & West, M. (2001). Minority dissent and team innovation: the importance of participation in decision making. *Journal of Applied Psychology*, 86, 1191–201.

De Vries, R.E., Van den Hooff, B., & De Ridder, J.A. (2006). Explaining knowledge sharing: The role of team communication styles, job satisfaction, and performance beliefs. *Communication Research*, **33**, 115–35.

Dickinson, T.L., & McIntyre, R.M. (1997). A conceptual framework for teamwork measurement. In C. Prince, M.T. Brannick & E. Salas (Eds), *Team Performance Assessment and Measurement: Theory, Methods, and Applications* (pp. 19–43). Mahwah, NJ: Lawrence Erlbaum Associates Publishers.

Doyle, J.K., & Ford, D.N. (1998). Mental models concepts for system dynamics research. *System Dynamics Review*, **14**, 3–30.

Driskell, J.E., Salas, E., & Johnston, J. (1999). Does stress lead to a loss of team perspective? *Group Dynamics: Theory, Research and Practice*, **3**, 291–302.

Druskat, V.U., & Pescosolido, A.T. (2002). The content of effective teamwork mental models in self-managing teams: Ownership, learning and heedful interrelating. *Human Relations*, **55**, 283–314.

Durso, F.T., & Gronlund, S.D. (1999). Situation awareness. In F.T. Durso (Ed.), *Handbook of Applied Cognition* (pp. 283–314). New York, NY: John Wiley & Sons Ltd.

Dwyer, D.J., Fowlkes, J.E., Oser, R.L., Salas, E., & Lane, N.E. (1997). Team performance measurement in distributed environments: The TARGETs methodology. In M.T. Brannick, E. Salas & C. Prince (Eds), *Team Performance Assessment and Measurement: Theory, Methods, and Applications* (pp. 137–53). Mahwah, NJ: Lawrence Erlbaum Associates, Inc.

Edwards, B.D., Day, E.A., Arthur, W., & Bell, S.T. (2006). Relationships among team ability composition, team mental models, and team performance. *Journal of Applied Psychology*, **91**, 727–36.

Einhorn, H.J., & Hogarth, R.M. (1978). Confidence in judgment: Persistence of the illusion of validity. *Psychological Review*, **85**, 395–416.

Eisenhardt, K.M. (1989). Making fast strategic decisions in high-velocity environments. *Academy of Management Journal*, **32**, 543–76.

Eisenhardt, K.M., & Tabrizi, B.N. (1995). Accelerating adaptive processes: Product innovation in the global computer industry. *Administrative Science Quarterly*, **40**, 84–110.

Ellis, A.P.J. (2006). System breakdown: The role of mental models and transactive memory in the relationship between acute stress and team performance. *Academy of Management Journal*, **49**, 576–89.

Ellis, S., & Davidi, I. (2005). After-event reviews: Drawing lessons from successful and failed experience. *Journal of Applied Psychology*, **90**, 857–71.

Endsley, M.R. (1988). Design and evaluation for situation awareness enhancement. In *Proceedings of the Human Factors Society 32nd Annual Meeting* (pp. 97–101). Santa Monica, CA: Human Factors Society.

Endsley, M.R. (1995). Measurement of situation awareness in dynamic systems. *Human Factors*, **37**, 65–84.

Endsley, M.R. (1995b). Toward a theory of situation awareness in dynamic systems. *Human Factors*, **37**, 32–64.

Entin, E.E., & Serfaty, D. (1999). Adaptive team coordination. *Human Factors*, **41**, 312–25.

Espinosa, J.A., Lerch, F.J., & Kraut, R.E. (2004). Explicit versus implicit coordination mechanisms and task dependencies: One size does not fit all. In E. Salas & S.M. Fiore (Eds), *Team Cognition: Understanding the Factors that Drive Process and Performance* (pp. 107–29). Washington, DC: American Psychological Association.

Faraj, S., & Sproull, L. (2000). Coordinating expertise in software development teams. *Management Science*, **46**, 1554–68.

Faraj, S., & Xiao, Y. (2006). Coordination in fast-response organizations. *Management Science*, 52, 1155–69.

Fiske, S.T., & Taylor, S.E. (1991). *Social Cognition*, 2nd (Ed.). New York: McGraw-Hill.

Fleming, P.J., Wood, G.M., Gonzalo, F., Bader, P.K., & Zaccaro, S.J. (2003). *The locus of shared mental models: Whence does the sharedness come?* Paper presented at the 18th Annual Conference of the Society of Industrial and Organizational Psychology, Orlando, FL.

Fracker, M.L., & Vidulich, M.A. (1991). *Measurement of situation awareness: A brief review.* Paper presented at the 11th Congress of the International Ergonomics Association, Paris, France.

Fussell, S.R., & Krauss, R.M. (1989). The effects of intended audience on message production and comprehension: reference in a common ground framework. *Journal of Experimental Social Psychology*, 25, 203–19.

Gaba, D.M., Howard, S.K., & Small, S.D. (1995). Situation awareness in anesthesiology. *Human Factors*, 37, 20–31.

Gentner, D. & Stevens, A. (Eds) (1983). *Mental Models: Hillsdale*. Mahwah, NJ: Lawrence Erlbaum Associates Publishers.

Gersick, C. (1991). Revolutionary change theories: A multiple exploration of the punctuated equilibrium paradigm. *Academy of Management Review*, 16, 10–36.

Gersick, C.J.G., & Hackman, J.R. (1990). Habitual routines in task-performing groups. *Organizational Behavior and Human Decision Processes*, 47, 65–97.

Griffith, T.L., & Neale, M.A. (2001). Information processing in traditional, hybrid, and virtual teams: From nascent knowledge to transactive memory. In B.M. Staw & L.L. Cummings (Eds.), *Research in Organizational Behavior* (pp. 379–421). Greenwich, CT: JAI Press.

Gugerty, L.J., & Tirre, W.C. (2000). Individual differences in situation awareness. In M.R. Endsley & D.J. Garland (Eds), *Situation Awareness Analysis and Measurement* (pp. 249–76). Mahwah, NJ: Erlbaum.

Gurtner, A., Tschan, F., Semmer, N.K., & Nagele, C. (2007). Getting groups to develop good strategies: Effects of reflexivity interventions on team process, team performance, and shared mental models. *Organizational Behavior and Human Decision Processes*, 102, 127–42.

Gutwin, C., & Greenberg, S. (2004). The importance of awareness for team cognition in distributed collaboration. In E. Salas & S.M. Fiore (Eds), *Team Cognition: Understanding the Factors that Drive Process and Performance* (pp. 177–201). Washington, DC: American Psychological Association.

Hackman, J.R. (1987). The design of work teams. In J. Lorsch (Ed.), *Handbook of Organizational Behavior* (pp. 315–42). New York: Prentice Hall.

Hackman, J.R. (2003). Learning more by crossing levels: Evidence from airplanes, hospitals, and orchestras. *Journal of Organizational Behavior*, 24, 905–22.

Hackman, J.R., & Wageman, R. (2005). A theory of team coaching. *Academy of Management Review*, 30, 269–87.

Harrison, D.A., & Klein, K.J. (2007). What's the difference? Diversity constructs as separation, variety, or disparity in organizations. *Academy of Management Review*, 32, 1199–228.

Hauland, G. (2008). Measuring individual and team situation awareness during planning tasks in training of en route air traffic control. *International Journal of Aviation Psychology*, 18, 290–304.

Heath, C., & Luff, P. (1992). Collaboration and control: Crisis management and multimedia technology in London underground line control rooms. *Journal of Computer Supported Cooperative Work*, 1, 24–48.

Heath, C., Svensson, M.S., Hindmarsh, J., Luff, P., & vom Lehn, D. (2002). Configuring awareness. *Computer Supported Cooperative Work (CSCW)*, 11, 317–47.

Helmreich, R.L., & Schaefer, H.G. (1994). Team performance in the operating room. In M.S. Bogner (Ed.), *Human Error in Medicine* (pp. 225–53). Hillsdale, NJ: Lawrence Erlbaum Associates, Inc.

Henry, R.A. (1995). Improving group judgment accuracy: Information sharing and determining the best member. *Organizational Behavior and Human Decision Processes*, 62, 190–97.

Hinsz, V.B. (2004). Metacognition and mental models in groups: An illustration with metamemory of group recognition memory. In E. Salas & S.M. Fiore (Eds), *Team Cognition: Understanding the Factors that Drive Process and Performance* (pp. 33–58). Washington, DC: American Psychological Association.

Hinsz, V.B., Tindale, R.S., & Vollrath, D.A. (1997). The emerging conceptualization of groups as information processes. *Psychological Bulletin*, 121, 43–64.

Hodgkinson, G.P. (1997). Cognitive inertia in a turbulent market: The case of UK residential estate agents. *Journal of Management Studies*, 34, 921–45.

Hodgkinson, G.P. (2005). *Images of Competitive Space: A Study in Managerial and Organizational Strategic Cognition*. Basingstoke, UK: Palgrave Macmillan.

Hodgkinson, G.P., & Healey, M.P. (2008). Cognition in organizations. *Annual Review of Psychology*, 59, 387–417.

Hodgkinson, G.P., Maule, A.J., & Bown, N.J. (2004). Causal cognitive mapping in the organizational strategy field: a comparison of alternative elicitation procedures. *Organizational Research Methods*, 7, 3–26.

Hoffman, L., & Maier, N. (1961). Quality and acceptance of problem solutions by members of homogeneous and heterogeneous groups. *Journal of Abnormal and Social Psychology*, 62, 401–7.

Hogg, D.N., Folleso, K., Strand-Volden, F., & Torralba, B. (1995). Development of a situation awareness measure to evaluate advanced alarm systems in nuclear power plant control rooms. *Ergonomics*, 38, 2394–413

Hollenbeck, J.R., Ilgen, D.R., Tuttle, D.B., & Sego, D.J. (1995). Team performance on monitoring tasks: an examination of decision errors in contexts requiring sustained attention. *Journal of Applied Psychology*, 80, 685–96.

Hollingshead, A.B. (1998a). Communication, learning, and retrieval in transactive memory systems. *Journal of Experimental Social Psychology*, 34, 423–42.

Hollingshead, A.B. (1998b). Retrieval processes in transactive memory systems. *Journal of Personality and Social Psychology*, 74, 659–71.

Hollingshead, A.B. (2000). Perceptions of expertise and transactive memory in work relationships. *Group Processes and Intergroup Relations*, 3, 257–67.

Hollingshead, A.B. (2001). Cognitive interdependence and convergent expectations in transactive memory. *Journal of Personality and Social Psychology*, 81, 1080–89.

Hollingshead, A.B., & Fraidin, S.N. (2003). Gender stereotypes and assumptions about expertise in transactive memory. *Journal of Experimental Social Psychology*, 39, 355–63.

Huber, G.H.P., & Lewis, K. (2010). Cross understanding: Implications for group cognitions and performance. *Academy of Management Review*, 35.

Huey, B.M. & Wickens, C.D. (Eds) (1993). *Workload Transition: Implications for Individual and Team Performance*. National Research Council, Washington, D.C.: National Academy Press.

Hutchins, E. (1991). The social organization of distributed cognition. In L.B. Resnick, J.M. Levine & S.D. Teasley (Eds), *Perspectives on Socially Shared Cognition*, Vol. 13 (pp. 283–307). Washington, DC: American Psychological Association.

Hutchins, E. (1995). *Cognition in the Wild*. Cambridge, MA, US: The MIT Press.

Ilgen, D.R., Hollenbeck, J.R., Johnson, M., & Jundt, D. (2005). Teams in organizations: From input-process-output models to IMOI models. *Annual Review of Psychology*, 56, 517–43.

Jehn, K.A., Northcraft, G.B., & Neale, M.A. (1999). Why differences make a difference: A field study of diversity, conflict, and performance in workgroups. *Administrative Science Quarterly*, 44, 741–63.

Jentsch, F., Barnett, J., Bowers, C.A., & Salas, E. (1999). Who is flying this plane anyway? What mishaps tell us about crew member role assignment and air crew situation awareness. *Human Factors*, 41, 1–14.

Johansson, O., Andersson, J., & Rönnberg, J. (2000). Do elderly couples have a better prospective memory than other elderly people when they collaborate? *Applied Cognitive Psychology*, 14, 121–33.

Johnson, T.E., Lee, Y., Lee, M., O'Connor, D.L., Khalil, M.K., & Huang, X. (2007). Measuring sharedness of team-related knowledge: Design and validation of a shared mental model instrument. *Human Resource Development International*, 10, 437–54.

Johnson-Laird, P.N. (1983). *Mental Models: Toward a Cognitive Science of Language, Inference, and Consciousness*. Cambridge, MA: Harvard University Press.

Kaempf, G.L., Klein, G., Thordsen, M.L., & Wolf, S. (1996). Decision making in complex naval command-and-control environments. *Human Factors*, 38, 220–31.

Kanawattanachai, P., & Yoo, Y. (2007). The impact of knowledge coordination on virtual team performance over time. *MIS Quarterly*, 31, 783–808.

Kanki, B.G., Folk, V.G., & Irwin, C.M. (1991). Communication variations and aircrew performance. *International Journal of Aviation Psychology*, 1, 149–62.

Keck, S.L., & Tushman, M.L. (1993). Environmental and organizational context and executive team structure. *Academy of Management Journal*, 36, 1314–44.

Kellermanns, F.W., Floyd, S.W., Pearson, A.W., & Spencer, B. (2008). The contingent effect of constructive confrontation on the relationship between shared mental models and decision quality. *Journal of Organizational Behavior*, 29, 119–37.

Kerr, N.L., & Tindale, R.S. (2004). Group performance and decision making. *Annual Review of Psychology*, 55, 623–55.

Kieras, D.E., & Bovair, S. (1984). The role of a mental model in learning to operate a device. *Cognitive Science*, 8, 255–73.

Kleinman, D.L., & Serfaty, D. (1989). Team performance assessment in distributed decision-making. In R. Gibson, J.P. Kincaid & B. Goldiez (Eds), *Proceedings of the Symposium in Interactive Networked Simulation for Training* (pp. 22–7). Orlando, FL: University of Central Florida, Institute for Simulation and Training.

Klimoski, R., & Mohammed, S. (1994). Team mental model: construct or metaphor? *Journal of Management*, 20, 403–37.

Kozlowski, S.W.J., Gully, S.M., Nason, E.R., & Smith, E.M. (1999). Developing adaptive teams: A theory of compilation and performance across levels and time. In D.R. Ilgen & E.D. Pulakos (Eds), *The Changing Nature of Performance: Implications for Staffing, Motivation, and Development* (pp. 240–92). San Francisco, CA: Jossey-Bass.

Kozlowski, S.W.J., Gully, S.M., Salas, E., & Cannon-Bowers, J.A. (1996). Team leadership and development: Theory principles, and guidelines for training leaders and teams. In M. Beyerlein, D. Johnson & S. Beyerlein (Eds), *Advances in Interdisciplinary Studies of Work Teams: Team Leadership*, Vol. 3 (pp. 251–89). Greenwich, CT: JAI Press.

Kozlowski, S.W.J., & Klein, K.J. (2000). A multilevel approach to theory and research in organizations: Contextual, temporal, and emergent processes. In K.J. Klein & S.W.J. Kozlowski (Eds), *Multilevel Theory, Research, and Methods in Organizations: Foundations, Extensions, and New Directions* (pp. 3–90). San Francisco, CA: Jossey-Bass.

Kraiger, K., & Wenzel, L.H. (1997). Conceptual development and empirical evaluation of measures of shared mental models as indicators of team effectiveness. In M.T. Brannick, E. Salas & C. Prince (Eds), *Team Performance Assessment and Measurement: Theory, Methods, and Applications* (pp. 63–84). Mahwah, NJ: Lawrence Erlbaum Associates Publishers.

Krauss, R.M., & Fussell, S.R. (1991). Constructing shared communicative environments. In L.B. Resnick, J.M. Levine & S.D. Teasley (Eds), *Perspectives on Socially Shared Cognition* (pp. 172–200). Washington, DC: American Psychological Association.

Kray, L.J., & Galinsky, A.D. (2003). The debiasing effect of counterfactual mind-sets: Increasing the search for disconfirmatory information in group decisions. *Organizational Behavior and Human Decision Processes*, **36**, 362–77.

Langan-Fox, J., Anglim, J., & Wilson, J.R. (2004). Mental models, team mental models and performance: Process, development and future directions. In *Special Feature: Distinguished Paper Series, Human Factors and Ergonomics in Manufacturing*. Hoboken, NJ: Wiley Inter Science.

Langan-Fox, J., Code, S., & Langfield-Smith, K. (2000). Team mental models: Techniques, methods, and analytic approaches. *Human Factors*, **42**, 242–71.

Langfield-Smith, K. (1992). Exploring the need for a shared cognitive map. *Journal of Management Studies*, **29**, 349–68.

Lant, T.K., Milliken, F.J., & Batra, B. (1992). The role of managerial learning and interpretation in strategic persistence and reorientation: An empirical exploration. *Strategic Management Journal*, **13**, 585–608.

Larson, J.R., & Christensen, C. (1993). Groups as problem-solving units: Toward a new meaning of social cognition. *British Journal of Social Psychology*, **32**, 5–30.

LePine, J.A. (2005). Adaptation of teams in response to unforeseen change: Effects of goal difficulty and team composition in terms of cognitive ability and goal orientation. *Journal of Applied Psychology*, **90**, 1153–67.

Levesque, L.L., Wilson, J.M., & Wholey, D.R. (2001). Cognitive divergence and shared mental models in software development project teams. *Journal of Organizational Behavior*, **22**, 135–44.

Levine, J.M., & Resnick, L.B. (1993). Social foundations of cognition. *Annual Review of Psychology*, **44**, 585–612.

Lewis, K. (2003). Measuring transactive memory systems in the field: Scale development and validation. *Journal of Applied Psychology*, **88**, 587–604.

Lewis, K. (2004). Knowledge and performance in knowledge-worker teams: A longitudinal study of transactive memory systems. *Management Science*, **50**, 1519–33.

Lewis, K., Belliveau, M., Herndon, B., & Keller, J. (2007). Group cognition, membership change, and performance: investigating the benefits and detriments of collective knowledge. *Organizational Behavior and Human Decision Processes*, **103**, 159–78.

Lewis, K., Lange, D., & Gillis, L. (2005). Transactive memory systems, learning, and learning transfer. *Organization Science*, **16**, 581–98.

Liang, D.W., Moreland, R., & Argote, L. (1995). Group versus individual training and group performance: The mediating factor of transactive memory. *Personality and Social Psychology Bulletin*, **21**, 384–93.

Lim, B.-C., & Klein, K.J. (2006). Team mental models and team performance: a field study of the effects of team mental model similarity and accuracy. *Journal of Organizational Behavior*, **27**, 403–18.

Littlepage, G., Robinson, W., & Reddington, K. (1993). Effects of task experience and group experience on group performance, member ability, and recognition of expertise. *Organizational Behavior and Human Decision Processes*, **69**, 133–47.*

Littlepage, G.E., Hollingshead, A.B., Drake, L.R., & Littlepage, A.M. (2008). Transactive memory and performance in work groups: Specificity, communication, ability differences, and work allocation. *Group Dynamics: Theory, Research, and Practice*, 12, 223–41.*

Lorch, R.F., Lorch, E.P., & Klusewitz, M.A. (1993). College students' conditional knowledge about reading. *Journal of Educational Psychology*, 85, 239–52.

Lord, C.G., Ross, L., & Lepper, M.R. (1979). Biased assimilation and attitude polarization: The effects of prior theories on subsequently considered evidence. *Journal of Personality and Social Psychology*, 37, 2098–109.

Lyles, M.A., & Schwenk, C.R. (1992). Top management, strategy and organizational knowledge structures. *Journal of Management Studies*, 29, 155–74.

Macmillan, J., Entin, E.E., & Serfaty, D. (2004). Communication overhead: The hidden cost of team cognition. In E. Salas & S.M. Fiore (Eds), *Team Cognition: Understanding the Factors that Drive Process and Performance* (pp. 61–82). Washington, DC: American Psychological Association.

Majchrzak, A., Jarvenpaa, S.L., & Hollingshead, A.B. (2007). Coordinating expertise among emergent groups responding to disasters. *Organization Science*, 18, 147–61.

March, J.G. (1991). Exploration and exploitation in organizational learning. *Organization Science*, 2, 71–87.

Marks, M.A., Mathieu, J.E., & Zaccaro, S.J. (2001). A temporally based framework and taxonomy of team processes. *Academy of Management Review*, 26, 356–76.

Marks, M.A., & Panzer, F.J. (2004). The influence of team monitoring on team processes and performance. *Human Performance*, 17, 25–41.

Marks, M.A., Sabella, M.J., Burke, C.S., & Zaccaro, S.J. (2002). The impact of cross-training on team effectiveness. *Journal of Applied Psychology*, 87, 3–13.

Marks, M.A., Zaccaro, S.J., & Mathieu, J.E. (2000). Performance implications of leader briefings and team-interaction training for team adaptation to novel environments. *Journal of Applied Psychology*, 85, 971–86.

Massey, A.P., & Wallace, W.A. (1996). Understanding and facilitating group problem structuring and formulation: Mental representations, interaction, and representation aids. *Decision Support Systems*, 17, 253–74.

Mathieu, J.E., Heffner, T.S., Goodwin, G.F., Cannon-Bowers, J.A., & Salas, E. (2005). Scaling the quality of teammates' mental models: equifinality and normative comparisons. *Journal of Organizational Behavior*, 26, 37–56.

Mathieu, J.E., Heffner, T.S., Goodwin, G.F., Salas, E., & Cannon-Bowers, J.A. (2000). The influence of shared mental models on team process and performance. *Journal of Applied Psychology*, 85, 273–83.

McGrath, J.E. (1964). *Social Psychology: A Brief Introduction*. New York: Holt, Rinehart, and Winston.

McIntyre, R.M., & Salas, E. (1995). Measuring and managing for team performance: Emerging principles from complex environments. In R.A. Guzzo & E. Salas (Eds), *Team Effectiveness and Decision Making in Organizations* (pp. 9–45). San Francisco: Jossey-Bass.

Michinov, E., Olivier-Chiron, E., Rusch, E., & Chiron, B. (2008). Influence of transactive memory on perceived performance, job satisfaction and identification in anaesthesia teams. *British Journal of Anaesthesia*, 100, 327–32.

Milliken, F.J., & Martins, L.L. (1996). Searching for common threads: Understanding the multiple effects of diversity in organizational groups. *Academy of Management Review*, 21, 402–33.

Minionis, D.P., Zaccaro, S.J., & Perez, R. (1995). Shared mental models, team coordination, and team performance. *Paper presented at the 10th Annual Meeting of the Society for Industrial and Organizational Psychology*, Orlando, FL.

Mogford, R.H. (1997). Mental models and situation awareness in air traffic control. *International Journal of Aviation Psychology*, 7, 331–41.

Mohammed, S., & Dumville, B.C. (2001). Team mental models in a team knowledge framework: Expanding theory and measurement across disciplinary boundaries. *Journal of Organizational Behavior*, 22, 89–106.

Mohammed, S., Klimoski, R., & Rentsch, J.R. (2000). The measurement of team mental models: We have no shared schema. *Organizational Research Methods*, 3, 123–65.

Moreland, R.L. (1999). Transactive memory: Learning who knows what in work groups and organizations. In L.L. Thompson, J.M. Levine & D.M. Messick (Eds), *Shared Cognition in Organizations: The Management of Knowledge* (pp. 3–31). Mahwah, NJ: Lawrence Erlbaum Associates Publishers.

Moreland, R.L., Argote, L., & Krishnan, R. (1996). Socially shared cognition at work: Transactive memory and group performance. In J.L. Nye & A.M. Brower (Eds), *What's Social about Social Cognition?* (pp. 57–85). Thousand Oaks, CA: Sage.

Moreland, R.L., Argote, L., & Krishnan, R. (1998). Training people to work in groups. In R.S. Tindale, L. Heath, J. Edwards, E.J. Posavac & F.B. Bryant (Eds), *Theory and Research on Small Groups* (pp. 37–60). New York, NY: Plenum Press.

Moreland, R.L., & Myaskovsky, L. (2000). Exploring the performance benefits of group training: Transactive memory or improved communication? *Organizational Behavior and Human Decision Processes*, 82, 117–33.

Morgan, B.B., Glickman, A.S., Woodward, E.A., Blaiwes, A.S., & Salas, E. (1986). Measurement of team behaviors in a navy environment, Tech. Report NTSC TR-86–014. Orlando, FL: Naval Training Systems Centre.

Mosier, K.L., & Chidester, T.R. (1991). *Situation assessment and situation awareness in a team setting*. Paper presented at the 11th Congress of the International Ergonomics Society, Paris.

Müller, A., Herbig, B., & Petrovic, K. (2009). The explication of implicit team knowledge and its supporting effect on team processes and technical innovations an action regulation perspective on team reflexivity. *Small Group Research*, 40, 28–51.

Murphy, G.L., & Wright, J.C. (1984). Changes in the conceptual structure with expertise: Differences between real-world experts and novices. *Journal of Experimental Psychology: Learning, Memory, and Cognition*, 10, 144–55.

Nadkarni, S., & Narayanan, V.K. (2005). Validity of the structural properties of text-based causal maps: An empirical assessment. *Organizational Research Methods*, 8, 9–40.

Neisser, U. (1976). *Cognition and Reality: Principles and Implications of Cognitive Psychology*. New York, NY: W.H. Freeman.

Nemeth, C.J. (1986). Differential contributions of majority and minority influence. *Psychological Review*, 93, 23–32.

Orasanu, J., & Salas, E. (1993). Team decision making in complex environments. In G. Klein, J. Orasanu, R. Caldewood & C.E. Zambok (Eds), *Decision Making in Action: Models and Methods* (pp. 327–45). Westport, CT: Ablex Publishing.*

Orasanu, J.M. (1990). Shared mental models and crew decision making, CSL Report, Princeton, NJ: Cognitive Science Laboratory, Princeton University.

Palazzolo, E.T., Serb, D.A., She, Y., Su, C., & Contractor, N.S. (2006). Coevolution of communication and knowledge networks in transactive memory systems: Using computational models for theoretical development. *Communication Theory*, 16, 223–50.

Patrick, J., James, N., Ahmed, A., & Halliday, P. (2006). Observational assessment of situation awareness, team differences and training implications. *Ergonomics*, 49, 393–418.

Pearsall, M.J., & Ellis, A.P.J. (2006). The effects of critical team member assertiveness on team performance and satisfaction. *Journal of Management*, **32**, 575–94.

Pearsall, M.J., Ellis, A.P.J., & Stein, J. (2009). Coping with challenge and hindrance stressors in teams: Behavioral, cognitive, and affective outcomes. *Organizational Behavior and Human Decision Processes*, **109**, 18–28.

Peltokorpi, V. (2008). Transactive memory systems. *Review of General Psychology*, **12**, 378–94.

Peltokorpi, V., & Manka, M.J. (2008). Antecedents and the performance outcome of transactive memory in daycare work groups. *European Psychologist*, **13**, 103–13.

Poole, M.S., Hollingshead, A.B., McGrath, J.E., Moreland, R.L., & Rohrbaugh, J. (2005). Interdisciplinary perspectives on small groups. In M.S. Poole & A.B. Hollinghead (Eds), *Theories of Small Groups: Interdisciplinary Perspectives* (pp. 1–20). Thousand Oaks, CA: Sage.

Porac, J.F., & Thomas, H. (1990). Taxonomic mental models in competitor definition. *Academy of Management Review*, **15**, 224–40.

Prahalad, C.K., & Bettis, R.A. (1986). The dominant logic: A new linkage between diversity and performance. *Strategic Management Journal*, **7**, 485–501.

Prince, C., Ellis, E., Brannick, M.T., & Salas, E. (2007). Measurement of team situation awareness in low experience level aviators. *International Journal of Aviation Psychology*, **17**, 41–58.

Pritchard, J.S., & Ashleigh, M.J. (2007). The effects of team-skills training on transactive memory and performance. *Small Group Research*, **38**, 696–726.

Rasker, P.C., Post, W.M., & Schraagen, J.M. (2000). Effects of two types of intra-team feedback on developing a shared mental model in command and control teams. *Ergonomics*, **43**, 1167–89.

Rau, D. (2005). The influence of relationship conflict and trust on the transactive memory: Performance relation in top management teams. *Small Group Research*, **36**, 746–71.

Reger, R.K., & Palmer, T.B. (1996). Managerial categorization of competitors: Using old maps to navigate new environments. *Organization Science*, **7**, 22–39.

Ren, Y., Carley, K.M., & Argote, L. (2006). The contingent effects of transactive memory: When is it more beneficial to know what others know? *Management Science*, **52**, 671–82.

Rentsch, J.R., & Hall, R.J. (1994). Members of great teams think alike: A model of team effectiveness and schema similarity among team members. In *Advances in Interdisciplinary Studies of Work Teams: Theories of Self-Managing Work Teams*, Vol. 1 (pp. 223–61). US: Elsevier Science/JAI Press.

Rentsch, J.R., & Klimoski, R.J. (2001). Why do "great minds" think alike? Antecedents of team member schema agreement. *Journal of Organizational Behavior*, **22**, 107–20.

Rentsch, J.R., & Woehr, D.J. (2004). Quantifying congruence in cognition: Social relations modeling and team member schema similarity. In E. Salas & S.M. Fiore (Eds), *Team Cognition: Understanding the Factors that Drive Process and Performance* (pp. 11–31). Washington, DC: American Psychological Association.

Rico, R., Sánchez-Manzanares, M., Gil, F., & Gibson, C. (2008). Team implicit coordination processes: A team knowledge-based approach. *Academy of Management Review*, **33**, 163–84.

Roth, E.M., Multer, J., & Raslear, T. (2006). Shared situation awareness as a contributor to high reliability performance in railroad operations. *Organization Studies*, **27**, 967–87.

Rouse, W.B., & Morris, N.M. (1986). On looking into the black box: Prospects and limits in the search for mental models. *Psychological Bulletin*, **100**, 349–63.

Rulke, D.L., & Rau, D. (2000). Investigating the encoding process of transactive memory development in group training. *Group and Organization Management*, 25, 373–96.

Rulke, D.L., Zaheer, S., & Anderson, M.H. (2000). Sources of managers' knowledge of organizational capabilities. *Organizational Behavior and Human Decision Processes*, 82, 134–49.

Salas, E., Cannon Bowers, J.A., & Johnston, J.H. (1997). How can you turn a team of experts into an expert team? Emerging training strategies. In G. Klein & C.E. Zsambok (Eds), *Naturalistic Decision Making* (pp. 359–70). Hillsdale: Lawrence Erlbaum Associates.

Salas, E., Prince, C., Baker, D.P., & Shrestha, L. (1995). Situation awareness in team performance: Implications for measurement and training. *Human Factors*, 37, 123–36.

Salas, E., Sims, D.E., & Burke, C.S. (2005). Is there a "big five" in teamwork? *Small Group Research*, 36, 555–99.

Sarter, N.B., & Woods, D.D. (1991). Situation awareness: A critical but ill-defined phenomenon. *International Journal of Aviation Psychology*, 1, 45–57.

Schwartz, D. (1990). *Training for Situational Awareness*. Houston, TX: Flight Safety International.

Sebok, A. (2000). Team performance in process control: influences of interface design and staffing levels. *Ergonomics*, 43, 1210–36.

Selcon, S.J., & Taylor, R.M. (1991). Decision support and situational awareness. *Paper presented at the 11th Congress of the International Ergonomics Association, Paris, France.*

Simons, T., Pelled, L.H., & Smith, K.A. (1999). Making use of difference: Diversity, debate, and decision comprehensiveness in top management teams. *Academy of Management Journal*, 42, 662–73.

Smith, K., & Hancock, P.A. (1995). Situation awareness is adaptive, externally directed consciousness. *Human Factors*, 37, 137–48.

Smith, W., & Dowell, J. (2000). A case study of co-ordinative decision-making in disaster management. *Ergonomics*, 43, 1153–66.

Smith-Jentsch, K.A., Campbell, G.E., Milanovich, D.M., & Reynolds, A.M. (2001). Measuring teamwork mental models to support training needs assessment, development, and evaluation: Two empirical studies. *Journal of Organizational Behavior*, 22, 179–94.

Smith-Jentsch, K.A., Cannon-Bowers, J.A., Tannenbaum, S.I., & Salas, E. (2008). Guided team self-correction: impacts on team mental models, processes, and effectiveness. *Small Group Research*, 39, 303–27.

Smith-Jentsch, K.A., Mathieu, J.E., & Kraiger, K. (2005). Investigating linear and interactive effects of shared mental models on safety and efficiency in a field setting. *Journal of Applied Psychology*, 90, 523–35.

Sohn, Y.W., & Doane, S.M. (2004). Memory processes of flight situation awareness: interactive roles of working memory capacity, long-term working memory, and expertise. *Human Factors*, 46, 461–75.

Stachowski, A.A., Kaplan, S.A., & Waller, M.J. (2009). The benefits of flexible team interaction during crises. *Journal of Applied Psychology*, 94, 1536–43.

Stanton, N., Stewart, R., Harris, D., *et al.* (2006). Distributed situation awareness in dynamic systems: theoretical development and application of an ergonomics methodology. *Ergonomics*, 49, 1288–312.

Starbuck, W.H., & Milliken, F.J. (1988). Executives' perceptual filters: What they notice and how they make sense. In D.C. Hambrick (Ed.), *The Executive Effect: Concepts and Methods for Studying Top Managers* (pp. 35–65). US: Elsevier Science/JAI Press.

Stasser, G., Stewart, D.D., & Wittenbaum, G.M. (1995). Expert roles and information exchange during discussion: The importance of knowing who knows what. *Journal of Experimental Social Psychology*, 31, 244–65.

Steiner, I.D. (1972). *Group Process and Productivity*. New York: Academic Press.

Stout, R.J., Cannon Bowers, J.A., & Salas, E. (1994). The role of shared mental models in developing shared situational awareness. In R.D. Gilson, D.J. Garland & J.M. Quince (Eds), *Situational Awareness in Complex Environments* (pp. 297–304). Dayton Beach, FL: Embry-Riddle Aeronautical University Press.

Stout, R.J., Cannon Bowers, J.A., & Salas, E. (1996). The role of shared mental models in developing team situational awareness: Implications for training. *Training Research Journal*, 2, 85–116.

Stout, R.J., Cannon Bowers, J.A., Salas, E., & Milanovich, D.M. (1999). Planning, shared mental models, and coordinated performance: An empirical link is established. *Human Factors*, 41, 61–71.

Stout, R.J., Salas, E., & Fowlkes, J.E. (1997). Enhancing teamwork in complex environments through team training. *Group Dynamics: Theory, Research, and Practice*, 1, 169–82.

Stout, R.J., Salas, E., & Kraiger, K. (1997). The role of trainee knowledge structures in aviation team environments. *International Journal of Aviation Psychology*, 7, 235–50.

Swaab, R., Postmes, T., van Beest, I., & Spears, R. (2007). Shared cognition as a product of, and precursor to, shared identity in negotiations. *Personality and Social Psychology Bulletin*, 33, 187–99.

Tanaka, J.W., & Taylor, M. (1991). Object categories and expertise: Is the basic level in the eye of the beholder? *Cognitive Psychology*, 23, 457–82.

Taylor, R.M. (1990). Situational awareness rating technique (SART): the development of a tool for aircrew systems design. In *Situational Awareness in Aerospace Operation (AGARD-CP-478)*. NATO-AGARD, Neuilly Sur Seine, France.

Trist, E., & Bamforth, K. (1951). Some social and psychological consequences of the Longwall method of coal getting. *Human Relations*, 4, 3–38.

Tushman, M.L., Newman, W.H., & Romanelli, E. (1986). Convergence and upheaval: Man- aging the unsteady pace of organizational evolution. *California Management Review*, 29, 29–44.

Tushman, M., & Romanelli, E. (1985). Organizational evolution: A metamorphosis model of convergence and reorientation. In L.L. Cummings & B.M. Staw (Eds), *Research in Organizational Behavior*, Vol. 7 (pp. 171–222). Greenwich, CT: JAI Press.

Van Den Bossche, P., Gijselaers, W., Segers, M., & Kirschner, P.A. (2006). Social and cognitive factors driving teamwork in collaborative learning environments. Team learning beliefs and behaviors. *Small Group Research*, 37, 490–521.

van Knippenberg, D., De Dreu, C.K.W., & Homan, A.C. (2004). Work group diversity and group performance: An integrative model and research agenda. *Journal of Applied Psychology*, 89, 1008–22.

Volpe, C.E., Cannon Bowers, J.A., Salas, E., & Spector, P.E. (1996). The impact of cross-training on team functioning: An empirical investigation. *Human Factors*, 40, 92–101.

Waller, M.J. (1999). The timing of adaptive group responses to nonroutine events. *Academy of Management Journal*, 42, 127–37.

Waller, M.J., Gupta, N., & Giambatista, R.C. (2004). Effects of adaptive behaviors and shared mental models on control crew performance. *Management Science*, 50, 1534–45.

Waller, M.J., & Uitdewilligen, S. (2009). Talking to the room: Collective sensemaking during crisis situations. In R.A. Roe, M.J. Waller & S.R. Clegg (Eds), *Time in Organizational Research* (pp. 186–203). London: Routledge.

Walsh, J.P. (1995). Managerial and organizational cognition: Notes from a trip down memory lane. *Organization Science*, 6, 280–321.

Walsh, J.P., & Fahey, L. (1986). The role of negotiated belief structures in strategy making. *Journal of Management*, 12, 325–38.

Walsh, J.P., Henderson, C.M., & Deighton, J. (1988). Negotiated belief structures and decision performance: An empirical investigation. *Organizational Behavior and Human Decision Processes*, 42, 194–216.

Webber, S.S., Chen, G., Payne, S.C., Marsh, S.M., & Zaccaro, S.J. (2000). Enhancing team mental model measurement with performance appraisal practices. *Organizational Research Methods*, 3, 307–22.

Wegner, D.M. (1987). Transactive memory: A contemporary analysis of the group mind. In B. Mullen & G.R. Goethals (Eds), *Theories of Group Behavior* (pp. 185–208). New York: Springer-Verlag.

Wegner, D.M. (1995). A computer network model of human transactive memory. *Social Cognition*, 13, 319–39.

Wegner, D.M., Erber, R., & Raymond, P. (1991). Transactive memory in close relationships. *Journal of Personality and Social Psychology*, 61, 923–29.

Wegner, D.M., Guiliano, T., & Hertel, P.T. (1985). Cognitive interdependence in close relationships. In W.J. Ickes (Ed.), *Compatible and Incompatible Relationships* (pp. 253–76). New York: Springer-Verlag.

Weick, K.E. (1979). *The Social Psychology of Organizing*, 2nd (Ed.) Reading, MA: Addison-Wesley.

Weick, K.E. (1990). The vulnerable system: An analysis of the Tenerife air disaster. *Journal of Management*, 16, 571–93.

Weick, K.E. (1993). The collapse of sensemaking in organizations: The Mann Gulch Disaster. *Administrative Science Quarterly*, 38, 628–52.

Weick, K.E. (1995). *Sensemaking in Organizations*. Thousand Oaks, CA: Sage.

Weick, K.E., Sutcliffe, K.M., & Obstfeld, D. (2005). Organizing and the process of sensemaking. *Organization Science*, 16, 409–21.

Wellens, A.R. (1993). Group situation awareness and distributed decision making: From military to civilian applications. In N.J. Castellan, Jr. (Ed.), *Individual and Group Decision Making* (pp. 267–91). Hillsdale, New Jersey: Lawrence Erlbaum Associates.

Wickens, C.D. (1984). Processing resources in attention. In R. Parasuraman & R. Davies (Eds), *Varieties of Attention* (pp. 63–101). New York: Academic Press.

Wiener, E.L., Kank, B.G., & Helmreich, R.L. (1993). *Cockpit Resource Management*. San Diego, CA: Academic Press.

Wiersema, M.F., & Bantel, K.A. (1994). Top management team turnover as an adaptation mechanism: The role of the environment. *Strategic Management Journal*, 14, 485–504.

Wittenbaum, G.M., Stasser, G., & Merry, C.J. (1996). Tacit coordination in anticipation of small group task completion. *Journal of Experimental Social Psychology*, 32, 129–52.

Wittenbaum, G.M., Vaughan, S.I., & Stasser, G. (1998). Coordination in task-performing groups. In R.S. Tindale, L. Heath, J. Edwards, E.J. Posavac, & F.B. Bryant (Eds), *Theory and Research on Small Groups* (pp. 177–204). New York, NY: Plenum Press.

Wright, R.P. (2008). Eliciting cognitions of strategizing using advanced repertory grids in a world constructed and reconstructed. *Organizational Research Methods*, 11, 753–69.

Xinwen, B., Erping, W., Ying, Z., Dafei, M., & Jing, R. (2006). Developmental characteristics of two types of shared mental models. *Acta Psychologica Sinica*, 38, 598–606.

Yayavaram, S., & Ahuja, G. (2008). Decomposability in knowledge structures and its impact on the usefulness of inventions and knowledge-base malleability. *Administrative Science Quarterly*, 53, 333–62.

Yuan, Y.C., Fulk, J., & Monge, P.R. (2007). Access to information in connective and communal transactive memory systems. *Communication Research*, **34**, 131–55.

Zaccaro, S.J., & Bader, P. (2003). E-leadership and the challenges of leading e-teams. *Organizational Dynamics*, **31**, 377–87.

Zajac, E.J., & Bazerman, M.H. (1991). Blind spots in industry and competitor analysis: Implications of interfirm (mis)perceptions for strategic decisions. *Academy of Management Review*, **16**, 37–56.

Zhang, Z.X., Hempel, P.S., Han, Y.-L., & Tjosvold, D. (2007). Transactive memory system links work team characteristics and performance. *Journal of Applied Psychology*, **92**, 1722–30.

INDEX

Note: Page numbers in *italics* refer to figures or tables

INTERNATIONAL REVIEW OF INDUSTRIAL AND ORGANIZATIONAL PSYCHOLOGY 2010 Volume 25

Edited by

Gerard P. Hodgkinson, *Director of the Centre for Organizational Strategy, Learning and Change and Professor of Organizational Behaviour and Strategic Management, Leeds University Business School, The University of Leeds, UK*

J. Kevin Ford, *Professor of Psychology, Department of Psychology, Michigan State University, USA*

This is the twenty-fifth in the most prestigious series of annual volumes in the field of industrial and organizational psychology. The series provides authoritative and integrative reviews of the key literature of industrial psychology and organizational behavior. The chapters are written by established experts and topics are carefully chosen to reflect the major concerns in both the research literature and in current practice.

Continuing the series' tradition of providing scholarly, up-to-the-minute reviews and updates of theory and research this twenty-fifth volume surveys developments in such familiar areas as the employee selection, team cognition and adaptation, leadership, and diversity management. Newer topics surveyed in the present volume include corporate communications, coaching, and positive organizational behavior. Each chapter offers a comprehensive and critical survey of the chosen topic, and each is supported by a valuable bibliography. For advanced students, academics, and researchers, as well as professional psychologists and managers, this series remains the most authoritative and current guide to new developments and established knowledge in the field of industrial and organizational psychology.

Contributors to Volume 25

Derek R. Avery, *USA*

James Campbell Quick, *USA*

Michael J. Cavanagh, *Australia*

Cary L. Cooper, *UK*

Olga Epitropaki, *UK*

Philip C. Gibbs, *UK*

Anthony M. Grant, *Australia*
Paul R. Jackson, *UK*
Laura M. Little, *USA*
Robert G. Lord, *USA*
Robin Martin, *UK*
Patrick F. McKay, *USA*
Debra L. Nelson, *USA*
Deniz S. Ones, *USA*
Helen M. Parker, *Australia*

Jonathan Passmore, *UK*
Sara J. Shondrick, *USA*
Geoff Thomas, *UK*
Anna Topakas, *UK*
Sjir Uitdewilligen, *The Netherlands*
Chockalingam Viswesvaran, *USA*
Mary J. Waller, *Canada*
Fred R.H. Zijlstra, *The Netherlands*

International Review of Industrial and Organizational Psychology

CONTENTS OF PREVIOUS VOLUMES